5.10

For Bob—

Each of us is born with the _TALENT_ to be remarkable at something—

Find that talent!

Fun working with you!

Don

DON'T WASTE YOUR TALENT

The 8 Critical Steps To Discovering What You Do Best

BOB MCDONALD, PH.D.
DON E. HUTCHESON

LONGSTREET PRESS
Atlanta

Published by
LONGSTREET PRESS, INC.
2140 Newmarket Parkway
Suite 122
Marietta, GA 30067

Printed in the United States of America

1ˢᵗ printing 2000

Library of Congress Catalog Card Number: 00-068575

ISBN: 1-56352-611-5

Book design by Jill Dible
Jacket design by Burtch Bennett Hunter

A LETTER TO THE READER

Dear Reader,

With over 10,000 participants to date in The Highlands Program, we decided to update our best-selling book, *The Lemming Conspiracy*, with expanded insights into how people and companies discover true success.

We have found wide acceptance of our programs in corporations since *The Lemming Conspiracy* was published. In the last few years, as the war for talent has become perhaps the number one issue in corporate America, the problem of keeping, motivating and fully utilizing the talent companies already possess has become critically significant. Recent research has shown that such 'soft' factors as satisfaction, balance and sense of personal connection to one's work have a direct and formulaic connection to the 'hard' issues of productivity, retention, customer satisfaction and profitability.

Part of what's different about this book—other than the title—is that we expanded the text to include three chapters on how people use The Whole Person Technology® in corporations, both individually and corporately. We also report on our research into what happens when people in corporations go through The Whole Person Technology®. Our research includes *long-term* outcome results, because the only change that makes any difference is change that sticks.

This book, like *The Lemming Conspiracy*, shows how individual people at any Turning Point, through the proprietary program of guided self-discovery we call The Whole Person Technology®, can create and use Personal Visions to transform their lives. Whether you are a high school student getting ready to go off to college, a college student getting ready to graduate, a person at midlife wondering what to do next, a young manager wanting to make the best choices for your career, a busy executive trying to have a whole life, or someone wanting to make the highest and best use of your retirement, you can find yourself in this book.

Many people, when they read this book, find that they want to know more about their natural talents and abilities. As we explain in Chapter 4, the only way to know *for sure* what your natural talents are is to take a carefully researched battery of ability worksamples, such as

The Highlands Ability Battery™. We have just completed translating this ability battery to a CD, which you can order by going to our website: www.highlandsprogram.com. It takes about three hours to complete, but will tell you objectively what your true gifts and talents are. It's information that no one should be without.

If you would like to learn more about The Highlands Program, whether for corporate application or for your own use, you can find us on the Internet at www.highlandsprogram.com.

Thank you for your interest in this book. We sincerely hope that you will find it transformative and enlightening.

Sincerely,

Bob McDonald

Don Hutcheson

ACKNOWLEDGEMENTS

So many people have contributed to the birth, growth and development of The Highlands Program that it would be impossible to list them all by name. We are profoundly grateful to our staff, our licensees, our investors and our friends and family—all of whom have hung in there through years of making the idea of The Whole Person Technology® real.

We would especially like to thank our Highlands Program staff, consultants and professionals. Their outstanding drive and professionalism have made it possible to deliver programs of consistently high quality. Rob Miklas, Rob Donovan, Kathi Russell, Scott Hornbuckle, Shelly Danz, LeAnn Ransbotham, Dori Stiles, Natalie Gold, Cheryl Mure, Joy Dawes, Lisa Cayce, Heather Taylor, Lisa Nayyar, Brooke Blackwell, Chris Bard, Wendy Baucom, Carla Lanham, Danielle Rubenstein, Ann Dangar, Lanie Damon, Andy Dishman, Barbara Doty, Charlotte Hayes, Micky Land, Cynthia Lynch, Linda Merrion, Holly Northrop, Amy Podurgal, Pam Reyes, Meg Smith, Elaine Wilco, Anne White, Gail Ostrishko.

We would like to thank our dedicated group of licensees who have made The Whole Person Technology® available to people all over the United States. Your insight in seeing the value of our technology in people's lives has been sustaining to us over the years of making the program work.

A number of corporate sponsors have not only believed in the power of our program, but also contributed significantly to our ideas about using The Whole Person Technology® in corporations.

Harris Warsaw, Jerry Cushing, Susan Rinaldi, Tom Smith, Joe Teplitsky, Bob Gonzalez, Gail Vail and Karen Donnalley of IBM. Each has experienced our programs and been willing to put themselves on the line as supporting a new idea and a new way of doing things. They have all believed in what we are doing and actively promoted our programs both in IBM and elsewhere.

Rich Podurgal, Jim Davison, Roger Hawley, Ken Russell, Rick Jones, Mike Arwari, Elizabeth Trotter, Mike Bennett, Kristy Johnson, Mark Thompson, Jerry Jones, Lou Esgro, Jim Lamb, Steve Rhoads,

Julie Wade, Mike Pucci, Ed Gallagher, Mason Brommer, Caterri New, Jeff Woodram, Routledge Cox, Clare McEntagart, Mary Boran and Benita McLean, Sherry Canbel, and Alice Swearingen of Glaxo Wellcome. Rich Podurgal and Jim Davison both showed instant insight about how our programs could help people at Glaxo Wellcome. Their wise coaching, mentoring and sponsorship have been invaluable.

Sue Bedford, Elizabeth Wolgin, LaVay Lauter, Julie Ward, Craig Gomez, Ed Paradise, Greg Akers, Andy Haggard, Bill Benson, Nancy Schwarm, Steve Hilla, Diane Adams, Carson Stuart, Karl Zurl, Paul Sikorski, Irving Tupe, Chris Olson, Mark Basinski, Hari Tewari and Shannon Nix of Cisco Systems. Sue Bedford and Elizabeth Wolgin have offered expert advice and counsel again and again on how to make our programs work in Cisco's culture.

Roy McAllister, Rob Lauber and Susie Howard of Cingular.
Darrell Ford and Lynn Parker of BellSouth Corporation.
Howard McCain, Bob Johnston and Kim Lang of Right Management.
Debby Selke and Melanie M. Hightower of Chase Manhattan Bank.
Ann Doster of Performaworks.
Debbie Morris, Rod Branvolt and Terry Ford of Nortel Networks.
Tom Brown of Printpack.
Carrie Welles and Dave Townshend of Marriott International.
Jim Huling of Matrix Resources.
Scott Kauffmann, Deborah MacArthur and Tony Clancy of Andersen Consulting.
Tom Blackstock and Joe Norton of Coca-Cola.
Dana Milner of Home Depot.
Monika Verazani of Prudential.
Allison Ehrler-Meyer of Wachovia Bank Card Services.
Sandy Vilas of Coachinc.com.
Michael Reene of Enterpulse.
Linda Frisby, Deb Warner, Judy Helstrom and Theresa Forbes of Hewlett Packard.

We would like to thank Elizabeth Lyon, Bridget Miklas, Wendy Baucom and Kathi Russell for their excellent editorial work with the manuscript, Steve Hilla for suggesting the idea of Chapter 10 and Rob Donovan, Kathi Russell and Amy Podurgal for their very significant help with Chapters 11 and 12. We want to especially thank the people at Longstreet Press who have been so important in bringing this book to life: John Yow, Scott Bard, Burtch Hunter, and Jill Dible. We would like to thank Robyn and Willy Spizman for their insightful and creative PR counsel.

We would like to thank some of the many people who have supported and encouraged us over the years: Jane Shivers, David Ivey, Jerry Brown, Laleah Henderson, Dick Henderson, Alf Nucifora, Alan Briskin, Bob Morrison, Ed Baker, David Rubinger, David Allison, Alexis Davis, Brad Kibler, Brenda Brown, Earl Gurr, Jacquie Damgaard, Libby Eason, Karen Tedeschi, Tracie Stein, Joe Dennis, Frank MacConochie, Patti Hulvershorn, Nigel Marson, Paige Moody, Kathy Doherty, Chris Miller, Todd Stansbury, Teresa O'Driscoll, Glenn Rupert, Lisa Schwartz, Diane Thomas, Deborah Mangum, Jere Harris, Tina Marie Davis, Mendy McConnell, Marcia White, Vicki Mowery, Elizabeth Chambers, Margaret Hutchison, Joy McCarthy, Ellen Wolchansky, Dianne Grove, Carole Smith, Robin Hirsch, Wieda Duncan—all have been important to us.

Bob: I would especially like to give thanks for my parents Adelaide and Pierce, my brothers, Allen and Paul and their wives, Ann Carter and Becky, as well as Allen III, Virginia, Porter and Neil. My family has always been my home base. I would like to honor and recognize my children, Erin and Peter, as well as Peter's wife, Ashleigh. I would also like to thank and recognize my teachers: Leo Droppleman, Charlie Cohen, Jack Barlow, Harold Fine, Wilhelmina Simmons, Don Williamson, T.K. Lee and Master James Fain. Special regard and thanks to Conor Loughridge, Pat Vecchio and Jake and Sarah Russell. Thanks for the light of the 7:07 Group – Jerry Brown, Bob Ostholthoff, and Curt Clause. I would like to thank Kathryn Vecchio Russell for a sustaining friendship that has brought me closer to Christ and God. I would like to recognize and thank my very good friends Don Hutcheson and his wife Lynda.

Don: I would like to thank the following people who have made this journey possible: My mother and father, Bettye and Don, from whom I inherited a keen mind and intrepid spirit. My grandparents,

Ralph and Mary Stallworth, who, by their example, taught me common sense and compassion. My sister, Linda Lee, extraordinary mother and defender of animals. My sister Pamela Bonning and her husband Ken—whose belief is unbelievable! My nieces Evan and Lindsay Lee and nephew Matt Lee—forever an inspiration. Alice and Earl Berkhan, Carol Watts, Jimmy and Glenda Hutcheson—Bless you for welcoming the black sheep back into the fold. Jacquie Damgaard and Sandy Vilas—who have saved me from myself too many times to count! David Ivey—the most level-headed, well-grounded business partner anyone could ever have. Brian Bailey and the Thursday Night Brotherhood—Ho! Jerry Brown—he also knows about redemption. My stepsons Will and Clay Shivers and my stepdaughters Kelley Hill and Kim Clark—who keep me honest. My lifelong friend, Bob—still the smartest guy I know, and ever steadfast. Lynda, my soul-mate and wife—who turned my life around more than I could have ever dreamed.

WE HIRE
People
FOR THEIR **Skills** BUT
THE
Whole Person
SHOWS
UP
FOR
Work.

Chester I. Barnard

Using Your Talent

We know two things for sure about success. You have to understand what you do best, and you have to find the right fit between yourself and your job. We founded a company, The Highlands Program, over ten years ago with the idea of helping people do just that.

We are not alone in our thinking. Peter Drucker, a widely respected management consultant and insight-provider about modern business, a man *Fortune* magazine called the "most prescient business-trend spotter of our time," agrees. For the last 10 years he has said this:

Success in the Knowledge Economy comes to those who do two things: identify and articulate their talents, and place themselves in positions to use them.

This book is about using your talent—not wasting it. It is about The Highlands Program and The Whole Person Technology®—the structure and process we developed because we believe that people deserve to be on higher ground in their lives and careers. We created The Highlands Program to do two things: First, to help you identify and articulate your natural gifts and talents. Second, to help you figure out the right fit between you and your career. You do this by creating a Personal Vision—a holistic map of what you're hardwired to do. A Personal Vision opens the doors to your creative insight, energy and talent and puts you on the clear smooth road to success *and* satisfaction.

Every one of us is born with unique talents and gifts. They are hardwired into us. We don't learn them and we can't forget them. They are just part of who we are. For some, talents are specialized and particular—a gift for music or design, for instance, or a gift for theoretical thought. For others, talents are more generalized—as a talent for leading teams, or abilities that make teaching, selling or writing easy. Some talents are mutually exclusive—talents that make you a naturally gifted manager are nearly opposite of talents that make you an insightful consultant or a creative designer.

The first step in using your talent is to figure out what your talents really are. Your talents are not something you just know about yourself.

You have to discover them on purpose. With the right tools, this is relatively easy and straightforward to do.

Knowing *what* your talents are is a huge accomplishment, but it's not enough. After you know what you're naturally gifted to do and how you're hardwired, you have to place yourself in a position to *use* your talents. This means finding the right fit, and it is a somewhat larger problem.

In 1990 we started wondering how people could discover work in which they could succeed *and* that they would find enjoyable at the same time. We were 42, right at midlife, and had successful, satisfying careers. Bob had been a psychologist for eighteen years and built a strong and lucrative practice. Don had been an entrepreneur, starting and running two profitable advertising agencies. We had been close friends since we were in the Army together as young men. At this midlife turning point we both wanted something different. Just as with most people at midlife, we wanted to use talents that our previous careers had ignored.

We discovered that most programs designed to help people figure out their best careers look at too small a picture of who people really are. We determined to create a program that would not just look at one or two dimensions of people, but would treat people and their careers holistically and honor their complexity.

Bob quit his practice and Don sold his last agency. We embarked on what would turn into two years of research on the questions—How do you figure out what you are good at? How do you get into a position where you can do that every day?

We discovered that most programs designed to help people figure out their best careers look at too small a picture of who people really are. We determined to create a program that would not just look at one or two dimensions of people, but would treat people and their careers holistically and honor their complexity.

Out of this research, we created The Whole Person Technology®. It is a way to get at *all* of the factors that influence the right fit between you and your career. Several things make it completely different from other programs, tests and processes.

It is multidimensional. We don't settle for a simple picture of who you are. You are more than your personality, more than your interests, more than your values, even more than your natural talents. If you don't take a whole picture of yourself into account, you run the serious risk of getting into a job or career that will end up feeling like it doesn't fit you at all. There are eight factors you need to take into account to find the right fit. The Whole Person Technology® presented in this book will help you identify and articulate them.

It is inside out, not outside in. We don't tell you what to do. If you are looking for an expert who knows more about you than you know about yourself, forget it. No matter how many tests you take or how many degrees some expert has, he or she will not know one thousandth of what you need to know to find the right fit. But you know the answers. They are inside you right now. The Whole Person Technology® helps you get to them, identify them and make them work for you.

It is structured. The value of The Whole Person Technology's® structured approach is that, if you follow the exercises in this book, you will get the promised result. The structure is designed to help you not leave anything out.

The Basic Plan Of This Book

The first three chapters deal mainly with why it's so difficult to know what your talents are and to figure out the right fit. They deal with The Lemming Conspiracy, the Stress Cycle, and career development over your lifespan.

The next six chapters show you exactly how to use The Whole Person Technology® to create a Personal Vision. A Personal Vision is a holistic plan that maps what you're hardwired to do based on accurately identifying your talents and figuring out how to use them most effectively.

The last four chapters show how to use The Whole Person Technology® individually at work, how corporations have used it in the workplace and how it can become a tool to use throughout your life.

People have used this book in several ways. What you get out of it is a product of your goals in reading it and also of the time and energy you put into it. Here are some goals you can achieve in reading this book:

Find out generally what natural talents are and how to get to use them. You can get this from reading the text and perhaps looking at the exercises. From this you will get a good idea about what natural talents are and what The Whole Person Technology® is.

Gain some personal insight about your career. You can get this from reading the text and doing whichever ones of the exercises appeal to you. All of the exercises yield highly interesting information, but if you don't want to go through all of them, just pick out one or two that you find interesting or that strike a chord for you.

Discover the right fit between you and your career. This is a bigger goal, but it's one that will pay off—both in terms of satisfaction and in terms of success. To do this, you have to take the time to read the text and systematically go through the exercises. We would suggest putting a little time into it every day. This is a process that could take a few weeks or a couple of months, depending on how thoroughly you go about it and how much time and energy you can put into it.

Identify and articulate your natural talents and abilities. Whatever your goals are, we strongly recommend that you take The Highlands Ability Battery™. You can order it from our website: www.highlandsprogram.com. This is a complete and thorough battery of ability work-samples that will tell you how you work best, as well as how you best communicate, problem solve and learn. See Chapter 4 for a more complete explanation of what abilities are and how we measure them. There is a charge for taking this battery, but the result is well worth it to you.

We have had numerous clients over the years that have come back to us after going through one of our programs or after reading the material in this book to tell us that The Whole Person Technology® changed their lives. Many people have told us that they use the knowledge they gained every single day. Our favorite endorsement, though, came from one of our earliest clients—a young man in his mid-20s who had been searching for a meaningful direction since finishing college. His father, tired of worrying about his son, paid for him to go through The Highlands Program. When he finished the program, he told his father, "Dad, this is the best thing you ever bought for me—including my car."

Creating a Personal Vision is perhaps the most important work you can do to make your life more fun, more productive and more meaningful. Gandhi had a Personal Vision. So did Churchill. So did Watson and Crick, who discovered DNA, and Benjamin Franklin, who shepherded the thirteen colonies through revolution. A Personal Vision can help you overcome almost any obstacle. Once you can see your goal, you can attain it.

Some people use their talents; others ignore them. Our philosophy is this: Don't waste your talent. It is your hardwired key to personal and professional success.

HOW MANY **MIDDLE-AGED** MEN
HAVE AWAKENED IN THE MIDDLE
OF THE NIGHT WITH THE
NIGHTMARISH REALIZATION THAT
THE WAY THEY ARE SPENDING THEIR
LIVES AND ENERGY FEELS
UTTERLY MEANINGLESS?
HOW MANY **MIDDLE-AGED WOMEN**
HAVE **SUDDENLY** SEEN THEIR LIVES
AS **WITHOUT MEANING** WHEN THEIR
CHILDREN LEAVE HOME?
OR HOW MANY HARD-DRIVING
PROFESSIONAL WOMEN
WAKE UP IN THEIR **LATE THIRTIES**
AND
REALIZE THEY FORGOT TO HAVE
CHILDREN?

THE LEMMING CONSPIRACY
CAPTURED THEM ALL AND
ANESTHETIZED
THEM.

The
Lemming Conspiracy
R E V I S I T E D

Why do some hugely talented people seem to bomb out of life? Why do the lives of others who seem naturally less gifted seem to be so much more productive and fruitful? Many people go through life with the strong suspicion that there must be some valuable part of themselves that never finds expression. Why is this? And more importantly, how can you make sure that you are *using* all of the talent you were born with?

This book helps you identify your true talents and figure out how to use them. It is based on work we have been doing for over ten years in helping people find the right fit in their lives, their jobs, and their careers.

Before we talk about how to find the right fit, though, we need to discuss why this is so difficult and why so many people are pulled subtly off track.

You might have heard about lemmings. In legend, these small arctic mammals band together from time to time and, running in vast herds, throw themselves over cliffs to their deaths. As a metaphor, it seems to describe how too many of us live our lives—the authors included.

Let us tell you about a conspiracy—we call it the Lemming Conspiracy—widespread and insidious, that controls what you do every day and even how you feel about what you do. It is a conspiracy that controls your perceptions of yourself and your options in your career.

This conspiracy routinely invades almost every aspect of our lives. Born of benign intentions, but almost totally hidden from our awareness, it operates outside of our conscious will and keeps us from understanding our real talents and what we could really do in the world.

Why do all of us settle for lives that are stressful, frenetic and often empty of meaning? Why do we spend our energy and time acquiring possessions that bring us so little happiness in the end? Why do we ignore people who are important to us, and ignore ourselves in the bargain? We behave in these "irrational" ways because the Lemming Conspiracy keeps us from experiencing ourselves as we really are.

We grow up learning to see a limited range of options as if it constituted *all* our options. Our schools, colleges, corporations, organizations, friends and families actively work—albeit unintentionally for the most part—to encourage this limited view throughout our lives. Why? Not because they are evil, certainly, but because they are *systems*. Systems create and carry out the Lemming Conspiracy.

The idea of *systems* and how they operate in cultures, corporations, biology, families, animal societies and human societies is very complex. Scientific treatments of systems are often rather densely unintelligible to the layman. If you can bear with us for a few paragraphs, however, you will begin to get the idea of what systems are and how they work. For us, as people living in society with each other, systems describe the rules by which our various family, work and friendship groups operate.

How Systems Control Our Perceptions of Ourselves

The fundamental fact about all systems is this: Any system of which you are a member has its own goals and interests, and those goals and interests are not the same as your goals and interests.

> NOTE: In this book, we will often talk about systems having goals, systems wanting things, or systems in other ways behaving as though they were alive. A system is a way of describing how people work together in stable groups like families or corporations. Obviously, a system is an abstraction, and has no will or wants of its own. But systems act as though they do have a life of their own. Many systems routinely produce results *exactly the opposite* of those that each and every person in the system wants to produce.

An Office System

At the very simplest level, everyone in a typical corporate office goes to work at about the same time every day, works steadily during the morning, takes off for lunch at about the same time, works steadily during the afternoon, and finishes the day's work at about the same time. All of the workers in the office know that they have choices about what they do all day long. But they act as though their choices are limited. In order to be members of this particular system—this office—they have to go by the rules. Otherwise the system will not function.

But other rules are less overt and therefore operate more powerfully. Some examples of the kind of *unstated* rules you might find in an office:

UNSTATED 'RULES'

- You should strive to make more money and gain a higher position in the organization.
- You must give up significant aspects of your personal life in order to be successful.
- If you don't get promoted, you are a failure.
- Work is not something you should think about enjoying; that's why they call it work.
- You should do whatever it takes to succeed, including 12-hour days and 75-hour weeks.

- Work hard, play by the rules, and you will be successful and happy.
- Happiness has something to do with how much you can buy.

These rules, powerful but covert, are different for every system, but they **make systems work**.

If everyone *didn't* act as though moving up the corporate hierarchy and being able to buy a better car were important, then the young people in the company wouldn't be scrambling all over each other trying to compete for the top spots. They wouldn't be willing to put up with drudgery and meaningless labor in order to please someone they might not respect. Middle-aged managers who want something more in their lives might begin to look outside the corporation. The collapse of the corporation would follow, with civilization not far behind—at least, this seems to be the driving fear that motivates systems to remain ever the same.

The *system* acts as though its rules are reality. It acts as though you as a member of a system fully buy into and share all of its rules. Systems are conservative; they don't change their rules easily or often. Surface appearances of change rarely, if ever, change the fundamental rules of any system. As a member of a system, you are under a great deal of pressure to believe, buy into and live out its rules. And most people do.

Subtly and silently, or overtly and crassly, systems encourage employees to forget about their real talents, interests and passions when they go to work, and to think of their life goals in terms of money and promotions. They are not encouraged to explore and develop natural gifts and talents. They are even discouraged from looking closely at their deepest values. At work people are often discouraged from engaging in any real self-exploration.

Systems act as though each person is a collection of skills and functions. They seem to operate most smoothly when you see yourself in this way, too. You remain distant from yourself, defining yourself firmly in one way, when the reality of yourself may be different entirely. This situation creates and perpetuates the Lemming Conspiracy.

How the Lemming Conspiracy Begins— The Family of Origin

The Lemming Conspiracy begins in the family of origin—the family in which we grew up as children. The families in which we grow up give us a primary sense of who we are. This happens outside of anyone's awareness, but it is a fundamental fact of development. Our perceptions of ourselves as smart, stupid, good-looking, capable, incapable, affiliative, distant and all of the hundreds of other ways we describe and think about ourselves start forming by about age four. They become solidified by the time we are 18 and ready to move out of our family homes into the wider world.

Children absorb a sense of who they are and what they "ought" to be doing in the world from their parents. The rebellious teen often rejects this influence: "I don't know who I am, but I know who I am not. I am not like my father." What is hidden from the teenager who might mutter this is that *his* father, when he was 18, probably had exactly the same thought about his own father.

Sometime around age 30 to 35, people often realize, with some horror, "I have become my parent." This recognition frequently occurs after they have children of their own. These people have, of course, been like their parents all along without realizing it. Their first conscious memories are of when they were 5 or 6 years old and their parents were 30 to 35. When recognition strikes, they are just recalling their first memories of their parents.

This process of acquiring a fully formed image of ourselves, a picture which includes both parents, is almost completely unconscious, but is one of the most powerful forces in our lives. It is called *identification*. It is the fully formed picture of who we are that we learn in our families of origin, and then take into adulthood. Without it, people could not grow up. They could not leave their families. They could not form ties and relationships in the adult world. They would not know the "rules" of adult life.

WHO WE ARE AND WHO WE ARE NOT

This image of ourselves gained through identification makes it possible to enter the adult world, and creating it is the main function of the family system. But this image also limits. We not only learn who we *are* in families, but we also learn who we are *not*. We learn, clearly, what role we are to play in the adult world, and we learn how to play it. Already, in the family system, we start to see divergence between how our *system* sees us and the potential we see in ourselves. Later, we will talk about the difference between our System Selves, the self that the system sees, and our True Selves, the person we are able to be.

The family of origin is a system. It is a closed circle of relationships that has its own history, rules, roles and customs. All of these remain stable over time. If you study a family for many years, you will see that certain roles and types keep reappearing generation after generation. When we leave home we take our "model" of the family system out into the world and recreate it when we start our own families.

Our family system is also the model for any other system that we become involved in, join or create throughout our lives. We join systems that "fit." We choose our friends, churches, synagogues, clubs, organizations, schools, companies and corporations, and they choose us, because they fit, and we fit. There is a role we can play in the system that we learned in our families of origin. This role may be exactly right for us. It may tap into every one of our natural talents and satisfy our deepest goals in life. It may perfectly express our fundamental values and involve aspects of life that we find intrinsically fascinating.

Or not. We learn roles in our families of origin that have more or less to do with our personal makeup. As we enter the adult world, we usually discover much more about ourselves than our families typically see. But our families, and other systems in which we become involved, persistently see us in the same interpersonal roles they always have. These perceptions don't change easily.

All systems strongly encourage you to see yourself as *they* see you. If you seamlessly fulfill your role, then the system operates more smoothly, if not more creatively. The problem is, *you* get lost, and it is difficult to get another view of yourself as long as you are involved in the normal systems of your life.

What follows is a true story about a person who did everything right. She went to the right schools, made wonderful grades, got a great job, and was successful at every turn. While she lived out a life her systems encouraged her to live, she steadily lost a true sense of herself and what she wanted from her life. Although she didn't realize it, she was a victim of the Lemming Conspiracy and stood in danger of wasting her most important talents.

NOTE: We will tell much of the story of this book through the stories of people's lives. In all cases, the stories are based on real people and the actual events of their lives; however, we have changed their names and any possible identifying information about them in order to protect their privacy.

Sarah's Story

Sarah grew up in a small town in Minnesota. An excellent student in high school, she had many extracurricular interests, including theater, which she loved. School came so easily that she seldom worked hard. Theater consumed a far more important share of her time and creative talent than academics.

Sarah's father, a successful computer systems analyst, had gone to graduate school right after college, intending to get a Ph.D. in history. At the time he dreamed of teaching. After he earned his master's degree, he did teach for a while.

Teaching made him happy, but he realized that he could never earn a high salary in this field. He had been married two years and had a little daughter for whom he was responsible. His father's image, that of a man providing well for his family, forcefully urged him to change.

Sarah's father switched to computers, and soon was doing well financially. When he took a job, he generally liked it at first, but it quickly became routine. There was nothing intrinsically interesting to him about computers or computer systems. When his unhappiness reached the breaking point, he simply found a new job. To him this did not seem unusual. He assumed most people didn't really like their jobs.

Sarah's mother was also a successful computer systems consultant. She didn't find her work rewarding either—just lucrative. She had stayed in the same job with the same firm for many years and was considered quite good at her role. She didn't find her work particularly interesting, creative or fun. It was work, and she did it, and was happy to have a job.

Sarah's mother had a love, too. She created handmade clothes for children. She had quite a following among her friends and had opened a shop to sell her creations. She loved all aspects of this endeavor—from the fabrics and their colors, to the design and creation of the clothes, to helping people find exactly the right garment for a family or a child. But she didn't call it work. It was a hobby. In her lexicon, "work" was what you had to do. Enjoyment was completely beside the point.

And so Sarah went off to college. She went to a small, select, liberal arts college in the South and did well—3.8 average. "I figured out very quickly what I needed to do to get an 'A'. I just took the right courses and paid attention in class and always did just enough to slide under the wire. I took history courses and English courses, but what I really enjoyed was drama. I got involved in a theater group the first semester I was on campus. It held the whole focus of my attention throughout four years of college. I loved the life of the theater; I loved the people in theater; I loved everything about it. It easily absorbed 90 percent of my attention and energy."

Sarah never thought about what she would do after college. Even well into her senior year, she did not have a real idea about what she would do when she graduated. An advisor, looking at her transcript, asked her if she had ever thought about law school. She had not. She had never, as far as she could remember, even known a lawyer. But this seemed like a plan.

Sarah applied to six law schools and was accepted by four, among them Yale. She decided to go there. Why? "It's Yale. You can't turn down Yale." She walked onto the Yale campus the next fall never having interviewed a lawyer, or worked in a lawyer's office, or even wondered too much about what a lawyer did. She just thought it would be a way to make money.

"I knew as soon as I started that I hated law. But, once again, I could make A's fairly easily. I did just as much as was necessary, nothing more. I joined a theater group right away, and the great majority of my time and energy went there. The saddest day of my life was the day I graduated from law school. It meant that I would have to stop doing what I really like to do in life and start working to pay back my law school debts."

Sarah's story was published on the front page of a major metropolitan newspaper, because she had secured a job in a distinguished law firm well before graduation, and because she had produced and directed a video about law students, which was broadcast on PBS. In the video, students talk about law and law school, and their feelings of anger and frustration at being trapped in a profession they don't like, have no real interest in, but which will pay them well anyway.

We talked to Sarah about a year after she started working for the firm. As a young associate she had had so little time that she couldn't be involved in the theater. She succeeded in the firm, but was already thinking that if she moved to New York City, she could earn more money, save it faster and eventually be able to do what she wanted.

SARAH'S FAMILY OF ORIGIN

Obviously, Sarah had absorbed a great deal from her mother and father. On the positive side, she worked hard and did well at whatever she set out to do. On the negative side, she had absorbed both parents' pattern of being in work they didn't like, had no interest in and that probably ignored their greatest talents. She would use her father's pattern of changing jobs in order to deal with her present unhappiness and dissatisfaction. And it would probably work no better for her than it did for her father. Her parents had given her the answers they habitually used, and she had taken them over without realizing it.

Sarah left her family of origin and established herself independently. By almost any yardstick she had succeeded, and her family had successfully performed its main role and function.

But no system ever challenged Sarah's basic assumptions or her decisions. Nor could it. This fundamental limitation of systems is the defining fact of the Lemming Conspiracy.

From the point of view of Sarah's high school, everything was fine. One of their brightest seniors went to an excellent liberal arts college. For them to challenge whether it was the right school, with enough options to explore what she really loved, would be madness. She had done well academically; she had been accepted to a strongly academic institution. Perfect.

At college, once again, everything appeared to be fine and on course. How could anyone think there was a problem? Sarah *herself* didn't think there was a problem. It was only when the end of her senior year loomed that any troubling thoughts came to her. What would she do *now?* Her advisor saw a bright, verbally oriented student with excellent grades, and one clear answer popped into his head—law school. She could get in, and it would make the college look good. The fact that she ended up going to Yale made it so much the better.

For the school to challenge this situation would be foolish in the extreme. As a small, very selective, expensive liberal arts institution, the school's survival depended on its graduates getting into graduate and professional schools. Getting graduates into *Yale* validated the fundamental premise of the school: "We are doing a good job because our graduates go on to high-quality graduate and professional programs."

Yale certainly never challenged Sarah's decision. It was happy to have such a bright student. It was even happier, as an institution, when one of its brighter and more talented students landed a good job four months before graduation. *That* makes a school look good.

The firm in which she landed saw its future in being able to attract smart, talented young lawyers who would work like demons for five to seven years until they are hooked into the financial rewards. Landing a Yale student near the top of her class, a *female*, was exactly what the firm wanted to do. And did.

All of these systems—high school, college, professional school, law firm—had their own goals and their own interests. Sarah was precisely fulfilling these interests and goals for each of these systems. But these systems' interests were clearly not the same as Sarah's interests—not even close. And Sarah had never looked at what her own interests and goals might be. Nor was she encouraged to. Instead, she was encouraged to think of herself as bright, successful and on the way to the top. When we, the authors, met her, she was unhappy and feeling trapped by debt. The only escape she could imagine was the exact answer her father had used to keep himself unhappy and trapped most of his career.

How We Get Out of Balance and How That Leads to Stress

Sarah's story, that of a young person who goes from success to success to success and yet ends up feeling trapped and unhappy, shows in clear relief how many people live out their lives in systems. While energetically jumping through hoop after hoop, they never stop to examine who they really are and what they really want from their lives.

With patterns and roles absorbed from our families of origin, we leap into the world in our early twenties. We find systems to join that fit our sense of ourselves and our sense of what roles we could play in life. This works well for systems, and it appears to work pretty well for us—for a while.

Throughout our adult lives, we experience regular cycles of stability and change. We launch ourselves into the beginning of our careers, just like Sarah did. At first everything may seem fine. We may feel that we are a good match for a system at the beginning. The system's values appear to match our own. Our lives seem interesting and exciting.

With each passing year, we grow and change. We become different on the inside. We have new ideas, meet new people, have new goals and new wants. But the systems in which we remain do not change their views of us. To our systems (and this includes our family systems), we are the same. Our systems assume we have remained on the same path, and that we have the same buy-in to the system's values and rules that we always did.

System Self, True Self and Life Balance

This increasing disparity between ourselves as our systems see us and ourselves on the inside—the difference between the *System Self* and the *True Self*—leads to our becoming increasingly out of balance. In general, we have a choice. We can either struggle with our systems about how they define us and how we define ourselves, or we can increasingly see ourselves as our systems see us. Very few people end up struggling with systems—at least, not for very long.

We *become* who our systems think we are. This invariably means that we are not attending to or putting enough energy into one or more critically important elements of our lives. Systems have only a limited view of us. We are whole people, but systems see only roles and functions. How many middle-aged men have awakened in the middle of the night with the nightmarish realization that the way they are spending their lives and energy feels utterly meaningless? How many middle-aged women have suddenly seen their lives as without meaning when their children leave home? Or how many hard-driving professional women wake up in their late thirties and realize they forgot to have children?

The Lemming Conspiracy captured them all and anesthetized them. These middle-aged people suddenly wake to discover what has really been going on for a number of years: their System Selves, defined by the role or function that the system demands, and their True Selves, the whole person that is possible, have grown irreparably apart.

The result of this disparity? Stress. Also anxiety, anger and often depression. When the stress or anxiety reaches some critical point, it often starts to seep into awareness. It is at these times of greater awareness— times we call Turning Points—that we seek new answers and change.

We *could* find creative answers and new directions at Turning Points, but too often we do not, because the Lemming Conspiracy still holds us captive.

Turning Points and Life Changes

As we reach the critical point of stress and anxiety, we arrive at a *Turning Point*. At Turning Points we feel ready for change. We actively seek new answers. One of the best-known Turning Points arrives at midlife, but there are actually eight of them. With remarkable regularity, they come every seven to ten years throughout our adult lives. These all-important crises of adult life can lead to positive creativity and change, but all too often do not.

At Turning Points, we often become aware of the increasing disparity between who we are and what our systems see. And we often try to change something. But what? The answers come from the family of origin. We will invariably make the same kind of decision, and for about the same reason, as one or the other of our parents made at the same age. We will talk more about Turning Points and how we typically make these decisions in Chapter 3.

In Sarah's story above, we can see the pattern of decision-making at Turning Points—both for Sarah and her parents. At the critical Turning Point at the start of adulthood, she decided to go into a field that was financially secure but offered little personal reward, just as her father did. Her sense of what work is and should be was formed by what she observed in her mother and father. She was well on her way to repeating her father's strategy of dealing with stress. We could predict that it would be no more successful with her than it was with her father.

We can see these same forces at work with a young man named Mitchell at a later Turning Point. He became increasingly aware of the disparity between his System Self and his True Self and was moved to change. The first answers he thought of came straight from his family of origin, just as they would for anyone. They could easily have led him to repeat Sarah's mistake, but Mitchell took a new path, and his story ends differently from Sarah's.

Mitchell's Story

Mitchell started working for a large technology firm straight out of college. He energetically pursued his career and achieved success early. He worked predominantly in sales. He came to the attention of his bosses and they wanted him on the fast track. "By age 30, I liked what I was doing. I liked my co-workers and clients. The company had been good to me, but I just felt this restlessness and uneasiness I couldn't put my finger on."

The firm could not help Mitchell with this problem. All of its answers are in the interest of the firm, not of Mitchell. Obviously, as long as Mitchell is productive, his firm will encourage him to "stay the course." It is in its interests for Mitchell to think that a good job, good pay, and good co-workers are enough. That is exactly what Mitchell thought. Or, more correctly, thought he should think.

Once this subtle misconception takes root, that a company's interests and a person's interests are the same thing, stress and imbalance loom on the horizon. Mitchell made this mistake when he tried to quiet his wish for change by admonishing himself to just grow up, settle down and endure. Mitchell's firm could not help him figure out who he was and what he wanted. Mitchell was only aware of feeling that he had to do something different, and the fact that he was obviously successful just made his wish for change more stressful. Mitchell's True Self had diverged from his System Self, but he had no mechanism to find and identify his True Self. He had no way to use a vision of his True Self to stand up to his systems.

Mitchell's family couldn't help. The message from his parents could not have been more clear: "Are you crazy? Stay with your job. It's secure." He strongly felt the responsibility of his young child. He couldn't do anything that would jeopardize her. And yet he needed to do something.

Here, Mitchell's story departs from Sarah's. Mitchell actively sought different answers by going through a structured process that systematically focused on all of the important factors of his life and career. It was crucial that the process did not involve his firm, his family or his circle of friends and colleagues. It was independent of all his systems and had no vested interest in the outcome of his search. As a result, it could help him come up with his own answers—what we call a Personal Vision—a fully articulated picture of his True Self. With a Personal Vision, Mitchell could escape the Lemming Conspiracy and start leading his own life.

What is a Personal Vision? What must it include to be effective in illuminating your True Self and defeating the Lemming Conspiracy? Eight critical factors must contribute. Leave one out, and you risk remaining entrapped.

Mitchell discovered what fit about his job and what did not fit, and why. Mitchell previously had some idea about his talents, but he couldn't articulate them in any detail. By learning exactly what his strongest talents were, he could more accurately focus and position himself. He knew what he wanted to move away from; more importantly, he knew what tasks and roles he should go toward. He also knew why his systems' answers, although compelling, were not right for him. He was able to create a plan and make a significant move in his career to a position and role that he felt expressed his true talents more exactly. He says of his change: "My clients are happy, and I get to play from my strengths and my love. It is truly a wonderful fit."

In this book, we take you through the structured process Mitchell used to change his life and career. We call it The Whole Person Technology®. We created this process, and thousands of clients have used it successfully. It leads you to self-discovery. You must find your true natural talents and pull your hopes and dreams to daylight. You must identify your most potent skills and even journey back to your original family system. Finally, you will be able to use this process to create your own Personal Vision—your vision of your True Self in the workplace.

Your Personal Vision should have a definite structure and form to be effective. Chapters 3 through 7 take you through each of the eight critical factors, explaining what each is and what significance it has for your life. You will go through them in a definite order—from objective to subjective, external to internal.

The Thought Experiments at the end of each chapter help you

translate the ideas of the chapters into a more practical reality. You can use these experiments as springboards for thought, or you can actually do the experiments. They are, at the very least, fascinating. They also hold the possibility of helping you transform your life.

Merely identifying and articulating the eight factors is not enough. A Personal Vision involves *creative integration*—a creative insight, if you will. Chapter 8 details the creative process we developed for our workshops and seminars. We call it *left-right-left*.

In the end a Personal Vision must relate to the real world if it is to help you live a balanced life. In Chapter 9, we describe the process we use to accomplish this integration—Surveying. Surveying has incredible power to kick your Personal Vision into motion, to translate it to the reality of the marketplace.

Through all of these chapters, we tell the stories of five actual people at different Turning Points, all of whom go through the process of the book by completing the Thought Experiments. After each Thought Experiment, we revisit all five to find out what they learned and how they use what they found out.

Chapter 10 shows how to use a Personal Vision to transform your experience of the workplace. Chapters 11 and 12 discuss how The Whole Person Technology® has found a place in corporations. You will see the results of our long term research in corporations utilizing The Whole Person Technology® as well as actual case studies from many different companies who have used it for retention, motivation, dealing more effectively with diversity, coaching and enhancement of team productivity.

Chapter 13 talks about Personal Vision at different Turning Points: how it can help propel you into a new job; or how it can make your present job work better for you. We end with a discussion of the power of Personal Vision to expand and open systems to make them more flexible, adaptable and human.

> **NEXT CHAPTER:** In the next chapter, we discuss the goal of The Whole Person Technology®, gaining a Personal Vision. A Personal Vision helps move you out of the cycle of stress, anger and depression we call the Stress Cycle, and toward the more vital cycle of inner-directedness and balance we call the Balance Cycle.

...the hallmark of the **STRESS CYCLE** is its **RELENTLESS RUSH**...you **NEVER STOP**...there is no time for such...

"**UNPRODUCTIVE**" work as thinking about your life or figuring out how you **REALLY WANT** to **SPEND** your **TIME**...

if you are in the **STRESS CYCLE**, it is virtually **IMPOSSIBLE**...

to identify your

TRUE TALENTS or to move

yourself into circumstances to be able to

USE
THEM...you never stop

2

The Stress Cycle
&
THE BALANCE CYCLE

The Lemming Conspiracy leads inevitably to the loss of real talent and to lives lived out of balance. Answers to the question of work and career learned in the family of origin help us move out into the adult world. But over time, they cease to be adequate because too much information is missing. Our systems prevent us from recognizing and changing this situation. Insofar as we let some important talent lie fallow, ignore some important aspect of ourselves, neglect a critical value, or do work for which we feel no intrinsic passion, we develop an increasing disparity between our System Selves and our True Selves. We come to live in the Stress Cycle.

Most of the people you know live in the Stress Cycle, as you probably do yourself. The Lemming Conspiracy produces the Stress Cycle for nearly everyone sooner or later. Over time the Stress Cycle comes to rule people's lives.

This chapter shows why the Stress Cycle eventually captures all of us and how it has such a profound impact. But this chapter also tells you about the alternative, the Balance Cycle, and what it means to achieve it. We will describe how to move from the Stress Cycle to the Balance Cycle and how a Personal Vision makes the journey possible. We will explain what a Personal Vision is and how you can create one for yourself. You'll learn how to beat the Lemming Conspiracy.

In the Stress Cycle, we feel like we are jumping through hoops. We work harder and gain little. Our day-to-day lives have little real meaning for us, even if we are engaged in work we *used* to enjoy. We have the uneasy feeling that something is missing, but it's difficult to identify what that might be. We have the definite sense that there is no time to think about any of this anyway. We barely have time to do what is absolutely necessary.

The hallmark of the Stress Cycle is its relentless rush. You never stop. If you are in the Stress Cycle you only have time to do the next task, or concentrate on the next project. There is no time for such "unproductive" work as thinking about your life or figuring out how you really want to spend your time.

More to the point, if you are in the Stress Cycle, it is virtually impossible to identify your true talents or to move yourself into circumstances to be able to use them.

If we operate in the Stress Cycle, we pass it on to our children. They see it as a normal and natural way for adults to live their lives. We can tell them a thousand times that they can choose to live their lives any way they want to, and they don't have to choose the same answers we did. But we see a great many high school students already caught in the Stress Cycle. Many try desperately to *avoid* living like their parents live. The hard fact is, if *we* are in the Stress Cycle, sooner or later, *they* will be in the Stress Cycle, too.

How does the Stress Cycle start? Obviously no one would willingly and knowingly choose to live like this. No one would want their children to live like this. So why does virtually everyone do it?

The Stress Cycle emerges directly from systems and the Lemming Conspiracy. As we move into systems from our families of origin, we feel an incredibly strong pull to *take the next step*. Declare a major. Graduate from college. Get a job, any job. Succeed. Earn more money. Buy more things. Move up in the organization. Complete the next project. Gain the boss's attention and approval. Become a boss. Retire. Die.

We are not talking about intelligence or character. We are talking about the universal pull of systems to engage us in the Stress Cycle. We are talking about how difficult it is to separate ourselves from this pull. Even people who routinely help others look at *their* long-term goals never think about whether their own lives are expressing a long-range vision.

So, what are the elements of the Stress Cycle?

ELEMENTS OF THE STRESS CYCLE

1. Short-term focus. Getting the next task done. "I'll just get this promotion, and *then I'll be able to live my life.*" Probably not. This focus on the task at hand means that you are never able to focus on a larger context. What about your real talents? What about your *life*? Most people spend far more time and energy focused on how they will spend their annual vacation than they do on how they will spend the next 20 or 40 years of their lives. *Systems want you to focus on the short-term goal. It is in their interest for you to do so.*

2. Status-driven goals. A new car would feel great. A new house. Maybe a second house. A promotion will mean that I'm getting somewhere in life. I want to dress like my bosses and drive their cars. I want to have the kinds of lifestyles that I see in magazines and on television. I want more responsibility, so I can have more say in what happens. I want to be in charge, so I can have a life. *Systems want you to feel all of this. They want you to work very hard to achieve something that is basically empty of meaning, so that when you achieve it, you will focus on the next goal.*

3. Outer-directed priorities. Someone else tells you what is important. New car? Promotion? More money? Getting a college degree, earning a lot of money, gaining a position of responsibility and power—these are all worthy goals, *if* they are a direct expression of your Personal

Vision. But, if they are not connected to anything larger in your life, they are empty, and you are being pulled along from hoop to hoop.

4. Reactive decision-making. Focusing only on short-term goals. Responding to everyday events as though to crises. When people concentrate only on short-term results, they become vulnerable to throwing all of their energy and creativity into problems that, in a longer view, may not be that important. Researchers in human behavior found long ago that getting people to concentrate on short-term reward resulted in increased short-term behavior. This narrowing of focus, however, inflates the importance of what may be trivial events. This inevitably leads to stress. How many people have led successful professional lives and accomplished each of their many goals only to discover, too late, that they never had a relationship with their children? Or their spouses? Or themselves, for that matter?

People in the Stress Cycle get caught up with achieving the next goal and accomplishing the next task. They feel too busy to worry about what their talents are or how to use them. Too busy to examine their lives and figure out what might be personally meaningful. But people do not generally start out in the Stress Cycle. It develops over time.

How the Stress Cycle Takes Over Our Lives

There are many high school students completely caught in the Stress Cycle. In academically competitive high schools, they are probably the majority. The Stress Cycle grips students even more firmly in college. As young men and women move out into the work world, marry, buy houses, cars, baby strollers and vacations, the Stress Cycle becomes as natural and normal as breathing. But answers that worked reasonably well in the family of origin, and even for a while in adulthood, eventually cease to function well at all. This is when stress develops.

When we live with chronic stress, we do not come up with creative answers. Our focus becomes short-term—we just want to get *this* job done, and then we can rest. We tend to focus on the goal in front of us. We do not feel we can take the time to think about what we are doing; we just need to do it. We tend to follow any direction presented to us. Unconsciously, we fall back on patterns learned in the family of origin. It is here that we start to become more and more like one or the other of our parents, because we make decisions exactly the way that parent made them at that age. What gets lost is you—and your own personal talents.

Below are the stories of two accomplished, successful professionals, Carol and Jane, both of whom had "succeeded" in the world through intelligence, planning, drive and character. You will also see that both were trapped in the Stress Cycle. Answers from their families of origin could not help them overcome the Lemming Conspiracy. Later in this chapter you will see how they figured out Personal Visions, came to a better understanding of their real talents and started living more balanced lives.

Carol's story, below, shows how answers that started off working well eventually led to the Stress Cycle.

Carol's Story

At 38, Carol was near burnout. She had been a hard-driving sales executive for 10 years, but she didn't think she would last two more years at her company. She didn't understand her stress and anxiety. She was still young; her job, if anything, was better than ever. But it just didn't feel like enough any more.

Carol's father had been a successful sales executive with a large company and had traveled throughout her childhood. A few years after she moved out of her family home, her parents divorced.

Like her father, Carol had always felt that her first responsibility was to be successful, but she had never challenged or even clearly articulated that perception.

Carol had never married or had a serious relationship longer than six months. She traveled three and four days a week. Almost anyone outside of Carol's family or network of busy professional friends strung out across the country could have told her that she would feel much better if she would create a life for herself outside of work. But her family and friends never challenged her assumptions—they couldn't, because they were living the same life. Her lifestyle prevented her from coming up with any creative answers herself.

Her bosses certainly didn't challenge her assumptions; from their point of view, Carol was perfect. She was a high performer on the fast track and probably had executive potential. The company had no way of knowing that Carol was considering quitting and that she was operating with markedly reduced efficiency and commitment. Indeed the company would never know until she walked out the door.

Carol had succeeded in forming an independent life for herself. She had succeeded in a competitive business and could go all the way to the top. But she was caught in the Stress Cycle. Taking on the next project, accomplishing the next goal, pushing ahead with her career plan, she had left herself out of the formula. Now she was experiencing the stress, anxiety and sense of crisis that normally develop.

It would be impossible for the company to help her with this. The company's interests were different from Carol's; it could not help her figure out who she was and what was important to her. Carol's response was absolutely typical; she redoubled her efforts, doing more of what she had always done. She used the same answers that had worked before.

These answers to her dilemma came from her family of origin; they could not help her. Carol's life mirrored her father's in many important ways. She had given over all her energy and focus to work, like her father, treating herself and her personal relationships as secondary to work. Also like him, she had not been able to develop a rewarding, fulfilling marriage or family.

Systems basically offer two answers at crisis points: Do more of the same, or quit. *As we have seen, Carol tried to do the first, and was considering the second as a real possibility. The next story is about Jane. It gives another view of systems' answers at Turning Points.*

Business, social and family systems all nurture the forces leading to the Stress Cycle. Jane's story illustrates how the Stress Cycle can develop completely outside of business—but not outside of systems.

Jane's Story

Jane had raised two children; both went to college. She had always seen her role as supporting her husband's law career, a role she performed very well. He had started a successful firm, and her talents in connecting with people had been crucial to that success. She believed it was her responsibility to be available for her children and her husband.

At age 50, Jane's carefully nurtured life began coming apart at the seams. Her youngest son came home in the middle of his junior year in college. He now had a job waiting tables. He spent most days watching MTV and soap operas and was out until very late at night with his friends. Her husband was seldom home. He sometimes worked seven days a week. She had no interests, plans or ideas about what to do with herself. She didn't have a clue about what she might be good at besides taking care of a household and raising children. She frequently had lunch with other lawyers' wives; their conversation felt pointless and mostly bored her. She started having migraine headaches that were stunningly debilitating.

Jane's mother had raised a large family in a small Southern town. Her father had been a minor public official. At about age 50, her mother developed a hip problem that prevented her from getting around. When her father died a few years later, it fell to Jane to take care of her mother full time, which she did until her mother died.

Jane was repeating her mother's life. A physical disability would take all choice away from her. Although her answers from her family of origin had worked well for years, they no longer helped her. Her husband couldn't help her; the Stress Cycle had ensnared him many years ago. Even her son was so caught in the family's stress that he could not form an independent life. It is interesting, and inevitable, that she would unconsciously choose her mother's solution to the problem—becoming incapacitated by illness—at about the same age her mother did.

Anyone can be a victim of the Stress Cycle, and in truth, almost everyone is at some point. But what is the alternative? We all live in systems. We all have to live in a stressful world. All of us get answers from our families of origin and then take them out into the world to start our lives. Those answers will eventually lead us to a crisis and a Turning Point.

These "crises" of our adult lives don't have to be negative. At these times we can become more open to change. We can look for new answers. Instead of adopting systems' answers or families' answers, we can use this openness to find our own answers. Over time, we can move from the Stress Cycle to the Balance Cycle. We can learn to recognize and use our most powerful talents every day.

Just as in the Stress Cycle, the elements of the Balance Cycle relate strongly to each other. One element leads to the next, and then to the next. Once you get into the Balance Cycle it perpetuates itself. And, you can pass along the Balance Cycle to your children—but only if you're living in it yourself.

So how does it work? What are the elements?

ELEMENTS OF THE BALANCE CYCLE

1. Long-term focus. Ultimately, anything you do should connect clearly to a fundamental value or goal. In the Balance Cycle, intermediate and short-term goals are steps toward a larger goal. In concentrating on a current project, it is important not to lose sight of why you undertook it in the first place.

2. Meaning-driven goals. What you do every day should contribute to giving your life meaning. If it doesn't, why are you doing it? The old saying runs: "No one ever got to the end of his life and wished he had spent more time at the office." The time at the office didn't provide any meaning. It wasn't connected to anything larger. It was just work. Meaning in work comes from its connection to the whole of what you want your life to be, not just a piece of it.

3. Inner-directed priorities. People in the Balance Cycle move toward goals *they* have chosen, not their systems' goals. As we have seen, it is often difficult to separate what we want from what our systems want us to want. This is why forming your goals using a structure that is *outside* your systems is so necessary and helpful.

4. Vision-based decision-making. An executive explained how he used his Personal Vision: "It is a template. Whenever an opportunity comes up, I match it up to my Personal Vision. If it will move me toward my Vision, I take it. If not, I politely decline. People often ask me how I can be so decisive and sure about important decisions. The reason is that I know where I'm trying to go, I know why, and I know it with a great deal of clarity and specificity."

People who operate in the Balance Cycle have a positive Personal Vision for the future. They feel that what they do makes the most difference in their ultimate happiness and satisfaction. They see satisfaction in a larger context than immediate gain. They actively seek and find meaning in whatever they do.

When you're in the Balance Cycle, you can create a life in which you can use your talents. Not just in the small context of your immediate job, but in a larger context of your life. Your talents are more or less constant throughout your working life, but there are many critical factors that change throughout your life to pull you away from your real talents and put you in danger of wasting your true strengths.

People in the Balance Cycle are not surprised by change. In the Stress Cycle, stress, anxiety and depression build to the point of crisis, and the crisis precipitates change. People in the Balance Cycle have already considered what may be next and why. Change becomes part of a whole Personal Vision or plan. People in the Balance Cycle approach Turning Points with a blueprint for making decisions. Above all, they approach Turning Points with the idea of *adding* significantly to their lives, not merely getting rid of things that are causing them stress.

The Balance Cycle may seem like a worthwhile alternative to the Stress Cycle, but how do we get there?

Personal Vision

The vehicle for moving from the Stress Cycle to the Balance Cycle is a Personal Vision for your life and career. A Personal Vision is an image of yourself in a future in which you are using your most powerful talents doing work that is meaningful and fulfilling. It connects you to your own future. It can help you at each Turning Point when you make decisions about your life and career. It can help you *every day* to make those small decisions that add up to the Stress Cycle or the Balance Cycle.

A Personal Vision, though it helps you see into the future, must be absolutely grounded in the present—in you. It must include every significant aspect of who you are, what you're hardwired to do and what you want from your life.

The Structure of a Personal Vision

I. A Personal Vision, to be effective, must comprise all important elements of your life and career. It should take into consideration:

A. Your natural talents and abilities. This is how you're hardwired. It's what you naturally do well—your inborn gifts. If you work against them, work is always labor. If you work with them, everything is easier and more fun.

B. Your skills and life experience. What you learn in life creates a hugely valuable asset to take to the next stage of your career. Your Personal Vision should help you use this asset as you grow older and your life changes.

C. Your interests and fascinations. What draws your attention, what *pulls* you. From this often-neglected factor springs the source of your most important creative energy.

D. Your interpersonal style. Accurately identifying and working through your personal style means that you can work more productively, expend less energy and experience less stress.

E. Your values. What you think is *worth* doing in life. Your values give your life an overall sense of direction and purpose.

F. Your goals. What you want to do in life. What you want to accomplish. Many people find out with a shock that they have been pursuing someone *else's* goals—too late. Figuring out your goals gives you steps to follow, way stations on your path.

G. Your family of origin. Some of the most fundamental concepts you take into adult life developed in the family in which you grew up. Including this in your Personal Vision gives it integrity, depth and meaning, often in profound ways.

H. Your stage of adult development. The Personal Vision of a high school student setting off to college will be different from that of a 42-year-old man who would like to do something different, or a 65-year-old woman planning retirement.

II. Your Personal Vision needs to involve both objective and subjective elements. The place to start is with a completely objective look at your natural talents—your basic hard-wiring. The only way you can really assess your talents is through objective measurements called *worksamples*. As you move through the elements of your Personal Vision, the factors become more and more subjective. The

life and direction of your Personal Vision will depend on more subjective factors such as interests, personality, values and goals.

III. Your Personal Vision should be based on a structure that is
outside of your current work, friend and family systems.
Advice from your family, friends or business associates, however wise
and well-meant, can only come from the perspective of your own systems. To gain a more objective and complete view of yourself, you need
to step outside your normal systems for a time. This is the only way you
can know for sure that your Personal Vision is not just another version
of your family's messages, or answers from your current systems.

IV. It should provide a blueprint for important life and career
decisions. People who have a Personal Vision are sure of
themselves. At important times, they can act and decide independently of their work and family systems because they have thought through
all of the important factors that influence their lives.

Having seen what a Personal Vision is, let's go back to Carol and
Jane to see how they developed Personal Visions and moved from the
Stress Cycle to the Balance Cycle.

Carol's Story, continued

*As you may remember, Carol had reached a point near burnout in
her career. She felt her only answer was to quit, and definitely
thought she would quit within the next two years. As she constructed her Personal Vision, she realized that she was, in many ways, ideally suited for her job. Her talents and abilities were a positive asset,
and she loved both the technology involved and the people she dealt
with every day. In looking at her natural talents, however, she understood that, in addition to sales, her talents were ideal for teaching.
She had thought she might like teaching and had thought at one time
that she could go to school, and eventually teach; however, having
objective knowledge of her talents gave her the courage to think she
could actually do something different.*

*When Carol did family-of-origin work, she realized that the pow-
erful messages she had absorbed from her family were still controlling*

her life. She realized that her company had no interest in changing these patterns, even though one could argue that it would be in the company's interests to help her do so. This would require a long-term focus that systems rarely exhibit. The only way Carol could change would be to take charge of and manage her own life and career.

As Carol constructed her Personal Vision, she realized that even though her present company was a great fit for her, significant aspects of her job needed to change. As she got a clearer picture of what she wanted to do, she began to create a position for herself that would meet her needs and the company's needs, too. She knew that her natural talents would help her as a teacher and trainer. Combining these with her desire for a helping role and a schedule that allowed her a personal life, she formed a plan.

She began working with the training department on a consulting basis. She found she was in fact a gifted trainer, and was able to shift more of her responsibilities there. Eighteen months later, she is much more satisfied and has no plans to quit. She feels she is a more valuable asset to the company because she now trains many others to sell as effectively as she once did.

By getting outside her corporate system, her family system and her system of friends and colleagues, Carol was able to come up with a new answer. She could continue to work in the company, but have more time for a personal life.

Jane's Story, continued

Jane's natural talents aimed her at management. In completing several exercises on values, Jane realized she had a strong wish to do something positive for children in her community. She joined a public-service organization that was devoted to helping young girls at risk stay in school, find jobs and discover new opportunities. She eventually became a board member, and finally ended up being executive director of the board. Her managerial talent was obvious to everyone.

Jane's headaches disappeared following one occasion when she insisted that she was going to attend an important board meeting over her husband's objections. Her son, perhaps realizing that if his mother could stand up to his father, she would probably take him on next, got off the couch shortly after this, and eventually graduat-ed from college. Her husband doesn't work on Saturday or Sunday any more. This entire family system was transformed by Jane's Personal Vision.

Creating a Personal Vision

The process of creating a Personal Vision and moving from stress to balance is vital. Nothing is easier than understanding the Stress Cycle, the Balance Cycle and how a Personal Vision can help you move from one to the other. Merely understanding the ideas and grasping the concepts will not accomplish anything as real as the profound changes in Carol's and Jane's lives we described above. Creating a Personal Vision that has the power to change your life must involve all of the following *behavior*:

1. You must stop. The Stress Cycle keeps you in constant motion. It keeps your mind constantly occupied. You must give yourself a period of empty time in order to do the work of getting to a Personal Vision. Not 15 minutes when you don't have any other appointments, but significant blocks of time over several weeks or months that are scheduled and inviolable. Chapter 3 deals with those natural times of crisis and change in which we are sometimes more open to stopping and looking for alternative answers. Even in the most compelling life crisis, however, nothing will happen unless you decide to stop.

2. You must get outside of your systems. Next to stopping, this is the most difficult step. You need answers different from those your family, friends or corporate systems can provide. Not because there is anything wrong with them, but because their stock of answers is vir-tually identical to your stock of answers. What you need at a Turning Point is the ability to take a fresh look at your answers and precon-ceptions. This book guides you through a process we developed to help you do this. It takes time and energy, but the payoff can be sig-nificant, in terms of both success and satisfaction. At the end of this chapter and each of the following seven chapters, we included a series of Thought Experiments. These Thought Experiments provide an action framework to help you create your own Personal Vision.

3. **You must engage in a structured exploration of all eight critical factors:** abilities, skills, interests, personality, values, goals, family of origin and stage of development. If you leave one out, you risk creating a blind spot in your vision that forces you to stumble back into stress and crisis at the next Turning Point. Chapters 3 through 7 explain how to explore all of the significant factors involved in a Personal Vision.

4. **You need to integrate creatively all eight of the significant factors.** This task is too complicated to perform logically. How do your values interact with your goals? How do both relate to your natural talents? These are not linear questions. In order to get to a Personal Vision, you must use your creative mind. Chapter 8 explains creative integration, and the Thought Experiment helps you use your right and left brain to create a Personal Vision.

5. **You need to make it work in the real world.** A Personal Vision that is just an idea is not complete. You need to bring in information from the real world in order to make it a useful tool for your life. In Chapter 9, we talk about Surveying, an extremely powerful process for translating your vision to real life.

Thought Experiment A:

A Personal Vision Notebook

The Thought Experiments included at the end of this and the next seven chapters are meant to guide you to your own Personal Vision.

Personal Vision Notebook. Buy a spiral-bound notebook of 50 pages or more. You will use this notebook to record and summarize everything you discover in the other Thought Experiments. If you think this sounds like it may involve a lot of writing, you're right. Forcing yourself to write down your discoveries about yourself makes your thoughts, feelings and ideas more usable. Each time you record your findings from Thought Experiments in your notebook, you set the stage for creative and integrative insights. Feel free to sketch or doodle in your notebook, or staple pictures, headlines, advertisements or articles in it. Use it any way that seems helpful to you. But also use it to record your findings about yourself *in words*.

For anyone for whom writing is a particular labor and who feels it would be an unproductive stumbling block, we suggest recording your responses into a tape recorder.

FOUR STORIES OF PEOPLE AT TURNING POINTS

After each Thought Experiment, we will tell continuing stories of four actual people as they proceeded step by step through the program outlined in this book. They will tell you—mostly in their own words—what they discovered from completing the Thought Experiments.

Tracy—23 years old

Tracy graduated from college nine months ago. Since graduating, she has lived at home and worked as a secretary in the law firm of her father's friend. In college, she majored in psychology, intending to earn a Ph.D. and become a psychologist. In her junior year in college she realized that, due to changes in managed care, it was becoming increasingly difficult for psychologists to have satisfying careers or even to earn a living. She gradually gave up her idea of going to graduate school in psychology, but had no alternative plan. When she graduated, she didn't know what to do next. She took the job in the law firm thinking that she could just earn a little money until she could figure out her next step, but nine months later she was no further along than when she started. "Since I graduated, I've been miserable. My parents are supportive, but I know they hate it that I don't seem to be able to bring myself out of this funk. I always did well in school, but this is something I haven't been able to figure out."

How is she feeling at this point? "Depressed. Discouraged. No self-confidence. Cynical about the work world."

Brian and Janet—both 30 years old

Brian works for a major telecommunications company in marketing. He started co-oping there while in college, and was offered a job immediately after graduating. He typically puts in 10- to 11-hour days and works most weekends. He has been married two years to Janet, whom he met at work. "At the end of the day, we are both so exhausted we don't want to cook dinner. We just fix a bowl of cereal and sit and read the paper. Janet wants to have children, but I'm thinking, 'We can't have children yet. I need to get another promotion under my belt.'" Brian looks at the people above him in the hierarchy, and most are just a little older than he is. One or two are younger. He feels that if he doesn't make his mark soon, he will lose his chance and be shuffled aside, or even out.

Brian's feeling now: "I want to get ahead."

Janet has been working in the same company for three years in customer relations. She has never been promoted. "I feel completely unfulfilled at work. I want to be successful there, but I don't like what I'm doing, and I don't really know how to get out of there. What else would I do? What department would I go to? It's confusing. I think if we had a baby, I would just quit and be a mother."

Janet's feeling now: "Tired. Discouraged."

Elizabeth—43 years old

Elizabeth is an executive in a large technology firm. "I work 75-hour weeks. I travel. I never see my child. My husband and I are strangers. There has to be another answer."

Her feeling? "I have to do something. Maybe this will help."

Carl—51 years old

Carl was vice president in Human Resources in a major entertainment company for nine years. Six months ago he was laid off as the result of a merger. This has not been as difficult for him as he thought it might be. "I was ready for a change anyway. This just meant that I have to change now, which, of course, isn't too comfortable. I have no idea whether I should go back into a large company or whether I should try to get a job in a smaller firm. Or maybe start my own consulting business."

His feeling now: "Interested. Hopeful."

NEXT CHAPTER: In the next chapter we begin to move toward a Personal Vision. We start with the adult development cycle—the predictable Turning Points of adult life.

AT
TURNING POINTS
PEOPLE UNEXPECTEDLY
BECOME OPEN TO
NEW IDEAS...
MEN MAY BECOME INTERESTED
IN **WOMEN'S ISSUES,** OR
WANT DESPERATELY
TO **CONNECT.**
A WOMAN
MIGHT SUDDENLY DECIDE
TO START A BUSINESS
OR **HAVE CHILDREN** FOR
THE FIRST TIME.
BOTH **SEEK WAYS** TO EXPAND THEIR
ARENAS OF COMPETENCE
AND **EXPRESS
THEIR TALENTS**
MORE COMPLETELY.

3

Crisis

&

CHANGE

Both Sarah, the young law student in Chapter 1, and Mitchell, the person in technology sales whose Personal Vision helped him use his talent more effectively, had reached normal adult Turning Points when they felt something must change. We saw Sarah move from high school to college, the first adult Turning Point, and then from college to the work world, the second. At this Turning Point, she wondered if her decisions had been good ones, but saw nothing she could do differently. Mitchell, at the Age 30 Turning Point, felt that his career, although a good fit in many ways, still lacked something that he had difficulty articulating. He used the structured process in this book to help him assess and create real change.

We all face Turning Points during our entire adult working lives, about one every seven to ten years. They don't even stop with retirement. We continue to have Turning Points every seven to ten years through our 60s, 70s, 80s and beyond.

Each Turning Point in adult development is initiated by crisis. One sense of "crisis" has a theatrical meaning: the many plot elements of a person's life come together in a decisive period of time. Another sense of "crisis" is a catastrophe. Turning Points have elements of both.

At Turning Points, the strands of our lives unravel slightly, and we decide how to weave them back together. Sometimes at Turning Points, however, we feel as though the entire cable severs, separating our lives into before and after. *In any case, at all Turning Points we make decisions that affect the course of the next seven to ten years of our lives for better or worse.*

What Are Turning Points and How Do They Affect Us?

Turning Points, in spite of the name, are not single points in time; they usually spread over one to three years. They signal periods of heightened awareness. At Turning Points people unexpectedly become open to new ideas. They may check out the self-help books in bookstores or the section on Eastern philosophy. At midlife men may become interested in women's magazines, or women's issues, or want desperately to connect. A woman might suddenly decide to start a business or have children for the first time. *Both seek ways to expand their arenas of competence and express their talents more completely.*

Turning Points and crises develop out of the Stress Cycle. As we get further and further into the Stress Cycle, we increasingly feel that significant talents and passions never got expressed. Our System Selves become increasingly different from our True Selves. The life we lead no longer expresses who we are, and we become aware of this fact. We recognize problems in our current lives, and consider alternative solutions. *At all Turning Points we start looking for answers and try to find something new.*

Unfortunately, at Turning Points most of us don't escape the Lemming Conspiracy. What does a 42-year-old man do when he wakes up one morning to find that he doesn't want to go to work that day? He can't stand the thought of doing what he does all day. This is not an unnatural feeling, nor is it uncommon. A person in this condition may find himself unexpectedly grasping for new answers and seeking new points of view.

A flurry of activity and change may follow. New clothes, new hairstyle or color, new car, new city, new wife, new family. These changes are all on the *outside*. Our 42-year-old in the midst of this flurry may *feel* that each new change expresses the "new him," but unless he has done some serious work on defining the True Self he is trying to express, most of these changes do not lead to any new or creative answers. They just end up throwing him into another round of the Stress Cycle.

Most divorces happen at Turning Points. People also tend to quit jobs or make sudden career moves. This is no accident. People want answers, and they mostly look for these answers in the *externals* of their lives. No creative solution emerges from these approaches. Simple change of externals rarely leads people any closer to their True Selves.

In order to discover answers that can really change your life, you must first look *inside*. You have to find out who you really are. Not your System Self, not the you of your family of origin, but your True Self—the self that powerfully wants expression at crises and Turning Points. After you have a clear sense of your True Self from the inside, you can look productively outside for ways to express it.

In Chapter 2, we described how crises develop from the increasing disparity between our System Selves and our True Selves and how this leads to the Stress Cycle. Let us see how the different crises and Turning Points develop over the adult life span.

The Eight Turning Points of Adult Life

At all Turning Points throughout our adult lives, we must solve the problem of a personal balance between connectedness and productivity. Between being and doing. Love and work.

At the earlier Turning Points, we tend to choose one over the other. Our major commitment and energy goes into our family and marriage, or into work and "making it." Traditionally, in our society, men have gone one way, and women the other. This traditional separation of men's and women's roles is no longer so predictable. When people speak of "having it all," they are referring to this traditional split between work and family; they want work *and* family. They do not want to make a black-and-white choice, but they often choose one over the other in spite of themselves. The wish for both frequently leads to frantic exhaustion in the pursuit of everything.

Balance implies choosing. We each have a limited stock of time and energy—a difficult concept for anyone 30 years old—and we must choose where to invest it. The more fully and completely we know our True Selves, the easier these choices become. At 30, at least for the authors of this book, choosing *less* of this and *more* of that represented heresy. At 40 or 50, these choices seem more reasonable.

After midlLife, lives can become less of an either/or proposition. Men, having made it (or not), may want more intimacy. Some women, perhaps having been intensely involved in family for years, may want to see what they can do out in the world. Other women, having invested their energies in the business world, may suddenly find that they want more intense involvement with a family. In any case, the either/or decision is a blind alley. It doesn't lead to a satisfying long-term resolution. We find that as people mature, as they encounter the Turning Points after midlife, they are increasingly capable of creating a solution that expresses both balance and choice rather than simply striving for everything. People who achieve this balance seem to have a calm and wisdom from which we can all learn.

Each Turning Point represents a window of time during which we have the energy and drive to examine our former solutions and try again to discover more satisfying ones.

High school to college (17-18 years old): Think back for a moment on how you decided to go to the college you attended. We know of a young man who went to Princeton. Why? Because it was Princeton. No other reason seemed necessary. Looking back on this important decision, it seems embarrassingly unconsidered to him. Princeton might have been the perfect choice or exactly the wrong one. But without any serious work on what he wanted to do with his life, or what he wanted to get out of college, how could he have possibly known?

Where to go to college is the first career decision most of us make. It begins the difficult but critical process of individuating from our families of origin. We often can't see its importance until we are older and look back, wishing we had explored a different opportunity, or not spent so much time on a dead end. High school seniors and their families typically make this decision with almost no real information about themselves. Most decisions about college are made by some combination of high school grades, SAT scores, teacher recommendations and the reputation of the college. All of these are outside factors; someone else passes judgment on the individual or the school. None of them tell the student anything about his or her *interior*—about such crucial factors as their true talents, their interests, their goals in life, or how their personality works. Indeed, most students at this age have never considered these interior factors in any detailed way, and have never been encouraged to. Yet their success in college, their success in the adult world, and how much they *enjoy* their lives depend far more on these factors than on grades and SAT scores.

The most important information high school and college students need is an assessment of their natural talents and abilities. This tells them how they are hardwired—what's going to be easy for them, and what difficult. We talk about this more fully in Chapter 4.

Students should also start addressing the "softer" issues and college is an ideal time to do this—interests, personality, family, values and even life goals. These all become increasingly important as we mature. If students get the idea that they are worth paying attention to, it can help them immensely in college and later.

We have talked to some adults who report themselves to be extremely happy with their careers over extended periods of time. They are markedly different from the driven young men and women in their 20s and 30s who work constantly, have no personal lives and tell you "Everything's fine!" These adults who have been so satisfied with their work lives always report the same thing: as teenagers, they were positively encouraged by their families to pay attention to and actively follow what they *enjoy*. They also had parents who actively followed this advice themselves. In these families, the family *value* was clear: the interior experience of what you did was paramount, not the result or the bottom line. We cannot stress enough that children absorb the actual values parents *live by*. If these values correspond to what the parents say, then children get a congruent message. If, however, parents live one message and proclaim another, the children always absorb the message their parents actually live. They also learn that what you say does not necessarily need to reflect reality.

High School to College: Two Stories

Ben went to a college-preparatory high school and did well. His grade point average, SAT scores and teacher recommendations allowed him to enter Cornell University. He was excited about going to his father's alma mater. At Cornell, he enjoyed his classes, but failed to find a peer group with whom he felt compatible. He became increasingly depressed, and when he came home for Christmas break, he decided not to go back.

Ben waited tables for several months after dropping out of college, but also became interested in showing his art. A talented artist, he started an artists' cooperative with two acquaintances.

Ben had never thought about his art in relation to college or to his career. He was indeed academically talented, but obviously there was much more that he could do. He had never considered exactly what he wanted to accomplish in college; it was enough just to go. He had put off thinking about a career altogether.

Patricia, on the other hand, went to college with several ideas in mind. She thought she might like to explore journalism. She was definitely interested in law and also politics. Patricia deliberately chose a college that offered her the ability to explore all three of her interests.

Patricia worked for the college newspaper for two years, becoming campus editor before deciding that her personality was wrong for newspaper work; she often felt she was forcing herself to capture an interview or a statement in a pushy way that she didn't like very much.

Patricia also worked in her state representative's office for almost a year as part of an internship. She wrote replies to letters from constituents. She enjoyed the feeling of doing something, and remained interested in politics. Her law courses really enlivened her, though. She became intensely involved in capital punishment and public-interest law.

Patricia graduated from college four years after entering. This put her in a minority. Of her group of seven friends from high school, she was the only one to graduate in four years. She went to law school and is now a practicing lawyer. She remains interested in politics, or perhaps in being a judge someday.

Ben ignored a hugely significant aspect of his natural talent when choosing a college. He was never encouraged to think about himself and what he wanted to do with his life. He was never encouraged to think about college as a springboard to his career or to think about how what he did in college might connect to him personally.

Patricia had been encouraged to figure out what she was looking for—in some detail. The college she chose was not the most prestigious one to which she was accepted. It was the one that offered her the clearest opportunity to experience personally the career fields in which she knew she had an interest.

It is important to understand that Patricia did not pull her thoughts about possible career fields out of the air. She went through a structured process like the one in this book while she was still in high school. She knew where she could use her natural talents (journalism, politics and law all heavily use the kinds of natural talents that Patricia has), and she knew where her interests led her. When she chose a college it was with a great deal of information about herself.

College to the work world (22 to 25 years old): This is, for many, the final step out of the family home. If successful, a young man or woman finally leaps into the adult world. If not, he or she falls agonizingly back into the family and can become dangerously stuck. A recent article in the *New York Times* indicated that almost one in seven males between the ages of 22 and 29 live at home with their parents.

Many factors conspire to make the transition to the work world more bewildering now than in the past. Although this has always been a difficult step, today there is no clear path. No one joins a large corporation out of college expecting to work there until retirement. Corporations expect young people to be free agents, hired for a finite period to do a particular job. For corporations, the premium rests on people who can clearly state their value to the company. Unfortunately, this is difficult for anyone who has never examined in any detail just what he or she has to offer an employer and doesn't know how he or she is hardwired in the first place.

College students and recent graduates can easily get caught up in externals. The imperatives are simple: Get into the work world. Start being a productive adult.

But what are the right questions to be asking? What pays the most? What industry offers the most security or the most stock options or the most growth potential? What career fields will capture headlines in the next century? What company provides the best benefits? Is there a secure career track? As important as all of these considerations are, they ignore the central questions: *Who am I, what do I want from my career and how can I put myself in a position to do what I do best?*

It's no wonder that college students don't typically pay any attention to the question of what to do after college until they are within months of graduating. Job? The work world? As a college student, it's easy to feel that these don't have anything to do with your life if you haven't done any work to figure out how you can use your talents in the adult world.

We talked to hundreds of college students as we researched the ideas in this book. The almost universal feeling among them is that when they leave college and enter into adult life, they will have to give up most of what they really enjoy about being who they are. They will have to settle down and work hard at a job that is essentially meaningless so they can earn enough money to buy the kinds of things that don't bring their parents much happiness. Many go to graduate school or professional school just so they can put off making a commitment for a few more years. Who can blame them?

College students first need to pay close attention to their natural talents. After their natural talents, they should look at their skills. What have they learned in life? How can they use that? Again, their interests, personalities, values and goals should play an important part in gaining a sense of *direction*. Ideally the first job would build upon experiences in college, internships and summer jobs, and be a positive step in a career direction that makes internal sense to the student. Simply joining the firm that sends recruiters to campus can lead to much unhappiness—and yet that is the predominant reason that college students choose their first jobs.

College to Work: Emily's Story

Emily majored in marketing at a good college. Her first job was copy editing for a publishing company. She moved from there to a music company and worked in marketing for them, but soon left. While looking for something more to her liking, she took a job as a receptionist at a real estate company. One day she woke up to discover she had been a receptionist at the same company for almost four years. She had never actively pursued anything else. This realization devastated her.

Emily, age 28, went through the program we describe in this book. She discovered that her natural talents, personality, interests and values all pushed her in the direction of counseling. At her Age 30 Turning Point, she started back to graduate school to earn a degree and eventually a license to practice counseling. The point is, Emily could have known this about herself at any time—before college, during college or after college. By expending concentrated effort and attention to figure this out, she could have made better use of her time in college. She could have worked in jobs that expanded her horizons and helped her career ambitions, and focused her energy on graduate school earlier, instead of trying desperately to make it in jobs that weren't rewarding to her. She didn't need to waste so much of her time and talent—and feel so bad about herself for so long.

Age 30 Assessment (28 to 33 years old): Regardless of the direction in which we launch ourselves in our early 20s, we do some reassessment around age 30. If we jumped right out of college into a job and started working like crazy, by this time we begin asking some predictable questions. Is this getting me what I want? Can I see myself doing this for another 10 years? How far can I go with this company? What else should I be doing? Should I make a move to get myself on the fast track? If our jobs seem to be getting us what we want, we start asking about lifestyles. Shouldn't I get a new car? Maybe it's time to get married. Maybe it's time to have a baby.

People always make *some* decision at this age. Just as with earlier Turning Points, most people look to the outside for their answers. The answer to the discomfort of the Stress Cycle is a new car, or marriage, or a child, or a new job or a promotion. *They almost never start by asking themselves who they are and what they would really like to be doing in the first place.* The significant questions at this age are more like these: Am I really using my most important talents? Are there some talents I have that I don't know about yet? Is this what I want to be doing? What doesn't fit? If my career keeps going in the same way it is now, where will I be in 10 years? Is that where I want to be? Why? What do I want to add to my life to make it fuller?

At this Turning Point, after the question of using your most powerful talents, the main issues revolve around goals. What do I really want in life? Is what I am doing going to get me that? If not, I need to do something different. If so, what else should I be shooting for? People who have been paying attention all along to the softer, interior issues like interests and values are in a much better position to use the creative energy of this Turning Point to position themselves in a career they will actively enjoy over the next 10 years or so.

The majority have not been paying attention. A great many young people in their early 20s get started in jobs that will not take them anywhere. How many young college graduates or dropouts do you know who are waiting tables or working at some other dead-end job? They are (perhaps) able to support themselves in an apartment, pay for gas, and pay for their entertainment. At the Age 30 Assessment, it suddenly dawns on them that these jobs cannot help them fulfill significant life goals. They can't get married, can't have a family, can't have anything like the life of their parents. Often young people at this age start over. They might go to school or become serious about finding a job with a future. We saw this pattern in Emily's story above.

The other main group consists of the young people who have started in a career or a profession and at this Turning Point start to get serious about it. It's not a lark any more. If they are going to get to the top, they have to do it *now*. The top, of course, is one of the fundamentally subversive myths of the Lemming Conspiracy. The top is understood without question or comment to be a positive goal and unquestionably worth achieving. Like all myths, it imparts a message about values and the way one should live. But it is a dangerous myth because it never addresses the interior of the person.

Regardless of how well or poorly people make decisions at the Age 30 Assessment, they move into their 30s and a period of stability. They may be miserable and hate their jobs, but they don't change course during these years. Even if the 30s are productive and satisfying, people inevitably come to midlife, a time of change, transition and starting over—especially for men.

Age 30 Assessment and Beyond: Paul and Melinda's Story

Paul and Melinda both worked in large corporations, Paul as a manager in a technology company, Melinda as an accountant in a large international accounting firm. Married at 25, they were now in their early 30s. Both Paul and Melinda sensed that time was running out. Melinda felt that if she was going to have children, it must be now. Paul felt that he had to get on the fast track in his company in the next two years, or he would never make it as far as he wanted to go.

They decided to have children, and their first was born when they were both 32. Another child followed a year later. Paul enrolled in an executive M.B.A. program; in addition, he asked for, and got, extra projects from his boss. Melinda was offered a promotion, but she would have had to move overseas, so she decided not to take it. They had money for the first time in their marriage; they moved into a new house and bought nice cars. They hired a nanny. Melinda was offered another promotion that required moving to another city. She felt she would have to take this promotion or see her career evaporate. Paul put in for a transfer to a city near the one where Melinda and the two children would be, but he felt this would definitely be a backwards career move for him. His boss was now actively interested in him and promoted his cause in the company. The new city would not have the kind of visibility that he now enjoyed. Paul already felt some resentment about being asked to make this choice.

The last thing either Paul or Melinda wanted to hear was that they should take a few weeks to sort through their lives and figure out what they really wanted. The Stress Cycle gripped both like an iron vise. Although each had goals, and they expended a great deal of energy toward attaining them, neither felt centered. They tried to pursue everything society and their families had laid out for them to do, thinking all the while they were fulfilling their own lives. The trouble is that neither had ever stopped to take a close and objective look at their lives and so they were being hammered by forces over which they could exert no control—and they weren't even aware of it.

Both Paul and Melinda made significant career moves and decisions during this Turning Point. Neither, however, dealt with limits. They wanted marriage and children and expensive things and career advancement and success and recognition. (How far? How much? "As far as possible" and "Everything" were their only answers.) They didn't want to choose between these goals.

By age 34, they were trying to maintain a marriage at a distance. Paul decided not to move so that he could continue working with his boss. His ambition settled on moving into the executive ranks. Melinda was being offered steady advancement in her firm, but this entailed a great deal of travel. They earned enough to have a full-time nanny who took care of the children. By their mid-30s, Paul and Melinda had grown far apart. They seemed to be waiting for a signal that it was time to divorce.

Eventually they will be brought up short. Paul may get downsized. Melinda might have an affair. One of their children might develop problems at school. They might get divorced. Any or all of these life events tell us one thing: "You have to stop." It sometimes happens at the Midlife Transition.

The Midlife Transition (38 to 45 years old): The Midlife Transition can be one of the most important and significant events in many people's lives. Or it can be an unmitigated disaster. It is no coincidence, certainly, that people in their early 40s in the midst of mid-life turmoil often have teenage children who are in the midst of the turmoil of leaving home. The parents and the teenagers are trying to solve the same problem. They both seek to create or recreate themselves so that they can function in the adult world.

Our society is used to thinking of midlife as a crisis, in the sense of a catastrophe. Midlife is really no more important than any of the other Turning Points. It may be just the first time many people become aware of any change in their lives. It is a catastrophe for many because they have ignored their True Selves for many years, accepting systems' answers for who they are and what they should be doing.

Eventually, most people become aware of the disparity between the person they feel themselves to be and the person through whom they function—their System Selves. When the disparity is large and the effort to keep it hidden from awareness is overwhelming, the realization can be sudden and intense. It can lead people to seek sudden and catastrophic answers.

Stories are legion. People at midlife have affairs. They get divorced. They suddenly derail from the fast track. Problems like drinking, drugs or gambling that have been lurking around for years suddenly become destructive addictions. They get depressed; they take Prozac. They want to buy sports cars or have surgery, or both. They may want to start their own businesses, change jobs or change careers. It's exciting. It's crazy.

It's scary. One of the worst outcomes of midlife is doing nothing. Many people, confronted with feelings of stress, anxiety and depression, choose to ignore them. It's too frightening. To open the door to change is to release demons and lose control over them forever. Better to simply endure.

In the short term, this strategy of perseverance appears successful. The upsetting feelings of midlife go away. People settle down to the life they were living before. But the feelings don't really go away; they just go underground. The True Self still needs expression. People who just endure have only given themselves a short reprieve. They often find that when the feelings of upset come back at the next Turning Point, they are much more intense and overwhelming. And solutions are correspondingly more catastrophic.

Besides figuring out how to use our talents, the main issues at midlife revolve around *values*. Usually, we know how far we can go in our careers by the end of our 30s. We know whether or not we can get to the top. We have a sense of how much income we can expect to bring in. We have a sense of what we can accomplish. We also turn an invisible corner sometime around age 40; half our lives are over. So a question begins to impose itself: Does what I am doing seem *worth* doing?

This is life's great question; wrestling with it makes us grow and figure out what we want. Too many people confront it, though, and try to forget about it. There doesn't seem to be any ready answer. Change feels unthinkable. And how do you figure out what's worth doing anyway?

It becomes increasingly important as you get older to feel that what you are doing is meaningful. What makes work meaningful is different for everyone, but too many people don't consider this question important. They feel that being an adult means holding down a job and providing for a family—and that's it. Often at midlife they are surprised by feelings that their lives aren't enough. What's missing is the interior—the True Self.

Midlife Transition: Steven's Story

Steven, age 44, was married with three children. The oldest was 15. He had been married 20 years. He had worked in banking since he graduated from college. He had been with the same bank for 13 years and was the manager of a department in the home office. One morning he read in the paper that his bank had been acquired by a larger bank in a complicated merger.

Within six months he was laid off because of the merger and restructuring of the two organizations. He had six months of severance pay and a good outplacement package. In the outplacement counseling, he was told that anger and depression were common reactions to his situation, but that the best answer was to dust himself off and get right back out there. Clearly the best way to jump back "out there" would be to land another job in banking.

Steven was suddenly acutely aware of his life and career balancing delicately between two paths, and that now he must choose. He could return to banking, a world he knew, or he could strike out in a different direction.

Steven chose to go through a program like the one presented in this book. He sorted through what made his life valuable and meaningful to him, and what seemed beside the point. In a practical sense, he knew he needed to capitalize on his banking knowledge, contacts and background. But in an emotional sense, he realized he would rather sell hot dogs than work for another banking conglomerate. In his program, he discovered natural talents in sales and strategic marketing that had never been evident to him. *He had long held that his family came first, and he determined that anything he did would not compromise that value.*

Steven ended up making a proposal to a smaller firm that outsources human resource services to large firms, such as banks. His contacts and experience in the banking world make him quite knowledgeable when talking to potential customers. He does not get paid as much as he made before, but he feels much more control of his life. Learning a new job and a new field has been very exciting. "I feel that I have gotten to try a whole new life—and I like it. I like the entrepreneurial feel of the company, and I like it that some days I go to work and I'm just making it up, because no one has tried what I'm doing before. I love that feeling!"

Age 50 Assessment (50 to 55 years old): You may notice that throughout the adult developmental cycle, the questions become increasingly complex and subjective. The Age 50 Assessment, just like the Age 30 Assessment, is a Turning Point in which we reassess the answers of the previous Turning Point. If those answers were grossly inappropriate, such as quitting basically productive jobs and rewarding marriages, we may start over at this Turning Point. If we did nothing at midlife, if we just had the feelings and simply endured, then the anxiety and depression of midlife come back in spades. If our solutions at midlife really brought the way we live closer to an expression of our True Selves, we may make small course corrections at this Turning Point.

By the Age 50 Assessment, it is impossible to pin down a single issue that is more important than the others, although attending to one's spiritual life seems to assume greater and greater prominence. Living a life that feels meaningful is the only real way to come to terms with the end of life. The alternative to meaning is despair.

Just as the Midlife Transition is particularly powerful for men, the Age 50 Assessment appears to have particular relevance and meaning for women. In fact, some evidence indicates that, for women, the true Midlife Transition may not be at 40, but instead at 50. Whereas men who have been trying to make it in the world suddenly at age 40 feel their isolation and begin grasping for connection, women who have connected all along, by age 50 are seeing many of those relationships change and disappear. Children leave home and start lives of their own. Parents die. Marriages break up. It is at this age that women's bodies say clearly, "Childbearing is over."

Many women whose focus has always been toward family and connection find that they move *outward* at this age, in the opposite direction from men. Now they want to see what they can *do* in the world. They want to make an impact. Women who have had successful careers may find themselves, like men at this age, wanting to make some changes to bring more balance to their lives.

Both men and women must find a different way to communicate inside their families. If they don't, and many do not, they run the significant risk of isolation. Children, now adults, no longer need their parents' constant time, energy and attention. Husbands and wives must find a new basis for their relationship. Many men, in an effort to create the intimacy they missed in first families, start new families. Many women look for a new "baby" to nurture—a business, a cause or a lover.

Both men and women need fuller lives at this age. Both need to achieve a balance between being and doing, relating and producing. Change is inevitable here, and just like at midlife, often catastrophic "solutions" like divorce are nothing more than attempts to deny and ignore change. Ideally, couples at this Turning Point can discover a partnership between equals. Once they have gotten over the fact that things are different, they can go on to figure out that *they* are different, and they have many more options to create different relationships.

By this age, our lives are the accumulation of all of our choices and decisions. It is difficult to take back earlier choices that limited us or kept us from expression of our True Selves, or kept us from even knowing who our True Selves were. But any choice we make at this Turning Point to help us know who we really are can open doors to express our True Selves.

Age 50 Assessment: Wade

When Wade was 52, his company asked him to take over a division in New York. It would mean a higher profile, being closer to the decision-makers at the home office. He refused. He did not want to move to the Northeast. He did not want to uproot his family. He did not want a more pressurized life. He knew his position in the company was secure, but that this decision not to move would take him off the fast track he had been on for much of his career.

Wade realized that he and his wife were virtual strangers after years of raising children and maintaining two careers. He also realized that, unless he did something, they would stay that way. He took some vacation time. He and his wife spent almost a month on a walking tour of England and Wales. It was the best time he and his wife had together since they dated in their 20s.

Age 50 Assessment: Marjorie

Marjorie, 53, was a successful counselor. She had been single for years and her children were now grown and out of the house. She enjoyed her counseling practice, perhaps more now than she had in years. She no longer felt so stressed by her clients. She liked them more and felt more warmth toward them. She had cut back her hours a little the previous year, and now cut them back again. She felt financially secure, although she was not wealthy.

At 50, Marjorie had started art lessons. As a child and young adult, she painted a great deal, but marriage, children, a career and divorce had drained her energy for art. Now she threw herself into art with great enthusiasm. She tried different media and experimented with different styles. She put her art in her office and home. She loves having her art around her. She has a network of friends who are artists also, some younger, some older. She finds this association with a whole different set of people from her academic and counseling friends very rewarding.

Marjorie does not think she will ever retire completely from counseling; however, she plans to cut back her hours even more, spend more time with art and perhaps travel a little with friends.

Pre-Retirement Transition (60 to 65 years old): Just like the transition from the family to the adult world in our 20s and the midlife transition of our 40s, at this transition, we again create a new life. Once again, the biggest mistake is ignoring the issue, assuming that retirement means the absence of work. Or assuming that if you have planned financially for retirement, that's all the planning you need to do.

Far from being a time of idyllic rest, retirement for many is a time of aimlessness and emptiness. People die from lack of meaning. If you don't believe that, look at statistics for death by suicide among senior citizens. But suicide isn't the only reason people die. When people feel no purpose to their lives, they tend to get sick and die within just a year or two in any case.

By this age, a fact of all lives is *loss*. We lose parents, spouses, friends, relatives, school chums, even children. We may stop working, and that is a loss. Our bodies may change; we become visibly older. We lose the strength, health and potency of middle age. We creep into the region inhabited by old people.

The most productive answers at all Turning Points *add* to life. They supply some important element we have missed until now. This general rule becomes even more critical as we grow older, when it is often so tempting to give in to loss.

The Pre-Retirement Transition sets the stage for one of the major movements of life. According to demographic statistics, people who live healthily to this age will probably live past 80. This means that at this Turning Point you make preparations for a period of over 20 years. This significant span of years can be mainly marked by emptiness, loss and meaninglessness, or defined by connection, meaning and productivity. The difference between one and the other relates directly to the quality of one's Personal Vision.

Ideally, the Pre-Retirement Transition, like all of the other Turning Points, should build on everything that has gone before. It should be an expression of all a person has learned, believed in, wanted to accomplish and *is*. But it should also be *new*. People looking at retirement should be thinking about what they want to continue doing in retirement, what they want to drop and what they want to add. They should be creating a Personal Vision for how their lives in retirement will be and what will be meaningful for them.

Generally, this is not something that a person should tackle after he or she has already retired. We feel that the process of thinking and planning for a life of retirement should begin at least five years before. (Clearly, this is true of the other Turning Points, too. As people become more aware of the regularity of change at midlife, we may find that they become more proactive about planning changes in their careers to make them less catastrophic and more productive.) The questions that are important have to do with summing up a life. What do I want to leave the world? What will be my legacy to the world for having been here? How will the next 20 years contribute to that legacy?

Having a Personal Vision at this age that answers these kinds of questions undoubtedly helps people live longer. But it also helps them live better, more fully, with more satisfaction. If you see those rare senior citizens who are vital, active and alert into their 90s, they have a Personal Vision. They have a reason to live and a purpose for pushing ahead. A Personal Vision can save your life.

Pre-Retirement Transition: Tom's Story

At age 60, Tom's company asked him to take a retirement package. He had a comfortable income from investments, a home that was paid for, and a wife of ten years who was 12 years younger than he. She was a physician with a successful practice.

Tom had always known he would retire, but had never thought about what he would do. *He was happy to be away from his company, but was angry about being shoved out. About a month after retiring, he decided to take up woodworking. He bought several expensive power tools and had some workmen come in to transform some unused basement space into a shop. He hovered over them as they worked, constantly criticizing their work. Several carpenters quit before the job was done. When the shop was finished and the tools installed, Tom had no idea what to make. He thought he would make some toys for his grandchildren, but became frustrated with several elaborate projects before they were done.*

Tom became increasingly morose and isolated. Calling a former business associate to have lunch with him was intensely humiliating. The former business associate could not figure out why Tom was calling him, and he didn't have a free lunch date open for weeks. "But let's stay in touch. Say, Tom, sorry, I have another call coming in. Let's talk soon." Tom started watching soap operas during the day. At night he talked about their plots with his wife.

Six months into retirement, Tom's wife knew he was clinically depressed. She was actually the catalyst for change: "If you don't figure out what to do with your life, I'm going to divorce you. Period." He went through the structured program we describe in this book. It was clear he was not ready to retire, and that he would be much happier working for a while longer. He took some consulting work in his old industry—enough to feel creative and productive. He and his wife plan to retire together in 10 years or so.

Age 70 Assessment (70 to 75 years old): The most important career questions at this age have to do with what you can give back to the world. By this age, you have a huge stock of knowledge and experience, but what can you do with it? All of us need to feel connected with others. In the same way, we also need to feel we are productive. This doesn't mean holding down a high-powered job, or earning mountains of money. We can feel productive if we are able to pass on our experience to a younger generation and help that generation grow and thrive.

Having a Personal Vision for these years can make the difference between living and dying, both emotionally and physically. We all need a purpose—a reason to get up in the morning and keep breathing. We all have this purpose inside, if we can identify and articulate it.

This Turning Point gives us a chance to assess and correct decisions we made earlier. Change comes rapidly during this period of our lives. Our bodies change, our friends' bodies change. People close to us die. If we have not accepted retirement, it is often forced upon us. People tend to separate into three groups by this age:

- The majority who settle down, become less active physically and mentally, and create familiar lives close to friends and family.
- A large minority who become increasingly isolated by distance, illness, poverty, death of significant others, and/or gradual personality change.
- A small minority who shift their activities into new arenas, but who remain physically and mentally vital. They do not release their holds on life, but seem intent on returning gifts from long and productive lives to the community as a whole. Jimmy and Rosalynn Carter, as well as Paul Newman and Joanne Woodward and many other people, both well-known and not, exemplify this kind of choice.

Age 70 Assessment: Robert's Story

For 35 years, Robert was the principal of a high school. He retired at 60. At this time, his wife became ill with bone cancer, and he cared for her full time for the next eight years until she died. Robert maintained a wide circle of friends in the small town where he lived. Many people there had been his students in high school; others had been friends since they and Robert were in school together.

Three years after his wife died, Robert met a woman slightly older than he who had been married to a well-known physician for many years. He had died of a heart attack the previous year. Robert and this woman began seeing each other regularly, having dinner together almost every night. They started dance lessons, and went dancing most weekends. They then started a dance group among their friends. Every few months they traveled—sometimes with a group to Europe or Asia, sometimes to see their children and grandchildren. Robert maintained a large garden and became an accomplished grower of roses. He volunteered his time with a neighborhood youth program and at the senior citizen center. He feels healthy and alive; he feels his life is busy and that what he does means something to others who are important to him.

Senior Transition (80 to 85 years old): Change continues. Here change involves the gradual shift from independence to increased dependence. Now your Personal Vision must help you make the utterly creative leap toward connection and productivity while dealing with appropriate dependence. Above all, one must achieve a working balance— remember, this means *choosing*—between appropriate dependence and remaining a vital actor in one's own life.

The factors that go into a Personal Vision are the same as those in earlier Turning Points. It is just as important here as at other Turning Points to seek a good balance between your personal growth and health on the one hand, and feeling productive and of benefit to others on the other. Figuring out how to remain physically active within one's physical limitations—through yoga, tai chi, walking, running or even weight lifting—becomes increasingly crucial to your health. Figuring out how to remain mobile—through walking, bicycling, public transport or hiring young people to drive you—again, within your limitations, can add immeasurably to your mental well-being. Figuring out how to *add* to the world by passing along your experience to younger people can help you feel that your life has a larger meaning than just the life and death of your physical body. In all of these areas, a Personal Vision that comprehends your talents, interests, personality, goals, values, skills and family of origin can make it far more easy for you to find what your passion is and create a life in which to express it.

It may be easy to ignore the fact that this transition is just as important and may shape just as much of your life as the other major transitions of your life. People who reach this transition and are healthy may be making decisions about the next 10 or 20 years of their lives. This is why it is so important to make plans and be proactive about keeping alive mentally and physically.

It is too easy to make King Lear's mistake. Lear decided he had graduated in life to the point that he should be taken care of, rather than take care of himself. He had accomplished much, given his children much and now he wanted to reap his reward of rest and passivity. The result was disaster, of course. Lear wanted to abdicate the role of actor of his own life. He felt he *deserved* to be cared for as he wished, without participating in that care.

This time in life can be an opportunity to *be*, to accept oneself and one's life as it is. We often see people of this age who are able to use their lives' balance and stability to give—not necessarily money, but a sense of reinforcement and reward to a younger generation.

Why Real Change Rarely Happens

As we have seen, each of the adult Turning Points is brought on by the Stress Cycle, the disparity between our System Selves and our True Selves, and the sense of crisis this engenders. We want change; our old answers cease to work well; we feel stressed. At these times we seek a better expression of our True Selves.

But rarely is anyone able to get outside of systems during these periods of openness and change. As we have seen, corporate and school systems cannot help anyone discover anything about True Selves. The System Self is all any system can deal with. Most of our "spontaneous" answers at Turning Points actually come out of our families of origin. As we have seen with Mitchell's story and Sarah's story, we will invariably use the same kinds of solutions for about the same reasons as one or the other of our parents used at the same Turning Point.

There are three common outcomes at Turning Points:

Endure. Ignore your feelings of stress and anxiety, tell yourself to grow up, and keep on doing what you are doing. As we have seen above, this effectively puts off the issue of change for five to seven years, but sets up an even more catastrophic change at the next Turning Point.

Appear to change. Many people, when confronted with the wish for change, do not know what to do with it. Systems urge us to pay attention to the outside, not to our interiors. A new car can be wonderful, but it won't make your life meaningful. Neither will a new job, unless it is connected to a Personal Vision. Even with a drastic change such as divorce, people usually find that the same issues of stress, anger, anxiety and depression come back. These external changes can't bring your True Self and your System Self any closer together.

Actually change. This is a rare outcome. It is always the result of getting *outside* systems and doing structured work on who you are and what you really want from your life. You have to sort out the messages from your family of origin that may be perfect for you from those that may not fit anymore.

Real change usually involves *adding* to your life. It is almost never a product of simply removing something.

With real change, your first goal is to figure out how your System Self and True Self have diverged, but ultimately the goal is to find the best expression of your True Self. This may involve giving up some aspects of your job or personal life that do not fit anymore. But this is never enough. You must *add* something to your life that is missing.

Real change is virtually impossible to accomplish alone. Any answer you discover on your own will probably be one derived from your systems: your spouse, your friends, your company, your church, your lover. They know you too well. They are all part of your systems. The answers we get from systems may feel real and obvious, but they don't lead to any real change at Turning Points.

Richard's Story

Richard, age 41, was a veteran 20-year insurance executive. He had worked for the same large international company since he graduated from college. On the fast track, he was definitely heading toward the top. He was well-liked by his boss and known to the management of the company.

"I sat at my desk with the door closed one day, going over my options. The only thing I could think to do was to quit. It seemed

like the only option that made sense. My boss and my friends at the company would have been very surprised if they had known where my thinking led me that day. None of them had any idea about these feelings, but they had become increasingly apparent and important to me."

Richard was at the Midlife Turning Point. His feelings were normal and made sense in a larger context. But they didn't make sense to him at the time. He could not articulate exactly what made contin-ued work for his company impossible. He knew he was just as pro-ductive as ever, but it wasn't fun anymore. He loved his wife and kids, and his job allowed him time and energy to be with them. But he didn't feel any challenge to life.

Instead of quitting, Richard "embarked on a quest." He read everything he could about change at mid-career and talked to all of his friends about what they were feeling. He found out that some level of discontent at his age is not only not unusual, but in reality is the overwhelming norm—for both men and women.

The Steps to Change

What is real change, and how does it happen? Richard, in the story above, didn't need a simple answer or new motivational talk. He also didn't need the answers coming from his systems: "Don't be a fool. Just keep doing what you're doing, and you'll be set for life." "You've got a good job with a good paycheck, a family to raise, and good prospects for the future. Don't rock the boat." These, or their variants, are the system's answer to Richard's dilemma.

In order for Richard to discover his own answers, he must first *get outside the system*. He must escape the Lemming Conspiracy. In the course of his research, Richard found a structured process to look sys-tematically at each factor of his career. This process was independent of his systems and its goals were fundamentally different from those of his company, his family or even his friends.

Systems kept Richard from really looking at himself and what he wanted. They asked him to focus on *results*, on the outside, his posi-tion, his possessions, his responsibilities. They did not, nor could they, ask him to focus on Richard. In order to beat the Lemming Conspiracy, Richard would need *new information*. He would need information that was not in his systems and that he didn't yet know about himself.

It turned out that one of the most crucial pieces of information Richard needed was about his natural talents and abilities—that inborn hard-wiring that makes it easy to do some kinds of tasks and difficult to do others. Richard found out that he had a natural problem-solving ability we call Classification. (We will talk about Classification in detail in Chapter 4.) He knew how he liked to tackle new problems, but he had not known what a powerful impact Classification had on his work life. As he looked forward to a comfortable life in the insurance industry, he saw no outlet for this ability to solve new problems and deal with rapid change. He understood that this could be the source of his unhappiness and sense of unfulfillment.

In the next chapter, we will talk about abilities in detail, specifically about the powerful Driving Abilities that shape so much of what roles we are particularly suited for, and what ones we are not.

Richard had known he wasn't happy. But he thought he should just grow up, buckle down and do his job. The *new information* he now had was that, objectively, his job would not make use of his most powerful and insistent ability. He could make a completely effective case to his boss, and his wife, because he had acquired information from outside the systems and had used this information to create a Personal Vision. We will see more of what happened with Richard in Chapter 5.

A Structured Process to Escape Systems

One of the most difficult aspects of gaining your own Personal Vision is sidestepping the Lemming Conspiracy—getting outside your own systems. We have found that the most effective strategy for defeating the Lemming Conspiracy is following a *structured process*. The process we developed includes *all* of the factors a person needs to consider at life Turning Points. Following a structure insures that you systematically take into account not only factors that are comfortable to you, but also ones that you might not think about otherwise. If you only include factors in your Personal Vision that feel "right" to you, or that you would think of yourself, you will only follow your own system. On the other hand, if you follow an external structure for creating your Personal Vision, the structure itself will force you to pay attention to what is important, whether it feels "right" in your system or not. This chapter and the next five chapters detail the structure we researched, developed, tested and have used with our clients.

GETTING OUTSIDE OF SYSTEMS—HARDER THAN IT MAY APPEAR

Your friends, your family, your colleagues, your boss, your relatives, your fellow church, synagogue or club members—they are all part of the Lemming Conspiracy. In spite of their most loving intentions, they are connected to you in a way that makes it impossible for them to help you gain a new perspective on your life. Basically, all they can do is help you keep doing what you have always been doing. Even if you change jobs, change cities or change marriages, you always eventually wind up stuck in the same place you have always been *unless you escape your systems*.

ESCAPING YOUR SYSTEMS: A PRIMER

We have discovered several factors that help people escape, briefly, the boundaries of their systems in order to see a wider picture.

One of the most difficult aspects of gaining a Personal Vision is *stopping*—setting aside a significant amount of time and energy to do the work. As we have seen, the Stress Cycle makes stopping seem impossible. The Stress Cycle makes it appear that everything is urgent and nothing can be put aside for a time so that you can figure out how you want to live your life.

The structured process we developed and describe in this book will help you get to all of the important factors you need to consider at the Turning Points of your adult life. It is thorough and effective. We did not create it to be a Band-Aid or motivational trick to excite you for a while, but lead nowhere. It is a process to use *now*, and at any future Turning Point, to help you envision the next stage of your life.

Doing the work of articulating each of the eight critical factors and then integrating them into a Personal Vision is not something you can do in a day, or even a weekend. You need to give your creative mind and logical mind a chance to work on the problem of getting to a Vision over a period of several weeks or months. As you tackle this work, you will find that you may labor over a problem—how to integrate values and goals, for instance—only to be frustrated by coming up empty-handed. A week later, you may be surprised to find you *have* an answer waiting for you. Your unconscious mind worked on the problem while you had been thinking consciously about something else. The Whole Person Technology® makes deliberate use of your creative unconscious. For the kind of complex problems we deal with—how to live your life fully and with enthusiasm—it is the most powerful part of your brain, by far. You will find that the Thought Experiments use your logical mind *and* your creative mind. You'll need both to create a transforming Personal Vision.

Thought Experiment B:

Your Developmental Time Line

In your Personal Vision notebook, make a page for each Turning Point of your life from the first one, High School to College, through the Senior Transition.

1. High School to College (age 17-18)
2. College to Work (age 22-25)
3. Age 30 Assessment (age 28-33)
4. Midlife Transition (age 38-45)
5. Age 50 Assessment (age 50-55)
6. Pre-Retirement Transition (age 60-65)
7. Age 70 Assessment (age 70-75)
8. Senior Transition (age 80-85)

Write answers to the questions below in your notebook. But *don't* write about them in past tense as though you are your age looking back; write in present tense as though you are looking forward. For instance, for your high school to college transition section, you might write, "I plan to be a doctor, but I am not sure, because I'm afraid it could turn out to be fairly boring. I just don't know what else to look at." Write either from your *actual* point of view at 18 or from the point of view of yourself as 18, but incorporating all that you have learned since then.

Proceed to each Turning Point, writing in each *as though you were that age*. Go backwards to all previous Turning Points. Do your present (or next) Turning Point. Go forward to all future Turning Points. Use the questions to get started, but write about anything that seems significant in how you were assessing your life at the time (or imagine yourself assessing it in the future) and in making plans for the next section of your life.

HIGH SCHOOL TO COLLEGE (AGE 17-18)

Answer these questions as though you are 18. What are the main issues on my mind? What are the main decisions I face now? What relationships are about to change (e.g., between me and my parents, or me and my high school friends)? In looking to the future, what are the most important factors I now think about? What are my plans for the future? Why? What plans do I have for a career? Why? How did I choose that direction among all the possible directions I could have chosen? What are my main talents? What dreams do I have about the kind of life I want? Why?

COLLEGE TO WORK (AGE 22-25)

What skills have I developed? What experience do I have? What kind of work am I most interested in? In choosing a career path, what is the most important deciding factor? What kind of lifestyle do I want? Is what I am doing leading me to that kind of lifestyle? What are my feelings about the adult work world? How do I think I will fit in?

AGE 30 ASSESSMENT (AGE 28-33)

What has been working about the course I chose? What hasn't been working? What do I want to achieve in the next 10 years? How will I do that? What would I need to change to put myself in a better position? What do I want my life to be like 10 years from now? What values do I need to pay attention to? What interests? What are my family goals? How am I balancing work and family? What would be most meaningful to me at this point in my career? What could I *add* to my life to make it more interesting and meaningful?

MIDLIFE TRANSITION (AGE 38-45)

How do I feel about my family? How do I feel about work? What changes would I like to make in the balance of work and family? How connected do I feel to others? What excites me about work? What has become old and stale? What else besides work would I find exciting? Or, what new direction in my life would feel interesting and fascinating to me? What could I pursue that would be interesting and meaningful? What values do I need to pay attention to? How can I carry that out? What goals do I have for the next 20 years of my career? What needs to happen to accomplish them? What experience and what skills of the first 20 years of my career do I want to be sure to take with me into the next?

AGE 50 ASSESSMENT (AGE 50-55)

Note for women: Many of the questions of the previous section on midlife may apply to you at this Turning Point.

What has been working about the course I chose? What hasn't been working? What do I want to achieve in the next 10 years? How will I do that? What would I need to change to put myself in better position? What do I want my life to be like 10 years from now? What values do I need to pay attention to? What interests? What are my family goals? How am I balancing work and family? Is what I am doing meaningful? If not, why not? How can I make my career more meaningful? What can I *add* to my life to make it more interesting and meaningful?

PRE-RETIREMENT TRANSITION (AGE 60-65)

How do I feel about my family? How do I feel about work? What changes would I like to make in the balance of work and family? How connected do I feel to others? What excites me about work? What has become old and stale? What else besides work would I find exciting? Or, what new direction in my life would feel interesting and fascinating to me? What can I pursue that would be interesting and meaningful? What values do I need to pay attention to? How can I carry that out? What goals do I have for the next 20 years of my career? What needs to happen to accomplish them? What experience and what skills of the first 40 years of my career do I want to be sure to take with me into the next phase? What can I give back to the world? How can I do that? Who could benefit from my knowledge and experience?

AGE 70 ASSESSMENT (AGE 70-75)

What losses am I contending with? What losses can I expect in the next 10 years? How can I provide enough reinforcement in life to keep me healthy and happy? What has been working about the course I chose? What hasn't been working? What do I want to achieve in the next 10 years? How will I do that? What would I need to change to put myself in better position? What do I want my life to be like 10 years from now? What values do I need to pay attention to? What interests? What are my family goals? How am I balancing work and family? Is what I am doing meaningful? If not, why not? How can I make my career more meaningful? What can I *add* to my life to make it more interesting and meaningful?

SENIOR TRANSITION (AGE 80-85)

What losses am I contending with? What losses can I expect in the next 10 years? How can I provide enough reinforcement in life to keep me healthy and happy? How do I feel about my family? How do I feel about my day-to-day life? What changes would I like to make in the balance of activity and family? How connected do I feel to others? What excites me about my daily life? What has become old and stale? What other kind of activity would I find exciting? Or, what new direction in my life would feel interesting and fascinating to me? What could I pursue that would be interesting and meaningful? What values do I need to pay attention to? How can I carry that out? What goals do I have for the next 10 years of my life? What needs to happen to accomplish them? What experience and what skills of my working life do I want to be sure to take with me into the next phase? What can I give back to the world? How can I do that? Who could benefit from my knowledge and experience? What forum or group could use my experience?

Wait for a few days, and then read over everything you have written about Turning Points. Do you see any recurring themes? What issues keep coming up? What new issues come up, and at what ages? What were the key decisions you made in your life? How did you make them? Were you always aware of what the impact of key decisions would be, or not? What key decisions can you see in the future?

FOUR STORIES: TURNING POINTS

Tracy

"At 18, I didn't know what I wanted to do; I just picked the best college I could get into. I guess I had always assumed I would be a doctor, but I didn't want to be as driven as my father, who is a doctor. The only kind of life I could imagine would be some kind of professional. I'm at a Turning Point now, and I still want to be some kind of professional; I'm just confused about how to do it. I imagine the future being just about like the lives of my father and mother. I'm a doctor or lawyer or something; I work all the time. I pull in a good income. I help people."

Feelings now: "I'm surprised at how hard this was. I'm also surprised at how the only thing I can really picture is my parents' lives. My main feeling is, 'How dull.'"

Brian and Janet

Brian: "When I was 18, I knew I wanted to go into business. I chose a college that had a good business school with a strong marketing department. My vision at the time was of going all the way to the top. I could see myself wheeling and dealing in a large company as a vice president or something. When I graduated from college, I already had a job, so I felt like I was right on track. I still feel on track at the Age 30 Turning Point, but now I have the sense of 'now or never.'

"As for the future, I play out two scenarios in my mind. In one, I keep going for the top, get promoted and end up in an executive office. I have plenty of money, but maybe I'm not married to Janet anymore. I know I want to have major responsibilities, but it's hard to picture myself in charge. It's also hard to picture the life I would be leading—except that I would just be working all the time. The second scenario is more troubling. I picture myself flopping. Not getting promoted. Maybe getting laid off and having to take another job I don't like as well. I picture myself anxious and getting more frightened as I get older and my options diminish. It's actually that scenario that drives me. It's a lot clearer to me than the other one. I can imagine how it would feel and what I would be doing. I work like a demon because I can't let that happen."

Feelings now: "Impressed with how powerful that negative image is. And how much I work to keep it from happening."

Janet: "When I went to college, I didn't know what I would study or what I would do after college. I don't even have any real clear memories of high school. I think I felt down or depressed most of that time. I think my parents probably were, too. When I went to college, my only goal was to make good grades.

"I interviewed with my company on campus in the spring of my senior year, and they offered me the job I'm in now. The main thing that happened in my life at this Turning Point was that I met Brian. We're such opposites, but it's like we had known each other for our whole lives. There was never a question but that we would get married.

"At future Turning Points, I see our marriage playing out. We have children; we stay married. The children grow up, and then they have children and live close to us, and as we get older we stay together *and have close relationships to our children and grandchildren. I don't really see the future too much in terms of my career. If I could quit, I would, so I feel that when Brian is successful enough, I won't be working, but just taking care of the family."*

Feelings now: "I found myself irritated by the questions at different Turning Points. I just see the future as being the same, not changing all the time."

Elizabeth

"When I was 18, I did not have a clue about what I would do. I figured I still had plenty of time in college to think about it, and I was having too good a time to worry. I figured, whatever I do, I'll succeed. Actually, the thought that I might not succeed never even once occurred to me. The winter of my senior year in college, some companies interviewed on campus, and that's how I got my start. I skyrocketed. It was then that I realized I was just like my dad. In fact, his image is in my mind a lot when I make decisions and go through my day. I feel I have this compass inside my head. I always seem to know exactly what the right move will be. It never fails me. At 29, I was put into the executive pool. One of the youngest. Everything has always seemed right on track—until now, that is. At this Turning Point, nothing seems clear. As I look to the future, I don't think I can keep on this course. I picture wanting more quiet and balance and fulfillment. I don't want my children to grow up without my ever knowing them. I would like to think at age 50 or 60 that I will have a close relationship with my husband."

Feeling now: "I realize that I have been doing everything pretty much as I planned it, but that I'm not very happy with the result. I want my life to be different in the future. But how?"

Carl

"I never planned too much. I just concentrated on taking advantage of the opportunities that presented themselves. I was not a sterling student in either high school or college. My first job after college was in a new business a friend was starting. I ended up running that business for about 18 years. I got married when I was 29—that was the 30s Turning Point. Then I got recruited when I was 40 for the

job I just got fired from. The future? I guess I'll just do what I've always done. The questions about retirement and later transitions made me think. I don't have any sense about what retirement looks like. Playing golf? Working? Living in a retirement village? None of it seems to fit me very well."

Feelings now: "Wondering where this is all going."

NEXT CHAPTER: In the next chapter we discuss the basic groundwork of your Personal Vision, your natural talents and abilities. Your natural talents tell you what kinds of tasks and roles you are naturally suited for, and which you aren't. This is the basic starting information you will need at each of your career Turning Points as you start to construct answers to what you will do with your life.

YOUR
Natural Talents
UNDERLIE **Any Job, Role** or **Career**
YOU UNDERTAKE
THROUGHOUT **Your Life.**
YET THIS **Objective Information**
ABOUT WHAT YOU NATURALLY DO
EASILY AND WHAT IS
Intrinsically Difficult
IS
ALMOST
Unknown
TO THE **VAST MAJORITY** OF PEOPLE
AS THEY MAKE **Critical Decisions**
AT
CAREER TURNING POINTS.

Our
Hardwired Talents
&
ABILITIES

Figuring out a Personal Vision may be the most complicated problem any of us ever has to solve in life. But the rewards of working through it are immense, whether calculated in terms of success or of satisfaction. As we described in Chapter 2, a Personal Vision, to have the most positive impact, must include eight critical factors: stage of development, abilities, skills, interests, personality, values, goals and family of origin—this is The Whole Person Technology®. In the last chapter we discussed how your age and life developmental stage influence your Personal Vision. The present chapter deals with the most fundamental aspect of what you bring to your career: your natural talents and abilities

—how you're hardwired to do some things with sublime ease and why other things will always be more difficult.

Before launching into natural talents, however, we want to be clear why it's so important to look at *several* factors, not just one. As powerful and rich in explanation as your natural talents and hardwiring are, they don't tell you everything. We invented The Whole Person Technology® because it was completely evident to us that people are more complex than just one or two factors. Generally, we find that more objective factors such as talent and skills help you make such basic decisions as how you go about work or how you position yourself in your job. Career *direction*, and, even more importantly, *passion* for what you do, come from the more subjective factors like interests, values, family and goals.

The Whole Person Technology® and Personal Vision

Many writers, test constructors, corporate program creators and motivational speakers seem to feel that *one aspect* of Personal Vision is sufficient when thinking about your life and career. Different ones tout values, goals, abilities, interests, stage of development, skills *or* personality. Each has been proposed as enough information alone to make career decisions or to formulate a career direction. The Lemming Conspiracy, the power of systems to control how you think about your life and career, means that these simple, unitary views are too confining. As powerful individually as each of these factors is, *none* is powerful enough alone to help you escape the power of systems and help you figure out a career direction that makes sense. We created The Whole Person Technology® to integrate all of the factors necessary to give you a Personal Vision that is a complete picture of yourself.

Another, more subtle issue works in many attempts to help people determine a life direction. Most experts in the field of career and job counseling see their roles in terms of gathering information about people and then telling them what to do. One of the first experts to break with this model was not a counselor or trained expert at all; he was just a businessman trying to solve a problem. He felt that an ideal job should be so specific to the person and to the marketplace that no one could tell you what you should do. You could discover your ideal fit by looking at enough information about yourself. The central insight was that a direction should come from the *inside*, not from the tests or insight of some expert.

The philosophy that informs this book is that you have the answer for your life's work inside yourself. The process we describe is a structure to help you identify it, describe it and put it into action.

Your natural talents underlie any job, role or career you undertake throughout your life. Yet this objective information about what you naturally do easily and what is intrinsically difficult is almost unknown to the vast majority of people as they make critical decisions at career Turning Points.

Your Natural Talents: What Are They, and How Do You Know Them?

Many years ago, an engineer at General Electric was given the task of figuring out what people should do when they applied for work at G.E. Should a prospective employee be a line worker? A supervisor? An engineer? A manager? What training would be most beneficial for a new employee? What kinds of jobs would an employee definitely *not* be suited for? This was before the era of universal college education, and so a person's educational background did not necessarily tell G.E. much about what a person could do.

With no preconceptions about the problem, the engineer started assembling tests that would measure what he called "aptitudes," or natural talents and abilities. He was not interested in what a person could learn through experience. Rather, he wanted to find out the special abilities and talents with which people were born.

A strong aptitude makes it easy for someone to master certain tasks. A weak ability makes it difficult for another person to do the same tasks. We are not talking about intelligence or motivation. Intelligent, highly motivated individuals can accomplish many things for which they have little or no talent. But they may not be happy or satisfied doing it.

The engineer discovered that certain *patterns* of talent make it easy for a person to work with tools and understand machinery. Other patterns allow people to understand processes and systems, or reveal natural salespeople. Some ability patterns mean that logical, step-by-step explanation of difficult problems is a piece of cake. Still others make managing people in organizations feel like second nature. These pat-

terns remain relatively stable over the many years of a person's working life. A person can't *learn* a pattern of abilities; he or she is either
born with it or not.

To the engineer, it became stunningly clear why organizations func-
tioned as inefficiently as they do. In *The Peter Principal*, Laurence Peter
forcefully draws a Monty Python-esque picture of organizations in
which people who perform excellent work are promoted rapidly and
continuously until they occupy positions for which they are totally
incompetent. There they stay until they retire.

Who has not heard a story about a legendary salesman, a killer who
would chew through doors to make a sale? His customers like and
respect him, and his numbers break all records. As a reward for work
well done, management promotes him. He now *manages* twenty salespeople—only to fall flat on his face. Sales plummet; his salespeople
hate him and quit; his former customers go elsewhere: a disaster. The
Peter Principal? Yes. But of infinitely greater importance, ignored abilities—and the Lemming Conspiracy.

The pattern of talents that makes selling easy is well-known. So is the
pattern that makes managing easy. *But they are completely different patterns.* It is as though we identified a player on a basketball team as a particularly effective rebounder and said, "I've got a great idea, let's make
him our ball-handler and play-maker!" Our salesman, so effective at closing a sale with a client, was totally at sea when asked to manage other people who were supposed to close sales. Not because he lacked motivation
or intelligence, but because it ran exactly counter to his natural talent.

There is another current in the story of the salesman. It has to do with
systems, and *The Peter Principal* describes accurately what happens. The
goal in systems is always to get to the next level. To stay in the same position is to stagnate. To move sideways is to fail. Up or out, that's the rule.

The goal of moving up in systems is external; it is part of the Stress
Cycle. Why? Because it has nothing to do with the individual. The
salesman would have been much wiser and happier had he remained a
killer salesman. But he didn't know that, and his system never brought
up the issue. From the perspective of the system, a bright, ambitious
young man must move up to get ahead in the organization.

Let us tell you about another man, Joseph, who faced a similar
dilemma.

Joseph's Story

Joseph, 41, was a senior partner in a large corporate law firm. He worked most weekends and many nights during the week. For several years he had been managing partner of the law firm. He was generally considered an excellent manager of the firm. He thought of himself as financially comfortable and successful.

Joseph also felt great stress. He did not enjoy his work. It took him away from his young family, but he didn't know what he could do about it. He felt his firm needed him as a manager. He felt his family depended on him to work hard and provide for them. Joseph had enjoyed law for many years after joining his firm, but for the last few years he had not enjoyed his work at all. It felt more like a burden. He worked longer hours now than when he started as a young associate.

Joseph was only vaguely aware of these problems. He probably would not even have described them as problems. From his point of view, what he experienced in his work life was just what everyone experienced. That's just the way things are. His firm was happy with him. His wife accepted the situation as a given and dedicated her time to their children. No system Joseph was involved with challenged his decisions.

Joseph went through a corporate program that used The Whole Person Technology® to create a Personal Vision—the same process we describe in this book. For him, one of the most interesting pieces of objective information he learned was that he had an extremely poor pattern of natural talent for management. His pattern of talent superbly fitted him for law and legal work, but management duties went completely against his grain. (We should note that natural talent cannot say whether a person can or cannot perform a role. Joseph, because he is intelligent and highly motivated, performed the role of manager in his firm exceedingly well. The problem was that it so far missed his pattern of talent, that he was forced to work twice as hard to achieve a result much less satisfying to him personally.)

Even though his role was dissatisfying and made him work against himself, it would have been easy for Joseph simply to keep doing what he was already doing. His firm benefited from it and expected him to continue. But he was not happy. He quit his role as managing partner—over the protests of the other senior partners. His wife worried over his decision; she was afraid Joseph would have less prestige and pull in the firm.

Joseph's systems tried to get him to stay in the Stress Cycle. They wanted him to have a short-term focus: He should not make a change because the firm would be upset by changing managing partners. They wanted him to focus on wealth, power and status; what about the prestige of being managing partner? They wanted him to take his direction from the system, not from himself. They wanted his decisions to be reactive, not meaning-driven.

Joseph's systems put this conservative pressure on him not because anyone—his friend and partner, his wife—wanted anything bad for Joseph. They did it because systems resist new information, new rules and new ideas.

Joseph insisted on the change, because he knew objectively he was right. He also set his priorities for his time. He was not going to work on weekends or evenings anymore. He would do this by concentrating on the kind of work he loved, and for which he was particularly well suited.

Joseph's partners were not wild about this change—at first. But after several months, Joseph's team was more productive, and he brought more business into the firm than ever. Besides that, he was happier. His team was happier. And they found another manager.

Astute readers might be asking themselves right now, Well, how did he manage to go up against all of his systems and make them listen to him? Resigning as managing partner was not something any of his systems was prepared to accept.

Joseph's decisions were more complex and involved more issues than abilities. Personality, interests and family of origin all strongly influenced his actions. We will take up Joseph's story again in Chapter 7 when we talk about the family of origin and its influence.

But just what are natural talents? And how do you discover yours? In the next section, we discuss the most powerful and influential talents, the Driving Abilities.

The Driving Abilities: What They Are and How They Affect Your Life

Driving Abilities are so important because they influence, or drive, you whether they are high or low. If you ignore them, you run the significant risk of getting into a role that doesn't use your strongest talents or that loads on a talent you don't have. Our experience has been that a great deal of dissatisfaction at work can be traced to having strong talents that you never use. We saw this above in Joseph's story. His strong abilities for law were not being used well in his role as a manager. He always felt dissatisfied, unfulfilled.

We will describe four Driving Abilities to give you some idea of what they are and how they relate to each other. The Thought Experiment at the end of the chapter includes a self-report measure to help you assess your Driving Abilities.

CLASSIFICATION

Classification uses your right brain to solve problems. This part of the brain takes information from everywhere—something you heard on the news, something you might have noticed without being aware of it, something somebody said—and pulls it all together at once into a solution. In Classification, your right brain takes a plethora of related and unrelated observations and arrives at a theory to explain them. This is inductive reasoning.

Classification is quick. People who have high Classification love to use it. It's fun. But this quickness and sureness of problem-solving also makes it difficult for people with high Classification to get along easily with people who have other equally valid ways of solving problems.

Let's drop in on the hectic world of Allison, a person with strong Classification ability. We can see how she solves problems, what kinds of tasks are easy for her, and what drives her crazy.

Allison—A Person with Strong Classification. Co-workers describe Allison as quick and self-assured. Given a problem to solve, she knows the answer before anyone even has a chance to explain it to her. She sometimes starts responding to what people say before they can finish their sentences. She has an irritating habit of being right and knowing she is right. She has little patience with people who are slower than she is at seeing the answers. She often feels she is metaphorically tapping her foot, impatiently waiting for her boss to see something that is completely obvious to her.

Allison is happiest when she is fully engaged by problems coming at her thick and furiously, with scarcely time to breathe. She is most miserable when she has nothing new to sink her teeth into.

Allison has high Classification. She doesn't solve problems logically or in a linear fashion; she solves them with her powerful right hemisphere, the one that doesn't speak. Pulling answers for problems together from many different sources simultaneously, people with strong Classification don't necessarily know *how* they get to an answer; they just know what the right answer is. Quickness of problem-solving is one of its defining characteristics.

When you hand a report to a boss, a report that you have worked weeks to make perfect, and he scans it briefly, remarking only that "I would change the order of the chapter titles," he is probably using Classification. People with strong Classification are quickly able to spot a problem with almost anything—to the general irritation of those around.

Classification demands to be used—more than any other strong ability. A person with high Classification who is stuck in a menial job that requires doing the same thing over and over will be very unhappy, perhaps even dangerous. One theory holds that many young people who become involved in delinquency as teenagers have high Classification, but low educational and cultural attainment—i.e., no prospects. The most they can hope for is menial labor, which will in no way use their high Classification ability.

People with high Classification who cannot use this ability at work often *create* problems for themselves, seemingly just to have the opportunity to make use of this powerful ability.

To test Classification objectively you must have a problem to solve—not just any problem, but a visual one that involves many separate elements. A problem like this loads almost exclusively on the right hemisphere. People with strong Classification go to the correct solution at once. People with other problem-solving styles must go through a much more laborious process to get to the answer. We cannot, of course, recreate an objective testing session in this book.

However, you can figure out an *estimate* of your Classification ability in the Thought Experiment at the end of the chapter.

CONCEPT ORGANIZATION

Concept Organization is the opposite problem-solving style from Classification. Concept Organization uses the left hemisphere to solve problems logically and linearly. Where Classification pulls information from anywhere and everywhere at once, Concept Organization deals with information one step at a time. It lines up parcels of fact and observation in a logical order, so that you can start with a theory and proceed to a logical conclusion—deductive reasoning.

The ability to line up facts logically is generally not as much fun as Classification, but it can do things that Classification cannot. People with high Concept Organization are able to see into the future in a way, because they can start with an idea about what they might want to happen and then logically construct a chain of events that can bring it off.

People with high Concept Organization are also able to communicate easily in words. Words are linear. They are small parcels of information that must be lined up in a logical sequence for communication to happen. You might have had the interesting experience of trying to relate a particularly vivid dream to someone. Dreams are holistic images created in the right hemisphere. They contain complex symbols, images and feelings. As you start to tell someone your dream, you may feel the vividness and richness of the dream evaporate as you attempt to put it into words. Words are simply unable to carry the enormously complex images and symbols that the right brain loves. What is left, except occasionally in poetry, is the rather thin and meager *content* of the dream. But without words, we could not even communicate the content. Without the logical and linear left hemisphere, we could not really communicate complex ideas at all.

Let us look at Jill, who has strong Concept Organization. What kinds of things can she do easily? What kinds of things are difficult? How does she feel about her talents?

Jill—A Person with Strong Concept Organization. Papers, files and folders spill everywhere around Jill's desk and office. A stranger would wonder how she could ever find anything. But if you were to ask her for a particular piece of paper out of all the piles in her office, she would go to it immediately. It is as if there is a filing system in her head. She knows where everything is according to a logical system that she created, but never thinks about. As a result, she feels no real need for an external system or external order to help her keep track of things.

When Jill's boss told her that they would need to prepare an annual report, she replied that it would take two weeks. She had immediately assessed everything else she was working on, re-prioritized all of it, figured out the tasks she would need to accomplish, and allowed some extra time for unknowns. All of this was completely obvious to her, but she had worked with her boss long enough to know that he didn't think like she did. He had worked with her long enough to know that if she said two weeks, this was probably the best estimate he could get, even if he didn't immediately see why.

Jill is able to organize the thousand details of her life and family without strain or noticeable effort. Sometimes, occasionally, things happen too fast at the office, or there are too many projects competing for her attention. At these times, she shows some strain and anxiety. She can't figure out what she ought to do *first* or, even worse for her, what she just ought to leave undone.

Jill can write more clearly and logically than her boss. But she likes it better when he gives her the direction he wants her to take in a letter. She knows that he sometimes has an idea that seems like it's from outer space to her, but that ends up being effective anyway. Jill doesn't like doing anything by the seat of her pants. When someone asks her what her gut reaction is to something, she will reply with a logical conclusion. She knows she works most effectively when she's given time to figure out conclusions logically. She knows she is least effective when she is overwhelmed by multiple tasks that need to be handled all at once.

Jill's ability to solve problems logically feels almost invisible to her. Often she is not aware of using it, nor is she often aware of how powerful it is for her. She assumes that everyone probably thinks the same way she does.

Objective measures of Concept Organization give participants a logical, linear, verbal task to perform. The left brain can do this task quickly and with ease, but it is almost impossible for the right brain to tackle it. You can get a sense of your Concept Organization ability with the self-report quiz in the Thought Experiment.

TWO FREQUENT ABILITY PATTERNS

Steve—A Consultant's Pattern of Abilities. Steve is a corporate consultant who sees executives all day long in one-to-one mentoring relationships. He constantly thinks on his feet. His clients ask him about business concerns, personal problems, tricky staff questions, tactical issues and long-term strategies. He never really knows what a session will be like beforehand. Steve is good at this, and he likes it. He has both high Classification and high Concept Organization.

When a client asks him about a problem, Steve usually knows how to tackle it before he or she finishes talking. He describes it as having a picture of the answer. This is his strong Classification ability. But when Steve responds, it is not with a picture or in any kind of impressionistic way. Rather, he gives a closely reasoned, carefully thought-out summary of his point of view with his thoughts and arguments compellingly marshaled. When Steve first solves the problem—when he gets a picture of the solution—he uses Classification. When he presents his point of view, he uses Concept Organization.

Steve works by using both Classification and Concept Organization. This is most efficient and productive for him. He could do his job with many other talent patterns, but he would have to go about his job differently to be equally satisfied and productive.

John—An Executive's Pattern of Abilities. One of Steve's clients is John. He is older than Steve, and has been an executive in his company for many years. He started as a young trainee right out of college and worked his way up through the layers of the organization. He says of himself that he has made every mistake in the book—some more than once. But he developed an instinct over the years that now makes it easy for him to provide clear and accurate direction for the people he manages.

When someone asks John his gut feeling about something, he responds immediately with his gut feeling. He has an unerring sense of what people should be in what jobs, and he has a sure ability to provide the kind of work environment in which people can do their most productive work. John is an experiential problem-solver—he scores low on both Classification and Concept Organization.

There has been a great deal of interest among psychologists about these experiential problem-solvers. They arrive at an answer to a problem by checking with their *experience* of similar problems in the past. What psychologists have found, often to their surprise, is that this is often a much more direct and efficient route to a solution than trying to solve it through logic like someone with high Concept Organization or by coming up with a new solution to every problem, like a person with high Classification.

People with high Classification and/or high Concept Organization are often one step removed from their experiences. They often feel and act as though their thoughts and conclusions were more real than actual reality. People who are low in both of these abilities are able to access their *experiences* more easily than others.

Steve was often struck by John's ability to say, "*This* is what is important here. I won't worry if we never get to *that*." But when John started with the company as a young man, he was sometimes overawed by others his age who seemed quicker or more able to handle complex projects. He tried a lot of different roles, failed a lot when he first started, but rose steadily because he was able to manage people so effectively. To him, this talent was like breathing. "What's the big deal?" But his ability to lead a team, give it a goal and vision, and create the conditions for each person in which he or she could function most effectively made him able to rise much higher than many of the bright stars he started with.

John discovered how he worked best, and it was different from how others work. John's pattern of talent make it supremely easy for him to manage, motivate and direct the work of other people. An important part of that overall pattern of talent is that John is such a strong experiential problem-solver. This pattern made it slower, perhaps, for John in the beginning—experiential problem-solving requires experience—but he eventually discovered that by working through others, he could make his best and highest contribution. And be a lot happier.

IDEA PRODUCTIVITY

When high, Idea Productivity is second only to Classification in its impact on a person's life. Idea Productivity describes the rate of flow of ideas. A person with high Idea Productivity, if asked to think of solutions to a problem, might come up with 25 different ones in the space of five minutes. A person with low Idea Productivity might come up with two in the same period of time. Idea Productivity refers to *quantity*, not quality or creativity. It might be that both of the ideas of the person with low Idea Productivity would end up being useful, while only one of the high Idea Productivity person's many ideas might ever help. High Idea Productivity *alone* does not predict how creative a person's ideas are. People with high Idea Productivity find that ideas and thoughts come to them constantly, even when they wish they wouldn't.

Andrew—A Person with Strong Idea Productivity. Andrew loves selling. He can sell anything to anyone. He loves finding just the right "hook" to get someone interested. He loves hearing their objections so that he can deftly steer them around the obstacle. He never knows what he's going to say; he always flies by the seat of his pants when he's making a sale. He picks up on nuances of meaning and speech and uses them to help his customer hear his pitch. He is overjoyed when a potential customer has a new objection because it gives him a challenge. The challenge is to develop, instantaneously, exactly the message that *this* potential customer will be able to hear. Andrew is a master at this.

What he does not do well is keep records. This involves too much detail. He might get started on lists for his customers, only to drop them and start on something else in less than 60 seconds. A few minutes later, he will drop that, too. Andrew has a hard time paying attention to details for long periods at a time, but not because he is distracted by outside noises. He is distracted from the inside, by his own thoughts. As soon as he starts working on something, a completely unrelated thought strikes him and takes his attention. No sooner does he start thinking about that, than another thought interrupts.

Andrew's friends sometimes get irritated because he is always interrupting them. Andrew's boss has noticed that he is a wonderful salesperson, but has his limits when asked to think about strategy. Andrew will generate ten alternatives, none of which seem particularly creative or useful. But Andrew can persuade anyone to come around to his point of view. That's what makes him such a powerful and effective salesperson.

Idea Productivity is such a powerful ability because it demands to be used almost constantly. A person with high Idea Productivity who is asked to concentrate on the same task all day long will be miserable and unproductive. A person like this may wonder why his or her concentration is so bad, but actually it is just a poor use of his or her talent.

To measure Idea Productivity objectively, you simply count the number of ideas that occur to a person when given a standard problem to solve in a given span of time. You can get a rough sense of your Idea Productivity from the Thought Experiment quiz at the end of the chapter.

SPATIAL RELATIONS

Spatial Relations ability is the best understood and most researched of all of the abilities. It is the ability to manipulate and envision three-dimensional objects and three-dimensional space in your mind. When we measure Spatial Relations, we give participants a task in which they are required to "see" a three-dimensional object in space and then mentally rotate it to "see" how it would look from the other side.

In all studies in the literature, men score higher on Spatial Relations as a group than women do. This is deceptive, however, because many individual women score extremely high on Spatial Relations, and many individual men score low. Without actually measuring it, you can't tell exactly how high or low on Spatial Relations any one person is.

In general, high school courses and most college courses do not use Spatial Relations ability. Many people score high in Spatial Relations on objective measures who had absolutely no knowledge or sense of this ability. It had been invisible to them because they had never had an opportunity to use it.

People who are high in Spatial Relations have a particular affinity and feel for *things*. They like to work with tools. They enjoy making things. They are interested in how things work. They like to figure out how things are constructed. They are interested in the structure of things. They often are engineers, physicians and scientists. For a person with high Spatial Relations ability, abstract concepts never seem real. A chair feels real. But dealing with abstractions like feelings and relationships, like a counselor might do all day long, would eventually feel empty to a person high in this ability.

Some experts feel that if you are strong in Spatial Relations ability, you need to use it in your work. If you don't, you run the risk of never feeling fully engaged with what you do all day long.

Elaine—A Person with Strong Spatial Relations Ability. Elaine is a successful architect. She went all the way through high school and most of the way through college taking liberal arts courses, never realizing that she had strong Spatial Relations abilities. She could never identify what she wanted to do in life, and when she was a junior in college, she decided to take a year off. She spent this year teaching skiing in Aspen. During this year off, she met an architect, and talked to him at length about what he did and how he got to do what he did.

Elaine was fascinated. She began reading books and inquiring about architecture schools. She found a program that would admit her, but she had to spend an extra year in college. She then got a master's degree in architecture.

Elaine now designs and builds visitors' centers for several Native American tribal councils. This job challenges her to help people of European, African, or Asian cultural backgrounds understand something of an alien Native American culture through the architecture of the centers. This task requires all of her abilities and background. She must envision the structure and the space that people will occupy. She must be able to see it from the point of view of someone looking at the building from the outside *and* from the point of view of someone inside, looking at the exhibits.

It is interesting that even Elaine's background in liberal arts has been helpful to her. She has had to spend a great deal of time with Native American tribal councils listening and learning what is important to them and figuring out how to extract that and interpret it to people with cultural backgrounds that have no real point of reference to Native American cultures.

As Elaine moves from the design to the actual building of the projects, she will be more engaged with the materials and structure of the buildings themselves. She is able to envision how each of the materials contributes to the overall look, stability and strength of the projects. She also deals with the scheduling and timing of the projects and how to get the buildings to come together in a rational, orderly way.

Spatial Relations ability makes it possible for Elaine to do all of these tasks easily and well. In fact, the only difficult part for her is communicating her vision of the space and structures to people who do not see mentally in three dimensions as easily as she does.

A fit in one's career as precise and creative as Elaine's is seldom really an accident, nor is it simple. It weaves together many strands of the person's life into a whole fabric. Your natural talents are the place to begin your Personal Vision, but they are never *enough* to make accurate and creative decisions about your career. All eight factors are vitally important, and weaving them together may require an epic creative leap. This is why it is so important to follow The Whole Person Technology® when creating your Personal Vision. You can be sure this way that you are getting to all the pieces.

Thought Experiment C:

Driving Abilities

NOTE TO READERS

If you wish to make full use of the Thought Experiments in this book, we urge you to order The Highlands Ability Battery™ on CD. The self-report measures below can give you some indicators of your Driving Abilities, but the objective, carefully validated measures of The Highlands Ability Battery™ can give you much more information, more objectively. In addition, you can find out about many other, more specialized abilities. You will receive a detailed written report on your results. If you wish, you can also arrange to have an individual two-hour feedback session from one of our specially trained consultants. If you are contemplating any significant career decisions, this can be critically valuable information, and will give you a complete and objective view of your natural talents—your hard-wiring. It is the ideal foundation upon which to build your Personal Vision.

You can order a CD to be sent to you directly from The Highlands Program. Contact information appears on the back page of this book.

SELF-REPORT MEASURES OF DRIVING ABILITIES

You can get an idea of your Driving Abilities by answering the following questions about yourself.

The Highlands Program Driving Ability Quiz

In your Personal Vision Notebook, using the scale below, write down the number of how well or poorly each of the statements describes you:

Not at all like me		Mostly not like me		Sometimes yes, sometimes no		Somewhat like me		Exactly describes me	
1	2	3	4	5	6	7	8	9	10

1. I *like* problem-solving and arrive at solutions very quickly.
2. I sometimes feel restless waiting for others to 'get it.'
3. I usually know exactly how to solve a problem.
4. Mostly I know what someone will say before they finish talking.
5. My solutions are usually the best ones.
6. I can organize and explain information easily.
7. I can plan quickly and well.
8. I appreciate a logical order to things.
9. It's easy for me to see the logical steps for future plans. I can easily see how to get there from here.
10. I feel more comfortable thinking through things step by step than just leaping into a solution.
11. When trying to solve a problem, I know I'll think of many ideas.
12. I am good in brainstorming sessions.
13. Ideas come so quickly to me that sometimes I interrupt others who are talking.
14. Ideas frequently crowd my mind.
15. Sometimes I am distracted by my own thoughts.
16. I am often interested in how machines work.
17. I have an intuitive understanding of machines and structures.
18. I like to work with tools.
19. I enjoy working with things I can touch and see.
20. I like to have a real product or 'thing' to see and touch when I finish something.

ADD UP YOUR SCORES AS FOLLOWS:

Questions 1-5 _____ Classification

Total score, questions 1-5:	Low	5-30
	Medium	31-40
	High	41-50

Questions 6-10 _____ Concept Organization

Total score, 6-10:	Low	5-30
	Medium	31-40
	High	41-50

Questions 11-15 _____ Idea Productivity

Total score, 11-15:	Low	5-30
	Medium	31-40
	High	41-50

Questions 16-20 _____ Spatial Relations

Total score, 16-20:	Low	5-30
	Medium	31-40
	High	41-50

You should be aware that no self-report quiz can provide the same kind of validated, precise and accurate measurement of abilities as measurements using objective worksamples.

When you complete the quiz and add up your scores, you can use the paragraphs below to find out what your abilities mean.

HIGH CLASSIFICATION

If your self-report score is in the high range, this can mean that Classification is a powerful ability for you, and may influence almost every aspect of your working life.

This is an ability that demands to be used if you have it as strongly as your self-report score indicates. Almost anyone who has this ability strongly gets positive enjoyment from using it. The flip side of that statement is important to remember, however. If you find yourself in a position that does not use this ability, you may be unhappy with your work.

The high Classification person loves to solve problems and to figure things out. This person enjoys change and challenge. There is nothing he or she likes better than taking on a new task, because learning something new uses this ability.

MEDIUM CLASSIFICATION

Your self-report score is in the mid-range in this ability. Classification is a powerful ability and your score in the mid-range indicates that you should take it into account when thinking about your work role. In a sense, you have more choice about using your Classification ability than if it were either high or low. You should be able to work in fast-paced environments or more stable, less chaotic environments. It may be that you will choose one type of work environment over another for reasons unrelated to Classification. Being in the mid-range on this ability gives you that option.

LOW CLASSIFICATION

Your self-report score indicates that you may find any work situation stressful that is chronically chaotic and that requires rapid-fire problem-solving with very little information. You will be happier and more productive in a work environment that is more stable and more structured.

The strength of your score in Classification is that you have the ability to persevere long enough to become proficient. You can become expert by acquiring increasing levels of knowledge and experience.

HIGH CONCEPT ORGANIZATION

Your high score in Concept Organization suggests an aptitude for any planning activity. In being able to see the logical sequences of events, you can predict, order and plan schedules for when things are going to happen. Even more important, this is the primary ability needed to communicate ideas to other people. Since you may be able to arrange ideas easily into a logical sequence, creating written materials and presentations of ideas that make sense to others may be easy for you. You may be able to see how all of the pieces of a project fit together to make a coherent whole. You will be able to use this ability effectively in any work in which there is a recurring need to organize materials or information.

People who are high in Concept Organization find that they want to use this ability often. Most people have ample opportunity to use it in their everyday lives, both at home and at work, and so we don't see people who are tremendously unhappy if it is not a part of their jobs.

MEDIUM CONCEPT ORGANIZATION

In the workplace, Concept Organization is a fundamental ability. Your self-report score indicates that you should be able to perform essential work and office tasks—planning, predicting, scheduling and communicating—with relative ease.

LOW CONCEPT ORGANIZATION

Your self-report score on Concept Organization can be an advantage in an environment that places a premium on action. If a person must act quickly and decisively, the kind of logical planning that is the hallmark of Concept Organization is actually counter-productive. It delays action.

Your score in Concept Organization means that it is relatively laborious for you to plan, organize and prioritize internally. It is much easier for you to use various external means of organization. These could include schedules, lists of priorities or lists of tasks to accomplish. People who are in the low range in Concept Organization frequently like to have their external world fairly neat and orderly. This helps them stay focused on what they feel is important.

HIGH IDEA PRODUCTIVITY

Your self-report score on Idea Productivity indicates that you may have many ideas flowing through your thoughts during any given period of time. It is important to remember that Idea Productivity is not an ability that you can turn off at will. These ideas occur to you whether you want them to or not. Whenever possible, you will be much happier and more productive when you can use your Idea Productivity in rapid idea production, problem solving and adjusting to new ideas, rather than trying to struggle against it.

Conversely, you will feel very confined by a task that requires long attention to meticulous detail, or highly detailed follow-through on someone else's plans and ideas. You are possibly capable of such concentration, but you will be constantly struggling against your Idea Productivity to achieve it. You will feel much more involved and fulfilled in your work if you have a real outlet for your flow of ideas during most of your working day.

MEDIUM IDEA PRODUCTIVITY

Your score in the medium range in Idea Productivity indicates that you will have some of the advantages of a high score, as well as some advantages of a low score. You are able to come up with ideas at a sufficient rate to be useful to you in solving problems and overcoming objections. You will enjoy being able to use this skill at times. Your rate of idea production is such that you probably feel somewhat confined by a task that requires long attention to meticulous detail, or highly detailed follow-through on someone else's plans and ideas. You are capable of such concentration, but you will not enjoy it as a complete description of your work day. You will feel much more involved and fulfilled in your work if you have some outlet for your flow of ideas during some portion of your working day.

Some uses for your rate or flow of new ideas can be in dreaming up solutions for problems, or in "selling" your point of view to others. You are in an ideal position to have enough concentration to work out a solution to a problem and dream up alternatives, and then adroitly overcome others' objections.

LOW IDEA PRODUCTIVITY

Idea Productivity confers an advantage whether you are high or low, provided you choose the appropriate work environment. Your self-report score in the low range in Idea Productivity may indicate that you are able to focus well, and work without undue distraction on a given project for a considerable length of time. You will probably work most effectively in a stable, rather than a volatile, work situation, where your ability to maintain focus undistracted is a positive strength. You will probably want to avoid being in situations in which you persuade or sell to others in an impromptu manner.

In work areas requiring a high degree of concentration, a low score in Idea Productivity is a distinct advantage. Your score in Idea Productivity will be helpful to you in any task that requires you to pay attention to details and follow through to a conclusion on ideas and plans.

HIGH SPATIAL RELATIONS

This is an extremely valuable ability in many areas of business. It is, of course, a fundamental ability for someone interested in science, design, construction, manufacture and technology. This ability allows a person to experiment mentally with different options or arrangements of elements or objects without actually having to see them.

An important consideration to keep in mind, however, is that eventually someone who is high in Spatial Relations will want to see the physical result of what he or she is doing. People who score high in this ability need to have their hands on something or produce something. They are most at home with provable facts, products, machinery and tools. Many roles at work do not deal in such tangibles. Roles and tasks that deal mainly in ideas, relationships, information or influence can end up feeling quite unreal to a person high in Spatial Relations. Some experts in the field of abilities consider this one of the most important factors to take into account when planning a work role.

There is a compelling quality to Spatial Relations/ Visualization in the sense that people who are high in it eventually feel pulled to use it. Often this pull does not make itself felt until a person is middle-aged. It is most often experienced as a wish to do something real—to have a tangible result of one's efforts at the end of the day.

MEDIUM SPATIAL RELATIONS

A score in the mid-range on this ability is sometimes difficult to interpret. Typically, people either have this ability or they don't. People who are high in Spatial Relations usually want to see the results of their actions in a concrete and immediate way. If they manage a business, they are more satisfied if the business produces a concrete product such as a chair, rather than an abstract product such as information. Your score in the mid-range on this ability indicates that you may have the ability to visualize the concrete results of what you are doing in your work. If so, you may want to consider being sure to use this ability on a daily basis.

LOW SPATIAL RELATIONS

A self-report score on this measure in the low, or abstract, range has several important implications. People in the abstract range are typically quite comfortable in work that deals with people, relationships, information or influence. They do not usually experience a strong wish to be involved in the concrete world of physical objects in their work. Training, managing, counseling, law and accounting are all examples of typically abstract work roles.

FOUR STORIES: ABILITIES

Tracy

"I have all of the Driving Abilities very strongly. It means I can do anything, basically. It's called a multi-ability pattern. The good side of it is that I have a lot of strong abilities. The bad side of it is that it makes it hard for me to choose anything that will use all of those abilities. At least I don't feel so crazy that it's been hard for me to figure out a direction.

"Finding out about my abilities was interesting, because I never thought of myself as a scientist or anything. But I could do science or medicine. It might be that law or even psychology would not use all of my abilities. I guess I don't really know that much more than when I started, but at least I know I can do something else. I realize now why I hate my job so much. It doesn't use any of my abilities. I guess I had lost a lot of confidence. After I graduated, I suddenly realized, 'I don't have a clue here.'"

Feeling at this point: "Better. More hopeful."

Brian and Janet

Brian: "Well, my abilities were right on target. High Classification, High Idea Productivity. It's no wonder I thrive on the pace at work. I feel like I have ideas and energy running out my fingertips. Whatever I do, I need to be in a work setting like the one I'm in. It seems perfect for me."

Feeling at this point: "I feel good about my job. Maybe why I feel so stressed is other things besides the job itself."

Janet: "The main thing I found out was that I like to take my time and solve problems logically. I have very high Concept Organization. I get frustrated with customers because they are so unreasonable. I can show them exactly why something happened, but it doesn't make any difference to them. It drives me crazy. I think my ability pattern is a hindrance rather than a help in my job."

Feelings at this point: "Interested. More confident."

Elizabeth

"I'm at the mid-point in both Classification and Concept Organization. My Idea Productivity and Spatial Relations are both low. I like to have problems to sink my teeth into.

But not too many at the same time. I can see why I like my job— when it's not totally overwhelming. I can also see why it's so easy for me to deal with problems."

Feelings now: "This means a lot to me. I know how to position myself better at work. I feel encouraged."

Carl

"I have low scores on all the Driving Abilities. This means I am an experiential problem-solver. I don't stop and figure out a logical solution. I usually solve problems at work by thinking of some situation I was in before that this reminds me of. Then I have a good idea about what to do. I know I have a strong innate understanding of what makes people tick. If you put me in a group of people, they always seem to elect me the leader. People listen to me. At least they have ever since I turned 35 or so."

Feelings now: "Still hopeful. Still wondering where all of this is going. Getting a little impatient to find an answer."

NEXT CHAPTER: In the next chapter we continue the construction of your Personal Vision with more pieces of The Whole Person Technology®, your skills, interests and personality. As you continue to add pieces, your Personal Vision will increasingly become a useful, working tool.

FOR
MANY
PEOPLE
"INTERESTS"
AND
"WORK"
ARE LIKE TWO SEPARATE BOXES.
THERE IS **RARELY** ANY
CONNECTION
BETWEEN
THEM.
BY TAKING A **CAREFUL LOOK**
AT WHAT YOU ARE
DRAWN TO
AND
FASCINATED BY,
YOU CAN DISCOVER YOUR
REAL SOURCE OF
CREATIVITY
AND **ENERGY.**

Skills, Interests
&
PERSONALITY

Just knowing what your talents are is not enough. You have to make sure that you can *use* them every day in the work you do and in the life you lead. We developed the concepts of The Whole Person Technology® and Personal Vision to make sure you would be able to take information about your talents and translate it to your life.

A Personal Vision should have a definite structure and internal coherence. It should embrace and comprehend your whole life, not just the hours you spend making a living. It's often easy to "forget" part of your life— just leave it out of your plans. If you leave a piece out, you run the risk of being subtly trapped by your systems into the Lemming

Conspiracy—and possibly ending up wasting your most important talents. This is why The Whole Person Technology® is so important.

As we saw in the last chapter, your natural, inborn talents and gifts form the base, or foundation, of your Personal Vision. In this chapter, we build on this base of talent. We start with relatively more objective factors of your Personal Vision: your skills and experience, your interests and fascinations, and your personality—how you habitually interact with others.

Skills and Experience: What Have You Learned in Life?

When Dan was 42, he had a sudden insight: He hated his job, and he would rather do anything than go to work that day. Everyone may have this feeling from time to time, but for him, the feeling didn't go away. In fact, it got worse. Eventually, he was sure that the only way to save his sanity was to quit his job altogether, move to the beach, and, using his retirement money, open a shop for tourists. He went so far as to check real estate listings at his favorite beach resort and to call his pension manager to find out how much money he could withdraw when he quit.

Fortunately, Dan didn't do that. He had been a corporate lawyer for 16 years, had never sold anything to the public, had never run an entrepreneurial business, and didn't really know the first thing about retail trade. It was a fantasy of a more relaxed, easier life, without the stress and greed that he encountered every day in his clients and their adversaries.

Dan faced a number of problems with this dream of a beach-front surf shop. But the main one was that it didn't take into account the enormous wealth of education and experience that he had so carefully built over the 42 years of his life.

Most people are unaware of the richness of their own skills. Many simply overlook their most powerful and effective skills, because they have always used them so effectively. Their most significant skills don't seem like important assets, because they're so easy. When asked to name their best skills, most people will name something that was particularly difficult for them to learn. Dan would have said, for instance, that the only thing he had learned in 16 years of lawyering was how to plug most loopholes in most contracts.

In a Whole Person Technology® seminar, Dan told a story about some events from his childhood that meant something to him. He had nearly flunked math in the eighth grade, but by dint of labor and will had managed to press on in math through high school with mostly B's and C's—the first time that he had been unable to earn virtually effortless A's. At the time, he felt tremendously frustrated, since he believed that school was really the only thing he could do, and now that wasn't going particularly well. Eventually, he decided that maybe he should try something besides school. And he did. He learned to play the guitar, started a rock band, crafted music and lyrics, wrote humorous pieces for a school magazine and ended up as editor-in-chief of the school newspaper during his senior year.

Dan didn't see what was special about this story. It was just what he had done in high school. It remained mildly embarrassing to him that math was almost totally beyond his ability to understand. But other people, people outside Dan's systems, saw much more in this story than laboring through a difficult school subject. You, the reader, can undoubtedly see much more, too. It was just invisible to Dan.

Dan's story is actually quite rich. The other participants in the seminar turned up dozens of skills and talents Dan had clearly shown in an event he thought of as a failure. For starters, he had transformed this frustration in high school into a positive, meaningful event in his life. By accepting a limit, he had been able to branch out into other, nonacademic pursuits. He loved music and enjoyed playing in a band with others. His real talent was writing, though. He wrote most of the band's songs. He wrote for the newspaper, and made people laugh at themselves in very funny columns. Later, as editor-in-chief, he was able to get other writers to meet deadlines and to organize all of the hundreds of tasks that went into a finished newspaper. He assumed the responsibility of directing stories and editing writers' copy easily. He could tell writers that they had to cut their stories in half, or that a story didn't have enough back-up information, in a way they could accept. He got them to work within limits, instead of fighting them.

As the seminar participants told Dan what they recognized in his story, it occurred to him that he helped his clients see alternatives where they saw none, and he helped them accept realistic limits where they didn't want any limits at all.

Dan had never ascribed any importance to the fact that he had formed and led a band of high school boys. Nor had he thought much about his role as editor of the school newspaper. What both of these roles had in common was holding people with strong personalities and strong agendas together and steering them toward a common goal—a goal he had first articulated and set out to accomplish. This, of course, was exactly what he so deftly managed when he negotiated agreements between clients. Realizing this gave Dan an entirely new perspective on his skills. His skills made him a great corporate lawyer, but he could also use them in many other fields. As he engaged his experience and skills, attempting to figure out how to use instead of discard them, the fantasy of a beach-front shell shop made less and less sense.

Dan realized that the beach shop was an expression of a goal: a less hectic and stressful life. He knew he would be throwing away some of his most important assets if he were to throw out corporate deal-making altogether. He pondered how he could reach his goal but also stay with his firm and a job that fit him so well. By working with his partners, setting clear limits and sticking to them, he was able to cut back his stress significantly. He now spends more time at the beach. He recently published a story in a literary monthly.

You can see that a crucial part of Dan's story, once he figured out how important his skills were, became naming and ordering his life goals. In Chapter 6, we talk more about articulating and prioritizing goals. Another crucial part of this story has to do with setting boundaries on your life—even when your systems definitely don't want you to. We will talk about setting boundaries in Chapter 10.

In the Thought Experiment at the end of this chapter, you will find a variation of the exercise Dan used to discover his real skills. It will help you understand your skills and experiences and how they contribute to what you do well. Remember, Dan's most important skills remained invisible to him until he did a specific exercise. This is true of virtually everyone. We designed the exercise in the Thought Experiment to help you see the most important things you have learned in your lifetime.

In the next section, you'll learn about one of the most overlooked factors of all: interests. Yet interests sometimes define the most direct path to your creativity and enthusiasm.

Interests: Direct Line to Where You Really Live

"Follow your bliss." Joseph Campbell's oft-quoted line could not offer a better or truer piece of advice. When we talk to people who have led particularly full and satisfying lives and ask them how they managed to find just the career that suited them best, they all say some version of the same thing: "I always did exactly what interested me." What appears to be extraordinary luck or the product of unusual confluence of talents is actually neither.

When you pay attention to what you find personally interesting and fascinating, you get to include this magical pull in your career. You can be more creative, happier and more enthusiastic. Work doesn't have to seem like work. The fact that somebody pays you to do it can seem like the most extraordinary luck of all.

For many people, "interests" and "work" are like two separate boxes. There is rarely any connection between them. By taking a careful look at what you are drawn to and fascinated by, you can discover your real source of creativity and energy.

When people assign their passions to a box labeled "not work" and relegate it to those times when they are not utterly exhausted by the routine of their days, it often takes some focused attention to bring interests to the forefront and make them important. Sometimes successful executives in the middle of a Whole Person workshop have looked up suddenly in surprise and said, "I never realized that my interests could have anything to do with work."

Richard's Story, continued

You may remember the story of Richard, in Chapter 3, the 41-year-old veteran insurance executive who had thought his only alternative was to quit. It turned out that his interests became a key to discovering satisfaction in his job. He had many passions in life but felt he could never get to them if he kept working as he had been. We have seen how finding out about his Classification ability made some of his discontent make sense to him. But what should he do?

Richard completed a long-term exercise on interests very much like the one you will find in the Thought Experiment at the end of this chapter. He realized that the hundreds of ideas, images and people that came his way every day fascinated him. From long habit, as soon as some idea grabbed his attention, he just as quickly let it go. He couldn't deal with it. He had no energy. He had a responsible job, a family, a life. He had no time to pursue anything like that. He became just a little more resigned inside.

In the exercise, Richard began to "catch" the many images, thoughts, ideas, words, stories, pictures, articles, people and events that momentarily grabbed his interest. He cut them out, wrote them down, and made brief notes about them. He became adept at holding onto a spark of interest long enough to identify it and make a record of it. He saved all of his records.

After a few weeks, he sorted the records into groups. Almost all of his interests lumped together into three broad categories: music and dance, art and photography, and one that he labeled loosely "adventure." These categories had remained stable for years. He had always been interested in them.

It dawned on Richard that his interests and fascinations, so long ignored and pushed down in the name of adulthood, could give his life more texture and substance. He decided to take them more seriously. He wanted to build a life in which they could play a role.

Once that goal was clear, things changed rapidly. As so often happens, when Richard knew what he wanted clearly enough, a way opened for him to obtain it. Actually, a way had always been there; he had just never noticed it until he realized he needed it.

Richard's insurance company had instituted a policy of flex time for employees several years previously. He had been aware of this policy, but as an executive he had understood that the policy had nothing to do with him. It was for tellers and bookkeepers, mostly women who had to deal with child care.

As Richard ruminated on the question of how to pursue his passions in life, a memo came across his desk about flex time. Inspiration struck. He could use flex time just as well as the administrative staff. He put in a request to his boss to work four days and take Wednesdays off. He would work the same number of hours, but not Wednesdays. He would then be able to pursue other ideas and interests outside of work.

The reaction was volcanic. His boss explained carefully, as if to someone slightly dim, that the policy was not for employees like

Richard. Richard knew he could win, though, because, as it happened, his boss had written the policy. It had been a political move to make the company seem more forward-thinking. Of the company's 20,000 employees, fewer than 30 had put in requests.

This is an example of the Lemming Conspiracy at work. The insurance company had a limited number of answers and actively resisted any new ones. No one behaved malevolently. But a system does not care what Richard wants from his life. Had Richard quit his job, his boss and friends would have been surprised, and his co-workers would have been momentarily disturbed. But there would be a new person in his spot soon, and the system would proceed, having learned nothing.

Before his quest, Richard's boss, friends and co-workers, and Richard himself, for that matter, defined Richard's options as the options of the system. It was only when Richard got outside the system and went through the Whole Person Technology® process for gaining a Personal Vision that he was able to see himself more clearly and see that many more options existed than those the system offered.

Richard did win. He now takes Wednesday off, and has for two years. He plans to pick something each year from one of his major groupings of interests to pursue and explore. This year music takes center stage. He is learning to play the violin and he and his wife are learning to dance. He doesn't know where this will lead, and he doesn't care. It adds joy to his life; he feels more productive at work.

Richard feels his life is completely different now than it was two years ago. His heightened sense of creativity is a perfectly normal byproduct of actively pursuing his fascinations. He is just as productive, but a lot happier. The insurance company benefited because it kept one of its most valuable employees. Richard benefited because he feels he is living his life for the first time in years.

But there is more to Richard's story. In defining his Personal Vision, that is, getting a complete picture of what he wanted his life to look like over time, Richard became very clear about the kinds of jobs he liked to do at work and also the kinds of projects that made best use of his particular set of talents and abilities. Now, if a project comes his way for which he knows he is not suited and would not enjoy, he turns it down. On the other hand, when someone proposes a project that Richard knows will be perfect for him, he jumps at once. Co-workers often express surprise at Richard's certainty. Sometimes he is more enthusiastic about a project than the person who tentatively proposed it in the first place. He has become something of a guru among his contemporaries in the company. Often, someone will pull him aside in whispered tones and ask him how he did it. The most difficult part of explaining his story is trying to convince people that the key is not in how he put it to his boss or in the structure of his proposal, but rather in learning about himself.

When we learn about our interior selves to create a Personal Vision, it is important to understand how we relate to others. This is the next building block of Personal Vision, personality.

Personality: The Interpersonal Environment

Many people have become excited and enthusiastic about personality, only to draw a blank when faced with using this information in a day-to-day setting. A popular personality inventory workshop becomes the talk of the office for a few days. But a month later everyone has forgotten about it, and not much has really changed. Experiences such as these may lead to cynicism about the usefulness of personality measures; however, in the context of the whole person, personality is an important piece of the puzzle.

One of the most limiting aspects of personality, as it has been used in business and corporate settings, is that it is so often used in isolation. Zealots proclaim, "Hi, I'm an ENTJ," or "Hi, I'm a Proactive-Idealist," as though this were sufficient introduction. Some feel that this kind of shorthand explains all there is to know about themselves. Nothing could be further from the truth. This is an example of using one of the building blocks of Personal Vision to stand for the whole structure. But it's not enough.

Personality testing carries at least two other burdens. First, almost all traditional personality testing is self-reported. You tell the test about yourself, and then the results of the test tell you what you just said. Obviously, no one knows you as well as you do yourself. On the other hand, you can't very well have an objective view of yourself, either. Furthermore, consultants and others have often used personality testing to predict patterns of behavior and predict how well a person will perform on a given job. Many more factors than personality affect job performance. Unless all of these factors are taken into account, any prediction is subject to some error. This said, when personality testing is used by individuals as one aspect of judgment about their own lives and careers, it can be powerful and informative.

The idea that certain patterns describe how we habitually interact with our fellow humans is an extremely old one. From the Greeks on, philosophers and pundits have described types of people engaging in more or less consistent patterns of interacting.

Some people love to talk to others; some prefer to be by themselves. But even the most garrulous extrovert likes to be alone sometimes. And even the most intense introvert gets lonely eventually. We are not really talking about something that can be measured with 100 percent accuracy. Personality traits are usually described by two ends of a continuum. Extroversion, for instance, is at one end of the continuum, introversion at the other. People are located somewhere between the two.

We will describe two personality dimensions we have found to be particularly helpful in thinking about what you might want to do with your life: extroversion vs. introversion and generalist vs. specialist. In the Thought Experiment we included a brief self-report quiz you can use to form an estimate of where you are on each of these dimensions, and a short summary of how your score describes your pattern of interacting.

INTROVERSION-EXTROVERSION

You can think of Introversion and Extroversion in terms of energy. Where do you get your energy? When an extrovert is tired after a busy day and wants to recharge, he or she wants to talk to someone. The extrovert gets energy back from the interaction. For very strong extroverts, nothing seems very real unless they have discussed it with someone. Often strong extroverts think through their ideas as they talk them over with a friend. Talking about an idea is an important part of the whole process of thinking for the extrovert. Extroverts like being around other people, being in groups and being in the know. At parties, extroverts get around and see everyone.

Not so the introvert. For the introvert who is tired after a day at the office, nothing is so restful and recharging as coming home, going through the mail, petting the dog, reading the paper and not talking to anyone. No matter how skillful and comfortable in interacting with others the introvert learns to be, it is always work. There is always energy going out. Introverts like to think ideas through before they share them. When they share ideas, especially personal ones, introverts feel best when they have a long history of trust with the other person. Introverts don't enjoy groups. When at parties, they often have a good time by finding an old friend and spending the evening talking to that one person.

No personality dimension is absolute. However, we have found that understanding the direction of your own tendency can be important when figuring out a compatible and productive work environment. If an extrovert is asked to sit alone in an office, working on projects all day long, day after day, he or she will feel profound stress. The source of the stress may not be apparent, but forcing extroverts to be non-interactive cuts them off from their most productive work style and causes everything to feel somewhat incomplete and unreal. In the same way, forcing introverts to interact all day long also leads to stress.

Margaret—An Extrovert. Margaret is a sales representative for a large private hospital. She had originally wanted to be a psychologist but, after earning her master's degree, she realized that being a therapist did not involve interacting freely with people. It involved keeping most of your thoughts to yourself. To be effective, you had to let the patient see just what was good for them to see. Frankly, it drove Margaret crazy. She was never sure what she should say and what she should hold back. She felt she was spending the whole day sitting on her hands.

As a sales representative for a psychiatric hospital, however, she was in her element. Her training and degree gave her credibility; she obviously knew what she was talking about. But her job now asked her to call on companies and insurance providers who were important sources of potential business for the services of the hospital. As Margaret saw it, her job was to form relationships with key people in these companies—people who would know her, remember her and call her when they were thinking about something the hospital could do for them.

Margaret loves this job. She likes talking to people all day long, she likes knowing them and they like her. When she has a meeting with someone important, getting to know this person, getting to like him or her and getting that person to like her occupies her primary attention. She can spend an hour and a half at lunch with an important client and never mention the hospital. Because of her ability to connect, Margaret has been successful at her job—and happy.

Mark—An Introvert. Mark is a corporate consultant. He has a Ph.D. in industrial psychology and has been in practice 15 years. He has two partners, both of whom are Ph.D.s. He likes to start his day by drinking coffee and reading the paper with his office door closed and his phone blocked. After about a half-hour, he emerges and begins his workday. He typically works with one or two corporate clients each day, talking to their executives, working with system problems, writing reports, talking to staff. After lunch, Mark likes to close his door and shut off his phone for another half-hour or so to recharge for the afternoon. Mark interacts with people all day, except when he is analyzing data or writing reports, but all of his interactions are structured. He is an expert; his clients seek his help, and he provides it. When he has lunch with a client, they mostly discuss the company, its problems and its future goals. The only time Mark really talks about his personal life is with his wife and with one or two old friends. Mark likes his job. He feels he is very good at it, and it suits him perfectly.

Mark and Margaret are at the two ends of the continuum between introversion and extroversion. They have both found positions in which their personalities are a positive force in their work. Margaret's ability and drive to connect at a personal level make her an exceptionally effective representative. Her sales contacts sense her desire to connect personally. They trust her because she's not trying to hawk the hospital all the time. She wants to know who they are and what their problems are.

Mark's introversion makes him able to assume the rather lonely role of expert. It also has the subtle effect of making him seem more trustworthy to his clients. They feel he will not say anything merely for effect. He means exactly what he says. He never becomes a part of any organization he helps. And that is fine with Mark. He enters an organization, provides his expertise and leaves.

Introversion and extroversion, like other personality styles, do not in general determine what kind of work a person should do. Rather, they determine how a person goes about doing what he or she does. Margaret and Mark could trade jobs and undoubtedly be effective, but only by going about their jobs in a totally different way.

The next personality dimension, generalist-specialist, is equally important, but not nearly as well known as introversion and extroversion.

GENERALIST-SPECIALIST

If you were to ask 1,000 people in the United States what is the first word they think of when you say "table," about 280 of them would respond "chair." Other responses, like "lamp," "cloth," or "floor" follow in terms of frequency. Some people, given this same stimulus word, respond with a fundamentally different kind of response: "Dalmatian," or "clock," or some equally idiosyncratic response. When asked the connection, they reply with something highly personal. "When I sit at my dining room table, my dog, a Dalmatian, always comes over and lies down at my feet."

This observation forms the core of the difference between specialists and generalists. Generalists comprise about 75 percent of the population. They are the ones who answer "chair." The defining characteristic of generalists is their gut-level understanding of how other people respond to things around them. They understand because they respond to things the same way. When generalists are in meetings, they don't need to worry about whether participants have arrived at consensus. They know. All they have to do is check their gut reactions. Generalists have a clear sense of what is going on with other people. This makes the generalist brilliant at understanding, motivating and leading other people in organizations. The generalist functions supremely well in groups, teams and systems.

The specialist is a different breed. The highly personal and idiosyncratic response noted above is how the specialist goes about life. It's important for specialists to own what they do—almost completely. The name *specialist* refers to their long-observed tendency to find a particular area of knowledge and pursue that one subject for an entire career. In organizations, specialists do not generally fair well. In fact, a true specialist is like an interplanetary alien who has somehow stumbled into the organization's world. If specialists do make it in an organizational structure, it is because they have found some particular area of expertise that is necessary to the system's functioning and have somehow managed to stick with that one particular specialty. They concentrate on that one area until they know more about it than anyone else. They rise in organizations because their special area of knowledge is crucial. What generally happens, of course, is that a specialist who is really performing well and who probably loves what he or she is doing will get promoted. At this point, specialists lose that vital personal connection to their jobs that makes them want to get up in the morning. When this happens, they frequently become depressed and dispirited, frequently without knowing why.

Specialists and generalists have two fundamentally different views about work. When you ask a generalist what he or she does at work, they are likely to describe a big picture. The company produces this; the team is working on that product; the department is moving in a new direction. The reason generalists function so well in organizations is that they can see what they are doing in terms of an overall result that is the product of many people working together toward a common end. They don't fundamentally care whether they are doing this piece of the work or that piece of it; they mainly care that the team or organization is doing what it set out to do, and that they are rising comfortably in the organizational hierarchy.

Specialists are concerned with what they, personally, are doing. When you ask specialists what they do, they tell you about the element of the particular project that they are personally working on. It's the only thing that makes any real difference to them. Specialists often have a real passion for what they do; that's what makes them so competent in the areas they have chosen.

Joseph, the lawyer we talked about in Chapter 4 who was managing partner of his law firm, but unhappy with it, was unsuited by abilities to be a manager. He was also unsuited because, like many lawyers, he was a specialist. He couldn't care less about the overall organization of the firm or the direction it was moving; he just knew he could manage deals with his clients better than anyone on the planet, and that's what he wanted to do.

Specialists tend to populate professions like medicine, accounting, law and dentistry. These professions have defined areas of expertise, and practitioners function within these areas for their entire careers. They tend not to be parts of large business organizations. If they do form professional groups out of financial necessity, these groups are best described as collections of independent practitioners. Artists, writers, actors, teachers and performers are mostly specialists. Again, these are people who get ahead because they completely own what they do.

David—A Generalist. David is a manager in an international technology company. He has been on the sales side for many years. He sees his job as motivating his people. At this he is a master. He supports them, pushes them, moves them, finds the right roles for them or helps them move on to a better fit if they can't find a good role with him. He has been a top producer for years, but is somewhat bemused by this. "I love to get the right person in the right job. I seem to know just how to get people moving and involved in what they are doing, but it's not something anyone taught me. It's like I've always known it. As far as what I know, I know a little about a lot of things. People who work for me know a lot more about their areas than I do. That's fine with me. They love this stuff, but I leave it as soon as I walk out the door."

David is an extrovert with a manager's ability profile. He is the quintessential manager. Recently he was transferred to production. This is fine with David; what he does won't change. Like most generalists, he sees progress in his career in terms of the organization's structure. Production will be a useful springboard upward in the company. This is quite unlike the specialists who often work for David; they see progress in terms of exercising more control over the one job they want to do.

Specialist-generalist is an extremely important dimension in envisioning a career. Asking a specialist to be a manager is an organizational bad joke. Lacking that gut instinct about others that is the defining characteristic of generalists, specialists often do not have a clue about how to motivate anyone. Basically, they have never seen motivation as much of a problem. They are motivated. Isn't everyone? Specialists' leadership style, when effective, could be called charismatic. The specialist believes totally in his or her mission and gathers people around who believe, too. These "believers" are usually generalists.

Specialists' defining characteristic of owning what they do makes them generally lousy managers. "Do it my way. This is my project, so don't screw it up. Here, let me show you how to do it. Just do it like I tell you to. I'll do it." These are all utterances of specialists, and utterances that would probably never even occur to a strong generalist. A team of specialists working on the same project (or more likely, on their personal pieces of the same project) can be a beautiful study of accomplishment and efficiency—as long as a manager is in charge. Could the atomic bomb have been built by scientists alone? Not without General Groves.

Interestingly, the reverse problem of generalists landing in "specialist" jobs does not come up very often. Given any choice in the matter, most true generalists aren't that interested in specialists' jobs. They would feel pigeonholed and limited; leave that for the experts. If, by some happenstance, a generalist does land in a specialist job, he or she will almost always go about it differently. Generalists in the professions, for instance, tend to become involved in the organization of the profession—in the professional societies or the state regulatory boards. That's fine with the specialists, because they aren't interested in that stuff anyway.

In the Thought Experiment, you will find a short self-report questionnaire designed to give you a sense of where you fall on the two dimensions of personality we discussed here: introvert-extrovert and generalist-specialist. Taking both of these dimensions into account will give you a picture of the kind of work environment in which you will feel most at home. There is also a short interpretive section so that you can see what the results of the questionnaire mean for you.

A Note about Anxiety

At this point in the process of creating a Personal Vision, when you are studying all the pieces and trying to put a picture together of what you want your career to look like, most people start getting anxious. At the beginning of this process, people make fascinating discoveries about themselves. They discover new talents they didn't know they had before, or didn't know the meaning of. They see themselves in new and unexpected ways. They reexamine assumptions that they didn't even realize they were making.

So where does the anxiety come in? You may have all sorts of new information, but it's hard to tell yet where it's all going. There's no picture yet. You can't know yet what it all really means. "I keep adding new bits of information and new insights, but where is it all leading?" Intellectually, you may know clearly that this is a big job that will take a while to figure out, but you may still feel anxious now.

We know that this anxiety is an important part of the creative process of building a Personal Vision. When you start feeling this anxiety, you know that both parts of your mind, the left and right hemispheres, are engaging fully in the problem of how to put all of this information together. It is as though your unconscious, creative mind is worrying the problem, turning it over, pushing it this way and that, trying to figure it out. Your logical, linear, problem-solving left brain wants an answer. And it knows that it can't provide one.

Researchers who study creative people with the idea of delineating the process of creativity itself invariably comment on this anxiety. The first stage of the creative process involves information gathering and logical attempts at solutions. As the problem takes shape, as the scope and extent of it become clearer, the creative person starts to feel anxiety. It is perhaps the mind's way of prodding itself to make a creative leap. This is the beginning of the second stage of the creative process.

The only thing to do is trust yourself. And keep plugging away at the problem. You need three more pieces to your Personal Vision—values, goals and family of origin. Then you will be ready to integrate them and form your Personal Vision.

Thought Experiment D:

Skills, Interests and Personality

1. UNCOVERING YOUR SKILLS

You will have to trick yourself to take a fresh look at your skills. You will need a tape recorder so that you can record one or two stories about yourself.

Think of an event in your life when you were younger, one that you feel positive about in retrospect. Think about what happened right before and right afterwards. Think about what you felt, what you did, and what happened. This can be a small event that would only be meaningful to you, or it can be a bigger event that anyone would recognize as positive.

Now tell the whole story into the tape recorder. Be sure to include details of what led up to it, what you did, what you felt, what happened next, how other people responded and how they felt.

Now record a different story, again one from when you were younger. This time, make it a story about an event which you found frustrating or disappointing. Be sure to include the same details as in the first story.

Now leave your stories for at least two weeks. Don't listen to them or even think about them if you can help it. When the two weeks are up, listen to the stories again. If it helps, pretend they are about someone else's past. In your notebook, as you listen, write down every positive skill you hear in the stories. Many people write down 15 to 20 different skills in even a simple story. Even in the negative story, be sure to find and write positive skills. You may find that you see the same positive skills in both stories.

If you get stuck trying to find positive skills in your stories, give them to someone else to listen to and find skills in them.

What skills appear in both stories?

Are there themes? Do your skills fall into natural groups? How would you name these groups?

2. FINDING YOUR INTERESTS

Start an Interest File: Get a file folder or a box and put it someplace where you'll see it. Use your box or file to collect notes about anything that gets your attention: articles, pictures or even random thoughts about what really interests you in life. You don't have to be choosy here. You're not wedded to anything you put in this file; the more you can play with it, the better. What looks like fun? What would be really interesting—even if you don't know anything about it? What would you like to find out more about? What has always fascinated you? Make a note; put it in the file.

Keep Your File at Least a Month: Longer is better. Don't look in it. Just keep putting stuff in. If you are surprised by anything, particularly delighted by something, or if something doesn't turn out the way you were expecting—these are all clues to what you might find interesting. Put a note in your file. Some of the best items are pictures that catch your eye. You don't have to know why it's interesting; just add it to the file.

Don't Try to Make Sense of It Right Away: Give yourself time. This is one of the most important secrets of creativity. Just add to your interest file; you don't have to explain it, justify it or make sense of it for now. You want to get as wide a sampling as possible of everything that gets your attention all day long. These will be directions in which you are actively drawn, not just things that you have to do.

After a Few Weeks, Open Up Your Interest File: This is where it starts to be fun. Pull everything out that you have been collecting and spread it out on the floor. Arrange it in piles. Sort out all the items into groups. What interested you about that story? What was fascinating about this picture? How are they related? If you don't get any real groupings, put it all back and keep collecting for a few more weeks. Try again.

Name Your Groupings: Identify some categories for your interests. You need a name for them, because it will help you focus on what you are interested in. Make a list. Put it in order of things that interest you most, if you want to.

Compare Your Interest Groupings with Your Skill Groupings: Any similarities? Any differences? What important skills would you definitely include in your Personal Vision? What interests?

3. SELF-REPORT OF TWO PERSONALITY DIMENSIONS

Read each item and then use the scale below to indicate how accurately the statement describes you. Write your answer in your Personal Vision notebook.

Not at all like me		Mostly not like me		Sometimes yes, sometimes no		Somewhat like me		Exactly describes me	
1	2	3	4	5	6	7	8	9	10

1. At parties or in social groups, I like to find one person and talk to him or her.
2. People have a hard time knowing what I feel about things.
3. I would prefer reading a good book to going to a party.
4. I give a good deal of thought to things before I say them.
5. I have one or two very close friends, as opposed to a great many acquaintances.
6. I often initiate conversations with strangers when we are thrown together.
7. Sometimes I don't really know what I think about something until I talk it over with someone.
8. I find parties and social gatherings relaxing most of the time.
9. I like to work around others all day.
10. People usually know what I'm feeling.
11. I like working on my own particular projects.
12. It makes me nervous to delegate anything.
13. I don't like working on teams as well as I like working on my own project.
14. I have some specific areas of interest and expertise.
15. I have my own particular way of going about things.
16. When given a task, I try to figure out who can do it best.
17. I like working on a project with others. I'm a good team player.
18. It usually doesn't matter to me what part of a project I take, as long as I contribute to the overall goal.
19. It wouldn't matter too much to me to be transferred to another set of responsibilities.
20. I enjoy the thought of working with other people on a project.

To develop a score for yourself:

I.   Add your scores together for items 1-5, 6-10, 11-15 and 16-20 (four separate scores in all).

II. With your totals for items 1-5 and 11-15, subtract each total from 50. If your total for items 1-5 was 10, you would subtract this from 50, yielding a score of 40.

III. Add your score for 1-5 (subtracted from 50) to your score for 6-10. Add your score from 11-15 (subtracted from 50) to your score for 16-20.

IV. Your total score for items 1-10 is for the introvert-extrovert dimension.

V.   Your total score for items 11-20 is for the specialist-generalist dimension.

VI. On the introvert-extrovert dimension, rate yourself as follows:
     A. Score: 10-44, Introvert, Paragraph A below.
     B. Score 45-65, Combination introvert-extrovert, Paragraph B below.
     C. Score 66-100, Extrovert, Paragraph C below.

VII. On the specialist-generalist dimension, rate yourself as follows:
     A. Score 10-44, Specialist, Paragraph D below.
     B. Score 45-65, Combination specialist-generalist, Paragraph E below.
     C. Score 66-100, Generalist, Paragraph F below.

INTROVERT-EXTROVERT

Paragraph A: Introvert. As someone who exhibits Introversion, you get energy and renewal from time spent by yourself. You can learn to be quite adept at social situations and very skillful at handling interactions with others. You must always keep in mind that no matter how skillful you become, interactions with others always have an element of work. Long periods of social or business interaction, no matter how satisfying or enjoyable, will always leave you feeling somewhat drained.

On the positive side, Introverts are able to concentrate on tasks that require solitary effort for long periods of time without undue stress. You can handle social situations by learning to be skillful and adept with them, and this means you can be with other people with very little stress provided you allow yourself enough time alone to regenerate.

Paragraph B: Combination Introvert-Extrovert. You report some characteristics of Extroverts and some characteristics of Introverts. In general, this position on the scale means that you have more choice about your interpersonal environment.

You have a good intuitive understanding of social situations and you enjoy interaction with other people. You are able to listen well to others and easily guess what they are feeling. On the other hand, you are able to be alone some of the time and enjoy this. You are able to concentrate on tasks that can only be done by one person, and not feel too much stress from this. Obviously, the two sides are somewhat incompatible. You will probably find that you lean more in one direction than the other. However, your score indicates that you participate to some extent in both.

You will probably need to allow a good balance in your life between being with others and being by yourself. If you are around people interacting for extended periods, you will probably feel some renewal by being alone. If you are alone for extended periods, you will probably find yourself wanting to be with others.

Paragraph C: Extrovert. You get energy from being with people and you like being around others through a good part of the day. If you were to get into a job that required you to be alone most of the time, or in which your interactions were so stereotyped that you could not really relate to others, you might well find it stressful and unsatisfying. The reason for this is that you would not be having enough contact with other people in the day.

You have excellent intuitive understanding of social situations and you enjoy interaction with other people. You are able to listen well to others and guess easily what they are feeling. Many people who exhibit Extroversion use interactions with other people to help them understand their own thoughts and feelings. Quite often, a thought or idea does not feel "real" to an Extrovert unless it has been shared with someone else. You will always be happier in a position if you have some way to interact with others.

SPECIALIST-GENERALIST

Paragraph D: Specialist. Specialists look at the world in a unique way. The Specialist will always see things somewhat differently from anyone else. This is a clear strength in the right setting, and with the right expectations. If you are expected (or expect yourself) to be part of the herd, or to come up with the "regular" response to problems, you will always be working against yourself. Your strength is that you may have a different slant on things and a different way of looking at things.

Being a Specialist affects how you perceive others and how you communicate. You tend to like the independence and autonomy that come with having total mastery of a body of knowledge or a skill of your own. Specialists often have clear ideas of what they wish to accomplish, and work with dedication and personal commitment.

Paragraph E: Combination Specialist-Generalist. You report characteristics of both Specialists and Generalists. Specialists like coming up with original answers to most problems and making unique contributions. Generalists are expert in judging how others in a group respond and contribute. You may well be able to do both to some extent.

You probably enjoy being an expert and having an area of expertise that fascinates you. If you can make this part of your job, it can be a tremendous benefit to you. You are also able to work effectively with teams and groups. This dual characteristic can be extremely valuable in corporations. You can gain a definite position or specialty, but also work effectively in the team atmosphere needed in most business environments.

Paragraph F: Generalist. Generalists like to work with people and through people. The Generalist usually thinks in terms of the overall goals of the organization, rather than strictly in terms of his or her own specific area or job. A true Generalist can move easily from job to job, and often does, just as long as he or she is furthering the goals of the team. The Generalist does not constantly live and breathe the job, like the Specialist. For the Generalist, the job is a tool, like a hammer, to be picked up and used for an end, and then laid aside when it is over.

Generalists like being part of a team. They are able to think broadly about the overall functioning of the organization, and not be so bound to one particular specialty. A Generalist can be willing for others to have their areas of specialty and expertise, because that can help the team. Whereas the Specialist operates through a particular area of expertise, the Generalist operates through the group.

FOUR STORIES: SKILLS, INTERESTS AND PERSONALITY

Tracy

Skills: "I told a story about organizing a paper-recycling project at my high school when I was a freshman. The school, of course, produced reams of paper every day, and they just threw it into the landfill. I thought, 'We can do something about this.' I got about 10 or 12 people in my class to come over on several Saturdays and we made boxes. Then we got all the teachers to put paper in the boxes. Then we organized collection and got a recycling service to pick it all up. I've always done that. I just look around and think, 'What needs to happen here?' and then set out to do it. I could have told a dozen other stories about things I did in high school and college both. I think when I really feel passionately about something, I am good at getting others interested, too."

Interests: "I've always been interested in the natural world and the environment. The pictures and articles I cut out to put in my file were about everything under the sun, but it always kept coming back to animals, the environment, nature, science."

Personality: "I am half-extrovert and half-introvert. No surprise. I like people, but I like being by myself to think every once in a while, too. What was interesting was that I am a total specialist. There have always been some things that really interested me. What I enjoy most is going into those subjects totally. There are some subjects I've been interested in for years. I guess that's another reason I don't like my job very much at the law office. I just have to do whatever they tell me to; I don't ever get to have a project or something that's just mine."

Feelings now: "I'm getting more excited. I'm seeing more patterns here. I don't know where it's going yet, but I think it's going somewhere."

Brian and Janet

Brian's Skills: "When I was a kid, my mother would have garage sales. She always liked me to help her because I was so good at getting people to buy stuff. I could always find exactly the right thought to bring someone around who was wavering about buying. I enjoyed the puzzle: What does this person want? How can I say it so he will want to buy it?"

Interests: "My interests are mostly in people or sports. I like to read about people who are doing things. I like interesting ideas. It's intriguing to me to see a particularly well-done print ad. I like to scope out how it catches my attention, and then what it promises. I'm always interested in how you 'hook' people."

Personality: "I am a total extrovert and generalist. It's like I was born knowing people and what makes them do what they do. Put me in a room full of people, and I'm not really happy until I have gotten around to all of them to find out what they think about things."

Feelings now: "Confident. It's amazing how much better I feel knowing how well my job fits me."

Janet's Skills: "The story I told was about doing a senior thesis in college. The school required a thesis for graduation, and most of the other seniors dreaded it. I got interested in the economics of political reform in nineteenth-century England. It was fascinating once I got into it. It combined a lot of different disciplines—history, politics, economics, law—and I had to learn about all of them. Then I had to turn it around and make it understandable to others. I had a great major professor. He kept saying that I knew more about some of this than he did. I got high honors, and he said I should publish it."

Interests: "I really love detective novels. I probably read one or two a week. I like to figure them out before the hero does. I also like reading the news. I like to try to figure out what is really going on. When the president or the treasury secretary says something, I like to predict what the reaction will be in the press."

Personality: "I am a complete introvert, and half-specialist, half-generalist. The introvert part is right. I like people, but just one at a time. When I go home, I like to read a book. When I got my scores, I showed them to Brian and said, 'See, that's why I don't like to go *around and talk to everyone every time we go out.' I like having one friend, or two. The specialist-generalist score is interesting. Maybe I would like my job better if I weren't feeling pulled in all different directions all the time."*

Feelings now: "Very interested. This is fascinating—the same themes keep coming back from the different exercises. Hopeful."

Elizabeth

Skills: "My story was about my senior year in high school. I was president of three organizations and a member of about six others, including cheerleaders. I made good grades, too—almost straight A's. The story really wasn't about all those accomplishments. It was more about how I handled stress. My day was going to meetings, classes, talking to my friends, more meetings, study, talk to my friends, a little sleep. I don't remember feeling tired or stressed, but I can hear my mother's voice, 'Honey, you don't have to do everything.' I guess my life's always been the same. Too much to do. Always on the edge of falling apart."

Interests: "I'm interested in my child. I'm interested in day care. Almost everything in my interest file had to do with child rearing or day care for children. There is so much that could be done with effective day care, but it is almost a total wasteland. Think of what really good day care would mean to lower-income families. I get so angry when I go pick up Frederick, my son, because half the time he's just sitting in front of a television. It's not the day care's fault, though they don't have any budget."

Personality: "In personality, I'm mostly a generalist and mostly an extrovert. I've always liked working with people in groups. My managerial style is collegial. I like everyone on the team to take an active part in decision-making. I like everyone to feel they have had a say in what happens to them. I have to say, though, that things usually go the way I think they should. As a team, we've been working together for a long time. We don't have much wasted effort. We're the top producer in the division."

Feelings: "Hopeful. I feel like everything I learn adds a new piece to a puzzle. I just want to see what the next piece will add."

Carl

Skills: "I told a story about volunteering at the Free Clinic at my church after I got laid off. For about one day, they had me sorting out donated pills and bandages. Then they put me in charge of organizing the pharmacy. Now I'm organizing the whole volunteer schedule. It has always worked like that with me."

Interests: "I've gotten a lot more interested in my wife and two boys. I have one son who will graduate from college this year, and another who is married and will have a child soon. Since I've been off work, I talk to my sons every week. I try to go over to see the one living in town. It's interesting to find out what they think about things. I'm also interested in the Free Clinic. I think that's a really worthwhile thing to do."

Personality: "In personality, I'm a complete generalist and more extroverted than introverted. I like organizations and teams of people. I like working with them and getting them all moving in the same direction. I know I'm good at that."

Feelings now: "A little impatient. I am finding out a lot about myself, but it doesn't feel new or different. I still don't know where a job is going to come from. I feel I had a pretty good fix on my talents and so forth before."

NEXT CHAPTER: In the next chapter, we start to give your Personal Vision more coherence. Your natural talents are the foundation. Your skills, interests and personality lend it substance and structure. But your values and goals give real life and direction to your Personal Vision.

WHAT
BLOCKED **ANNE**
WAS HER FAILURE **TO LOOK** INSIDE
TO EXPRESS WHAT WOULD BE
MOST MEANINGFUL
FOR HER.
ALL OF HER **GOALS** WERE SET UP
BY HER SYSTEMS.
SHE
NEVER STOPPED
TO QUESTION THEM OR DECIDE HOW
THEY **MATCHED UP** WITH HER
**PROFOUNDEST
BELIEFS.**

Values
&
GOALS

While the objective factors of natural talent, skills, experience and personality form the substrate on which to grow a Personal Vision, the subjective factors like interests, values and goals really animate it. In the last chapter, we saw how to begin capturing and using the drive and creativity that come with your interests and passions. In this chapter, we talk about how values and goals start to give your Personal Vision direction and purpose.

In the process of creating a Personal Vision, identifying your values and goals propels the difficult leap from the Stress Cycle to the Balance Cycle. You may remember from Chapter 2 that the Stress Cycle is outer-directed, motivated by wealth and status, focused on short-term issues, and reactive. In the Stress Cycle, you never stop; you just jump through the next hoop. To be in the Balance Cycle, you must have an interior sense of who you are and what you want in life. In order to grapple with your values and goals, you must look at your life from the inside and find out what directs and motivates your energy and what gives your life meaning.

With values and goals, you must also look at time. This chapter examines two different kinds of time: the immediate time you live in and the future time you plan for. With values, the day-to-day time you spend living out your immediate life determines how "in sync" you feel with yourself. With goals, however, you need to look into the future—10 and even 20 years ahead.

A Question of Values

Values are one of the most common sources of stress for people between the ages of 38 and 45. Increasingly, as we reach the invisible mid-point of our lives, as we start looking ahead and seeing a limit, we start wondering if what we do all day long is worth doing.

Most people do not have this question while they are raising children. Time, energy and money spent towards launching children into the world seem well spent to most people. By midlife, though, people can see the end of raising children. The question arises, what now? What is going to seem equally worth my energy and time?

This is not a trivial question. Answering it can prolong your life, increase your joy and energy, and move you a long way toward meaning—that ineffable commodity that separates the living from the waiting-to-die. Even the business world, ever concerned with the bottom line, has begun to recognize that employees who pay attention to their values are more productive. When people's minds and hearts are involved in what they do, they perform more fully. They are more involved in their lives and work.

Anne's Story

Anne, 45, was an executive in an international public relations firm. She started with this firm after college and moved steadily upward. She had transferred from the New York to the San Francisco office and had achieved a number of prominent successes. She was "second chair" on the new business team—the vital group of high performers that routinely made pitches to new clients. Anne was married, with two children. One would start college next fall, and the other would follow the next year.

"I couldn't imagine doing anything else. Everything seemed to be going just the way I had planned when I was 25. I liked my job. I could see a path upward. I liked the other people I worked with."

Something had been nagging at her, but she could not articulate what. "I basically just wanted to see if I was missing anything or if there were some other way to go with my career. I knew I wanted something, but I didn't know what."

Anne took a Whole Person Technology® seminar to gain a Personal Vision. She quickly discovered why she was so successful in her role in public relations. An extrovert and a specialist, she was a natural performer who liked painting vivid, compelling pictures of the world as she saw it for clients, bringing them in and letting them see it the way she did. With high Classification and high Concept Organization, she was able, in flashes of insight, to understand and overcome a prospective client's objections to a pitch. Then, using an inexorable tide of logic, she turned the client to her point of view. For her, public relations was perfect.

In the course of discovery, Anne examined influences from her family of origin. (We will talk about how to work with your family of origin in the next chapter.) Her mother and father had been missionaries. She had lived a large part of her first 14 years in China. Anne had absorbed an important value as a child, powerfully communicated by both of her parents: "You should give something back to the world."

Her family did not present this value as a mere homily. When she interviewed her mother and father, Anne discovered that her father, shortly after marrying, had spent two or three years working for a bank as a manager-trainee. He was dissatisfied, though, and at age 25 entered a seminary. He was assigned a small church, but applied to be a missionary because he felt the need was greater. He and his family moved to China when Anne was only two years old. He felt that quitting the bank and embarking on this risky venture that never paid him quite enough made his life feel more vibrant and worthwhile.

Hearing her father and mother's story, some of it for the first time, put many of Anne's nagging doubts into sharper focus. "Public relations was right for me, but I started to see how helping large clients sell more product was not going to be enough. I want to feel that I am contributing more actively to society."

Some months after completing work on her Personal Vision, a memo came across Anne's desk. An international relief agency was looking for someone to be director of public relations. Pay was roughly half of what Anne took home from her present job. "Normally, I would ignore a memo like this. If someone I knew were looking for a job, I would pass it along. Otherwise, it would go into the trash can."

This time she didn't throw it away. "As soon as I saw it I began thinking about giving something back to the world and how important that had become to me. I went home and discussed it with my husband. We thought that with my savings from bonuses over the years we would not have a difficult time putting our kids through college. Otherwise, our two salaries should be fine."

Anne applied for and got the job. She is now director of public relations for the relief agency and routinely travels all over the globe. "I'm now doing work that is inherently meaningful. It makes use of all of my abilities and my experience and skills. It makes everything I've done up to now make sense."

To make values work for you, you must compare your strongest values—what you personally hold most meaningful in life—to how you actually spend your time. That is what Anne did.

Like many people, Anne had never taken the time to articulate clearly her most important values. Articulating values requires a disconcerting shift of focus from the outside to the inside. Anne, like most people her age, had spent the majority of her career jumping through hoops. She had gone after a college degree, a good job, a better position, more pay, a path to the executive suite. Each of these goals had focused her entire attention and energy outside of herself.

Let us be clear. None of the hoops Anne so competently jumped through were wrong in and of themselves. What blocked Anne was her failure to look inside to express what would be most meaningful for her. All of her goals were set by her systems. She never stopped to question them or decide how they matched up with her profoundest beliefs. She was a victim of the Lemming Conspiracy.

For Anne, the trip inward started when she interviewed her parents. As we shall see in Chapter 7, there are many positive reasons for interviewing your parents. Without question, it is one of the most powerful things you can do for yourself as an adult. Our values originate in our families of origin. We absorb them fully before we even start school. The most important values are the ones our parents live out—not the values they speak to us in words. This holds equally true for yourself—your important values are the ones you live out in action in your life.

You can clarify your values initially without your family of origin. The Thought Experiment at the end of this chapter will help you articulate the values that most strongly direct your life. Then you can use that information to see how your priorities match up with how you spend your time.

What troubled Anne was that when she did articulate her most important values, she realized she didn't invest any time into living them out. In working with values, we start by establishing priorities. What is your most important value? What is next?

The critical and difficult question comes next: How do you spend your time? How do you actually live your days? A value, even a dearly held one, feels fundamentally hollow unless you act upon it in real time in your real life. The second part of the exercise in the Thought Experiment helps you compare your most important values with how you spend your time.

Having a fundamental value to live a healthy life and take care of your physical body may be important to living a balanced life. But having this value will do nothing unless you translate it into time and actions. Having health as a primary value, but not spending any time in exercise in a normal week, creates a continual disjunction between your values and your life. It is this kind of disjunction that leads to the "hollow men" of the modern world, people who live lives of no meaning to themselves.

In coming to grips with values, we have begun to accumulate enough objective and subjective information to begin to move from stress to balance. In the next section we show how goals form the concrete stepping stones leading out of the Stress Cycle and into the Balance Cycle. Goals create this path *only* if you link them to all of the information, objective and subjective, you have been gathering about yourself. Once again, as with values, time is the medium through which goals move.

Whose Goals? Yours or Your Systems'?

The Lemming Conspiracy insidiously blinds us to the difference between our systems' goals and our own goals. Anne, in the story above, felt absolutely sure she was charting her own course in life. She had a plan, she was following it and she was on schedule. The nagging doubts she felt at odd moments didn't stop her. In fact, nothing stopped her. As we have seen, stopping is the one thing the Lemming Conspiracy will not let you do. The Lemming Conspiracy keeps you grinding away at the Stress Cycle without ever looking up to see what else you might want to do with your life.

Anne assumed her goals were her own. But when she examined these assumptions, she realized that her goals had nothing to do with her most deeply held values. She had left that part of the equation out. Her goals did not reflect who she really was.

As it happened, Anne's goals were a close match for her natural abilities. They took into account her many skills and interests, as well as capitalizing on her interpersonal style. In many ways, Anne's goals fit perfectly, but in one crucial area they missed. In this section, we will talk about how to match your goals to what you know about yourself. The closer you match your goals to *every* aspect of yourself and what you want out of life, the closer you move toward a Personal Vision and the Balance Cycle.

We designed the Thought Experiment at the end of this chapter to help you articulate your goals. What do you want to accomplish in the next five years? Ten years? Expand your goals beyond the limits of work. Your life is bigger than work. What do you want to accomplish in regard to your family? Your friends? Your spiritual life? Your physical self? All of these critical elements enliven and enrich your life just as much, or at times more, than work. Later, as you move toward integration, the difference between your own goals and your systems' goals becomes increasingly apparent.

Over time, you may change some of your goals, eliminate some of them, or add others. It is important to start where you are now. Don't expect yourself to get to answers on the first try. We know from experience that you can't create a Personal Vision from logic alone. There are too many competing pieces to this puzzle. Attempting to pin down your goals is an important preliminary step to the creative work of integrating a Personal Vision.

Goals That Can Be Achieved—One Way Out of the Stress Cycle

Goals are the smaller way stations on the path to a Personal Vision. But some goals can keep you fixed in the Stress Cycle, while other goals can move you away from stress and toward the Balance Cycle. As you might imagine, goals that originate in your systems keep you enmeshed in the Stress Cycle. Goals that originate from you create stepping stones toward a more balanced life.

"I want to be comfortable financially." "I want to be healthy." "I want to be a good father." These sound like fine goals; it's hard to argue with any of them. But as stated, they are not goals at all. They are really more like value statements—a statement about what is important to you. As goals, however, they don't work, because they are endless. They must be more clear to help you. To articulate goals that work better for you, you have to understand: 1) how to know when a goal is reached, and 2) your time frame for finishing it.

SETTING GOALS YOU CAN ACCOMPLISH

For the goals above, what does "comfortable" mean? How much money? When? What does "healthy" translate to in terms of behavior? How many workouts per week? How long? Or what does it mean in terms of blood pressure or cholesterol level? By when? What does "good father" mean for you? Time with your children? How much? How often? How will you know you have succeeded?

Goals are tricky. We tend to feel that once we name a goal, we're done with it. When you deal with goals that might or might not actually be your systems' goals, it is trickier still. One way to recognize a goal that is your systems' rather than your own is that you can never know when you achieve it.

As an example, look at the goal of being financially comfortable. This is a worthy goal, and an important one for anyone in our society. But what does it mean? For most people, there is no end point to this goal. It just means more: more money, bigger house, better car, better job. This is a system goal. It pins you in the Stress Cycle.

To make it your goal instead of your systems', you have to translate it into concrete terms for your own life. What are you going to use money to buy? Retirement, house, car, education for your children, security? You can connect an amount of money to each. You can figure out how much and what is enough.

Next, you need to think about when you need money. When is retirement for you? When do your children need educational money? These questions may sound obvious and trivial, but they are not. Most people do not ever bother to figure out what is enough money. As a result, most are like rats on a treadmill, endlessly running and never getting anywhere.

As we saw earlier in Anne's story, a critical piece of her being able to do what she wanted to do with her life was sitting down with her husband and figuring out what money they needed to accomplish their goals. Before she did this, she had never considered the question, "What would be enough?" But without this step, she would never have made the change she made without feeling anxious about it. As it happened, figuring out and agreeing with her husband on what amount of income would be enough for them was an enormously freeing act. It allowed her to pursue her Personal Vision and change her life for the better.

GOALS AND TIME

The second part of making a goal yours instead of your systems' is putting it on a time line. You have to know not only what you want to accomplish, but when. In the Thought Experiment, you will see an example of a time line. There are only two ways to go with time: forward and backward. In thinking about goals, it is often most useful to go backwards. Start with what you want to accomplish. Put it on the time line. Then start to fill in behind. 'In order to accomplish *this*, what else will I need to accomplish? When?' Put that on the time line. As you keep working on your time line, it can become an important working document for your career. It should never be static. To make it live and breathe, refer to it; update it; add to it. This can become an important part of your written plan for your life.

Systems' Goals vs. Goals That Integrate

Besides being unachievable, another sure sign of a system goal is one that is single-dimensional. "I want to earn $5,000,000 before I'm 50." You clearly know if you accomplish this. You know when you want to accomplish it. But is it a system goal, or yours?

It is totally one-dimensional. If a client were to state a goal like this, we would ask, "Why?" The answer might have something to do with power, prestige or things he or she could buy. These are outer-directed goals that leave people in the Stress Cycle. They don't lead anywhere and don't really have anything to do with the person, only with his or her systems.

On the other hand, the answer could have something to do with security, children or the ability to tackle a lifelong ambition. This is better. People who answer this way are at least thinking about themselves and what they want from their lives. But in this case, the goal becomes security, or having adequate money to educate children, rather than $5,000,000 before 50. If you address these issues in your goals, you will go a lot further toward moving yourself out of the Stress Cycle.

We talked to a lawyer once, the founding partner of a successful corporate law firm. He stated his goals this way: "I have spent nearly 60 years amassing a fortune. In a few years, I'll retire, and my goal is to spend it." This lawyer has one of the finest strategic minds in the field. He has made his fortune because he is so adept at keeping his clients out of the very kind of trap into which he has fallen himself. He is a victim of the Lemming Conspiracy. He told us in the same interview that he particularly enjoys working late on Saturday night because no one is in the office to bother him. He is in the Stress Cycle, and his goal will not help him out. His whole universe is bounded by his role as a lawyer. If he is not that, what is he?

Many things. But he won't be able to know that unless he breaks out of the Lemming Conspiracy.

Ideally, all of your goals should relate directly to all or most of the important factors of your life. For instance, as you define what security means for you, how does it relate to your abilities, interests and personality? How does it relate to your skills and experience? How does it relate to your values? To see how all of these factors work together with a person's goals, let us tell you about a young woman with a fairly specific goal—she wanted a job within six months.

Ruth's Story

Ruth had been a buyer of women's clothes for a department store chain for five years when a bigger chain of stores bought her company and she lost her job through restructuring. She had not liked her job very much, finding it stressful and unrewarding, so she wanted a job in a new field. She had no idea where or how to start looking.

Ruth had enough money to live for six months without going too deeply into her savings. At the beginning her goal was simple and straightforward: Get a job, any good job that paid about the same as she had been making, but in a different field, before her savings cushion ran out.

As she found out more about herself, her goals changed. She discovered natural artistic talents of which she had been previously unaware. She also discovered much about her previous job that she liked and that suited her well. She liked the travel and contact with people; she also enjoyed working with different kinds of fabric and cloth. She had always been fascinated by fabric, and had for a time thought about becoming an artist in cloth and natural fiber. She didn't think she could make enough money with this kind of work, however. One aspect of her previous job she did not like was the boring kinds of cloth and clothing she was required to handle. As you might imagine, she discovered she was a specialist, so her interest and fascination with cloth made more sense to her. Her dissatisfaction and discomfort in the large organization she had been working for also made more sense.

So her goal became more specific: she wanted a job in an artistic field, with a small company, or perhaps with an individual, that involved working with specialized cloth, and that made use of her skills and experience acquired as a buyer. This goal related strongly to her Personal Vision, and encompassed several critical factors she had discovered and wanted to express in her life.

Ruth used a process called Surveying to make her goal real. We will discuss Surveying in more detail in Chapter 9, and we will talk in detail about how Ruth carried out her Survey project.

In Surveying over four months, Ruth received three job offers that fully met her first criteria: good job, decent pay, different field. But she knew they didn't match her goals. They would not satisfy her in the long run. She turned down all three and pressed on with her Survey. She found this surprisingly easy.

Ruth finally connected with an architect who had an interior design studio. He wanted a person to buy unusual and artistic cloth from Italy and France for his customers wanting something different in their homes. He had been looking for someone to do this for almost a year. Ruth got the job in one interview because she could tell the architect, in detail, exactly how her goals, interests, fascinations, skills, experience and personality worked together to make her perfect for what he wanted her to do. She took this job and is still happily buying cloth.

Ruth's story illustrates several principles we feel are crucial.

1. *The best answers—the ones that lead to the greatest satisfaction in the end—come from inside you.* No counselor, no matter how well educated, administering no matter how many tests, could have advised Ruth to seek and find the job she ended up with. No one else could possibly know enough about her to give her this advice. Her previous employer could not know; an outplacement service could not know; a career counselor could not know. But Ruth knew. It was always inside her; it just needed a process to bring it out and make it plain to Ruth herself.

2. *First finding out about yourself defines and lays out the most direct and efficient route to finding a satisfying job or a satisfying fit in your present job.* Many people feel or act as though looking at themselves were a waste of time in the practical business of finding the right job or the right fit. Not only is it the most efficient way to proceed, but it can help you avoid wasting years of your life in pursuits that don't fit you at all.

3. *If you create a clear goal that includes enough about yourself, and keep that goal in front of you as a target, you can generally find what you are looking for.* Reread Ruth's story above. Until she articulated a clear enough goal, she couldn't find the right job. Once she had stated her rather definite goals, though, she was in fact able to come up with a job that met almost all of them.

4. *By creating a Personal Vision and using it as a template, you can know clearly which opportunities to accept and which to turn down.* One of the most freeing aspects of creating a clear Personal Vision is being able to know clearly what does *not* fit. No matter how attractive a promotion or a project might look, if it doesn't fit you and your Personal Vision, then maybe it's part of the Lemming Conspiracy, the Stress Cycle, and is not something you really want to touch. The other side of it is equally important. With a Personal Vision, you know immediately when you run across an opportunity that you want to jump on.

Ruth's initial goal—find a job, any job—was a product of the Stress Cycle and would undoubtedly keep her in it. By the time she had turned down three jobs that met her first criteria, she knew more clearly what she wanted and how that was different from what her systems would choose for her. Ruth's Personal Vision, and the goals she developed out of it, allowed her to break the Stress Cycle and move toward the Balance Cycle.

Thought Experiment E:

Values and Goals

1. YOUR VALUES AND YOUR TIME

How can you know what's important to you? How can you know if you are out of sync?

Go to the values lists below. Read over the entire list.

Start with the Priority list. Think about the importance of each of the values on the list. What are the most important ones from your point of view? What values do not seem as important?

Now number the values, 1 being most important to you, 2 being next, and so on until you have numbered the entire list of 16 values from the most to the least important.

Values List—Priorities

(number from 1-16 according to your own priority)
—— Security
—— Monetary Success
—— Family
—— Position
—— Wisdom
—— Health
—— Stability
—— Productivity and Competence
—— Creative and Artistic Work
—— Spiritual Fulfillment
—— Authority and Decision-Making
—— Excitement
—— Innovation
—— Physical Challenge
—— Friendship
—— Change and Variety

Now go to the Time list. Carefully go through your calendar for the last two months and count up the hours you spent directly working toward each of the values on the Time list. If you spend 10 hours at work each day, for instance, you might count this toward monetary success, position, authority and/or security, but it would probably not go to family, health or spiritual fulfillment. Now rank the values on the Time list according to your Time, Energy and Focus, with 1 being the value toward which you put the most of your actual time, energy and focus, down to 16, where you put the least.

Values List—Time
(put number of hours spent directly working on each in last month, rank according to time, energy and focus, 1-16)
—— Security
—— Monetary Success
—— Family
—— Position
—— Wisdom
—— Health
—— Stability
—— Productivity and Competence
—— Creative and Artistic Work
—— Spiritual Fulfillment
—— Authority and Decision-Making
—— Excitement
—— Innovation
—— Physical Challenge
—— Friendship
—— Change and Variety

Compare the two lists—what you consider your priorities versus where you put your actual time, energy and focus.

If your high priority values (1, 2 or 3 on your priority list) are low time/energy/focus values (13, 14 or 15 on your time/energy/focus list), this causes stress. This lack of inner direction, of course, is a major function of the Stress Cycle.

In the same way, if your low priority values (13, 14 or 15 on your priority list), are high time/energy/focus values (1, 2 or 3 on the time/energy/focus list) this also signals disjunction in inner directedness, and also causes stress. Again, as you get older, the stress increases.

Stress due to disjunction between what you hold meaningful and how you actually live your life tends to force itself into consciousness for the first time at the Midlife Transition (age 38-45). However, young people feel this stress, too, even if they are not paying attention to it. The sooner people pay attention to their values and work to bring them in sync with their daily routines, the more alive, productive and enthusiastic they tend to feel about their work.

2. PLACING YOUR GOALS IN TIME

First of all, write down all the goals you can think of in your Personal Vision notebook. Near goals, far goals, personal goals, work goals, family goals, health goals, money goals. Don't worry about grouping them yet.

When you have a significant number of goals covering different aspects of your life and career and different times in the future, start grouping them. Connect ones that go together, creating subsets within categories. You may find that you have a few large goals and that many of the others are smaller goals leading to the larger ones.

In your Personal Vision notebook, draw a line. At the beginning of the line, put your age now. At the end, put 100. Now fill in your Turning Points, every 10 years between the age you are now and 100. Mark ages 22, 40, 60 and 80 with heavy lines, as they tend to be major transition points for most people. Some people use a large poster for this exercise; some people tape several sheets of paper together to create a large foldout in their Personal Vision notebooks. Feel free to create your time line in any way that makes it come alive for you.

Place your major goals on the line at the age you wish to attain them. Feel free to be as creative with this as you want—it's your career, and your time line. Put pictures on your time line if you want to, draw diagrams, use colors. Your line doesn't even have to be straight. If you want hills, valleys, circles or spirals, put them in.

After you have your major goals on the time line, fill in the smaller, intermediate goals. Again, let yourself have some freedom to create. Fill up your sheet with goals and connect them to a time line.

As you continue with your exploration and work on your Personal Vision, you might find that you want to change some of your goals, add new goals or take some goals out altogether. You may find that after you have done the creative Thought Experiments in Chapter 8, you want to do another time line, taking more of your life into account. The main task is to create a working document that you will be able to use and refer to as you make your Personal Vision real.

FOUR STORIES: VALUES AND GOALS

Tracy

Values: "The values were interesting. My highest values were productivity, excitement, innovation and change. My lowest were security, money, position and stability. All of my time, though, is spent holding down a job that's exactly the same drudgery day after day just so I can earn enough money to live on. I'm pursuing my very lowest values with all my time and energy. It's no wonder I feel so discouraged."

Goals: "My most immediate goal is to figure out what I'm going to do next. I've given myself three months. I need to get out of my job at the law firm yesterday. Even more than that, I need to be aiming in some direction that will yield some of the excitement and change I want so badly. I want to be involved with what I do."

Feeling now: "Determined. Confident. I know more what I'm looking for."

Brian and Janet

Brian's Values: "My strongest values were monetary success, family, competence and decision-making authority. My weakest were artistic work, spiritual fulfillment, physical challenge and health. I guess I would rather watch a game on television with a gang of friends than run or exercise. When I look at my time and energy, it looks about the same, with the exception of family. It's one of my highest values, but I don't put any time into it at all. That bothers me. The health one being on the bottom bothers me, too. I guess I'm just taking health for granted."

Goals: "My goals are these: make the million-dollar club this spring, get at least two older executives to know who I am and be interested in my career and be in the fast-track pool by next spring."

Feelings now: "Thoughtful. I wonder why I don't want to spend any time or energy toward family."

Janet's Values: "My highest values: family, security, money and stability in that order. I would also put friendship in the highest group. Lowest: position, authority, physical challenge and change. I think family is really the number-one priority for me, but when I look at my time, it's totally different. I don't put any time into family. I just work to make money, so that's in line, I guess. But I don't care at all about promotions and getting more authority. I look at the people in charge, and they seem a lot more stressed than I am. They certainly don't seem happy."

Goals: "Have a family, get a different job or else quit entirely."

Feelings now: "Kind of trapped. Maybe a little confused about what I want."

Brian: "I notice how different we are on our goals. I'm totally focused on work. Janet is totally focused on family. Most of our values are similar, I think. We both want to have a good lifestyle, and we both feel that family is important. As far as family goes, neither one of us is putting much time into it right now. I don't feel I will ever be able to put much time into it and still reach my goals. So I guess it's nice that it's so important to Janet, because she can sort of make up for me."

Janet: "I'm glad to see that Brian and I have some of the same values. I really see how important family is for me, and how we're not doing anything about it right now. That's sort of worrisome to me."

Elizabeth

Values: "My top values: family, stability, spiritual fulfillment and friendship. I can tell you right now, I'm not putting my time into any of these. They are all pretty much at the end of my time list. My bottom values: monetary success, position, excitement and variety. These are what I put my time into. My life is upside down. I have been working, working, working for all the things that I value least. What I value most barely gets any of my actual time."

Goals: "Change this situation. Now. Immediately. I just don't exactly know how. My only option seems to be to quit, and I am not going to do that—yet."

Feelings now: "Mad. Determined."

Carl

"My primary values are family, wisdom, health, position—in that order. Lowest on the list (but not unimportant, certainly) are excitement, innovation, creative and artistic work and physical challenge. I am spending more time with my wife, and it is very rewarding. I talk to my children regularly. It makes me think about what I missed while I worked so hard for my company. The same with health. I am working out regularly for the first time since college. Maybe this will all make me a little wiser. Actually, the only thing missing from my top values is position, of which I have none, of course. I do work on it every day, but it's discouraging to think that I may have to take less pay and benefits than I had before. One thing I think about is that I don't want to get back into a rat race when I take a new position. I don't exactly know how I would pull that off, but I feel better now than I have in years. I'm closer to my wife, and closer to my children. I don't want that to go away."

Goals: *"Get a new job. Soon. I'm beginning to think, though, not just any job I can find. I want it to be one that fits me."*

Feelings now: *"I can see what I was missing before. I don't want to make the same mistake again. I'm afraid that if I get back into a job, the same forces that drove me to work 60-hour weeks will drive me to do that again. To tell the truth, sometimes I don't really want to go back."*

NEXT CHAPTER: In the next chapter, we talk about the final factor you need before integrating all of them into a Personal Vision: your family of origin. Just as the Lemming Conspiracy begins in the family of origin, so the family provides by far the greatest energy for breaking out of it. By understanding your family of origin's impact and working with it in a structured way, you may have your best tool for moving your life to the Balance Cycle.

Our **Parents'** KEY DECISIONS AT TURNING POINTS FORM THE

Model

FOR HOW **WE MAKE DECISIONS** AT TURNING POINTS. **Understanding** THE **HOW** AND **WHY** OF OUR **Parents'** DECISIONS CAN HELP US START TO LIVE OUR OWN LIVES INSTEAD OF **RELIVING** OUR **Parents'**.

Family
Of
ORIGIN

There is no more powerful influence on our lives than the family in which we were born and grew up. We form our personalities here, largely before age six. We learn our sense of limits here. We learn what work is and how people go about it. So much of what we learn in the family is unconscious that it is sometimes difficult to know the extent of its influence. Most of our learning about systems takes place as children, and as adults we conveniently forget most of what happened before age six. While we may have no recollection of exactly what we learned, the lessons become part of our emotional and social DNA.

Psychologists may sometimes blame parents or families for much of what's wrong. We have never found this approach to be particularly productive. Figuring out what *positive* things you learned in your family, finding out what makes you unique, and, most of all, asking how your parents made key decisions at Turning Points in their lives moves you into new territory. This new information transforms you and your systems.

Our parents' key decisions at Turning Points form the model for how *we* make decisions at Turning Points. Understanding the how and why of our parents' decisions can help us start to live our own lives instead of reliving our parents'.

Our parents are the source of the most valuable information we can have about ourselves, but tapping into it requires particular effort. Normally, a great deal of the most significant information in families is *not* spoken of. It is "understood," or not seen to be as significant as it is. Often, our roles in families come to take precedence over our individual selves. It may be more important for me to be "father" than it is for me to be a living person with hopes, fears, inconsistencies, mistakes, ambitions and ambivalence. Families often don't know how to talk about the most important matters because they never get much practice. It's not through any conscious withholding, but merely from force of habit. We have taught thousands of people in our programs how to return to their families of origin and find out some of the most fascinating and significant information they will ever discover. You can, too.

Families of Origin and the Lemming Conspiracy

If the Lemming Conspiracy starts in the family of origin, the family of origin also helps us escape it. As we saw in Chapter One, our family systems form the model for all future systems in our lives. We learn how to make decisions at critical junctures in our lives, and we learn how to handle such normal aspects of living as work, disappointment, success, the future, balance and families themselves. None of this learning is conscious. In Chapter 1 we spoke of the psychological process of *identification*. We absorb our parents, and they remain part of our social and emotional selves forever. That's what allows us to function and succeed in the world. This unspoken influence on our emotional and social lives is far more valuable and pervasive than all spoken messages combined in terms of our ability to live our lives. But identification with our parents is also what leads us to make errors at Turning Points—decisions about our careers that keep us enmeshed in the Lemming Conspiracy.

Mitchell's Story, continued

We met Mitchell in Chapter 1. He had worked in a large technology firm, but found a much better fit for himself in a smaller, more entrepreneurial company. Before he did family-of-origin work, Mitchell unknowingly repeated important decisions his father had made 25 years earlier.

When his father was 30, exactly the same age Mitchell was when he felt so dissatisfied, he worked for a large insurance company. Also dissatisfied, his father wanted desperately to start his own business. But he was newly married and had a small child, Mitchell. After much anguish and soul-searching, he decided he could not make this jump. It was too risky. He continued with the insurance company, buried his feelings, and soldiered on.

But the dissatisfaction came back 10 years later, stronger than ever. When Mitchell's father was 41, he decided to start his own entrepreneurial business. Mitchell remembers this time in the family's life. There was never enough money. His father was never home. His mother exuded stress and anger. Mitchell left for college, and his father continued the business for four more years. But it was never successful and eventually failed. To support his family, Mitchell's father went to work in the insurance agency of an old friend.

Mitchell's father never escaped the Lemming Conspiracy. He ignored his feelings when he was Mitchell's age and kept working for the large insurance company. At midlife, he made a precipitous jump for which he was unprepared in terms of capital, experience or per-sonality. It was not quite a disaster for the family, but close. He ended up in a job he did not like, far more stuck than he was before, and with an even more limited view of his options.

Even though he didn't know it, Mitchell had absorbed all of this as a child. As a 30-year-old man with a young family working for a large international company, Mitchell had been successful. Thoughts of starting a business of his own also came to him, and he also rejected them as too risky. He felt trapped and stuck—much like his father at the same age.

At this point, instead of swallowing his feelings, Mitchell embarked on The Whole Person Technology® to create a Personal Vision. He has this to say about his interviews with his father: "It was like a door opening. My father telling me how he had struggled and suffered with this decision was like looking into my own life. I could see that I was set to make exactly the same mistakes that he did—and regretted. It was interesting because his advice was: *"Don't leave your company." But when I asked him to tell his story and describe why he decided to do what he did, it was clear that he saw only two options: leave or stay. His advice to me was to stay. It was well-meaning and based on his experience of the world, but it was from the same either/or point of view that he saw in his own life. Once I realized that, the clouds began to clear and I decided that there was probably another middle way that he just didn't consider. Incidentally, it also helped to know that there were reasons I wanted to leave my company and go to a smaller one. It wasn't just some ego-driven, arbitrary wish on my part. It had to do with my natural abilities, personality and interests. There were some* objective *reasons why the fit in my job wasn't right. So in that sense I had an advantage my father didn't."*

Mitchell ended up in a smaller, entrepreneurial, technology firm. He could make full use of the skills and experience acquired in his previous job, but expand into other areas of interest and take on more roles than he ever would have been able to otherwise. He had at least as much security as he did at the larger company. Even though he did not earn quite as much as before, he felt the new company afforded more long-range potential. For Mitchell it was a good compromise. He had beaten the Lemming Conspiracy.

Mitchell's feelings were almost identical to those of his father at the same age. He would have, in all likelihood, made the same decision, and for the same reason his father did at that age. And it would probably have been as big a mistake for Mitchell as it was for his father. Mitchell had absorbed his father's limited point of view without realizing it. If he had not asked his father specifically what life decisions he had made and why, Mitchell would have continued operating from this point of view.

Mitchell's story exemplifies all of our lives. We take over the worldview of one or the other of our parents—even when we consciously want to do anything but. All of us absorb information from both parents. However, we tend to have a worldview and feelings very much like only one or the other parent—often the parent of the same sex as ourselves. When we change and grow in life, we tend to broaden our behavior and perspective. Often this widening of viewpoint involves allowing information from the other parent to emerge.

When Mitchell took the time to ask and listen to his father talk about his life, many things changed. It was as if he could see his father for the first time. This was not *father*, but a *person*, a person who had been a young man once, just like Mitchell. A person who had been anxious and depressed at times, had had a young family once that he wasn't sure he could take care of, who didn't know what the future would bring, and who just took his best shots at life decisions and hoped they were the right ones.

Just as he saw that he and his father were a lot alike and had many similar thoughts and concerns, Mitchell also saw that they were different. One advantage Mitchell enjoyed was that he knew more clearly what he wanted. For another, he saw that he didn't need to be bound any longer by his father's either/or point of view. This freed him to make decisions different from those of his father.

Going Against Systems—How the Family of Origin Helps

We all live in systems and will continue to do so. No system will voluntarily change. It will keep flowing in the same circular channel—and keep channeling its members into the same roles—unless it is dragged, kicking and screaming usually, into a new channel by someone inside it.

It is obviously difficult to go up against systems and even more difficult to effect any lasting change. But it can be done. Let us tell you more of Joseph's story. Joseph was the lawyer we met in Chapter 4.

Joseph's Story, continued

Joseph decided not to continue as a managing partner. He had been excellent at that role, from the point of view of his firm. When he became aware of how unhappy he was with the role, he thought about quitting it. But quitting felt momentous, and he knew that many of his partners would be unhappy. He also knew that his wife would question it and be unhappy. She felt his position cemented her husband's influence in the firm.

Joseph felt stuck. He knew what *he wanted to do, and he knew* why. *It made sense, but it felt like too big a leap. He felt the Lemming Conspiracy's pressure to keep him on track. The system had a role for him; the system provided goals; the system wanted Joseph to continue to see its point of view, not Joseph's.*

Joseph interviewed his father about his life and decisions at important Turning Points. His father had been a successful physician in general practice and had done well financially and professionally. He was part of a large group of general practitioners in a city in Texas. He told Joseph that when he was 40, he went through a period of boredom and malaise. The work was always the same. One day he felt that if he saw one more kid with a sore throat and runny nose with a depressed, strung-out, lonely mother, he would scream. He went so far as to think about applying for another residency, perhaps in psychiatry. He dismissed it as impractical. It would cost him a lot of money; he had a child, Joseph, getting ready to go to college; he would be giving up a successful practice to start all over again; everyone would think he had suddenly lost his mind. There were a hundred reasons why it wouldn't work. He might not even be able to get into a residency.

Eventually, Joseph's father settled down to his career. He told Joseph that it was soon after this that he had his first affair outside of his marriage. It was with a patient. He had others; sometimes he felt that only this excitement kept him functioning. Now close to retirement, his practice remained busy and profitable, but he felt that perhaps he drank too much. He had no plans other than to keep practicing until he died.

Joseph: "I felt like I had just had a prophetic dream. I could see how my father had struggled with exactly the same feelings I had when he was my age—we both realized our jobs were killing us, even if the reasons were different. He had the same abilities and personality I do, and I could see that he needed the same kind of stimulation in his work that I do. When he gave up trying to get that stimulation from his job, he got it in other ways, ways that he feels bad about now. I don't think he really sees the connection between feeling stultified and trapped at work and starting to have affairs, but I see it clearly. He wanted his life to be more interesting. Me, too."

When Joseph realized the power of these messages from his family of origin, and when he saw what he knew would be his own future, his vision became clear. He wanted to quit as managing partner—for many good reasons. He wanted to concentrate on work that he enjoyed and that stimulated him, not on work that felt like drudgery. He wanted to be an active presence with his wife and children.

As Joseph became more certain of his ideas, he started letting his wife and partners know what was coming. No one was very enthusiastic, but Joseph's belief and certainty that it was right for him *carried him through. At first, both his wife and his partners acted as though nothing would happen—until Joseph turned in a letter resigning his role as managing partner. In two months, the person he had chosen to succeed him (*not *the person next in line of seniority; rather, the person Joseph felt had the abilities and personality that fit the job) took over. That day, Joseph left early. He didn't work any more weekends.*

Some of Joseph's partners were so mad that they talked among themselves, but when they realized the firm was not collapsing and that revenues were not dropping, everything settled down. Some months later, some of the partners realized that the firm was being run better. Some of Joseph's partners started talking about leaving at six o'clock themselves and not working so much on the weekends. The system adjusted to new information and became more open.

"It was the same with my wife," Joseph said later. "One day I came home around 5:30 and she was trying to get the kids' dinner ready. She was mad and the kids were hanging on her legs. They were all tired and cranky. I took the kids outside and we shot some baskets while she finished dinner. It was a blast! Sometime later my wife came out and called us all to dinner, but she was obviously angry. I tried to find out why, but she wasn't talking. Finally, later, it all came out. She had had to raise the kids by herself all these years and now I decide to have a mid-life crisis and come home at a decent hour and have fun *with them and her life is just as boring as ever. Sometimes* she *would like to have a mid-life crisis and do something different. I thought that sounded pretty reasonable."*

Joseph is describing systems' reactions to change. First, the system tries to keep roles and relationships the same. If a person in the system tries to change, the system works subtly to move that person back in line. If faced with the threat of real change, systems work more overtly to return things to normal. Sometimes systems exert this pressure crudely and powerfully. Often people in systems feel angry when someone challenges the system's rules. It is important to keep in mind that if you decide that you can have more choices in life than you felt before, this throws a challenge up to *everyone else* in your systems. If you have more choices, then maybe they do, too. Rather than look at that rather frightening thought, sometimes it's easier to convince the errant member that he or she *really doesn't* have any other choices.

For systems the final solution is to reject. Throw the heretic out. Hire someone else who fits. Divorce. But Joseph's systems adjusted.

If a person changes *and* stays, the system must change. It must eventually adjust to the new information. This happened with Joseph's systems. His wife and children adjusted to having a more active and present husband and father. His wife started to take better care of herself. She is now planning to do freelance design work—a field she had been in before her marriage. Joseph's firm adjusted to a new manager, but more importantly, it adjusted to the added possibilities Joseph introduced. Partners didn't necessarily have to work until late at night and on weekends; they didn't necessarily have to fail in their marriages.

Joseph's systems became more *open*. That is, they had more options available, and they could be more responsive to new information from the environment. No system is totally open—if it didn't have rules, it would not be a system. Many systems are highly rigid and closed, but all human systems must be at least somewhat open to new information to survive. The most difficult obstacle facing people who want to set their own courses in life is the Lemming Conspiracy—the power of systems to control their thoughts, feelings, and actions—even when it runs counter to self-interest. Once a person has gathered and integrated enough information about himself or herself, once he or she has started to chart a course, it is time to go to the beginning of the Lemming Conspiracy, the family of origin. That is what both Joseph and Mitchell did. This is what you can do.

Going Back to the Family—Why? And How?

Both Joseph and Mitchell learned crucial information, instrumental in standing up to pressure from their systems, by interviewing their parents. How does this work? Why would asking your father and mother about what they did and thought when they were teenagers have anything to do with you now? Don't you know that stuff already? And would they talk to you about it anyway?

Interviewing your parents, if you have done the right preparation, can be a fascinating experience. It can help you to see yourself and your systems in a new perspective, one that is outside usual channels.

The most difficult problem you will face in doing family interviews will be setting them up in such a way that you really move *outside* your usual interactions. The interactions must be different to be effective in giving you new information to take back to your systems. In the Thought Experiment, you will see detailed and specific instructions for setting these interviews up and carrying them out. Following them closely can help you break out. This is a situation in which your instincts will naturally lead you into your usual circle of interactions. They will keep you inside the Lemming Conspiracy.

It is also important to be ready for the interviews. It's tempting to feel that if this is the most powerful exercise, then let's just do this one and be done with it. But all that comes before is crucial to conducting your family interviews. Preparation helps you understand what is unique about you and your career.

In interviewing your parents, your goal is to learn to see them as distinct from what your system has taught you to see, and thereby to see yourself distinctly as well. As Joseph remarked, "It was like I saw my mother and father for the first time."

Thought Experiment F:

Interviewing Your Family of Origin

Undertaking family-of-origin interviews can be a mind-opening, enjoyable experience in which you find out a lot more about two of the most important people in your life. But only if you set them up well. We recommend following all instructions exactly; each one has a definite purpose.

WHOM TO INTERVIEW:

Ideally, you want to interview both of your natural parents in separate interviews, with no one else there besides the two of you.

If you were raised by a stepparent for a significant part of your childhood, you would also want to interview the stepparent. If one or both of your parents is not available for interview, because of death or severe disability, then you should interview a substitute. This could be (in order of desirability) the deceased or disabled parent's brother or sister, a close personal friend or cousin or an older cousin of yours. Failing all of these, your brothers or sisters can substitute. You would conduct this interview just like you would with your parent—asking the substitute about *his* or *her* life, not about your parent's. Only after talking about the substitute's life in detail, just as you would have asked your parent, would you turn to asking what they might know about your parent's life.

WHEN TO INTERVIEW:

After you have done all the Thought Experiments leading up to this one.

HOW TO SET UP THE INTERVIEWS:

Call your mother or father. Let's say you start with your mother. Tell her that you would like to talk with her in about two or three weeks. She would be doing you a great favor and you would like to have the conversation when it would be most convenient for her. You would like to set aside about one or two hours to ask her some questions about her life. You will be coming just to do the interviews, not for any other reason. You won't be bringing anyone else with you.

This sounds simple and straightforward, but it represents a shift *out* of the family system. Some typical responses to this request, and your answers:

What do you want to ask? I just want to find out some things about your life. Sort of like *Roots*—a family history thing.

Why wait two weeks? Let's do it tomorrow. No, I would rather plan ahead so that we can be sure we both have the time put aside. Also, I want to make sure that I have my ideas and questions ready.

Is this going to be some kind of confrontation? Absolutely not. I just want to find out some more about your life. It would be a big help to me.

Will you be bringing your wife/husband/children? No, it will just be me.

Are you going to interview Father? Will you interview us together? Yes, I will definitely interview Father, too. No, I want to interview you separately so I can concentrate on you one at a time.

You should end by saying that you want to be sure you can interview her without being interrupted. Then, talk to your father in a separate conversation and set up the same kind of interview with him.

WHAT YOU TALK ABOUT:

Below are some questions, but you should think of these as starting points. If anything grabs your interest, pursue it. Make sure you ask your parent how he/she *felt* about whatever happened. Also ask for the *reasoning* behind whatever your parent did. What was his/her plan? What was he/she thinking about?

Let's assume we are talking about your interview with your mother again. You can follow the same questions and format with your father.

Usually it's best to start with your mother's parents:

1. What did your father do for work?
2. How did he come to do that?
3. What particular skills or abilities made him good at that?
4. What kinds of things came easily or naturally to your father? [not necessarily work-related]
5. Did he have a hobby or avocation?
6. What did your mother do for work?
7. How did she come to do that?
8. What particular skills or abilities made her good at that?
9. What kinds of things came easily or naturally to your mother?
10. Did she have a hobby or avocation?

Next, you would ask about your mother herself, generally following a time line in your interviews.

Take her back to the age of the first Turning Point in her mind:
1. What was going on when you were 17?
2. Who were your friends?
3. What were you thinking your life would be like?
4. What were you thinking you would do with your life?
5. How did you feel about that?
6. How did you decide what to do immediately after high school? Why?
7. What happened then?
8. What did your parents think about your choices?

For whatever she decided to do (go to college, for instance, or go to work, or get married), ask the following questions:
1. What skills made you good at it?
2. What came easily? What was more of a struggle?
3. What were some problems you encountered? How did you respond?
4. Did you ever wish you had done it differently? How? Why?
5. Describe a bad day. What made it bad?
6. Describe a very good day. What felt rewarding about it?

In this way, go through each major Turning Point of your mother's life listed below. Taking her mentally back to that age, asking questions about what her life was like, what decisions she made, why, and how she felt about them before, during and after.

- High School to College—age 17-18
- College to the Work World—age 22-25
- Age 30 Assessment—age 28-33
- Midlife Transition—age 38-45
- Age 50 Assessment—age 50-55
- Pre-Retirement Transition—age 60-65
- Age 70 Assessment—age 70-75
- Senior Transition—age 80-85

You may want to tape-record your interviews. They may be a valuable reference for you or your children.

FOUR STORIES: FAMILY OF ORIGIN

Tracy

"I interviewed both my mother and my father for about three hours each. It was amazing. My mother went to nursing school and met my father when he was an intern in the hospital where she was. She never actually worked as a hospital nurse. She worked in a doctor's office to make money while my father finished his residency, and then to make ends meet when he started a practice. It was a stable job with regular hours, and that's what they needed at the time, since they had a young family. But she hated the routine of it. When she could, she quit, and has never worked since. She's had some problems with depression—especially since the children left home. I sort of knew that was going on, but it felt great to talk to her about it. It turns out, she has been feeling that she should do something, work somewhere, but doesn't know what to do, either.

"My father has been like a total force of nature. He still works 12-hour days, just like when I was a kid. He says he has always loved practicing medicine. He gets mad because he says the profession is changing so much. He was really against my going into psychology because he said I'd never be able to make a living. I asked him about retirement. He said he will never retire. Just work until he dies."

Feelings: "It's a little much to put together right now. I can see myself in both of my parents. When I was going strong in psychology, I was just like my father. But then when I lost focus, I became just like my mother, kind of depressed. I can see some problems with some decisions they made, and I could see myself doing the same thing. I can see that I need to have something of my own to sink my teeth in. But I don't want it to be my entire life, like my father."

Brian and Janet

Brian: "My father runs an insurance office in my home town. He has always been pretty successful, though not amazingly so. People like him and trust him, and he keeps customers forever. He had to go out at night a lot. He just felt it was part of the job; he had to do whatever it took. He said he felt like his major duty as a father was to earn a good living and provide for his family. That was what his father did. His father lost his business because of the Great Depression. My father said that he never recovered. It just wiped him out—financially and spiritually. He got work again, but he was never the same. I think that left a profound impression on my father. It's like my father said, 'That's never going to happen to me.' I don't get the sense that he has enjoyed his life very much.

"My mother was a housewife and took care of me and my two sisters. I don't think she was terrifically happy either, but I felt a lot closer to her while I was growing up. She never graduated from college. She met and married my father and then left college to go with him. Her main thing was raising us kids. Since we left home, she doesn't seem to know what to do with herself. She wishes now she had completed college."

Brian's Feelings: "Thoughtful. I'm just like my dad. He worked and worked to get ahead. That's what I'm doing. I feel I'm going to make some terrifically bad mistakes if I'm not careful. I look at my mother, and I think, she could have done so much more. I don't want that to happen with Janet."

Janet: "My father and mother divorced when I was 15. I interviewed my mother face to face, but I had to interview my father on the phone, because he lives in another city. I think my mother's not as mad about the breakup as she used to be. She never remarried, but she's been dating someone for a year now. When my father left us, she got a job with a publisher. She has ideas all the time about books and what books the publisher should bring out next. When she gets an idea, she proposes it to the publisher. She then goes out and gets some expert to write about it. She's very successful. And she loves it. She's like Brian; she would work all the time if she could.

"My father is an engineer and works with one of the Bells. He has always liked the research work he does, and has published several articles. He remarried a few years ago, and they have two children. He seems to have more to do with that family than he ever did with ours. He seems more relaxed than I remember him when I was growing up—not so removed."

Janet's Feelings: "Hopeful. I can see in personality and abilities that I'm a lot like my father. I love it that my mother was able to find a job that she liked so much. I also love it that my father has found a happier family life. It gives me hope that I could find that for myself."

Elizabeth

"My father just retired in the last six months. It hasn't been a great adjustment. He was the king of the hill in his company. He worked for an automobile manufacturing company for almost 40 years and retired as a vice president. Since retiring, he doesn't seem to know what to do with himself. He was the classic executive workaholic. He would do anything for the company, and they rewarded him hand-somely. We had to move around the country a good deal because of his job, so most of his friends were business associates. Since retiring, he's gotten more angry—almost bitter.

"My mother just managed the household. About 20 years ago, she got into a lot of volunteer work. She has now worked for years on the executive board of Planned Parenthood and travels all over the country giving speeches and talking to political types. She's totally committed to this work. I asked her why she suddenly started doing that. Her answer was interesting: 'I had to do something. I knew your father would never change, and with you kids gone, I needed something else to be interested in. I was lucky that I had the financial security to do whatever I wanted to. I am committed to the organization and helping young women have more chances in life. It's very fulfilling.'"

Feelings: "I have always identified with my father. But I can see that, as much as I love my father, I really admire the way my mother has made a life for herself. They seem like a good business partner-ship. I would probably like more feeling in my relationship with my husband than they seem to have in theirs. More fun, too."

Carl

"My father died two and a half years ago. My mother is still alive and lives in an assisted living complex. I've never seen anyone so delighted to do anything as she was to tell me her life story. It's like *she had been waiting years for me to ask. My father was a fairly well-known Episcopalian minister. My mother said that the first time she saw him, she knew they would get married. She played the rather demanding role of minister's wife about as well as anyone could. She never made me or my brothers do anything just to make my father look good. I always appreciated that. She insisted, sometimes over my father's strong objections, that we be allowed to think for ourselves. When he retired five years ago, he had been depressed off and on for years. He drank too much, too. He and my mother remained together through all of that. I think there was always a good deal of mutual appreciation and respect. My mother always had a wide circle of friends and when my father died, it was really nice for her to have them. A group of them moved into the same complex a few years ago. My brothers and I have remained close to her and close to each other.*

"A major change happened in my mother's 'career' when she was 41. She said that up until then she had tried to be perfect. Lead all the church women's groups, host teas, entertain my father's guests. At this point, though, she decided that she needed to have a life of her own. She took classes at a community college, took up gardening in a big way, and started teaching in the local high school to add to the family's income. She was different after this. More sure of herself, I guess.

"I interviewed my father's younger sister. She told me an interesting story about their father, my grandfather, whom I barely knew. He worked for the railroad his entire life. He was a die-maker in the huge shops where they built locomotives and railroad cars. He started there when he was 15 and ended as a supervisor. She told me that he was highly respected among the men. His integrity and honesty were above question. He never made the first political speech, but he always represented the men in the shop to the Union. The dies he made were the patterns that they made tools from. His tools were considered some of the very best because they were so elegantly and precisely made. His sister gave me one of my grandfather's tools she had been keeping. It's very precious to me. The spirit that made him make those tools so much better than they had to be, that is what I feel was passed on to my father, and now to me."

"When my mother told me about her change at 41, I started thinking about myself at 41 or 42. That's when I was recruited by a head-

hunter to be a vice president in the entertainment company. It was quite a ride. My whole career changed like I shifted into another gear.

"I feel I am a lot like my father. If I got depressed, I could see myself drinking too much like he did. I take care of my health better than he did; I would like to live longer and be healthier."

Feelings: "Moved. Impressed with my mother's and my father's lives. Proud of what I 'inherited' from both."

NEXT CHAPTER: When you have finished your family-of-origin interviews, you are ready for integration. Your unconscious mind has been working on integrating since you began reading this book and working with the Thought Experiments. Now it is time to bring your creative unconscious work to light and use it to create a Personal Vision. Each element of Personal Vision is important. Each element is also individually complex. To pull them together into a coherent focus that can direct your career is a mammoth task. But your creative mind can do it, if you access it. The next chapter deals with the creative process and how to make purposeful use of it in forming a Personal Vision.

MANY PEOPLE THINK OF **creativity** AS A **mysterious gift** THAT SOME HAVE AND MOST DON'T. MANY ASSOCIATE CREATIVITY ONLY WITH **purely artistic pursuits.** IN REALITY WE ALL HAVE **creative minds** AND ACCESS TO ENORMOUS **creative talent.**

WE JUST HAVE TO **know how to use it.**

8

Creative

INTEGRATION

To be effective, a Personal Vision should combine all the elements we have been discussing: stage of development, natural talents, skills, personality, interests, values, goals and family of origin. Your creative mind can perform this kind of integration. Your logical mind cannot. To make creativity work, however, you still need your logical left brain. In this chapter, we describe the creative integration process we developed for our clients to use with The Whole Person Technology®. We call this process *left-right-left*. It uses both sides of your brain, the logical *and* the creative, to help you achieve useful creative insights and also to make them work in the real world.

We will show you how creative integration combines *all* of the critical factors of career decisions into a Personal Vision. We will also give you an example of an actual Personal Vision that a person has used for years to guide his career. You can use the Thought Experiment at the end of the chapter to start your own left-right-left integrative process.

Creativity—Where Does It Come From?

Many people think of creativity as a mysterious gift that some have and most don't. Many associate creativity only with purely artistic pursuits. In reality, we all have creative minds and access to enormous creative talent. We just have to know how to use it.

If you boil down creativity to its pure essence, what remains is simple: A creative insight puts ideas together that no one had thought to put together before. Edison used lamp-black for a filament in an incandescent light bulb. Pasteur realized that invisible microbes in milk cause it to sour. Marie Curie realized that radiation was not a chemical reaction, but intrinsic to the element itself. Wilbur Wright suddenly understood that controlling a vehicle in the air, in three dimensions, requires a completely different guidance system than controlling a vehicle on the ground, in two dimensions. Rachel Carson realized that the poisons we spray to kill weeds and insects eventually kill everything else. The utter obviousness of truly creative ideas often stuns us—*after* somebody thinks of them.

Consider artistic endeavors—painting a landscape, carving a sculpture, or writing a poem. Each of these works involves a creative insight; that is, a vision of what the painting should look like, or what the sculpture will be. That sudden connection between previously separated ideas springs from the right brain.

How do you teach your mind to think creatively? How do you learn to join two unrelated ideas to form a neat, easy solution to an "insoluble" problem? Actually, you don't have to teach your mind to do this at all. Your right brain thinks like this all the time. You just have to put it to work on the problem you want to solve.

Your right brain naturally thinks *holistically*. It solves problems by latching on to what it needs—what you remember, what you see, what you hear, what you think. The right brain does not know or care about time, and it doesn't have a strong fix on reality, either. Past, present, future, real, imagined, impossible, good, bad, profitable, impractical—they are all the same to your right brain. It doesn't make distinctions like these.

If you think about your dreams, you'll have a sense of how the right brain works. Your nighttime dreams don't make any logical sense. They are a mish-mash of seemingly unrelated images, feelings and events. Some dream images seem taken from life. They feel so real that you wake up and think they actually happened. Some seem to have no connection with reality at all. We know now that dreaming is our right brain's way of solving problems from day-to-day life. Psychoanalysis bases its treatment on understanding dreams and using them to make unconscious, insoluble problems both conscious and solvable.

Each of the seemingly unrelated images and events in a dream holds a complex meaning. The deeper you go into a dream the more profound and multifaceted its meaning. You can have a simple dream about a trip in a car, but the car can represent many layers of meaning. It can be, at one and the same time, simply a car, a symbol for power and control, a representation of your father and an image of yourself. Each time we dream (and experts believe that most of us dream every night whether we remember the dream or not), we create worlds and visions as complex and enlightening as the *Mona Lisa* or *Hamlet*. At night, we are all Michelangelos, Emily Dickinsons, and Mozarts.

Where is all that creativity? Why don't we feel it when we are awake? Our waking minds live in the left brain, not the right. The left brain works through words. It operates something like a digital computer. It lines up facts like parts on an assembly line and puts them together to end in a logical solution. The left brain lives in the *present*; it remembers the *past*; it thinks about the *future*. It makes clear distinctions between real and not-real, possible and impossible, profit and loss, practical and unrealistic. The left brain can plan, it can learn new facts, and it can figure out logical solutions. It's the home of the *ego*, our adult selves. It is the author of civilizations. If you think about the words on this page—lined up in logical order to express a particular meaning and no other—you have the left brain.

In contrast, look at how words are used in a poem by e.e. cummings:

*Thy fingers make early flowers of
all things.
thy hair mostly the hours love:
a smoothness which
sings, saying
(though love be a day)
do not fear, we will go amaying.*

Here you see words used by the right brain. The logic is slippery and the meaning could go down any number of paths. It's not like a digital computer. It's like the colorful images of Georgia O'Keefe, or the dark symbolism of Picasso's *Guernica*, or the baffling melting watches and clocks of Salvidor Dali. It's playful, subtle, complex, hidden and perhaps a little dangerous. It's creative.

The creative process doesn't *just* happen in the right brain. The left brain is the unsung hero. While creativity undoubtedly springs from the right brain, we don't think of people who live just in the right brain as creative at all. We think of them as schizophrenic—people who cannot tell the difference between reality and fantasy.

Most people who consult on creativity concentrate on helping people achieve a creative insight. But the power of creativity comes only through attention to three distinct steps involving both sides of the brain. Leave one step out and the whole process fails.

The sequence to any creative work, no matter how large or small, is always the same: *preparation, creative insight, execution.* Left-right-left. The left brain prepares the problem for the right. The right brain has the creative insight. The left brain must then translate that insight into the reality of life. What could Leonardo have done if he had not painstakingly taught himself to draw? Or if he had not taken infinite labor to learn the engineering of his day? His insights and visions would have borne no relation to reality. They would have been the ravings of a madman. Or what would we know of Tolstoy if he had not written draft after draft of *War and Peace*? Nothing. Edison's dictum that invention is 1 percent inspiration and 99 percent perspiration captures the whole truth.

In *The Mustard Seed Garden*, a traditional Chinese text that teaches drawing with pen and ink, one section deals with the creative process.

"First, however, you must work hard. Bury the brush again and again in the ink and grind the inkstone to dust. Take ten days to paint a stream and five to paint a rock. If you aim to dispense with method, learn method. If you aim at facility, work hard. If you aim for simplicity, master complexity. If you wish to draw bamboo, draw bamboo every day for ten years. Then forget about bamboo entirely. When one day you feel inspired to draw bamboo again, its pure essence emerges from the end of your brush." Left-right-left.

The left brain prepares you; it sets up the problem for you. The right brain comes up with the creative insight. The left brain must execute the insight. In The Whole Person Technology®, we consciously use this left-right-left process to help people solve one of the most complex and intricate problems imaginable, creating a Personal Vision for their careers.

Creating a Personal Vision—Preparation

Your left brain, even though it can't come up with the creative insight, can set up the problem. It can help you prepare. Each of the previous chapters of this book has set up a different part of the problem. Each of the Thought Experiments was part of the preparation, helping you identify and articulate a parameter of the problem. Even though you might not know exactly what your Personal Vision may look like, you can begin to *describe* it. For instance, "I want to be sure the fact that I am a specialist and an introvert is a positive help to me and that I don't get into a position in which I'm working against myself. That would mean I would be working in an environment in which I can spend a lot of time concentrating on one kind of task that really grabs my interest and attention."

Each time you do one of the Thought Experiments, the information is there for your left brain to use in your daily life. But it is also there for your right brain to fold into its creative musings. Doing the Thought Experiments puts your *unconscious* mind—your right brain—to work on the problem.

In our Whole Person Technology® seminars, participants spend four to five weeks preparing. They learn about each of the eight factors we have talked about in this book—abilities, skills, interests, personality, values, goals, stage of development and family of origin.

As we add information and factors, the problem of integration becomes more and more difficult. Participants begin to wonder where the process is leading, or if they will ever be able to put everything together. For most people, some kind of inspiration strikes midway through the process. Each creative exercise produces more "ahas!" and participants start to see a path ahead. They have the beginnings of their Personal Visions.

As we noted at the end of Chapter 5, some anxiety is not only normal, it can be an important part of the creative process. Your right, unconscious brain produces anxiety as it starts to engage the problem. As a general rule, creativity happens where you are most *involved*. In The Whole Person Technology® we are talking about your *life* and how you want that life to be. It's worth getting involved.

Creating a Personal Vision—Inspiration

The problem of creativity is very much the same as the problem of falling asleep. You can't make yourself fall asleep. The harder you try, the more awake you become. You can't force it, but you can set up the conditions in which it can more easily occur. You can't *make* it happen, but you can *let* it happen.

Once you set up the problem and complete your preparation, you are ready to let your right brain work on it. When you try to make creativity happen, you are using your left brain—the very brain you want to turn off so that the right brain can work. To let your right brain swing into action, we use a three-pronged approach:

- Create an *environment* in which creativity can happen.
- Put your left brain to sleep.
- Give the right brain a task at which it can excel.

CREATE THE RIGHT ENVIRONMENT

Setting up an environment for creativity is just as important as setting up a problem. For a creative environment, you must let go of your left brain's control for a while. You need to promise your left brain that if it will let the right brain work on the problem, it will eventually get the problem back.

How do you let go with your left brain? One way is by letting go of *results*—temporarily. Demanding that an answer be perfect and must solve all problems *now* won't gain you any creative insight because your left brain isn't letting go of the problem. Remember, your left brain thinks in terms of the right answer, the correct solution, perfect results, even the bottom line itself—terms that make no sense whatsoever to the right brain. Your right brain can discover a new way to put the elements of your life and career together, a way that solves several different problems simultaneously. But it will take your left brain to make this insight work in your actual life. If you let the right brain work on the creative insight, trusting that your left brain has the talent and ability to translate that insight to the real world, you will have moved a long way towards creating the internal environment you need to enhance creativity.

PUT THE LEFT BRAIN TO SLEEP

What is the experience of shutting down the left brain and working with the right? Most of us know this feeling, even if we don't recognize it as such. In the 1960s, some psychologists were fond of inducing an "alpha" state. A person in the alpha state felt more relaxed, lost track of time, often experienced images and sometimes insights. Today meditation is more fashionable as a term, but the state is the same—working with the right brain. In these states, we do not experience conscious thought; the logical left brain does not speak to us in words. Rather, the right brain produces dream-like images, perhaps with some words thrown in, but not in the logical manner of the left brain.

Albert Einstein once remarked that he had to be very careful not to cut himself while shaving in the morning. Not because he was clumsy, but because an idea often ignited his imagination while he was in the middle of that routine daily chore. Ideas came to him so suddenly and forcefully that they startled him.

When we lapse into a reverie, when our minds drift without apparent purpose, we are using our right brains. Our left brains fall asleep. We often experience this kind of reverie when listening to soothing music, or watching the movement of water or enjoying a peaceful walk in a park.

To see how to put your left brain to sleep on purpose, let's look at meditation. People who practice meditation every day carefully set it up. They use a certain room at a certain time of day. They sit in a prescribed position and breathe in and out in a prescribed way. They may say a mantra over and over to themselves. Notice the similarity to the routine and preparation for falling asleep. A certain room, a certain time, a certain preparation (change clothes, brush teeth, put out the cat), a book to read instead of a mantra. In these cases, we simply *bore* the left brain until it gives up and goes to sleep.

In the Thought Experiment at the end of this chapter, you will see that the first part of it puts your left brain to sleep. In the second part, the fun begins.

GIVE THE RIGHT BRAIN A TASK AT WHICH IT CAN EXCEL

There are some tasks that are difficult for the left brain and quite easy for the right. Driving an automobile would be impossible if you tried to do it logically. But your right brain enjoys this kind of spatial, multifaceted task and does it easily.

As you access your right brain's creative power, you seek an *initial creative insight*, not the final answer. Your right, creative brain can only make the initial connection. Your left, logical brain makes an idea real and practical.

A young engineer had been struggling to design a truck that could be driven through rugged country to search for oil in some of the barren wastes of the West. So many different needs conflicted with so many different functions that, after six months working on the project, he was hardly further along than when he had started. His boss demanded that he present the results of his work in just two weeks, but the engineer knew he had nothing to show. In despair, he sought the help of a psychologist. After listening for an hour, the psychologist told him to come back next week and present the *worst* possible truck he could design for the purpose, a truck that would be impossible to use. The engineer feared he was wasting his time and money, but seeing no alternatives, he complied. He returned at the next session with drawings and sketches of the most outlandish contraption imaginable. He laughed so much while drawing the sketches that his wife feared the worst.

The engineer had almost not returned for that second session. There was no need. He was now working furiously on the sketches for the real presentation. While in the middle of creating the horrendous design, an insight leapt, full-blown, into his mind. "I suddenly knew where everything should go. I immediately started drawing the real designs. It was as though there were a photograph in my head and I just took the design from the photograph." The oil exploration trucks he designed are still in constant use today in Texas and Oklahoma.

The psychologist gave the engineer a task that bypassed the left hemisphere. It wasn't logical. In fact, the only way to do it was to heave logic out the window. But in doing the illogical task, the engineer's right brain gained the crucial insight into the organization of the many pieces of the engineering puzzle.

So which tasks use the right brain and bypass the left? There are an infinite variety, but we have discovered several types that are particularly successful in helping people gain an initial insight into a Personal Vision. These tasks make use of the right brain's ability to break with hard reality and think "as if." The right brain can play with ideas and thoughts; it doesn't require logic or practicality. That's why it can come up with such creative associations.

Does this mean that whatever association the right brain develops will be valuable? Almost any strong image your right brain creates probably has some meaning for you. Messages from your right brain are never random. The complexities of your life profoundly determine each detail. They may be exceedingly difficult to translate, however. Think about the difficulty of unraveling a dream. Your left brain must translate the message.

An accountant did an exercise in which, after relaxing and allowing himself to follow a guided imagery passage, he described an ideal day. This exercise occurred after he had done a great deal of work on identifying and articulating the pieces of his Personal Vision. That is, he had already set up the problem. His image of his ideal day, as delivered by his right brain, was of himself as a circus clown: funny outfit, greasepaint, big shoes, bulbous nose—making people laugh.

Did this mean he should leave his job and join the circus? No. He lived near a circus training site, and so the sheer repetitive experience of seeing circus performers may have planted an image for his right brain to use. The accountant understood the message immediately. For many years he had been fascinated by storytelling. His grandfather had told traditional tall tales that delighted him as a child. He took every opportunity to seek out particularly good storytellers to listen to and record their stories. A strong introvert, the accountant had never thought about what he could do with his interest. It just never occurred to him to think of it as anything but a meaningless pastime.

In looking at his natural abilities, however, he discovered that he fit a performer's profile. His personality and thinking style came together in a way characteristic of people who perform in front of others— teachers, presenters, marketing representatives, trainers and actors.

In his image of the clown, he realized that he enjoyed making people laugh and enjoyed molding his material in response to his audience. He also realized that the clown hides behind his face paint. The clown is a little removed; he is not *interacting* with the audience, but *performing*. The accountant realized he could hide, a little, behind his stories. And that he would enjoy telling them.

He is actually a gifted performer. He has not stopped being an accountant, but he has *added* something new, exciting and meaningful to his life.

A Personal Vision

At age 42, the Midlife Turning Point, Edward, a consultant in human resources, went through The Whole Person Technology® process we describe in this book. He examined all the factors—abilities, interests, skills, personality, values, goals, stage of development, family of origin—and finally went through a series of integrative exercises. This is how he describes his Personal Vision:

"My Vision came in stages. The first insights came when I got feedback on the ability battery. This was extremely enlightening—even for someone such as myself who had been through virtually every kind of development program as a part of my job. I realized that my role at work really capitalized on my natural abilities. I felt much more confident, even though I have always been successful at what I tried. It said what I had always *felt* to be true, but there it was in black and white.

"As useful as it was to know about my abilities, this did not help me make the leap to a Personal Vision. It helped fill in a few pieces, though. More pieces followed: interests, skills, personality. I started noticing a pattern. The same ideas kept emerging. When we did an integrative exercise, my Personal Vision started to take on a definite shape.

"Until that point, most of my thoughts were concerned with the structure of my job. The integrating exercises helped me broaden that perspective. In creating a Personal Vision I became more concerned with my role at work, but, just as important, *what my life would look like* as I lived out my career.

"I realized that I would need to hold several aspects of my life in balance. From my family of origin and my subsequent values, I knew my family must take an overwhelming priority. If this sounds obvious, it was not always so with me. There were times as a young professional when my family took a back seat. It was only when I consciously thought about values and priorities that I realized the personal importance of time and commitment to my family.

"My interests and talents led me toward art, which surprised me. I had never realized how important this had become to me. I suddenly "remembered" that my mother had been an artist. Also, I had never thought of myself as having anything to do with design or visual representation. But I uncovered a talent for creative design and words that has been helpful in my job and satisfying to myself. I realized I wanted to take a few more risks at work—I could be more creative in consulting with clients.

"I knew from my experience and abilities that I could create the role I wanted at work. I also knew without any doubt or hesitation that there were some roles I could be asked to fulfill that I did not have the experience, the personality, or the inclination to carry out. I knew people who could, and who would love to do it, but it wouldn't be me. This was a great insight because I had always felt it necessary to be able to do everything. Realizing there were some roles that fit me well and other roles that didn't was enormously freeing.

"All of these elements came together in a picture I drew of my future career. I drew myself both creating and using a new technology while doing something beneficial for the world. My family was with me, and part of my attention went to them. Off to one side, I was painting, and there were sculptures that I created. As simplistic as this picture sounds when rendered in words, its *meaning* has guided most of my decisions since the day I made it."

Thought Experiment G:

Creative Integration

We especially adapted this series of integrating exercises from simi-lar ones that we do in the course of our Whole Person Technology® programs. Carefully following the instructions will help you access your right creative brain—not an easy task to do alone or on purpose.

STEP 1: PUT YOUR LEFT BRAIN TO SLEEP

Find a tape recorder you can use to record the following text. You can record it in your own voice, or you can have a spouse or friend record it for you. This will form the lead-in to all of the subsequent integration exercises. Remember that your task is to put your left brain to sleep temporarily. Your verbal left brain can relax and let go of its role in speaking to you and guiding your actions for a short time in order to let your right brain engage a problem for which it is sublimely suited.

Record the following in a slow, relaxed, well-modulated voice. Leave some pauses in your reading to give yourself a chance to picture and experience the images. We will put a note like this: [pause] where you should especially pause for a second or two. Don't worry about following the script word for word; the important thing is to relax.

RELAXATION SETUP

I want you to take a deep breath and let it out. Now take another, in and out. And as you let that one out, be aware of all of your mus-cles relaxing and letting go for a few minutes. All of your muscles usu-ally have to have a certain amount of tension in them to hold you upright and help you walk around. But now they can relax for a little while and let go of their usual roles. Let your arms relax. Let your torso relax. Let your hips and legs relax. Let your neck and face relax. Let yourself drift for a little while. Let yourself drift for a moment and just enjoy this feeling of being relaxed. [pause]

Now think about a place—it can be imaginary or it can be a real place—where you feel utterly safe and secure. In your mind, get a pic-ture of that place. [pause] Now think of yourself there, alone. What do you hear? [pause] What do you see around you? [pause] What do you smell? [pause] What are the sensations you have on your face and arms? [pause] Your back and legs? [pause] Just relax for a few minutes and enjoy the amazingly calm feeling of being in this place and enjoying all of your sensations. [pause]

You can use this tape whenever you want to work on integration. Just play it for yourself, listen to your own voice, and follow its simple instructions. This can help your left brain let go for a few minutes and let your right brain work on an exercise designed to help it make connections that would be difficult for your left brain.

This tape-recorded relaxation will be the setup for the integration exercises that come next. After the end of the relaxation sequence, wait just a few seconds, and then record the instructions you are given for the exercise you want to do.

After you do any of the exercises, *write* what you unearth in your notebook, *tell* someone else what you discovered, and/or *say* what you discovered out into a tape recorder. Don't worry if you don't know what an image means right now. Just describe it in words. You might have to do several integrative exercises before you "understand" the message your right brain is trying to communicate.

Make this effort to describe your image in words in order to bring your left brain back into the picture. Remember that the whole process of creative integration is *left-right-left*. You have done the preparation in the previous Thought Experiments. These exercises help your right brain integrate, but to *claim* your right-brain discoveries, you must translate them to your left brain.

STEP 2: CREATIVE INTEGRATION

We suggest you read the following exercises and decide which one most strikes your imagination. The more you can approach any of the exercises with a feeling of "Let's just see what happens," the more open you can be to whatever your right brain may have to give you. Don't worry if you can't see the sense in an image or thought right now. Trust your left brain to decipher it later. In the next chapter on Surveying, you will learn how to make your vision work in a practical sense in the real world. For now, you can just let your right brain play with the pieces of the puzzle without getting too uptight about its final form.

EXERCISE A: GUIDED IMAGERY

Record the following after your relaxation setup:

Now, in your imagination, I want you to get up gradually and look around. Again, sense how safe, secure, and comfortable you are feeling. Notice a path leading away from where you are. You don't exactly know where this path leads, but you feel it would definitely be worth your while to find out. You decide to take this path. It winds through some territory that is familiar to you and some that is new. You have a pleasant sensation of moving, feeling your legs step confidently one after the other and feeling your footsteps plant solidly and strongly one after another on the path. You hear the leaves around you stirred by a cool breeze and feel the pleasant and cool air on your cheek. You still feel totally safe and secure. Your feeling is that of exploring a new and fascinating territory and making interesting discoveries.

Finally you come to a large body of water. It is calm, but you can't see the other side. There is a boat nearby. It is exactly suited for the purpose of carrying you safely to the other side. You get in and push off. You guide the boat yourself. You feel entirely in control of it.

Soon you see the shore. Gradually it comes more clearly into view. Finally you feel the prow of the boat crunch gently into the sand. You step out and realize that you are in a different place. It is a place where you always wanted to be, even if you never quite realized it before. You look around and realize that this is the place where you will be living your life sometime in the future. It is your fullest, most satisfying, and most complete life. All of the important elements are here, and all of the important things you want to do are ready for you to take up and do. All of the important people that need to be here are here.

What is around you? [pause]
Where do you live? [pause]
Where do you work? [pause]
What is the main feeling of your life? [pause]
Who is here in this place with you? [pause]
What do you do with your days? [pause]
What is a typical day like? [pause]
What is the most important thing you do in a day? [pause]
What is next? [pause]

What are your most important relationships? [pause]

What is the role you play in your relationships? [pause]

Just enjoy this life for a few minutes, and when you are ready, wake up and write in your notebook everything about your image you can remember, no matter how unimportant it may seem. Include your answers to the questions asked. If you want, you can also tell someone important to you about your image, or record it on tape. Again, try to describe the image in detail, even if the meaning is not clear to you right now.

EXERCISE B: TAKING AWAY AN IMPEDIMENT

Record the following instructions after your relaxation setup:

Many people seem to live life habitually as though they were *forced* to do everything they do. "I have to go to work to earn money to support my children and spouse. I have to put up with work I don't find particularly meaningful because if I didn't, I wouldn't have a job. My boss is abusive but if I don't endure it, I'll be fired."

We find that people have far more choice in life than they usually think they do. They live life as though forced to endure it, but when they decide what they want, and go after it, they often succeed.

We designed exercises like this to give you the sense of choice. If you could choose to do anything, what would you do? [pause]

Imagine that you woke up one morning and found that the life you thought you had been living was actually a dream. Your actual life, the one to which you just woke up and now realize is the real one, is almost exactly like the one you had dreamed, except for one key difference. You realize you have a bank account that you can draw on any time you want and this bank account has many millions of dollars in it. You realize that you never have to worry about earning money again. You have all the money you can possibly ever need or that anyone close to you can possibly need. You can start each day asking yourself, "O.K., what do I want to do today?" And then do whatever comes to you.

What would your life be like? [pause]

How would you spend your time? [pause]

What would your relationship with your spouse or partner be like?
    [pause]
What about your children? [pause]
How about with your parents? [pause]
Who would be your friends? [pause]
What would you talk to them about? [pause]
How would you feel about your days? [pause]
How would you feel about your life? [pause]
Now describe a typical day as you would live it. What would you do?
    [pause]
Where would you go? [pause]
What would give your life meaning? [pause]
What would be the most important thing you would do with your life?
    [pause]

Now open your eyes and write down all that you can remember of your images and the answers to the questions in your notebook. Write down anything else that seems important from your image. Remember that it doesn't have to make any sense right now. Any message your right brain comes up with may be something your left brain will be able to use. Again, if you prefer, you can tell someone important, or record it on tape.

EXERCISE C: LOOKING BACKWARDS

Record the following instructions after your relaxation setup:

Now I want you to imagine that you are much older and have lived a very long and productive life. You are still quite healthy and active. You have accomplished the many things you set out to do with your life, not only in your career, but also in your family life and in your personal life. You feel content and satisfied. Your life has been remarkably full and interesting.

A teacher in a local junior high school has given her pupils an assignment: interview an older person about his or her life and find out what advice, ideas and wisdom he or she would like to pass on to a younger generation just starting out in life. One of the pupils, 12 years old, comes to interview you. Here is what the young student would like to know:

What are the most important things you have accomplished? [pause]

How have you changed over the years? [pause]

What used to be important to you that isn't so important now? [pause]

What used to be *not* important that feels a lot more important to you now? [pause]

What are your most important relationships? [pause]

How have you nurtured and maintained them over the years? [pause]

How have you managed to stay so healthy and vital all these years? [pause]

How have you managed to stay so alert and interested in life? [pause]

What is the most important piece of advice you could give to someone just starting out about how to live life? [pause]

What else would you like to say about your life? [pause]

What other advice would you give to a young person? [pause]

Now open your eyes and write down all that you can remember about your answers to the questions and about your thoughts and feelings during the exercise. If you prefer, you can tell someone or record your impressions.

FOUR STORIES: INTEGRATION

Tracy

"This was fun. I did all three of the exercises and got something interesting from all of them. Science kept emerging. And the environment. Also different cultures. I could see myself investigating interesting problems about the environment and producing something that would be of significant benefit to the world. When I gave advice to the 12-year-old, I was a scientist who had made some important discoveries about the habitats around the coral reefs. I told the young boy that he should find something that was completely fascinating and pursue it like crazy. Don't worry too much about money. Worry more about doing something meaningful that you feel passionate about."

Brian and Janet

Brian: "When I did the exercise about removing an impediment I got a rude awakening. If I had all the money I needed to live on—more than I could spend—I wouldn't have anything to do. I could almost picture myself being like my mother: directionless, flat, trying to find something to occupy my time. I did the exercise on giving advice, too. The main advice I gave was, 'Find something worth living for.' Neither my parents nor Janet's parents have had very strong marriages. Unless Janet and I do something different, we could easily drift apart, too. I could see agreeing to have a baby just to give Janet something to do, turning the entire parenting thing over to her, and then ending up just like my mother and father. I'm rethinking this whole deal. Maybe I've been missing something important."

Feelings now: "Very, very thoughtful."

Janet: "When I did the exercise on an ideal day, I had this clear image of doing a research project. I would ask people questions about what they wanted and how they liked things, and then figure out from their answers how to make them happier with our service. I could work on my own projects and think about them as much as I wanted to. The whole image makes me happy. When I described it to Brian, he said, 'Why don't you do it?' At that moment I realized that's exactly what I could do. I could do detailed research on customers so that the company would be able to avoid some complaints and pitch its services more toward what people already want. Brian said that marketing could use that kind of information. This is all tremendously exciting to me. For the first time, I felt I could do a job that was really me."

Feelings now: "Very excited."

Elizabeth

"When I did the exercise about my ideal day, the image I had was of working hard, solving problems, doing something interesting, quitting at 5:30, and going home to be with my children and husband. And I don't mean taking a big briefcase home with me, either. I mean really being with my family. It was a wonderful image. I told my husband about it, and he said, 'Sure, honey. You could no more do that than fly to the moon.' I started thinking, 'Why not?'

"The second image I had was when I did the exercise on looking back. The advice I gave was, 'Find something you're really passionately interested in, and make it happen.' What's interesting was that in the image of myself in this exercise, I was a famous innovator in children's day care."

Feelings now: "Excited. Energetic. I think I know what I want to do. First of all, I'm going to start working more normal hours. I will make that happen. Second, I'm going to look into day care at our company. Maybe there are a whole range of child-related services the company could offer its employees. I know of some innovative programs. I'll find out about them."

Carl

"This was easy. My ideal day was working for the Free Clinic. I enjoy it and enjoy the people there. I feel like I'm doing something for people that they really need. The feeling I get working there is exhilarating.

"When I did the 'taking away an impediment' exercise, I was still doing something like the Free Clinic. I was in charge of it. Which is interesting, because the executive director of the last 12 years is leaving in three months. They've already offered me another job on staff. I'm thinking about looking at that executive director position.

"My advice to the student was this: Do something you enjoy. Do something you find meaningful. Don't wait around until you're old before you realize you ought to enjoy what you do."

Feelings now: "Excited. I haven't felt this enthusiastic about anything in at least a couple of years."

NEXT CHAPTER: The ideas and images you gain from these exercises may help you start to crystallize a vision—an image of what you want your future to look like and how you want to live in it. As you start to get an image of this future, you are ready to Survey. Surveying is a practical, reality-based, hands-on way to translate your image or picture into substantive reality and into a solid path to get you there. In the next chapter we describe Surveying. The Thought Experiment will help you carry out a Survey interview.

Surveying MAKES THE **Vital Connection** BETWEEN THE **Reality Of Yourself** AND YOUR DREAMS, AND THE **Reality Of The Marketplace.**

IT HELPS YOU FIND YOUR **Exact Fit.**

9

Surveying

The most difficult part of creativity may happen *after* the creative insight. In fact, lack of attention to this step is probably what sinks most creative ideas. You can have the most imaginative Personal Vision of all, but it won't help you unless you connect it to your real life.

Surveying is a tool we use to help bridge the gap between integrative insight and reality. It is powerful, subtle and remarkably effective. Let's look at how it worked with Jim, a young manager.

Surveying

Jim, a production manager, had a creative idea for tightening production schedules. His idea came to him in a dream. The whole production process could be organized more efficiently with little additional cost and a reduction in total manpower needs. He couldn't wait to get to work to tell his boss.

When he launched into telling her how production should be reorganized, he was surprised and disconcerted as his wonderful idea seemed to melt away. What came out was only a pale shadow of his whole idea, and the more questions his boss asked, the thinner and more insubstantial it became. He finally realized that she was just listening politely and didn't get the power of the idea at all.

Jim did have a creative idea, but he had not done any work to make it real. The idea came out of his right brain; it came from a dream. To explain it to anyone else, he would have to translate it to the left hemisphere. He would have to put it into words.

People generally have the same experience as Jim when they try to put their most creative thoughts into words. What at its inception was a rich, colorful idea becomes one-dimensional, ordinary, and limited. In spite of this, it is only by translating an idea into words that we gain control of it, that we have the ability to use and exploit it.

Frustrated by his first attempt to convince his boss, Jim worked through his idea again.

First of all, he drew a picture of this plan to reorganize production. Then he wrote it down on a flow sheet. The flow sheet detailed every aspect of production affected by the changes. He practiced talking about the changes with his wife, explaining his chart point by point. He told her about the problem his changes were designed to help, and how his idea would improve overall production. His wife didn't know anything about the production process, but asked Jim questions that sent him back to his flow sheet to reorganize and solve some major problems in his proposal.

As Jim got more excited about his idea and determined to see if it would be helpful, he noticed an article in a trade magazine in which a manager talked about organizing information systems. The recommendations the manager proposed were structurally very much like those that Jim proposed.

Jim called the author of the article. They talked for several hours over four different conversations. Jim felt energized. For the first time since his original conception, he *knew* his idea would work.

With his boss's permission, Jim then went to other people in the production process who would be affected by change. He talked to a number of them, explaining to each one what he saw as a problem, and then discussed his idea. Each time he did this, he further refined his original idea. He had not taken into account some important details in his first conception. In some instances, the changes Jim proposed would create new problems.

When Jim returned to his boss, it was with a written proposal for change. He detailed not only exactly what he thought should be changed and how, but also what he projected the results would be. He addressed the kind of real-world detail that adds richness and texture to a proposal. He also addressed potential problems and how to solve them.

At this point, to his boss, the decision was obvious. What Jim was proposing would save a great deal in time and effort, cutting out needless redundancies. Jim had thought about it from every angle and it looked quite promising.

It is important to keep in mind that the basic proposal Jim described to his boss the day after his dream was *exactly the same proposal* that his boss later thought was a no-brainer. What changed was that Jim made the creative idea real.

The Process of Making an Idea Real

The process Jim used to transform his original insight into an effective, compelling presentation may seem far removed from figuring out what to do in your career, but it's not. If you are to make any move in your career, you will need to convince someone else. You will need to make a compelling case for whatever you decide you want to do, whether it is to shift to a new responsibility at your present job, let go of a task that drives you crazy, change jobs altogether, go to graduate school, or jump into a field right out of college. Whatever you want to do, you will have to tell some critical people and convince them it's a good idea. Even if you realize you want to stay precisely where you are, you still have to make a compelling case to *yourself.* Otherwise you are trapped.

Surveying makes the vital connection between the reality of yourself and your dreams and the reality of the marketplace. It helps you find your exact fit.

To begin Surveying, you must have an idea. We designed the previous Thought Experiments to bring in all of the important career factors and help you creatively integrate them and figure out a Personal Vision. Your Personal Vision can give you direction and focus, or simply someplace to start looking. Without this kind of focus, Surveying can't happen.

So let's say that you have an idea about what you are looking for, or what you would like to be doing with your life, or how you would like to be living. If your idea sprang from a strong connection to yourself, then it can form the nucleus of your Survey work.

The Steps of Surveying

Step 1: Write it down; force yourself to put the idea, as completely as possible, in words in your notebook. Get the flow and sequence right. Put it on a time line. When do you want to be doing this? What are the intermediate steps? What will you have to do first in order to arrive where you want to be? Put those on a time line also.

Step 2: Tell someone outside your systems. It has been said that you don't really know something until you can explain it to a reasonably intelligent seven-year-old. A person outside your systems has no agenda or preconceptions about you and your career and doesn't know anything about the issues or the problems with which you are dealing. You will find out a great deal by talking to a person like this about your plans. You can use this information to revise your original idea.

Step 3: This is the critical step of Surveying: *finding someone who is doing the same thing, or close to it.* Once you have a clear, verbal conception of your idea, you can find someone doing something very close to your idea. It may be in a different arena, or with a different process, but the *idea* may still be similar. Interview this person and find others to interview. The Thought Experiment at the end of this chapter deals with this Survey Interview. It can save you hours of planning and going down dead-ends. It can be the most powerful and useful step you take in making your idea real.

Step 4: After considerable Survey work, make a presentation. This should combine all of the elements of your creative conception with how you have molded and modified your idea to work in the real world. This presentation should start with what your idea has to do with you. What abilities, skills and interests of yours does it relate to? What values and goals does it fulfill? How does your personality aid you in carrying out your idea? What does your idea relate to in your past or in your family of origin?

Then the presentation should shift to the marketplace. You must be able to tell the person how your idea will help him or her. If you were making a presentation for a business, for instance, you would need to have learned enough about the business and the marketplace through your Survey Interviews to know exactly what needs your idea will fill. You will need to know enough to overcome all of the inevitable questions.

So how does it work? Let's pick up Ruth's story from an earlier chapter.

Ruth's Story, continued

You may remember the story of Ruth, the buyer of Italian cloth, from Chapter Six. She didn't just stumble into a perfect job. She had done all the work of creating a Personal Vision. She had written down what she knew of it. You may remember that the idea she started with, although well connected to her abilities and other personal factors, was vague and ill-formed. She wanted to work in an artistic field. She wanted to use her skills acquired in her years as a buyer. She had a particular affinity for the artistic qualities of cloth and fiber. She wrote down everything she could to describe the position she sought, even though she did not know yet what that position was.

Ruth told her idea to people outside her systems. This is an important step, often overlooked. Ruth first proposed her idea following an integration exercise. "I had this crazy idea of working with cloth. You know, buying special cloth." She was ready to reject the idea entirely and go on to something more practical. The other people in her workshop weren't in her systems, though. They didn't see what was crazy about it. They saw how well it matched much of what she wanted in life. In our programs when people have really creative ideas, they frequently want to reject them at first. But people outside your immediate systems can often see creative solutions as genuine innovations.

Ruth determined to make her idea real. She started Survey Interviews. She started a chart to record her Survey work. Using the interview format you will find in the Thought Experiment, she interviewed people in positions suggested by her description of her ideal career. She interviewed two museum directors and several curators and museum archivists. She interviewed several creative and design people from advertising firms. She interviewed many interior designers and decorators.

Each time she interviewed someone, she found out first about that person, as an individual, then about that person's job, then about the company that person worked for, and finally about the whole field in which the person worked. (As you will see in the Survey Thought Experiment, this is a useful order for asking questions in a Survey Interview.) Although during the course of her survey work Ruth always insisted from the beginning of each interview that she was not looking for a job or asking for one, she was offered three different jobs by people who were impressed with her knowledge and intelligence. Ruth was prepared for this, because it frequently happens during surveys. She knew what she was looking for clearly enough to turn these offers down and keep on pressing. She was not ready to make a formal proposal yet because she didn't know enough about the area of business she was finding out about.

Ruth interviewed designers and buyers for design shops. With every interview, she learned more about the tight little circle in which she had become interested, and she found more people to interview. She filled up several posters with her Survey notes. When she understood how difficult it was for upscale design studios to find unusual art cloth, she saw that many had a problem for which she was uniquely qualified to provide an answer.

At this point, Ruth met and interviewed the architect to whom she would eventually make her proposal. Long before this, she had noticed a change in her interviews. She often knew more about what was happening in the field and in her area of interest than the people she interviewed. Often they asked her *questions about what was going on because she was so clearly knowledgeable.*

In the course of her interviews, Ruth met a person who had tried to import art cloth, but could never find a ready market. Ruth was sure she had enough contacts to create and sustain a market for this cloth. She felt ready for a presentation. She saw the architect as having the most pressing need, so she decided to start there.

Ruth scheduled another interview with the architect—this would be her third. This time she told him that she wanted to make a presentation to him that would be of interest. She outlined her whole idea, starting with herself, moving to the architect's need for unusual art cloth, to how she would propose to work with him. For the architect, it was obvious. Ruth had known it would be.

Surveying, as a process, is much like a funnel, large at the top, smaller and more focused as you progress. Starting with a largely unfocused idea, Ruth was yet able to use it to begin her Survey work. In the course of almost 50 interviews over several months, she eliminated a number of dead-ends and uncovered several likely avenues. As she continued to explore, her focus narrowed. As she found out more and more about a progressively narrow field, her idea became more precise and more attuned to marketplace demand. When she made her proposal, it was exactly suited not only to what she wanted to do, but also to what she knew the market needed.

Surveying at Turning Points

At every Turning Point we need a Personal Vision. At every Turning Point we should Survey. The better idea we have of the road ahead, the better we can make decisions about our lives.

Starting in 1990, we, the authors, both 42, both at the Midlife Turning Point, spent more than two years Surveying. Beginning with an idea for a new business, we interviewed anyone we could find who did anything remotely similar to what we had in mind. We personally went through any program we could find that related to the issue. We interviewed hundreds of potential competitors, potential customers, and business people in other fields entirely, but who used a business structure we might want to use. At each interview we took away invaluable information. Even if it turned out that a person did nothing remotely similar to what we had in mind, we focused our thoughts, narrowed our ideas, and became more precise and knowledgeable in presenting our case each time we talked to someone.

Our experience in helping people launch new ideas in their

careers—whether they have ideas for whole new businesses or only for a slight shift in job responsibilities—is that they ignore this step too often. The more Survey work you do *before* your presentation, the stronger your case will be and the more confident and solid you will feel in your presentation.

Let's take the case of Sharon, an advertising director at a large public utility.

Sharon's Story

Sharon went through The Whole Person Technology® and created a Personal Vision. What she found out startled her. She had many more abilities than her staff position made use of. She had realized before that she was not interested in her job and that it failed to challenge her or push her to grow. Knowing this about her abilities helped her focus on what she wanted. She wanted her job to express more of her unique talents.

Often managers ask us what the company gets out of letting its employees go through a process of gaining a Personal Vision. Some feel that if employees really looked carefully at what they are expected to do, they would quit and do something else. Some feel that their employees are already highly motivated. Our overwhelming experience is that people who create a Personal Vision feel more connected to their companies and their careers because they learn exactly how to position and utilize their unique talents. They also feel less stressed and less burned-out for the same reasons.

Soon after Sharon went through The Whole Person Technology®, an internal memo came across her desk: The company wanted to hire a national accounts manager. Making such a shift would be unusual, but Sharon knew she had the right mix of abilities, talents, personality, and interests for the job. Over a period of two weeks, Sharon pulled out her Personal Vision statement and used it to craft a careful description of how she saw herself carrying out the new job. She then interviewed the person who had just vacated the position, three people who were in similar positions in the company, and five people who would be reporting to her should she get it. After each interview, she revised her plan and wrote down what she had learned.

Sharon applied for the job. One of the people who interviewed her was someone she had interviewed about it just the week before. She had become knowledgeable about the position and the system by interviewing others. She used her Personal Vision to make a compelling and clear presentation for the job. She started with her interests—even her interest in managing detail as a young child. She then went to her natural abilities, her personality and her demonstrable skills, and continued with her strong values. She showed clearly how all these different aspects of herself interlocked and made her qualified, not just by her skills, but by her heart and talents. The case she made was airtight— a slam dunk. She is now a national accounts manager.

She would never have thought about this opportunity had she not looked carefully at her career and life to understand more fully what she wanted. Her Personal Vision was like a template. When the right job came along, she recognized it instantly. By Surveying, Sharon made her Vision real.

Thought Experiment H:

Surveying Interview, Survey Presentation

Surveying is the most powerful tool we have for making creative ideas real. You can never know enough about a market or a field. Each time you do a Survey Interview, even if it seems that you didn't find out anything new, you force yourself to challenge your ideas against the reality of the marketplace. You become sharper, more focused and more realistic in what you can and cannot do.

The Survey Interview
WHEN TO INTERVIEW

The Survey Interview can serve several purposes in the whole process of career self-management. At the beginning, you can use it to make your Personal Vision more focused and related to the marketplace. Starting with even a vague notion, so long as it gives you some direction, you can interview people to find out about them, their jobs and careers, and the fields they are in. Each time you do this, you will narrow your focus by making your Personal Vision more realistic.

You can continue this process of narrowing your Personal Vision almost indefinitely, making it more precise until your idea crystallizes. When you feel more certain about what you want to do, you can continue to use Surveying to gain valuable knowledge about the field and about systems. As noted in the body of the chapter, when people you interview start asking you questions because they recognize your knowledge and expertise in the area, you know you will soon be ready to make a presentation. This may take several months, as in Ruth's case, or over a year, as in the authors'.

WHOM TO INTERVIEW

Let your Personal Vision guide you. Even if it seems ill-formed and unfocused, it can give you clues about whom you should interview. At first, you can gain valuable insight from anyone who does anything even remotely like what you have in mind. As you do each interview, you will learn more and find other people to talk to. You will also become increasingly precise about *whom* you interview and *what* exactly you are trying to find out.

SETTING UP THE INTERVIEW

Setting up the interview lays the tone and groundwork for the interview itself. Paying attention to details in the setup can insure a successful outcome.

Call the person and state who you are and how you were referred. Let's say this person is a woman who manages an organization in a style similar to the way you are interested in managing. When you call, tell her that you would like to meet for 30 minutes or so at her convenience. You are not selling anything. You are not looking for a job. You are only interested in the way she manages her organization. Explain how you found out about her. Make every effort to accommodate her schedule and time.

CONDUCTING THE INTERVIEW

Start with the person herself. How did she decide to get into her present career? What were the decisions she made at Turning Points? What was her reasoning at each?

College to Work (age 22-25)
Age-30 Assessment (age 28-33)
Midlife Transition (age 38-45)
Age-50 Assessment (age 50-55)
Pre-Retirement Transition (age 60-65)

How did she move into her present position?
What does she like about it? What does she dislike?
How did she come to adopt her present management style?
How would she describe it?
Describe a recent day that she felt was productive and that she enjoyed.
What made it enjoyable?
What made it productive?
Describe a recent bad day or one that was unproductive.
What made it bad?
What made it unproductive?
What does she see for her own future?
What does she see for the future of this field (industry, company)?
What has helped and guided her most over the years?
What advice would she have for someone just starting out?

Again, just as with the family interviews, use these questions to give yourself a springboard for the interview. If anything strikes your interest, pursue it. Remember, you are asking this person, as a favor to you, to talk about the most fascinating subject on earth—herself and her opinions. You don't have to agree with everything she says; just listen. If you approach it openly, you will learn a great deal, even from interviews in which you thoroughly disagree with every point your subject makes. Your job is not to change this person's mind, but to learn something that will be valuable to you in making your Personal Vision real.

When you have done enough Survey Interviews to be thoroughly knowledgeable about the field and what you want to do in it; to recognize the best fit for your abilities, personality, interests, values and goals; to understand others' needs that your Personal Vision could contribute to; and to plan how you want to go about implementing your Vision, you may be ready for a presentation.

YOUR PRESENTATION

Start your presentation with yourself. Ideally, list what you have learned about your talents, interests, personality, skills, experience, values, goals and even family of origin and stage of development. This is the most effective way to communicate who you are, what you have to offer, and why. Next, talk about what you know to be the needs of the organization or the person to whom you are presenting. Your Survey work will pay off here if you can speak knowledgeably and cogently. Link yourself to the company's needs by means of your Personal Vision, showing how the sum total of your personal career factors contributes to fulfilling a need in the company. (If you find you can't make this link, or that it appears weak, this may be a signal that you need to do more Surveying.) You should have a clear vision for this job—what it entails, how you would work and with whom, what the potential problems might be, and what the factors are that will make it successful. Your job in the presentation will be to communicate the essence of this vision, to be able to answer any questions that may come up, and to transmit the enthusiasm and passion that you can bring to the job.

FOUR STORIES: SURVEYING

Tracy

"I have interviewed about 10 people so far. I started with a micro-biologist at the university. He was interesting and let me tag along with him for a day to see what he did. I knew from that that I wasn't interested in pure science. I need to see some result that is closer to the real world. He pointed me in the direction of a friend of his who is a behavioral biologist. Her work is almost all theoretical. But it was interesting to talk to her about how she sees it being useful to people— eventually. After her, I interviewed a biochemist. He introduced me to some people running a primate research lab. That was more like it. I interviewed several of their research people and talked to them about their projects. I liked the whole feel of the place, and I was interested in what they are doing. After I had had two or three inter-views there, and been back to spend a day with one of the researchers, one of them told me to apply to be a tech assistant there. So I did. And now that's what I'm doing, working full time. I am also plan-ning on taking a graduate course in primate biology and evolution at the university. I am pretty sure I will go to graduate school in the next couple of years, but I feel the experience I'm getting now in hands-on research is wonderful, so I'm not in a crashing hurry. The scientists I'm working with have connections all over, and I'm sure they can help me get into a good graduate program when I'm ready. I don't think I'll spend my career in primate research, but I know I will go to graduate school in some area of biology. Lately, I have become fascinated with marine mammals."

Feelings now: "For the first time since I quit psychology, I feel like I know what I'm doing. I know I have a long way to go, but that's OK, because I have this clear image of doing something interesting and meaningful."

Brian and Janet

Brian: "My first question was, whom do I interview? I'm already doing what I like. Then, as I got to thinking about it, I realized that the real question for me was how to have a life besides work. My father never has. When I put it this way, I thought of a story someone *had told me about an older guy in Human Resources. He had refused some assignments because it would take him away from his family. At least that was the story. I found out who the guy was and called him up. When I said what I wanted, he immediately suggested we have lunch. It was fascinating. He decided early in his career that he would not let his work take him from his family and that he would not ask his family to move around unreasonably. I asked him if he felt it had hurt his career. He said, in the short run, yes, though not as much as you might be afraid it would. In the long run, he's accomplished much of what he wanted to do in his career and has ended up in charge of a major portion of Human Resource services nationwide. I would like to end up like him. He gave me the names of a couple of other executives in different departments who have done the same thing. I called them and talked to both of them a long time on the phone. The more I talked to them, the more I realized that it is more possible to have a family life than I thought. It's going to be rough for the next five or six years, but if I don't start making room for a family now, I could wind up divorced like about half the people I know.*

"Next, I took my boss to lunch and set out the whole deal to him. I went through my abilities, interests, personality, values, goals— even what I found out about my family. After that I told him what I wanted to do and why, and asked him if he could help. He was actually very sympathetic and quite helpful. He likes my work a lot and feels that I have real promise with the company. He said I would have to set limits on my time myself, but that he would help by making sure I got some good projects. He doesn't know what effect this will have on my being chosen for the fast track."

Brian's feelings now: "Determined. I feel I am sort of sailing into unknown territory. The company would like it if I worked 24 hours a day. To tell the truth, a part of me feels I should work around the clock if the company needs it. But I need a whole life, too. So does Janet. If we are going to have a family, we have to make it a priority for both of us."

Janet: "I did some research and found out there is a company in town that does market research. I called them up and got to talk to one of their senior researchers. He was very happy to talk to me when

I explained what I wanted. We met and talked probably two hours about what he did. This was fascinating. It was like doing a research project for your work. He gave me the names of two other people in the field, and I interviewed both of them. One of them gave me the name of someone doing market and customer research in a large corporation. This would be more like my own situation, so I was eager to interview her. She helped, because, as it turned out, she had started her own little unit of customer research in this company about 10 years ago. She had been able to show tremendous benefit to the company over that time for very little outlay. This would give me a strong case to my bosses. She offered me a job there, but by this time, I was already feeling I could get my own show going in my company. Over the next three months, I continued interviewing. I also started some preliminary talks with some people in my company about what I had in mind and why. I wanted to get an idea about what roadblocks I would probably run into. I finally wrote up a proposal in which I showed what other companies' experiences had been with ongoing customer/market research. I made a formal pitch and they are going to let me proceed on a trial basis. This whole project is the most exciting thing I have ever done."

Janet's feelings now: "Tremendously happy and proud of what I've accomplished. Brian and I are planning to have a baby after next year. I want to get this project rolling. I am finding out something new every day and I couldn't be happier."

Elizabeth

"The first thing I did was go to my boss and tell him that I was out of here at 5:30. I was not going to travel, and I wouldn't work at night. That was rash, I know, and I was holding my breath after I said it. He looked at me and said, 'OK.' I didn't know whether I'd be able to stick to it or not, but mostly I have. I've had to travel some, but I have also been able to turn down some travel. I do leave between 5:30 and 6:00 every day. My family responded immediately. Things have been much less stressed at home. I have had to force myself to be more organized and to be clearer about my priorities. I also delegate better. I think I am actually working so much more effectively that I get everything that absolutely needs to be done accomplished.

"The second thing I have been working on is company-sponsored day care. I've probably interviewed 50 people, from day-care operators to consultants to human-resource people to architects. This has been interesting. I know we'll win eventually. I have my own team of people from all over the company who are now working on this project—all on our own time. The company hasn't quite understood the idea yet; nor do they see the benefits. Other companies are sponsoring day care for employees' children, and we will have to solve a number of significant problems to bring it off, but I am sure we are right. Anyway, the whole project is very exciting."

Feelings now: "Excited. Creative. Alive."

Carl

"I went right away and interviewed the executive director of the Free Clinic. It is very intriguing. Resources are quite limited, and a large part of the role is fund-raising and public relations. I have a lot of contacts in the business community, and I think I could build some corporate sponsorships. The only thing holding me back is the pay. It would be a lot less than I had been making. On the other hand, my wife and I are pretty well set as far as retirement, and college for the kids is nearly over, so I think we could make do with less. I am pretty sure from talking to the Board members of the Free Clinic that I would have a good shot at the position, and I think I will ask them to consider me for it.

"I feel I could always go back into business somewhere, but I realize I would be disappointed to do so. The opportunity to work at the Free Clinic is much more exciting to me, even if it won't pay as well."

Feelings now: "Happy."

NEXT CHAPTER: One of the biggest problems facing people who create their Personal Visions and then set out to make them real is creating boundaries. Elizabeth had to create boundaries in the story above; Richard did the same in Chapter 5; and we saw it in Joseph's story in Chapter 7. The first step of creating boundaries is the hardest one—figuring out what you want. That is what this book has been about up until now. The next steps in creating boundaries involve stating what you want your boundary to be and then making it stick. That is what the next chapter is about.

EXERTING A **BOUNDARY**
GIVES YOU THE OPPORTUNITY
TO MAKE
AUTHENTIC STATEMENTS
ABOUT **YOURSELF.**

IT GIVES YOU THE OPPORTUNITY TO SAY:
"THIS IS WHERE **I Start** AND
            THE
    Corporation Ends."

10

Creating Personal
BOUNDARIES

A very successful manager in one of the fastest-growing high-tech companies in the world spent about forty to fifty hours going through all of the exercises in this book. How he came to do that is an interesting story in itself.

"My work has always been rated 'Excellent' by my managers. I have been with this company for five years, which is generally considered to be two or three lifetimes because of the stress level here. At each career juncture, I was offered a promotion to more and bigger managerial responsibilities. I don't really know how many hours a week I was working, but there were many nights when I slept on a cot in my office. The reason I read this book and took the trouble to go through the exercises in it was what happened one (rare) day when I was actually at home. I was watching my young daughter and her friend play with their Barbie dolls. My daughter took the male doll and tossed it over her shoulder into a box. 'Dad's at the office sitting in front of his computer,' was her explanation. I knew then that something would have to change in my life. I just didn't know what. It was very soon after that that someone gave me this book."

After going through all of the exercises and creating a Personal Vision, this manager realized something: "I knew what I wanted to do, but I felt like the only way I could do it would be to quit my job and start somewhere else. I desperately wanted to follow through and create the life I had envisioned—a forty-hour work week, a job I felt I could actually manage and enjoy, no nights, no weekends—but the culture at this company views a job like that as a vacation, not an actual job."

Systems and Rules

What the manager had come up against was what everyone who goes up against a system eventually faces—how to make his reality stick as opposed to the system's reality. His system had a clear, simple, but unstated rule that covered engineers' time: You will be available at any time and all times to answer the needs of our customers. If you're on vacation and a customer needs you, then you will come back. If the customer needs you to work 24 hours a day for three or four days, that's what we have sleeping cots at the office for.

Almost every story we've told in this book involved someone changing. And those changes almost invariably involve systems that do not want anything to change. Furthermore, part of what makes a system a system is that it has built-in self-correcting mechanisms. If one part of a system (you, for instance) strays too far out of line, then the system reacts. It will try to pull the errant part back into line. If the straying part doesn't respond, the system will up the ante, finally getting to the point of rejecting the rebel altogether.

As we discussed in Chapter 1, all systems have rules, and this includes all work systems. The rules that are easiest to manage and deal with are the ones that are clearly and overtly stated: All employees will wear white shirts and ties (men) or conservative business suits and stockings (women) every working day. You may not like this rule, but since it's so clearly stated, you can decide whether you want to live with it or not before you sign on.

The rules that lead to far more stress and binding anxiety are unstated, covert, 'understood' rules. These are legion—a good example of one is provided in the example of the engineer's company. These rules powerfully control our behavior, but they are hard to fight or even understand very clearly, because they are never overtly stated. If you were to look up the stated company policy in the HR manual, you wouldn't find the rule for engineers about being available 24 hours a day. But everybody in the company behaves as though the rule is absolute.

What this means is that in order to fit in, you have to submerge yourself. You have to allow the company to take over some of your life. You have to give up some of your decision-making power and sense of control. The net effect is to give up something of your personal identity.

Whenever you are involved in a system, you have to give up part of yourself. The important questions are: How much of yourself and what parts of yourself do you want to give up to be in a system? The flip side to these questions is equally important: What are you *not* willing to give up about yourself in order to be in a system? Having clear answers to these questions is an important part of your Personal Vision.

Boundaries

Boundaries are the means by which we create our identities in the first place. It starts when we are young, in our families of origin. When our parents set a limit with us—"No you can't go out after dark, because you're too young"—we have a clear and definite response to it. Limits make us angry. We know what we want; we just can't have it. The process of having a limit set and having a definite response that is *our own*, not our parents', creates a boundary. We gain a sense of who we are and what reality is. *I* want to go outside. *Reality* says that I can't. As we get older we take over setting our own limits, so instead of having parents who set limits and make boundaries for us, we have to do it for ourselves. By setting boundaries for ourselves, we carve out a clear and continuing sense of our own identities.

The reverse is also true. When we *don't* set limits and *don't* create boundaries, we begin to lose our sense of identity. In corporations, that is another way of saying that we fall victim to the Lemming Conspiracy. The Stress Cycle involves taking our direction from outside and submerging ourselves in the direction our systems want us to pursue. It usually means that we are caught up in spending our time and energy pursuing goals and ends that ultimately don't matter very much—to us. As adults involved in corporations, all of us get caught up in systems and start to feel the stress of being a System Self instead of an authentic True Self.

The Balance Cycle involves taking our direction from the inside, planning ahead for our careers, finding worthy values and principals to guide ourselves and making decisions from a Personal Vision.

> **"Boundaries define us. They define *what is me* and *what is not me*. A boundary shows me where I end and someone else begins, leading me to a sense of ownership."**
> **—Cloud and Townsend, *Boundaries***

When you create a Personal Vision, it is a picture of your True Self operating within a system. But to make it real, you have to exert a boundary. It's not enough to have your Personal Vision in your thoughts. Your system will never be able to respond to your True Self unless or until you say, "This is my limit. I will do this, but not that." The question is, how do you get to the point where you can create a boundary in a corporation or system, and how can you be sure that the system won't turn around and throw you out because you broke the rules?

We have found that setting boundaries is one of the most important hurdles facing people after they create their Personal Visions. A manager at IBM realized that he was most interested in and worked best in environments that were a bit chaotic. He liked to be assigned to brand new teams with lots of problems to solve because that was how he could use his natural talents most fully. When management asked him to take over a unit that was doing well and that had a long history of making its numbers, he smelled trouble.

"I knew from doing the work on my Personal Vision that the fit would be bad. Even though the new assignment would be a promotion, I was very hesitant to take it because I knew it wouldn't interest me. Eventually, I would get bored. Finally, I told them no, I didn't want it. I used my workbook from my Whole Person Technology®

seminar to explain my decision to my boss. And his boss. It ended up working in my favor. They could see the truth of what I was saying about myself. They could see that I wasn't being capricious or uncooperative. I was just telling them an authentic truth about how I work best and what the best fit for me in the company is. Later, I got another assignment from them that was much more in line with who I am and what I have to offer to the company."

Exerting a boundary gives you the opportunity to make an authentic statement about yourself. It gives you the opportunity to say, "This is where *I* start and the corporation ends." If you look at your Personal Vision as a complete, authentic and true statement about yourself, then when you exert a boundary in order to make it happen in your actual life, you are taking a step to establish a clear personal identity in relation to the corporation or the system.

Exerting a boundary can also make you feel vulnerable when you go up against a strong and seemingly unified culture. Questions arise. Is it fair for me to assert a boundary that no one else does? What if my boundaries are totally unreasonable? What if they are perceived as unreasonable? What are my choices then? Am I then faced with caving in or quitting? What if they just think I'm too much trouble and fire me?

These kinds of questions and anxieties are fairly normal when you take on a system at work. Let's look at some practical ways to deal with boundaries that can help you know when you want to assert some boundary for yourself and how to go about it.

First, Know Yourself

The first and most important part of setting boundaries is to know what boundaries you want to set. This is an important goal in creating your Personal Vision. In our seminars with corporate clients, the last day of the seminar deals with what we call a Focused Vision. The participants spend the first two days of the seminar creating their Personal Visions, but the last day deals with how their Personal Visions will play out—in specific terms—in their corporations. This is the Focused Vision.

You might think that people in corporations who go through The Whole Person Technology® end up with extreme Personal Visions that couldn't possibly work in any rational company environment. In fact, we don't find this to be true. We do sometimes have participants who, through the Lemming Conspiracy, have strayed far away from their True Selves and are living out a System Self that is essentially crazy—like an executive who went through our program a couple of years ago who routinely worked 95 hours a week. When these people do the work of creating a Personal Vision, they often find that they want to make changes. But even in these cases, the changes people generally want to make are specific and focused.

The executive above who was working 95 hours a week—Lauren—was completely amazed when she did the Values portion of the Whole Person Technology® seminar she attended. "I realized that the values I was actually living out were exactly backwards from the values that I hold to be most important. I was putting the *most* energy and time into my least important values—money, position and power—and the *least* energy and time into my most important values—my children and marriage. I knew that something had to change.

"Before I started the Whole Person Technology® seminar, I thought, I'll just keep working at my present job for another year or two, and then quit. I felt so much stress that I was beginning to doubt that I would even make it six more months. I also felt that my company did not really care about me or about what was important to me.

"In the seminar, though, I realized that I didn't want to quit my job. I like it. I'm good at it. It really uses my most important abilities. I like the people I work with. Many of my life goals are definitely related to my job. What I really needed to do was make my work more manageable—more human, I would say."

A year after Lauren finished the seminar, we talked to her about what she was doing. She was still working at the same company and in the same job, even though there had been at least two major reorganizations. "I work about 55 hours a week now. And I'm still on my numbers. In the last week I have been told that I am a better manager, better executive, better parent and a better wife than I was nine months ago. You guys saved me before I crashed and burned."

Interestingly enough, the story doesn't end there. We talked to Lauren again about nine months later. We got some inkling about what was going on when we called her office to make an appointment with her. As it happened, we called about 5:25 in the afternoon. Her secretary told us that she would take a message, but Lauren wasn't there, since she always walked out the door at 5:00. We thought this probably boded well for her life. It was obvious that she had set and maintained a clear boundary.

When we did catch up with her, she had this to say: "I work about 40 to 45 hours a week these days. I can't remember the last time I took work home. I almost never travel. The thing I'm proudest of is that I have not paid $1.00 in overtime childcare in the last six months. I am still on my numbers. I work more efficiently now than before I did The Whole Person Technology®. I use my real talents better, and I delegate better. I think a lot of what I was doing before I went through the seminar was spinning my wheels and wasting a lot of energy. I have a lot better feeling about my company. I feel that they care about me here. I'm not thinking about quitting any more. I could see staying here and moving up in my organization."

The company she works for is a global technology company. We have had a number of people tell us—in earnest—that you have to work at least 70 hours a week at at this company in order to keep your job. So how did this executive do it? Was it luck? Is this some special case?

No, it is not some special case. Lauren went through the same structure of The Whole Person Technology® that you see in this book. Part of the answer for her had to do with her natural talents and abilities. She saw that she never got to use some of her strongest talents because she wasted so much time in tasks for which she had little talent at all. These tasks absorbed 90 percent of her energy and creativity and gave her little pleasure or satisfaction. She also saw that her priorities were out of whack. When she interviewed her mother and father, a lot of her choices began to make sense to her; she was duplicating the life her father lived. He had been in sales and traveled a great deal when she was growing up. Her memory of him was that he was gone a good deal of the time. "I always hated it that my father never participated much in my life when I was growing up. You can imagine my shock when I realized that my own kids would probably say the same things about me."

Second, Be Clear About Your Goals and Priorities

After creating her Personal Vision, Lauren figured out goals related to it. As she set her goals, she took everything she had learned about her values, priorities, talents, interests and family of origin into account.

One of the best ways to identify the boundaries you want to set—at work, home or in your personal life—is to first look at your time. One of the basic boundaries that we all deal with in life is that we have only a limited amount of time—in a day, in our waking hours, in our lives—and no more. How you apportion that time makes a simple, powerful statement about how you live your life. Most of us who are caught in the Stress Cycle and the Lemming Conspiracy find that our time is sucked away from us in tasks that don't seem to matter. Tasks that *do* matter don't get their fair share of time. A critically important part of moving away from the Lemming Conspiracy is taking charge of your time. A basic law of systems and human relationships is this: Everyone else will control your time unless you take *active* control of it yourself.

After you look at your time, the next most basic and important factor to control in your life is how you apportion your energy. When we are young, we tend to think (or at least act as though) our energy is endless. If we need to exercise, we'll just get up earlier. If we need to finish a project, we'll just stay up later. But just as with time, energy is not endless. We have limits. Our bodies have limits. Putting energy into one set of activities means that you don't have that energy for something else. The more careful you are about controlling your energy and putting your energy into projects that are meaningful to you, the more productive and satisfying you will find your career. This means setting boundaries. Bob, who tends to do a lot of the actual writing for the two authors of this book, finds that he writes best in the morning. By the afternoon, he has a hard time coming up with anything creative. By setting and maintaining a clear boundary that he can't be disturbed or have appointments in the morning, he is much more productive in his writing, and a lot happier.

Once you have control of your time and energy, other boundaries become possible. If you're not spinning out of control in the Stress Cycle, you can begin to think about the quality of your relationships at work. You can begin to think about your *role* at work and how to move into roles and tasks that use your abilities better or that are more rewarding. You can even begin to think about *internal* boundaries such as how you want to act with co-workers or how you want to speak to them.

Lauren looked at several boundaries for herself. "The first thing I did was to be clear about my goals. After I worked on my Personal Vision, this was easy. Some of my goals were work-related. Some were family-related. Some of my work goals were about *how* I work. I knew I wanted to use my talents better and spend less time on tasks that had nothing to do with what I do best. The main goal, though, was that I wanted to spend less time at work. It had pretty much taken over my life and, even though I enjoy most of it, I don't enjoy it *that* much. This, of course, dovetailed with my personal goals. I definitely wanted to spend more time with my kids while they were still young, and I wanted to have more time and energy available to be with my husband. I knew I couldn't do it all at once—on either side. So I figured out some reasonable intermediate steps."

Lauren knew that her ultimate goal was to manage her career in a different way than she had. She felt it would put too much stress on her and on her systems—work and family—to try to move immediately to her final destination. After gaining a clear sense of her ultimate goal, she thought backwards to create a few intermediate way stations. Note that Lauren's goals were complex. Her goals for work related to and involved her goals in her family.

A Note on Systems

Perceptive readers might notice something interesting about the last paragraph. Lauren felt that a sudden, drastic change in her work schedule might put too much stress on her job *and* her family. One might logically think that if it were a good thing for Lauren to spend more time with her children and husband, then the best thing to do would be just to do it. The truth is that systems don't change very much or very fast. Even family systems. Lauren felt that if she just started showing up at home at 5:30 every day expecting that everyone else in the family would of course reorganize *their* schedules, she might be setting herself up for disappointment. She felt that if she eased her schedule by stages and discussed it beforehand with her family, then everyone might be able to accommodate the changes better.

Every system is different. And ways to approach change in systems are different. Sometimes it's better to introduce changes into a system all at once. Other times, it works better to introduce change so gradually that no one is really aware of anything new going on. One constant, however, is that if *anyone* in a system changes—that is, really changes the rules of the game—then everyone else in the system has to accommodate to those changes. Or else they must expel the member who is trying to change the rules.

Third, Identify Your Internal Resistances

When faced with creating change in a seemingly monolithic corporation, we all tend to think of resistance to change as coming from the corporation itself. In fact, many of the most important barriers to change will come from you, from your own thoughts and feelings. These are your *internal resistances*.

What are these barriers? Here are some typical thoughts that will almost certainly result in non-action:

• My boss would never go for this.
• This will result in more work for my co-workers.
• Everyone will be mad at me.
• No one has ever done anything like this before.
• What right do I have to do something different from everyone else?
• I'll feel guilty if I have it better than everyone else.

The common denominator with all of these statements of internal resistance is simple; they are all *externally focused*. They say, in effect, that I can't do what I want to do and what I feel is right for me because someone else would feel unhappy about it. Remember from Chapter 2 that this is also the hallmark of the Stress Cycle. As long as your concern is primarily with what others think or will think, you will indeed be stuck.

Our experience in helping thousands of people create Personal Visions and then take action on those visions is that as long as you are externally focused, you won't be able to see most of the real options available to you. On the other hand, the clearer you are about your goals and priorities and the more clearly you can state them—to yourself and to others—the more options you will see.

Find your own resistances. Find the statements you make to yourself that keep you stuck. In most cases, these will be statements that are focused outside of yourself like the list above. It might well be that your most powerful internal resistances to change come right out of your family of origin. As we discussed in Chapter 1 and Chapter 7, all of us learn how to work in systems from our family systems. When we grow up, we join systems that fit us, so it makes sense that we would resist change with tactics that we learned in our original family systems. A simple and useful way to find out what kind of influence your family of origin might have on your resistances to change is in the Thought Experiment at the end of this chapter.

As you become aware of internal resistances, write them down in your Personal Vision notebook. Don't let them just circulate in your mind. When you write them down, you start to gain some distance and control over them, and they will stop influencing your behavior and decisions so much.

You will probably start encountering internal resistance almost as soon as you become clearer and more specific about your Personal Vision. Your resistance might be in the form of simple statements like the ones above, or it may be more nebulous and complex. If you do the Thought Experiment at the end of this chapter, you may become aware of resistance that you didn't realize you had.

The more you pin down your resistances, and the more you write them down in your Personal Vision notebook, the less power they will have over you. The central key to real change is creating your Personal Vision in the first place. When you learn to focus on *it* to guide your decisions rather than focus on what you think others want you to do, you will be on your way to the Balance Cycle.

Fourth, Develop a Plan—'As If'

This step may help you if you feel you would like to set some boundaries but wonder if you can really do it. If you feel that you can go ahead and create whatever boundaries you need to make your Personal Vision real, you may not need to worry about this step. However, if perhaps you find yourself clear about the result you want, but you can't figure out how to make it happen, or if you find that the thought of creating a boundary (like Lauren's above—"At 5:00, I'm out of here.") makes you feel anxious, then this small exercise may help.

Start with your Personal Vision. Whatever your Personal Vision is, ask yourself, "If I were going to make this vision real, what would I have to do? Who would I have to talk to? What points would I have to make stick? What behavior would I have to carry out?" Notice that none of these questions implies that you would actually *do* anything. You just want to think about what you *would* do *if* you were going to carry out your Personal Vision.

What boundaries would you need to set and keep *if* you were going to make your Personal Vision real? Remember to think of the larger context of your career, not just of the job you are doing every day. What will you need to change at work? Think in terms of *time, energy, relationships,* and *tasks*. How do you want to use your time? How do you want to use your energy? What kind of relationships do you want at work? What tasks do you want to do; what do you not want to do? Write the answers to these questions in your Personal Vision notebook.

What about your personal life? What boundaries will you need to create in your family—even perhaps in your extended family? Remember to think of your goals in terms of your family, your marriage, and your personal and spiritual self. The more you can write down in your Personal Vision notebook, the better.

Remember that you don't *have* to do *anything*. Just because you write something down doesn't mean you have to do anything about it. You can help yourself by letting go, for a while, of any practical sense that you have to translate your boundaries into action. This will help you play with the ideas and play with the thought of setting boundaries and leading a different life.

The next part of this imaginary exercise is to pick out one boundary to work on. *If* you were going to set a new boundary, which one would you choose? Don't choose a large, far-reaching boundary. Rather, choose one that is small and easy to translate into action, like reducing overtime. Put your *as if* boundaries in order. List them from the easiest and smallest all the way up to those that will change great parts of your life.

This list is your action plan. The important thing to keep in mind is that you don't have to implement your plan all at once. As an example, if you want to set a boundary to leave the office at 5:30 every day, when you are now leaving at 7:00 every night, it might feel too difficult to institute all at once. But if you let everyone know that you

intend to leave at 6:30 every night from now on—and then do it—
you will be surprised at how much better you feel. The world doesn't
come to an end. In fact, you may find that you can move relatively easily to your next step, 6:00. And the next, 5:30.

Fifth, Setting Boundaries

The most important and significant part of setting boundaries is
that you are the only one who can do it. You cannot expect anyone else
to set boundaries for you. You can't even expect anyone else to be
happy with boundaries that you set for yourself. When and if you set
a boundary, you cannot expect anyone else to maintain it. If you want
to leave at 5:30 every day from work, you are the only person who can
make that happen. In fact, there will be some days when you feel that
you have to fight everyone in the office to make it happen. There are
ways to go about setting boundaries that can help, though.

The main tactic that can help is this: Talk to people. If you want to
set a boundary at work, for instance, if you want to take on this kind
of task but not that, then talk to the people that this boundary most
affects. Don't just talk to your boss; talk to your co-workers and subordinates. Talk to anyone on whom your boundary will have an
impact. Tell them how you came to think about this boundary and
why you came to the decision you did. Go into as much detail about
your whole Personal Vision as you want to. The more that people
understand why you seek change and exactly what changes you plan
to make, the more willing they will be to accept changes—and even
cooperate with them.

The manager in the high-tech company at this chapter's beginning
created a Personal Vision. He spent a good deal of time doing the exercises in this book and putting together a whole picture of what he wanted his life and career to look like. When he finished, it looked as if the
only answer for him was to quit. He didn't see any way he could work
at his company and live even close to the kind of lifestyle he envisioned.

But he decided nothing would be lost in trying. One of the first
boundaries he wanted to enact was around the kind of work he did. It
was clear from his work on his Personal Vision that he was not suited
by talent or personality to be a manager. "Being a manager drove me
crazy. There were so many different problems to take care of all at

once. I never felt that I could keep track of everything I felt I should do. It made me anxious all the time. The other part of it was that I really enjoyed working on the tech side. I liked to take on a really interesting tech problem and just work on it until I figured it out. As a manager, you never get to do anything like that, and I missed it.

"Beyond my role as a manager, I wanted to take control of my hours. I wasn't going to work every weekend and I wasn't going to work at night. It was clear from my values that my family comes first in my mind. I was determined to carry out those values in action.

"I talked to my manager first. I took him through the whole story—including watching my daughter throw the Ken doll in the box. I showed him the work that I had done on my Personal Vision and showed him what specifically my Personal Vision looked like. We started talking about ideas about how it could work in my company.

"We didn't solve all of the problems at once. The first time I talked to him, we didn't get very far at all. But as we continued talking, I could see that he really wanted to try to make something work. He could also see that I wanted it to work for him and the company as well.

"It turned out that the hardest boundary to set was to stop being a manager. I am actually still managing people in a very limited way, but I mostly get to work on the kinds of projects that I like. It seems like every month or so my big boss wants me to take over some management position or other, and we have to go back and forth on how I don't want to be a manager and I'm a lot happier working where I am.

"Setting boundaries around my time has gone a little easier. I talked to the other people on my team about what I had in mind. They were amazingly supportive. I had felt that if I left at a reasonable hour I would feel guilty and feel that I was increasing the work load of everyone else. That has not turned out to be true, but I've had to work at doing parts of my job more efficiently.

"The logical point stuck in my mind, though, and has stayed with me; if everyone just works late and on the weekends without setting any boundaries, then the management of the company is not getting the feedback that they need to hire more people or restructure the job. I know that management does not want to be abusive to people. On the other hand, they are not going to change anything unless people set boundaries and let them know what's really going on.

"I work about 45 hours a week. I don't work at night. I don't work on the weekend. Every few days something comes up that makes me think that I should just keep working past the time when I need to be home with my family. I just keep this image in my mind of my daughter throwing the doll in a box, and it helps me set a limit on my time and maintain my boundaries.

"I am still working for the same company and I am still rated excellently by my managers. I have just been offered a management job that I refused. I don't feel like quitting any more, and I feel that my company cares about me as a person. I feel that my job fits me and that I deliver the best work I can do to my company. And I feel that it is appreciated."

Boundaries in Systems

One of the main reasons that systems react so strongly when people set boundaries (and why co-workers often seem to undermine any boundaries that you do set) is that when you set a boundary or a limit, that same boundary becomes an option for anyone else in the system. In effect, when you set a boundary, you give other people in the system more choices.

This can be positive if others are ready for those choices. But if other people are not ready to look at their own lives and are not ready to see their own choices in life, they can react strongly to your taking control of your life.

If you want to create boundaries at work, taking other people through your whole thought process in creating the boundary—even enlisting others' input—can help a great deal in pulling in their cooperation. The more you have worked on your Personal Vision and the more of that work you share with others, the more they can feel a part of the boundaries you set.

Thought Experiment I

Resistances To Change

Much of our internal resistance to change originates in our families of origin. It is here after all that we learn how to deal with systems. Our sense of what is 'normal' and 'right' to do in systems comes right out of the families in which we grow up. It makes sense that when we start thinking about doing something differently, our first reaction might be to think, "I can't possibly do that." You can start to find out the sources of some of these internal resistances with the following simple exercise.

In order to complete this exercise, you will need to have already done some work on your Personal Vision. You will also need to have done some work on identifying appropriate boundaries as described in the body of this chapter.

1. Once you have figured out what boundaries you would like to establish, write them down in your Personal Vision notebook. For example, you might write: "I want to leave work by 6:00 every day." You might have a list of a dozen or more boundaries you are interested in enforcing.

2. For each of your boundaries, whether work-related, family-related or personally related, answer the following question: "How would my mother react to this boundary?" The best way to answer the question is to write your answer in your Personal Vision notebook *as though your mother were writing it.* Don't think that you already know what she would say and so there's no need to write it down. Write down her answer. You may surprise yourself with what your unconscious comes up with.

3. You can increase the sophistication of this exercise by considering your mother's response at two different times in her life. How would she have responded to this boundary at the age she was when you were about twelve? How would she respond to this boundary at the age she is now?

4. For each of your boundaries, answer the question: "How would my father react to this boundary?" Again, you can increase the sophistication of the exercise by answering the question at two different times in your father's life. Once again, write the answers in your Personal Vision notebook as though your father were writing them.

5. If you want to take another, very interesting step with this exercise, then call your mother and father and schedule times to come and talk to them individually. When you talk to them in individual interviews, tell each the situation at work and the boundaries you have in mind to put into place. Listen to how each one responds to each of your proposed boundaries. How do their responses differ? Does one think it's a great idea? Does it make one nervous? Does a parent discourage you or encourage you? Which parent mirrors most closely your own internal responses?

You may find that as you try to come up with reactions from your parents, you uncover some resistance—and perhaps some encouragement. Some people even find that the very words they use to resist change in their minds are the same words they imagine their parents using. Writing down these words will help you gain some distance on them and gain some choice about whether to proceed or not.

> **NEXT CHAPTER:** We created The Whole Person Technology® for individuals. However, in the new economy—the Knowledge Economy—corporations are increasingly recognizing that the path to thriving or even surviving involves helping individuals do what they do best and find the right fit in the company. These are exactly what research has shown that The Whole Person Technology® accomplishes. A program that helps individuals can end up helping the corporation be more profitable.

...WHEN INDIVIDUALS
HAVE ENOUGH
Information ABOUT **Themselves,**
THEY CAN BE
Proactive
AND INFORMED **Participants**
IN THE MANAGEMENT PROCESS—
MAKING
THE WHOLE CORPORATION
RUN MORE
Efficiently
AND
Effectively.

Corporations
&
THE WHOLE PERSON TECHNOLOGY®

McKinsey and Company recently published the results of a two-year study of talent in U.S. business. Their conclusions were somewhat sobering. Over the next fifteen to twenty years, there will be an increasing talent gap. The economy will try to expand at its usual rate, but the supply of young people to fill increasing numbers of positions will actually dwindle. This talent shortfall has already begun to affect companies in the high-tech arena. You can check it out in any major city by just driving down the freeway. Billboard after billboard advertises websites dedicated to helping people move up into

Rob Donovan provided significant help with this chapter.

high-tech professions. In Silicon Valley, the billboards are more direct—"If you're tired of your present job, call this number."

In this Knowledge Economy of the opening years of the century, success or failure will depend on talent: the talent that a company can bring to bear on a key problem or process, the talent that creates the new ideas that change how business is done, the talent to organize and manage increasingly separated elements of global money-making. McKinsey's numbers are cold and emotionless, but the statement they make is compelling: There won't be enough talent to go around in the next twenty years. The immediate corollaries are obvious: Make better use of the talent you already have—and above all, don't lose it.

"Talent will be the most important corporate resource over the next 20 years. It is also the resource in shortest supply."

**—Ed Michaels,
McKinsey and Company,
*The War For Talent***

There have been a number of recent books published whose purpose is to help business use talent more effectively (Jeffrey Pfeffer, *The Human Equation,* 1998; Heskett, Sasser and Schlesinger, *The Service Profit Chain,* 1997; Kaplan and Norton, *The Balanced Scorecard,* 1996; Edward Gubman, *The Talent Solution,* 1998). One of the most interesting of these is by Buckingham and Coffman, *First, Break All The Rules* (1999). Buckingham and Coffman, of the Gallup Organization, report on a number of studies that included over 80,000 managers in 400 companies. They sought to identify those attitudes in the workplace that led companies to be more productive and more profitable.

The Gallup Organization didn't look at company strategy. They didn't look at product advantages. They didn't even look at technological innovation. They looked at *people*. What were the attitudes of people in teams, divisions, sections, units, and companies that were more productive and profitable, and what were the attitudes in units and teams that were less profitable?

Two points stand out in Buckingham and Coffman's conclusions. First, people in more profitable companies and business units reported that they get to do what they do best every day. Second, people in more profitable companies and business units reported that they felt a connection between themselves and the mission of the company.

The conclusions Buckingham and Coffman drew were that the

path toward a better-functioning company or business unit *must begin* with two critical steps. First, companies need to place people in positions in which they can use their talents—where they can do what they do best every day. Second, companies need to insure that there is a good fit between the company and the person.

Buckingham and Coffman concluded that the critical difference between the more profitable business units and the less profitable ones had to do with managers. Highly talented managers put people in positions in which they could use their best talents. In addition, they somehow helped people feel a better fit between themselves and the company.

We feel that The Whole Person Technology® has implications for these conclusions. By driving information down to individuals, corporations have the ability, for the first time, to have a meaningful *dialog* between individual and manager about talent and fit. The effect of this dialog will be to make *any* manager function as one of the Great Managers of Buckingham and Coffman. As we will see, some companies have already seen that this highly profitable dialog can improve team functioning and the bottom line metrics of a variety of business units.

The Knowledge Economy

Peter Drucker started talking about the implications of the Knowledge Economy almost ten years ago. Here is what he said in a recent article in the *Harvard Business Review:*

Most of us, even those of us with modest endowments, will have to learn to manage ourselves. We will have to learn to develop ourselves. We will have to place ourselves where we can make the greatest contribution. And we will have to stay mentally alert and engaged during a 50-year working life, which means knowing how and when to change the work we do.

Drucker draws the clear, logical conclusions you have to draw when you start thinking about knowledge workers and the Knowledge Economy. The name for this economy stems from the fact that economic value no longer lies in *things*; rather, it lies in the special knowledge and talents that each individual brings to the job. 'Human capital' is a phrase we encounter more and more. But just because people use that phrase doesn't mean that this kind of capital is the same as the more traditional capital of machines, buildings and rolling stock.

Frederick W. Taylor once said to factory workers: "You are not paid to think. Other people are paid to think around here." Now, even in factories, there is an increasing expectation that *everyone* will be responsive to what is happening around him or her and make decisions accordingly. Now, almost everyone in corporations is being paid *primarily* to think and respond to a constantly changing business environment.

Increasingly, to compete effectively, all organizations need people who make decisions. Not just executives. Not even just managers. To deal effectively with a work environment that changes daily, *everyone* has to be alert to changes and react appropriately.

The fundamental fact about the knowledge worker is that he or she is not merely one among many interchangeable machines humming day after day on the factory floor. The knowledge worker is an individual with his or her own individual talents, experiences, connections and history. As corporations increasingly discover, these workers can always take their knowledge, experiences, contacts and relationships and simply go elsewhere.

In the Knowledge Economy, the company and the business are contained in the heads of the people who work there. Our point of view is that it cannot be left to Great Managers alone to place those people in the right positions so they can use their strengths. It cannot be left solely to Great Managers to make sure people feel a good fit between themselves and the company. Our point of view is that when individuals have enough information about *themselves*, they can be proactive and informed participants in the management process—making the whole corporation run more efficiently and effectively. Each person can be a Great Manager of himself or herself.

Success In The Knowledge Economy

Drucker has some ideas about what is needed for success in the knowledge economy:

First and foremost, concentrate on your strengths.

Put yourself where your strengths can produce results.

Figure out *how* you work best.

Figure out how you learn most effectively.

Figure out how your values impact what you do.

Figure out how your career will change over a 50-year span.

Mr. Drucker, writing years and decades ago, seems to foreshadow The Whole Person Technology®. Abilities tell you what your strengths are. They also tell you how you learn best as well as how you make decisions and solve problems most effectively. By working through the elements of The Whole Person Technology® and integrating them creatively, you can come to amazingly productive conclusions about *how* you work best, what your values say to you, and the best fit for yourself in the workplace. An important part of The Whole Person Technology® concerns how your career changes through your life cycle. There are predictable way points and issues that you can plan for and take into account *before* they become crises.

As if to emphasize the importance of seeing yourself as a whole person, not just a collection of skills and functions, Mr. Drucker has recently begun to stress the importance of the spiritual side of people in business. The implications of Mr. Drucker's thinking are clear: in our Knowledge Economy, people will be more effective, more productive, more satisfied and will last longer in their jobs if they can see themselves in a bigger way and see what they do in a bigger context. As Mr. Drucker is at some pains to point out, figuring out all of this about yourself is not a matter of filling out a few personality tests and attending a class or two. He describes a process that takes *years.*

The Whole Person Technology® that we describe in this book is a structure. It helps you get to all of the important factors that will impact you and your career at any given time in your work life. It allows you to be *proactive* in an economy and business environment that changes constantly. It allows you to concentrate on your strengths—as opposed to trying to be everything to everyone.

Above all, The Whole Person Technology® is a tool to help you articulate your highest and most important contribution to the company, to your family and to your own life. It allows you to articulate and deal in the truth about yourself. What you find out when you go through The Whole Person Technology® is not something that someone else tells you or that you just make up. It comes out of you. It *is* you.

We have found that being able to say with complete conviction and self-knowledge, "This is how I work best, and here is where my values lead me, and this is what I am really passionate about and this is what I see as my highest contribution" opens and creates many opportunities.

Why? Because there is enormous power in dealing with the truth. The Whole Person Technology® is about finding the truth about yourself. It's an objective truth that you can say to your spouse, your children, your co-workers, your subordinates and your boss.

The Whole Person Technology® in Corporations

We have been using The Whole Person Technology® in corporations for some time now, but when we first created it, we didn't think of it as a corporate program. We thought of it strictly as a tool for individuals. Many of the most important aspects of The Whole Person Technology® actually come out of that original conception.

- **We wanted it to be complete.** Since we weren't trying to please an HR manager who wants a program done in a half-day, we felt free to put all the elements we felt necessary into the program.

- **We wanted it to be inside out, not outside in.** The Whole Person Technology® would not be a series of lectures delivered by an 'expert.' It would be the guided self-discovery of the real expert—you.

- **We wanted it to be practically useful.** There would be no reason for individual people to undertake a program like this unless there were a direct and palpable benefit—one that they could feel and experience. This held us to a rigorous standard.

- **We felt strongly that the individual would own the information.** This is a program for the individual, not for anyone else. Only individuals can make decisions about their careers and these individuals ought to have the information.

- **We are not invested in the outcome.** We deeply care that people who go through The Whole Person Technology® receive the best possible and most complete program we can deliver. We are not invested in the specific outcome of what participants discover. It's not that it doesn't matter to us; it is because we would not presume to know what is right for a person. We presume that if a person honestly approaches The Whole Person Technology® and goes through with an open mind, that he or she will find the right answer.

These were all pretty big obstacles for using The Whole Person Technology® in corporate settings when we started out. Managers who were used to traditional training programs assumed we would share any data that came out of the programs with them. They assumed that they could use the data to hire new workers or to shift workers to new responsibilities. We explained that an important component of the success of the program is that the individual participant owns the information. Our point of view has always been that the individual, armed with enough information, can ultimately make the best decisions about his or her own career. We feel that individuals taking responsibility for their own careers and entering into a dialog with management results in the most positive outcome for both.

Managers often wanted to know whether the trainers who delivered the program could make it *interesting*. This was an arresting point. The managers knew that their people were used to motivational shows and energy-inspiring hype. They knew that if the speaker was dull, their people would simply drift away. Our response to this is that there is one subject on earth that you—the same as everyone else—find fascinating, compelling and endlessly absorbing: you. That is what The Whole Person Technology® is about.

How We Got Our Start In Corporations

A young man who worked at IBM was so disgruntled with his job that he decided to try our program. His idea was to figure out what else he could do besides what he was doing because he basically hated it. He was making a good salary and was named to be in the pool of young talent being groomed for the executive ranks, but his heart was not in his work. He did not understand why he was so unhappy, but he felt that if things didn't change, he would quit.

When we first started doing programs with The Whole Person Technology®, we thought that one way we could measure the success of the program would be by the number of people who quit their current jobs and got into whole new jobs in whole new fields. We found out quickly that that particular statistic did not tell us anything. Instead, we found that in the vast majority of cases, people did *not* switch jobs. Even people like the young man above who were markedly unhappy with their careers almost always figured out how to make their present jobs work better for them rather than quit and start over somewhere else.

The young man did go through The Whole Person Technology® and it was a life-changing event for him. He was so excited that he went to his boss with his notebook and took the boss through everything he had learned about himself, how he worked best, where his real strengths were, and what he saw as his best fit in the company. The young man was not thinking about quitting any more. He knew what he was looking for *at IBM* and felt that with his boss's help, he could find it.

This was one of the first examples of the kind of dialog between individual and manager that can happen when people have solid knowledge about themselves. We have seen a great many since.

The young man's boss was so impressed with the result that he asked us to develop a corporate version of the same program. We did develop this program using the same Whole Person Technology® you see in this book.

Research and Outcomes

From the very first seminars we delivered in corporations, we wanted to demonstrate what was happening as people went through the programs. We decided to develop a series of research scales covering significant measures related to profitability, retention, satisfaction and productivity. In addition, we determined to measure long-term outcome results rather than just immediate post-seminar outcomes. Our thinking was that the program should demonstrably have an impact on significant business metrics and that it was only long-term gains that were really meaningful.

We developed a questionnaire of some 220 items. From these items we derived nine different scales:

1. Ability Match: The perceived match between the person's natural abilities and talents and his or her major <u>roles</u> in the organization. There have been many hundreds of studies over nearly 70 years confirming the importance of Ability Match in productivity and job satisfaction.

- When <u>low</u> (weak match), positively related to <u>stress</u>
- When <u>high</u> (strong match), positively related to:
optimism
internal locus of control
connection to company.

2. Stress: The person's report of how much or little stress he or she is currently experiencing on the job. Stress has been studied by researchers for decades.

<u>High Stress</u> is related to:
- Poor job satisfaction
- Poor company connection
- Poor personal satisfaction
- Poor health
- Poor retention
- Poor overall productivity

3. Optimism: The person's report of how much or little he or she sees a positive future. Martin Seligman has spent much of his career in psychology studying the effects of optimism and what leads to optimism.

<u>High Optimism</u> has been positively linked to:
- Higher Productivity
- Lower Stress
- Better Management Decisions
- Higher Retention
- More Effective Sales
- Better Health

4. Internal vs. External Locus of Control: A measure of how much or little people feel that their own decisions affect what happens to them in life.

<u>Internal Locus of Control</u> has been positively linked to:
- Higher Productivity
- Higher Satisfaction
- Better Management Decisions
- Better Long Term Health

5. Connection to Company: A measure of the person's reported sense of his or her connection to the company and sense of the company's care and concern about him or her. Connection to Company has just begun to be studied in detail in the last ten years or so. Nevertheless, there have been valid and reproducible findings in this area.

<u>Higher Connection to Company</u> results in:
- Greater overall job satisfaction
- Better retention
- Higher Productivity

6. Vision: A measure of the <u>specificity</u>, <u>completeness</u> and <u>objectivity</u> with which a person looks forward to the future. A complete, specific vision for the future that you arrive at with some objective information is more predictive of both <u>success</u> and <u>satisfaction</u> than any other factor researchers have ever found.

7. Balance: A measure of the kinds of factors the person takes into account when figuring out personal and career goals. When people create career goals with some attention to <u>job</u>, <u>family</u>, and <u>personal</u> aspects of their lives, and when they fit these into an overall schema or vision, they are much less likely to burn out, derail or make precipitous career moves.

8. Satisfaction Index: An overall rating drawn from all of the previous scales of the person's present sense of satisfaction with his or her career. Strongest determinants:
- Role satisfaction
- Optimism
- Balance

9. Productivity Index: A rating drawn from all of the previous scales of the person's overall present productivity. Strongest determinants:
- Role Match
- Internal Locus of Control

The Highlands 220 questionnaire was administered before corporate participants started programs, immediately after they finished and then administered again after six months. This resulted in pre, post and six-month follow-up scores on all nine scales. A total of 165 people from corporations participated in the research over a two-year period.

The following chart shows the results:

Long Term Gains From The Whole Person Technology® (Corporate)

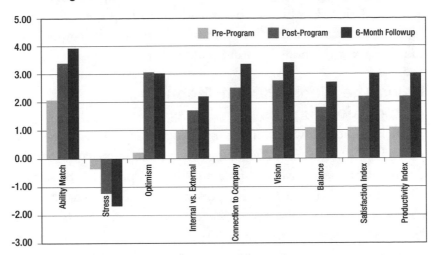

These results are also shown in the following table:

	Percentage Gains		
	Pre to post	Post to 6 mo.	Total Gain.
Ability Match	19%	7%	26%
Stress	-20%	-12%	-32%
Optimism	56%	-1%	55%
Internal vs. External	11%	8%	19%
Connection To Company	40%	11%	51%
Vision	47%	8%	55%
Balance	11%	13%	24%
Satisfaction	19%	10%	29%
Productivity	19%	10%	29%
Average	**27%**	**9%**	**36%**

Note that Stress is backwards—if Stress goes *down*, that is good. All changes pre- to post- are in the positive direction and statistically significant. All changes pre- to follow-up are likewise in the positive direction and statistically significant.

The interesting thing about this research is that a program we created and designed to be used by individuals to help them lead more fulfilling and balanced lives is now actively being used by corporations to help increased productivity and profitability.

Using The Whole Person Technology® In Corporations

We have worked with a number of corporations over the last five years. The Whole Person Technology® is a basic framework that different organizations have used for a multitude of purposes. By starting with the individual and how that person uses his or her talents, companies as diverse as IBM, Glaxo Wellcome and Chase Bank of Texas have used our seminars to deal with such critically important issues as diversity, team functioning, retention and organizational vision.

TEAMS—GLAXO WELLCOME

At Glaxo Wellcome, The Whole Person Technology® is being adopted as a tool to help improve productivity and profitability in an increasingly competitive and crowded marketplace. Rich Podurgal, Director of Corporate Learning and Development at Glaxo Wellcome, says: "I had my entire team go through the Whole Person Technology®. We measured both job satisfaction and performance pre- and post. I'm convinced that participation in the seminar can lead to improved job performance and satisfaction at the individual level. I believe using the process with an intact group can be a powerful way for a team to gain a better understanding and appreciation of one another, improve the manner in which they communicate, and adjust job activities to take full advantage of each individual's talents."

Post-program analysis indicated that the individual productivity of people on the team had improved an average of 8%. The overall productivity of the team had improved 7%. And the individual job satisfaction of people on the team had improved an average of 17%. Changes due to participation in The Whole Person Technology® seminar were isolated from changes attributable to other influences.

In the course of completing the seminar for this study, it became startlingly obvious that two people on the team were in roles that did not match their abilities and personalities well. The fact that this team was composed of experienced human resources professionals points out the difficulty of matching people with roles without objective information to go by. Carefully moving through the structure of the seminar made these role discrepancies apparent to the two people involved. This realization resulted in the kind of open dialog that often characterizes systems that work well. The two team members ended by radically redesigning their role assignments.

The difference in attitude and performance is startling. Both team members had performed well in their previous roles. In their new roles, they show the kind of spark and creativity that managers wish for. One of the team members has completely redesigned the structure of the programs they offer to eliminate redundancy and to follow a more logical path. Both team members have performed so well in their new roles that they are now in line for promotions and wider responsibility.

This team's story is an example of a phenomenon we see over and over again. Talented people in the wrong role can usually perform satisfactorily, even quite well. But the enormous effort required to do that means they're not going to enjoy their roles and are certainly not going to be very creative in them. From the outside, though, there is nothing particularly wrong with the picture.

The opposite situation reflects another universe. In this universe, people *fit* their roles by talent, interests, values, personality, skills and goals. In this world, people are happy; they come up with creative new ideas all the time; and they are hugely productive.

DIVERSITY – CHASE BANK OF TEXAS

The Chase organization is well known for its work in diversity. It is ranked as number 18 in *Fortune* magazine's annual listing of the Diversity Elite—the top 50 companies most active in incorporating and utilizing diversity in their workforce. Debby Selke, Vice President of the Diversity Group at Chase Texas, first heard about The Whole Person Technology® during a conference at which the two authors spoke. "As a part of Chase's diversity strategy, our aim is to attract, nurture, challenge and reward people who have a wide range of talents, experiences and perspectives. Vigorous and effective career development is integral to that goal, so our employees have access to an extraordinary array of development tools and resources. Yet the assessment instrument and discovery process outlined at the conference appeared to offer something unique. It seemed to provide a missing link, one that would enable Chase employees to clarify and articulate their natural talents and interests and then match them to the organization's mission and goals.

"I was spurred to try a pilot program by a comment from a participant in our Leadership Mentoring Program. This is a mentoring program in which high-potential mid-level people of color are paired with Chase Texas executives. He said he was unsure of his next career steps at Chase. I realized that until he could create and envision his own direction in the bank, he could not achieve the success of which he is capable, nor could Chase benefit fully from his talents.

"We completed a pilot program with a group of Leadership Mentoring protégés. Many have told me that it was a life-changing experience. And six months afterwards, their stories are even more powerful. Already Chase has benefited from participants' enhanced loyalty, productivity, communication skills and satisfaction. We are currently considering additional ways to offer the program in conjunction with succession planning, top talent development and intact team initiatives. By helping individuals know themselves better and clarify and communicate their vision, we have helped them connect with Chase, and this will result in tremendous long-term benefit to the organization."

ORGANIZATIONAL VISION – MATRIX RESOURCES

Matrix Resources is a fast-growing IT placement firm in Atlanta, Georgia. It has been on the *Inc* 500 list of fastest-growing companies in the country for three years in a row—a remarkably difficult achievement. Jim Huling is the Vice President of Corporate Services there and leads the team that manages all aspects of operations except for sales. "We've experienced 900% growth in four years. My management team consists of me and seven directors. We've been together as a team for about three years and I feel that as a team we were pretty tight before we ever did the Whole Person Technology® seminar. My goals for the seminar were for me and my team to gain a better understanding of ourselves and a better understanding of each other.

"We had three definite steps in our growth—each one significant. The first was when we went through The Highlands Ability Battery™ together. It made a huge impact almost immediately. I noticed a new level of self-awareness and a new level of self-confidence in the members of the team. I attribute this to two factors. First, individuals could see objectively that they really were good at some things. Second, and this is a little more subtle, people could see that they were *not* well matched for other things in terms of natural talent. It meant that you don't have to pretend you're great at everything. What a relief!

"The second step happened when I made copies of my Ability Battery report for everyone on the team. People found this so helpful in understanding how to work with me that everyone on the team ended up making copies of his own report for the other people on the team. Communication opened up. We reached a level of support and acceptance that we had never reached before.

"The third step happened in the seminar that followed. We did a number of modeling exercises and ended by creating a Vision Statement for the team. We came up with eleven principles that would be our vision for the leadership team. After the seminar we realized that this Vision Statement is pivotal and we began to flesh it out with examples and statements about how to carry it out. It is now a one-page document with the eleven principles and their supporting statements. The seven directors are now in the process of taking this Vision Statement to each of their teams to form the basis of their team visions. The vision that emerged from the seminar will ultimately be the basis of a statement of principle for our entire company."

RETENTION AND MOTIVATION – MARRIOTT INTERNATIONAL

The Alliance Accounts Organization at Marriott International is responsible for strategic accounts management. Their clients are the top 31 global corporate customers of Marriott, and they are responsible for over $700 million in sales. Carrie Welles, a member of the Alliance Accounts team first became aware of The Whole Person Technology® when she read the previous edition of this book. "It's evident that self-development is important. This seemed different from the many other things that Marriott offers. It seemed far more complete. It also seemed more powerful because it was self-discovery, not some expert telling me about myself. My thought was that our group has been together for three years. It is a very close and well-functioning team. If we could go through an experience like this together, it seemed to me that we could have a better chance of staying together as a team and have less chance of people moving off into a different career path just to do something different. I took the idea to my boss, David Townshend."

David Townshend is Vice President of Alliance Accounts and leads the team of 15 relationship managers. "When Carrie brought this idea to me, it seemed different. I wanted to see how we could be a more effective team. I wanted to raise the overall level of performance and I wanted to revitalize the group. For three years, this organization has been on the front of a paradigm shift at Marriott. This is sometimes frustrating work.

"I wanted the members of the group to be able to know each other individually and for the team to be able to draw on each other's strengths. The members of our team never see each other for most of the year and our experience with The Whole Person Technology® seminar was intense and very open. I feel we understand each other at a core level. The team is more focused and energized.

"Every member of the team has been at Marriott for many years. One always has the question, is there a better place to work outside of Marriott? The program helped bring from the back of our minds to the forefront: Is there alignment? And what exactly attracts and keeps people on board? With the war for talent out there, people can always go out and make more money. But maybe that's not the most important thing. One person on the team, as a result of the seminar, realized that she could not find a fit with her career and life goals at Marriott. The other members of the team completely understood her position and have been very supportive of changes she wants to make. All of the other members of the team felt more clearly and positively aligned with Marriott and with the team. I feel this was an exceptional use of time and exceeded my expectations."

COACHING AND THE LEARNING ORGANIZATION – PRINTPACK

Printpack is the largest privately held flexible packaging converter in the United States. It has about 4,000 employees in 18 domestic plants, and has about $1 billion in revenue. Tom Brown is the Director of

Organizational Development for Printpack. Tom has been interested in creating a coaching model for the development of front line leaders for some time. "Printpack is a manufacturing company. We wanted to create a program to develop our plant-level leaders that would take people off the floor as little as possible but that would allow us to grow a learning organization from the very lowest levels. Our model would depend on the development talents of people that we are training as coaches. We call it the Frontline Leadership Development Program.

"The Whole Person Technology® turns out to be the glue that holds the whole thing together. It makes us consider vital learning issues such as: How does this person learn? How does he or she solve problems? By understanding individual differences in learning and problem-solving channels, our coaches can better go out to the plant floor and meet the people on their own ground. They can work from the point of view that starts with the individual. We call the Whole Person Technology® part of the program Leadership From Within. There is no question but that it is extremely beneficial for the Frontline Leadership coaches to have the tool of the Whole Person Technology®. These coaches will be the delivery mechanism for development to our production supervisors. The Whole Person Technology provides a gymnastic-like floor mat—a platform from which to take off and land."

SUCCESSION PLANNING—BELLSOUTH CELLULAR

Roy McAllister is Vice President, Human Resources at BellSouth Cellular Corporation. He became interested in The Whole Person Technology® when he went through the ability battery himself. "I learned things about the way I work and how I pace myself. I better understood that not everybody works in the same way. As a senior manager, one of my most important jobs is the identification and development of the future leaders of BellSouth Cellular. I had noticed before that our most talented young people go about things differently. Partly that is a difference in generations. But an important difference is simply how they are uniquely wired.

"I felt it would be valuable for the young people who will be leading BellSouth Cellular to have the benefit of learning what things they can do easily and well, and what things they will have a hard time with. I also wanted them to be cognizant of how people are different. I wanted them to be able to become observers of how other people work, so that the program could help them as managers and better prepare them for leadership roles.

"The participants in the program have been uniform in their appreciation. One interesting sidelight was that they all felt more ownership of responsibility for their own development after the program. One person, after going through the program, realized why a current assignment was particularly frustrating for her. With her knowledge gained from The Whole Person Technology®, she could talk to her boss clearly about what was frustrating and what kinds of assignments would be more in her line. For several others, you could tell that the light bulbs went off when they started to understand why they worked the way they worked. I feel that this is extremely valuable knowledge for these young people to have in their development as leaders."

LEADERSHIP—IBM

Bob Gonzales is Vice President of Human Resources Operations at IBM. His focus is North America, with some global responsibilities. He leads a team of 20 people, all of whom are leaders and managers of other teams. "I was interested in The Whole Person Technology® because 70 percent of my team are new to their jobs. I wanted the team to do something that would bring us together as a team. I think the program helped us deal with our own talents as individuals. More importantly, it helped us see and appreciate and value our differences. Diversity does not have to pull us apart. By valuing our differences and the differences we see in others, our diversity gives us more strength.

"The experience with The Whole Person Technology® was emotional and memorable. It has stayed with us. We have a better understanding of our individual traits, but also the strengths of others on the team. It helped us see what we as individuals bring to the team that others don't. I think it has helped us use the strength of our diversity of styles and work types. It has helped us personally, but also helped our leadership skills and how we work together as a team."

Motivation In The Knowledge Economy

Researchers have known for at least fifty years that pay and benefits—beyond a certain baseline—are not particularly effective motivators for people in corporations. In spite of this, managers have up to now almost exclusively relied on pay to motivate people—probably because this is what they felt they had control over. In the past, this worked—or at least it worked well enough. In the Knowledge Economy, managers are increasingly faced with trying to motivate people for whom pay has ceased to be even a significant motivator.

What *does* motivate people now? If you ask people what they want, they frequently fall back on the same answers their managers come up with—pay. The problem is that most individuals haven't fully engaged the question of their own motivation either. In Silicon Valley, where companies desperately try everything to keep people from jumping ship, the answers they come up with are frequently bizarre: valet laundry, for instance, or on-site dentistry. As one HR manager pointed out, the effect of many employee-generated suggestions is actually to keep people at their desks working without so many interruptions. One company motivates executives by letting them use the company Humvee for the weekend.

Digging a little deeper into the problem yields more substantive answers. Generally, what people seek is success, but with a more balanced life, less stress and more enjoyment. The wish for more pay and more perks, on closer interview with individuals, translates to a wish for a better lifestyle. To quote Jeffrey Pfeffer:

> Creating a fun, challenging and empowered work environment in which individuals are able to use their abilities to do meaningful jobs for which they are shown appreciation is likely to be a more certain way to enhance motivation and performance—even though creating such an environment may be more difficult and take more time than merely turning the reward lever.
>
> —Jeffrey Pfeffer, *The Talent Equation*

Peter Drucker, Buckingham and Coffman, and Jeffrey Pfeffer, among many others, all point to similar conclusions. If you want to succeed, if you want to be profitable, you have to structure things so that people can do what they do best, feel a good fit between themselves and their jobs, and enjoy and feel engaged by what they do all day long. The Whole Person Technology® gives corporations a way to accomplish all of these goals. The only caveat is that they first have to think outside the dots of traditional skills-oriented, outside in, management and system-driven programs. They have to be willing to trust individuals with enough information about themselves to create a *meaningful* dialog between management and individual to gain these goals individual by individual. When enough individuals are doing what they do best and bringing their whole selves to work every day, then the system has changed, and everyone benefits.

The next chapter is about one company—Cisco Systems—that has gone a long way toward creating a new kind of business culture. One that we believe will be the model for how business moves into the future.

"WE HAVE THE OPPORTUNITY HERE AT **CISCO** TO TRULY HAVE AN ORGANIZATION IN WHICH **Everyone** WORKS IN **Roles** THAT **Fit Them** AND **Their Talents** AND IN WHICH PEOPLE GENERALLY **Love What They Do.** BUT ONLY IF PEOPLE ARE ABLE TO **Take Responsibility** FOR THEIR OWN DECISIONS. TAKING RESPONSIBILITY DOESN'T JUST MEAN MAKING CHOICES. IT MEANS MAKING **Strategic Career Decisions** BASED ON **Real Data.**"

Sue Bedford
Senior Manager
Human Resources
CISCO SYSTEMS

The
Culture Of The
F U T U R E

Cisco Systems has grown faster than any other company in history. It recently overtook General Electric and Microsoft for a few days as the most valuable business on earth. The Internet drives and defines the future of business. Cisco Systems makes the Internet work.

Everyone knows the business story of Cisco Systems. What may not be as apparent is that, in addition to creating great wealth, Cisco has also been creating the company and the business culture of the future. In many ways the culture Cisco created is just as important as the routers and switches it sells all over the globe.

Kathryn Vecchio Russell, M.S., provided significant help in writing this chapter.

Sue Bedford is Senior Manager, Human Resources for the Research Triangle Park facility of Cisco. "When we think about our day here, we don't think in terms of an eight-hour work day. We have to think about 24 hours. We do business all over the world. I might have a meeting at 9:00 at night with someone in Korea, or one at 3:00 AM with someone in Singapore. There really isn't any such thing as an eight-to-five day.

"There are a lot of different ways to look at the culture here. To some, it might seem that this is the technological futureworld gone crazy. To me, it seems like a huge opportunity. What it means is that it's up to the individual. When you eat, sleep, exercise, work, have time for your family or go to the grocery store is a matter of individual choice. You determine your priorities and how you want your life to be.

"The success of this new kind of culture depends on the individual knowing enough about himself to set his own boundaries. People who look at this kind of freedom and shudder are just thinking from an old point of view. Work-life balance at Cisco means flexibility. There is no such thing as work and life. They're merged into one. The question is, can we create environments and work experience for employees that accommodate the rest of their lives?

"If you understand yourself you can prioritize all of the different aspects of your life in a 24 hour day. In order to balance their lives, employees must know themselves because the responsibility is squarely on the individual to order his or her own life."

Ed Paradise is Vice President and General Manager of the Technology and Mobile Business Unit. He puts it succinctly: "I think of our employees here as volunteers."

There is much in Ed's pithy comment. Cisco has had generous stock option plans for employees from the beginning. Anyone who has been at Cisco more than four or five years is probably a multimillionaire. This means that, from a financial viewpoint, none of these people—arguably Cisco's most valuable employees—really has to work.

In today's work environment—at last count there were hundreds of thousands of IT jobs nationwide that employers cannot fill—the war for talent is particularly intense for exactly the kinds of engineers that populate Cisco's hallways. People who work at Cisco could work anywhere. The question on Ed and Sue's minds is, how do we keep these valuable people from leaving?

An Operations Manager for global engineering support heads up a project aimed at finding better ways to measure performance at the Technical Assistance Center (TAC) at Cisco. He talks about the sense of urgency and impatience at Cisco. "Many people here are in the work-drive mode. The overriding wish is to make something happen *now*.

"Cisco's culture is highly entrepreneurial. We allow people a lot of autonomy. We empower people to make decisions about their work even at a very low level. As Cisco grows larger, this is changing somewhat, but people can still make relatively large financial decisions to please a customer. The growth has been overwhelming. We focus entirely on growing market share through customer satisfaction.

"Most people who come here have never experienced anything like this before. There are so many things going on at once; it presents a challenge and an opportunity to master. Problems are being worked around the clock and around the globe. It's *always* on."

The rewards for mastering this culture and learning to balance this 24-hours-a-day work-and-life mixture are immense. As one manager put it: "I'll get rich; I'll work with the latest technology, and I'll be on the hottest career path going."

So how will Cisco keep these high-powered young engineers? Nancy, a Director who has been at Cisco over ten years—making her one of the elite group of very early employees—describes her experience:

"When I started at Cisco, it had $28 million in revenue. It's now at $18 billion and growing. It's always going at a crazy, hectic pace. Two years ago, I had gotten to the point that I was tired and frustrated all the time. I never felt like myself. I started thinking that I should do something else.

"I thought I would quit my job—I had already earned more money than I had ever dreamed I could earn in a lifetime. My only question was, 'What should I do next?' I didn't want to just quit. I wanted to go in a positive direction to something else that made sense. That's when I heard about The Whole Person Technology® from Sue Bedford. She told me about the value of understanding my abilities. It sounded like a good thing.

"What I found out was that I was really in the right place doing the right thing. I was just tired. I found out that some things I thought I wanted to do would not be right for me in the long run. It's scary now to think about it, because I had the resources to do whatever I wanted. Without this information I could have made some choices that were entirely wrong.

"I discovered that I really was in a good job. I just needed to pay attention to some different parts of myself. I needed to set some limits on my job. I also needed to get involved in some other aspects of life than just Cisco Systems. I am now on the Board of Directors of our local Food Bank. I'm also a fire commissioner for our county. I take better care of my health, and I am in a relationship that is very important to me."

Nancy is still at Cisco—two years after she went through the program. "It helped me come back and not be so frustrated all the time. I am able to keep my perspective better."

Managers are concerned about how to keep the young people on their teams involved and happy. As one says, "They're young; they've just been working at Cisco a short time. They're given an extraordinary amount of latitude and freedom to do their work the way they see fit. I want them to be able to know themselves well enough to take full advantage of the opportunity this culture offers them."

It is a culture that opens the potential for almost unlimited choice. You can choose how you want to work. You can choose when you want to work. You can often choose the kinds of projects you want to work on.

As Sue Bedford says: "At Cisco we don't reward effort. We reward results. How you get to a result is your responsibility."

Ed Paradise echoes this: "There are many ways to be effective here. Knowing how you personally can be most effective gives you a distinct advantage. This was my experience with the program."

Sue Bedford feels that if people know more about themselves, they will be able to guide their careers more effectively. "I see one of the major uses of the program is in career pathing. Not everyone should be a manager. Many people will be much happier and more productive as individual contributors. Some people will be superb managers. This program can not only help people get pointed in the right direction, it can help guide their learning opportunities throughout their careers.

"We have the opportunity here at Cisco to truly have an organization in which everyone works in roles that fit them and their talents and in which people generally love what they do. But only if people are able to take responsibility for their own decisions. Taking responsibility doesn't just mean making choices. It means making strategic career decisions based on real data."

Ed Paradise also sees this future. "This program means that people have more information about themselves to be more effective. If I'm working with someone, I have the opportunity to know how I work best, under what conditions, and in which roles. This program deals with the problem of how we work together better. It gives data points on how we work best, and how to work best with other people—with this type of problem-solver or that.

"Before, it was a guess. Before, I had to learn a lot about myself, and, hopefully, a lot about the other people on my team. This is a much quicker path to a solution.

"Face it, if people aren't having fun, the culture isn't going to work in the long run. If I'm *not* having fun, and I'm sitting next to someone who *is* having fun, then who's going to be more productive? Who's going to stay?

"Cisco is a team culture. We want people who are confident about what they have to offer, who know what they want, and who can learn from the rest of the team. These are the people we want to attract and keep. This program provides a clear path to those goals in a shorter time and by a more direct route."

A RESEARCH PROJECT WITH THE WHOLE PERSON TECHNOLOGY®

Cisco is a data-driven culture. Sue Bedford was led to sponsor a research project to measure the results of participation: "I was interested in demonstrating that a program that centers around the individual contributor can benefit the organization in real and measurable ways." The project drew participants from two different business units at Cisco. They all went through a Whole Person Technology® seminar and answered extensive research questionnaires at the beginning and end.

The preliminary results from this project are shown below:

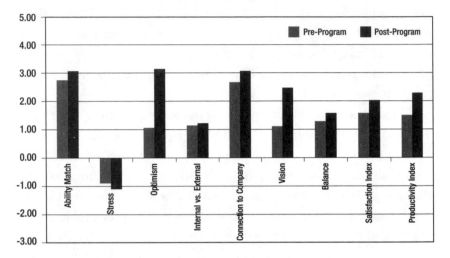

Cisco Systems Square One Results

These results are shown in percentile form below:

Percentage Gains From Square One® at Cisco Systems (Pre- to Post-Program)	
Ability Match	4%
Stress*	-5%
Optimism	32%
Internal vs. External	1%
Connection To Company	5%
Vision	20%
Balance	5%
Satisfaction	7%
Productivity	12%
Average	10%

*Note: Stress is backwards. If Stress goes *down*, that is good.

These results are interesting. We found that Cisco employees are better matched up with their natural talents to begin with than is common at other companies. We also found that they show a stronger initial connection to Cisco than we typically see. Cisco employees generally see themselves as more completely in charge of their own careers than average. The program resulted in gains in all of these areas, even though the starting point for each was relatively high.

Greater change was reflected in Personal Visions. By taking in more information about themselves and what they wanted from their lives, they gained a great deal in both vision and optimism. Both are strong predictors of satisfaction and long-term retention. Perhaps most interesting of all, the program resulted in significantly greater productivity. When people are happier and feeling more optimistic, they are also more productive.

OPEN AND CLOSED SYSTEMS—AND CISCO SYSTEMS

In the beginning chapters of this book, we described some of the rules by which systems work. We talked about how a system's interests are never really the same as the individuals' interests who compose the system. In Chapter 8, we talked about how to escape the rigid boundaries that systems impose on your thinking. To do that you have to use the creative part of your mind to integrate many elements from your life. In Chapter 10, we talked about how to create boundaries of your own so that, in effect, your systems have to adjust to *you*.

We describe systems as relatively open or closed. All systems are rule-bound. All systems accept some new information and reject other new information. If a system were completely closed, it would die sooner or later because it can't change. If a system were completely open, it wouldn't really be a system, it would be a constantly shifting bunch of people doing their own thing.

A *relatively closed* system rejects *most* new information and new ideas. "This is the way we do things here and if you don't like it, there's the door." The positive value of this kind of system is that it feels safe and comfortable. If the rules basically work in a wide variety of changing circumstances, a closed system can actually survive better in circumstances that kill more open systems. The Catholic Church is a good example of the positive value in keeping a system relatively closed. It has not only survived for centuries but continues to grow and develop. It has done so by developing a clear dogma and insisting that the church should hang on to it.

A *relatively open* system readily accepts *most* new information and most new ideas. An open system is more troublesome, not to mention troubling. Very open systems change so fast that it's hard to get your hands on what they are exactly because in two days or five minutes, something significant will be different. It's a constantly growing, developing, changing environment. Obviously, this is a kind of system that can react quickly to change. It's also the kind of system that encourages risk and creativity.

Most entrepreneurial companies start out as relatively open systems. As they get bigger, the openness of the young company to new ideas and new ways of doing things slowly starts to become more a liability than an asset. At some size and stage of growth, most companies must decide who they are and what their business is and cling to that, letting other visions pass them by. They have to become relatively closed because if they don't, they can't manage being big.

Cisco Systems long ago defined its business. Its path has been constant, straight, and true. The *culture* Cisco has created (it would be more accurate to say *is creating*) is different though—it is highly open and evolving. In some ways, creating this open culture has been necessary to carry out a business plan that involves acquiring new companies at a rapidly increasing rate. In some ways it is necessary because, as Ed Paradise and others have noted, so many of the most experienced people there don't really *have* to work there.

Elizabeth Wolgin is an HR manager in Customer Advocacy. She is also relatively new to the Cisco culture. "Cisco is the train and the Internet is the tracks, and it's going about a hundred miles an hour. People love it here because it's a culture that is fluid and open and responds immediately to change. It's a culture that's composed of the best and brightest people anywhere and it demands absolutely the best you can give.

"What I found most interesting—almost shocking—when I arrived is how open the system is here at Cisco. This is a culture that not only does not reject new ideas from a newcomer out of hand, but also actively solicits new information and new approaches. At first I was continually amazed with how much traction could be generated—and how quickly it could be generated—with a new idea.

"I think the people who end up at Cisco have two overriding characteristics: They want to make a difference to society and to the world in an entrepreneurial environment, and they have an uncompromisable need to feel challenged.

"I think the biggest challenge here is figuring out how to navigate in such an open system. Here they *want* you to make decisions for yourself and come up with new ways of doing things. It is incredibly satisfying. But the culture demands 100% of share of mind. I think what we are working out here is a new way of thinking about work and life—one in which we come up with solutions individual by individual rather than one size fits all.

"It puts the major burden of responsibility on individual people to design the way they want to mesh this 100% culture with the rest of their lives. That's where I see the value of the whole person approach. I think people's experiences in the seminars are deep, spiritual and profound. It's a process and a tool to help you figure out what values, interests and talents fit into this and the next part of your life. It helps you make a deliberate, conscious choice about where you want work in your life, where you want family and where you want your personal life. It helps people stay on this crazy train and love it and also not leave their families and personal selves behind. I see it as a way for people to come up with individual work/life solutions that are more innovative and creative."

MERGING CULTURES

Greg Akers is Vice President of Technical Support at Cisco. In the seven years he's been there, the number of employees has jumped from 1200 to over 32,000. "I was at Cisco when we made our first acquisition. Now we're making them almost monthly. Assimilating all of these new employees has been and continues to be a tremendous challenge. We try to take a positive posture toward the problem—trying to move people into roles with similar duties and titles. But the real problem can be assimilating into a new culture.

"The culture at Cisco is unique in my experience. It's very fast-paced and there are things happening all the time. Our acquisition managers can feel out of place at first. I have found that Whole Person seminars can help with this assimilation process. It gives the new managers a common language and a common ground to work with the other management teams and their approaches."

CHOICE AND CAREER PATHS

Another aspect of the Cisco culture that Greg sees every day is the huge array of choice open to individual contributors. The company has tried to create a culture in which there is a great deal of opportunity to move up. "Cisco likes to help people move into manager's roles if that's what they want to do. The company has grown at such a rapid rate that we are often promoting people to manager's positions who might be too young or inexperienced elsewhere. We like to keep about a 60-40 mix of experienced to relatively young managers. I have found the Whole Person seminars help the inexperienced managers come onto a more even playing field with the more experienced ones.

"I remember one young man in particular. He was doing a good job technically, but he desperately needed to come to grips with himself in the role of manager. He lacked the personal introspection he needed to excel. I suggested he do a Whole Person seminar. This was so successful for him that he actually outgrew his original role very quickly and went into a business development role. I think the seminar was a pivotal experience for him. It allowed him to think about himself in that role and what he could aspire to."

MOTIVATION

"People who have been at Cisco a long time—meaning more than a few years—at some point realize that they no longer have to work for financial stability. They start asking themselves, Why are they doing what they do? What's going to motivate and drive them? What will capture their interest? How will they continue to grow in the future? They need to think about the next 10, 15, or even 20 years. Not how are they going to achieve financial gain, but how will they make a difference. How will they get to do something exciting to them?

"I think this is a good use for the program. The introspection and insight gained through the seminars can help people come up with longer term goals. They can come to grips with change and create a plan that carries them into the future. Maybe they can go to different roles, maybe go back to school. The point is, that it gives people a chance and a structure to think about what they really want from their jobs at Cisco. I think that helps them and helps Cisco."

TEAMS

"One use for the Whole Person seminars that I have seen be quite helpful is with teams. When a team goes through the program together, it gives them a common, shared experience. This camaraderie and interaction is extremely valuable. It helps build a level of trust and approachability that improves communication.

"On one management team, for instance, there was a fairly new leader. He had great tactical and implementation skills, but had a harder time communicating his vision to his new team. When the team went through the program together, this type of communication improved tremendously."

CISCO CULTURE

"At Cisco we talk a lot about maintaining an entrepreneurial spirit and culture. To me, what this means is that we empower people. We encourage people to take risks—not only for the fruits of success, but also for the learning that happens whether one is successful or not. We give people a lot of choices. We want to give people the ability to come to themselves—what is it that I want to do and how do I go about doing that?

"If someone comes to me and says, 'I have this talent and this is what I would like to accomplish with it,' then what I want to do is help them develop it, especially if they are looking at themselves with a full perspective.

"At Cisco, motivation is different. People are motivated more by what they can do and the input they can have than by only money as in other environments. I like it when people can find something they want to do and can commit themselves to doing it. I think this culture gives people the opportunity to go into new areas and do things that are creative and unique.

"You can think of a traditional business as like an ocean liner. If you want to change, it takes a lot of effort, because you have to shift that entire huge mass at once. I see the Cisco culture as much more like a lot of rubber boats in fast moving rapids—each with a team. They can shift and turn and respond instantly to change. There are always boats out scouting the next rapid.

"We are not on a pre-prepared road here. We are building the road.

We of the senior management team are very interested in preserving this culture we've created here, no matter how big we get."

There is really no reason that getting big means getting staid and stodgy. The remarkable freedom and self-determination that Cisco has created for its employees has resulted in a culture that can react instantly to change and focus incredible amounts of talent on a problem. This is a culture that depends on people making decisions for themselves and taking strategic charge of their own careers. By learning how they work best, how to integrate best with the contributions of others, and by learning to broaden the sense of what is important to them to be more inclusive and more balanced, the individuals that make up this new culture can master the challenges of a new workplace and make it work in their lives.

The next chapter shows how people use their Personal Visions at different career Turning Points throughout their careers to make their lives more satisfying and productive. The more information you have about yourself and the more integrative work you do at any Turning Point, the better you set yourself up for future Turning Points.

PEOPLE
ALMOST ALWAYS HAVE
MANY MORE **Choices** IN LIFE
AFTER
THEY **Create** A **Personal Vision**
THAN BEFORE.
WHY?
IS IT BECAUSE PERSONAL VISIONS
Create MORE **Options?**
NO, ALL THE OPTIONS WERE
ALWAYS THERE.
RATHER, PERSONAL VISIONS
HELP THEM **Focus** ON WHAT
THEY **Really Want.** WHEN YOU
Know What You Are After,
YOU CAN ALMOST
Always
Find
It.

Personal Vision
As A
GUIDE FOR LIFE

Your Personal Vision is a way to see into the future and link yourself to a future that makes sense to you. It points the way, it works as a template for making decisions, and it draws you forward. One of the primary characteristics of happy, productive, successful people is that they *see themselves in a future that feels positive and attainable.*

The opposite is also true. A defining characteristic of people experiencing stress, anger, depression, boredom, ennui and burnout is that they do *not* see themselves in a future that feels positive. Any positive future they see feels like it's too distant or too difficult to attain. They don't like the way things are going, and they don't see things changing. They are caught in the Stress Cycle.

When people don't have Personal Visions they confuse their systems' goals and interests with their own goals and interests. The goals they seek are actually their systems' goals. They move toward a future that is not really their own, but their systems'.

Some Thoughts about Personal Vision

The more objectively connected your Personal Vision is to yourself, the better it can guide your career. Your Personal Vision must come from *inside* to be effective; no one can hand it to you. If you don't follow a *structure* to create your Personal Vision, you run the risk of leaving out key aspects of your life that may prove critically important later. You also run the risk of viewing yourself and your options through the distorting lens of your systems. The more solidly and objectively your Personal Vision grounds you in your present life, the more surely it moves you into the future.

No matter how accurate the Personal Vision you create now, change will occur. Our lives all move in regular cycles from Turning Point to periods of stability to Turning Point. No matter how satisfied we have been with a career, there are times when we long for change. No matter how dissatisfied and unhappy we are during periods of stability, we continue along the same path without changing—until we arrive at another Turning Point.

Work you do to create a complete and viable Personal Vision not only helps you at the present Turning Point, it also continues to help you at future Turning Points. Opening options at one Turning Point can give you more options at the next, just as shutting down options at a Turning Point can easily limit your options later.

As we move through our lives and careers, each Turning Point builds on the strengths and weaknesses of the process we used at the last one. Knowledge about your abilities, skills, interests, personality, values, goals and family of origin, as well as ideas and answers for putting them together, help you every time you face a decision. If you make career choices enlightened by a clear Personal Vision, these decisions can help you grow and experience your life more fully. When you get to the next Turning Point, you not only have a useful structure for figuring that one out, but you also have several years of fuller, more successful, more enthusiastic experience under your belt from which to draw.

If, when faced with change, you ignore increasingly negative feelings, you can certainly survive Turning Points intact. But you will not have found out any more about yourself. You will have missed one of the most powerful opportunities in life to figure out who you really are and what you really want.

The same can be said of unconsidered, radical or catastrophic change at Turning Points. This ostensibly sudden change only occurs after years of unrecognized and unexpressed unhappiness. The results of catastrophic change usually mirror closely results of doing nothing at Turning Points. Great sweeping changes throw away many advantages of long experience. Starting over from scratch means that you spend your time and creative energy getting back to the point at which you started, rather than exploring new territory. No real learning takes place. And an opportunity to figure out what could really feel productive and satisfying and create more meaning in your life goes to waste.

When people limit their options at Turning Points, it becomes more and more difficult to open new options later in life. Not because options aren't available, but because it becomes increasingly difficult to see anything outside of the Stress Cycle.

Creating the Balance Cycle

The nature of humans and systems is such that balance doesn't just happen. We have to create it consciously. We learn how to fashion our lives from our parents. Obviously, if our parents live stressfully, we learn to live stressfully, too. Any life outside the Stress Cycle would seem unnatural.

But what about parents who *do* balance work and family, productivity and connectedness—parents who grow and change throughout their lives, adapting effectively to changes in their environments and in themselves? This example is incalculably valuable for the child who is to become an adult. Parents like this have held steadfastly to an *interior* sense of themselves and what they want and consistently held this interior sense of self as more important than the self their systems see.

The children of these parents learn to create an interior sense of self, too. They also learn that this interior sense is more important than the self the system sees. But these children will need to be just as active in creating and retaining a Personal Vision as their parents were. They will have to move purposefully into the Balance Cycle—it won't just *happen* for them any more than it did for their parents.

Children in such families learn that they are not one person now and forever. Rather, our True Selves constantly learn, grow and change. Our systems, including our schools, colleges, corporations, and families, seize on *one* view of us—usually a fairly simple, one-dimensional view—and maintain that view through all manner of evidence that the person has changed and grown.

We must constantly assert our own view of ourselves, based on an interior understanding of who we are and what we want out of our lives. If we don't, our systems define us, and our systems determine our goals. And our systems suck us inevitably into the Stress Cycle.

The tool for creating the Balance Cycle is a Personal Vision. Derived from a close objective and subjective structure for understanding yourself, a Personal Vision gives you solid ground to stand upon, a secure fulcrum to help you move your life, and a way to be sure it is *your* life you are living, not someone else's. As parents, we can give our children tools by our examples to help them understand themselves and separate their True Selves from System Selves, but *they* must step out in their lives and create their own Balance Cycles for themselves. No one can do it for them. Their lives will be different from ours. The Balance Cycle they create will of necessity be a different one than we created for ourselves. The underlying certainty, though, is that the more and sooner we create balance in *our* lives and understand *ourselves*, the more powerful are the tools our children will have to do the same in their lives. Any option we open for ourselves automatically becomes a possibility for our children.

Personal Vision Through the Cycle of Adult Development

"Change is the only certainty." This wisdom comes to us from the past, but its lesson often eludes us. In any case, the cycle of adult development regularly alternates between change and stability.

Just as we must of necessity continually create and recreate the Balance Cycle for ourselves if we are to live in it, so must we periodically reassess our Personal Visions throughout our lives. A Personal Vision we create at age 17 before leaving for college can include certain areas of knowledge, like abilities, which don't change through our working lives. But a 17-year-old cannot create a Personal Vision that will work for a 25-year-old or a 30-year-old. The areas of experience that the 17-year-old cannot know are too many and too vast. Having a Personal Vision does not exempt us from the cycles of change; it just gives us a method for handling change more effectively.

We tend to make major changes in our lives and careers approximately every 20 years, starting in our early twenties. We tend to make minor changes and adjustments at the 10-year points. As noted by Gail Sheehy, Daniel Levinson and others, women may delay a mid-life change comparable to men's Mid-Life Transition for 10 years or so, effectively delaying the kind of change associated with mid-life until their fifties. However, we can usually look at our life spans as a series of 20-year cycles, with mid-point assessments and adjustments.

The jump from the security, structure and dependence on our families of origin to the way station of college and into independence in the work world is one of the largest we ever make. But the forces of change at mid-life are almost as great. Many people at mid-life literally set about recreating their careers from scratch, and many more wish they could. At the Mid-Life Transition, men and women have some advantages that younger people don't have. They know a lot more about themselves for one thing. People at mid-life also have a huge wealth of experience to draw upon, and they are often socially and financially more stable. On the other hand, people at mid-life often feel trapped by these same factors. They feel they shouldn't just throw away all the experience and stability they spent twenty or more years building.

At the Pre-Retirement Transition, we are once again faced with creating new lives. The lessons of the Mid-Life Transition continue to be important here. This Turning Point is just as inevitable as any other in our lives, and yet many people pretend it's just not going to happen. They think that if they have enough money saved up, that's all they need to consider.

As a general rule, the more gradual and continuous, as opposed to sudden and catastrophic, the change in your life, the better you will come out in the end. This is true even of great change such as the shift from being a student to being in the work world, or the shift from work to retirement. If a young person's first job after college builds naturally out of college courses, internships and work experience in college, chances for success and satisfaction increase dramatically. At the Mid-Life Transition, if changes build naturally out of interests, plans, experiences and values of the thirties, then you are no longer dealing with a *crisis*; you are dealing with a natural time of transition and change. Plans for retirement can build out of relationships, interests and activities already in place long before actual retirement. Retirement can be an opportunity to express passions and values or play out major themes in one's life, but in a different way or in a different venue. *Continuity* in life helps lend it substance and meaning.

The Senior Transition is yet another inevitable focal point of re-creation. As the balance of your life shifts gradually from *doing* to *being*, the sense that you have focused on themes that are important to you enriches your moment-to-moment existence.

A Personal Vision in Your Present Career

Most people who do the work of creating a Personal Vision and making it real find many good reasons for having chosen the career path they did. For most people, significant parts of their careers fit them well. As we have seen, when people start out in careers, their roles may initially fit well. As people progress in their careers, however, changes in themselves and rigidity in systems cause this fit to deteriorate. Feelings of stress, anger, boredom and lack of meaning follow. But regardless of the strength of these negative feelings about their present careers, a relatively small change in what they are doing or how they go about their careers can often make a disproportionate difference in how they feel. A highly focused 10 percent shift in work roles—adding something new that you find meaningful or interesting or letting go of something you find tedious or difficult—can make a 100 percent difference in feelings.

Moving from the Stress Cycle to the Balance Cycle does not usually or even ideally mean that you have to shake up your life violently. Carefully assessing and integrating all of the important aspects of your life to arrive at a Personal Vision and using your Personal Vision to make *focused and considered* changes leads much more directly to balance. Unless you have done the work to create a Personal Vision, it is next to impossible to know exactly what to change to direct you toward balance.

Failing to create a Personal Vision leaves you vulnerable. Without a Personal Vision, over time your various systems will almost certainly pull you into the Stress Cycle. When you arrive at Turning Points without a Personal Vision, you are highly susceptible to the two Big Mistakes: doing nothing, or making sudden, catastrophic and ill-considered moves that turn your life upside down. Both of the Big Mistakes lead to notoriously unsatisfactory outcomes. Having a Personal Vision gives you a tool of incalculable value to use now and in the future when you navigate change.

Let us look at those Turning Points at which we construct or reconstruct whole careers to see how Personal Vision impacts them.

A Personal Vision to Create a New Career

Young people must often choose a direction and begin their careers with very little information to go on. Considering that this is one of the most significant decisions anyone makes, it is surprising how little attention schools, colleges, corporations or the young people themselves pay to it.

Research has shown clearly that young people who have a positive vision for themselves in an attainable future are more likely to complete college on time and less likely to drop out or transfer. They make better grades, get more out of their college experiences, and feel happier, more satisfied and more enthusiastic about college. Later, they get better jobs that are more related to the work they did in college.

A Personal Vision begun in high school can frame and define a student's college experience. By figuring out what areas to explore in college—not an answer pulled out of a hat, but a real answer created and discovered *within*—students can know with a great deal more certainty what courses to take, what jobs and organizations to pursue on campus, which professors to contact, and what internships or summer jobs to attempt. Think of the experience of 18-year-olds who arrive on campus with no idea of what they will do or what they want to accomplish in school—and our research indicates that this is the majority. Taking one course after another with no idea how this work could relate to their lives, forced to declare majors for more or less random reasons, or

feeling compelled to decide upon a career such as medicine with virtually no knowledge of what that involves, it's no surprise that the majority do not finish in four years. The wonder is that any finish at all.

These students are all victims of the Lemming Conspiracy. Unless
they work purposefully to create a Personal Vision, they will continue
to be victims throughout their lives and eventually add their lives to
the statistics concerning stress, burnout and boredom.

The rare student who has a plan—one carefully constructed from
self-discovery and from first-hand experience of life—stands out from
this common herd. More focused, more sure, more confident, able to
benefit fully from what college offers, these students appear to cut
through life more easily than most. Perhaps by accident or family
encouragement, they have created something like a Personal Vision;
they have just done the work. But *this does not have to be an accident*.
Anyone can create a Personal Vision. And a Personal Vision can transform anyone's life.

Personal Vision At Midlife and Retirement

To some extent, we create new careers every 20 years. The 41-year-
old at mid-life is in just as much a quandary about what to do as the
20-year-old college student or the 62-year-old facing retirement. At
these major bends in our life streams, we need some connection to the
territory ahead. We need a vision that connects ourselves as we are now
to a future that makes sense. This is the job of a Personal Vision. There
is no short cut. The process for creating a Personal Vision merely helps
it emerge and helps make it useful to you.

One of the most interesting aspects of Personal Vision is its use to
corporations. The next section describes how corporations can use the
idea of the whole person to create more human—and more profitable—organizations.

Personal Vision in the Workplace

Stress pervades most people's working days. The higher you go, the
more stress takes its toll. The workplace does not usually encourage
families to thrive, nourish values or produce people who live full lives.

Employees grow and change. They arrive at Turning Points and
want more meaning. It is no accident that executive derailments,

transfers and loss almost invariably happen at Turning Points. Corporations cannot provide Personal Visions for employees, but they can provide conditions in which employees can create their own.

As we have seen, some businesses are beginning to see the interests of their employees as being in some ways the same as the bottom-line interests of the business itself. In all cases, though, the responsibility for living a fulfilling and satisfying life rests with the employee, not the corporation. Recently, however, some researchers have documented that there is a strong and replicable connection between satisfied customers and satisfied employees. Businesses have found that by retaining more key employees, they also retain more of the vital relationships between the business and its customers. Even small increases in customer retention translates to very large percentage gains in profitability and business health.

Investors pay attention to these connections. It has become apparent that satisfied employees mean increased efficiency and profitability, and this fact has assumed greater importance in investment decisions.

So what makes an employee fulfilled and satisfied? Money? Prestige? Power? *None* of these aspects of work makes it into even the top seven factors that influence employee satisfaction and retention. The key to retaining key employees? Balance and meaning.

People want to have whole lives. They want families and communities, and they want to feel productive and useful out in the world. When they don't have this balance and don't see any prospect for attaining it, they hit Turning Points and leave. Or they hit Turning Points and become less involved in work, or less satisfied with it.

Companies can't dictate whole lives. There is no set of commandments they can lay down, no matter how liberal or enlightened, to insure that employees achieve balance. It is only individual people who can examine their own lives and decide what they want to do.

Companies can help. In the rare cases in which companies actively encourage employees to do the work of creating Personal Visions, effectiveness, efficiency and profitability increase.

This also creates the new corporation. The new corporation does not work through the traditional totalitarian hierarchy.

In the traditional hierarchy, responsibility resides at the top. Orders and direction pass down the pyramid to the bottom. In this paternal model, if you keep your nose clean and do as you're told, you don't have anything to worry about. Daddy will do the thinking, and Daddy will take care of you.

The old model of corporation produced massive inefficiency, abuse and excess. In this model, the executive at the top—the one making all the decisions and taking all the responsibility—could and should make tens of millions of dollars while at the same time closing plants and laying off workers because of lack of profitability.

The new corporation is more efficient. It engages in a dialogue with the employee. The corporation says, in effect, "This is what I need you to do, and this is what I'm willing to pay for that service." The employee says, "This is who I am, and this is what I can do well and in a way satisfying to me, and this is what I am willing to do." The new element is *choice*, an element so powerful and effective that it transforms the corporation. What choice creates is the difference between someone who comes to work and just does a job and someone who *likes* to go to work because it creates *meaning* in life. "My work expresses who I am."

The Lemming Conspiracy And Leading A True Life

The positive power of systems makes civilizations possible. All of the advances in culture, comfort, productivity, security, longevity and health that civilization delivers were made available to us all through systems. However, individuals do not *live* in systems. They exist. They play a role. They provide a function. The real life of a person happens individually on the inside.

Creativity, energy, passion, wit and life are only expressed by individuals. The more we can express these parts of ourselves, the more fully human we become. We do not see the choice as either/or: "Either you express your true self, or you exist as an automaton of the system." Like most black-and-white statements, this is not a true choice.

It is possible to express a True Self *and* to fulfill your function as a member of systems. The difficult part is attending to the whole person. That is what we created the process in this book to do. Once you have delineated that True Self and figured out a Personal Vision to express it, it becomes entirely possible to find a place for that Personal Vision in systems. People almost always have many more choices in life *after* they create a Personal Vision than before. Why? Is it because Personal Visions create more options? No, all the options were always there.

Rather, Personal Visions help them focus on what they really want. When you know what you are after, you can almost always find it.

The Lemming Conspiracy keeps you from seeing yourself, and it keeps you from seeing the true options for your life. By keeping you focused on a System Self, believing that *this* is all there is, the Lemming Conspiracy limits you and causes you to waste your true talent. A Personal Vision is a way to find and express your True Self and fully use the talents you were born with. Once you can communicate your Personal Vision to others you have the option—the real choice— of expressing your True Self every day in the life you lead.

"I have learned this, at least, by my experiments; that if one advances confidently in the direction of his dreams, and endeavors to live the life he has imagined, he will meet with a success unexpected in common hours."

Henry David Thoreau, WALDEN

FURTHER READING

This book was not written to be a technical reference. However, readers who wish to pursue some of the subjects of this book are referred to the following excellent resources.

Amabile, T. M. *The Social Psychology of Creativity*. New York: Springer-Verlag, 1983. Excellent summary of research on creativity.

Bertalanffy, Ludwig Von. *General System Theory: Foundations, Development, Application*. New York: George Braziller, 1976. Highly theoretical treatment of the general properties and workings of any system.

Bowen, Murray. *Family Therapy in General Practice*. New York: Aronson, 1978. Readers are referred specifically to Chapters 20, 21, and 22 for an excellent general treatment of differentiation from the family of origin.

Caine, R. N., and Caine, G. *Making Connections: Teaching and the Human Brain*. Alexandria, Va.: Association for Supervision and Curriculum Development, 1991. Practical treatment of goals and behavior showing how internally motivated goals provide much more power for learning and behavior.

Campbell, Joseph. *The Hero with a Thousand Faces*. Princeton: Bollingen, 1949. Description of the process of change.

Covey, Stephen R. *The Seven Habits of Highly Effective People*. New York: Simon and Schuster, 1990. The classic work on values and their impact at work.

Csikszentmihalyi, Mihaly. *Flow: The Psychology of Optimal Experience*. New York: HarperCollins, 1990. A readable treatment of what it means to live a life expressive of one's True Self.

Erikson, Erik. *Childhood and Society*. New York: Norton, 1964 (reissued, 1993). One of the first works to propose stages of development beyond childhood.

Eysenck, H. J., and Eysenck, M. W. *Personality and Individual Differences: A Natural Science Approach*. New York: Plenum, 1985. A classic work on personality research and theory.

Gall, John. *Systemantics: How Systems Work and How They Fail*. Ann Arbor, Mich.: General Systemantics Press, 1986. A highly readable description of the workings of human systems.

Gardner, Howard. *Frames of Mind: The Theory of Multiple Intelligences*. New York: Basic Books, 1983. Theoretical treatment of abilities as opposed to traditional ideas about general intelligence.

Gawain, S. *Creative Visualization*. Berkeley, Calif.: New World Library, 1978. An excellent explanation of creativity.

Gazzaniga, M. S. *The Social Brain*. New York: Basic Books, 1985. A scientific examination of goal-setting and behavior.

Koestler, Arthur. *The Act of Creation*. New York: Macmillan, 1964. An excellent treatment of the *process* of creativity.

Levinson, Daniel J. *The Seasons of a Man's Life*. New York: Alfred A. Knopf, 1978.

———, with Judy D. Levinson. *The Seasons Of A Woman's Life*. New York: Alfred A. Knopf, 1996. Pioneering research on adult life span. Ground-breaking observations on the regularity of adult developmental stages.

Lowman, Rodney L. *The Clinical Practice of Career Assessment*. Washington, D.C.: American Psychological Association, 1991. Describes the state of research with regard to abilities, interests and personality.

McCrae, R. M., and Costa, P. T. *Personality in Adulthood*. New York: Guilford Press, 1990. Offers a five-factor theory of personality, considered the most complete treatment.

Sheehy, Gail. *Passages*. New York: Dutton, 1976.

——. *New Passages*. New York: Random House, 1995. Highly accessible works describing adult development through the life span.

Sternberg, R. J. *The Triarchic Mind: A New Theory of Human Intelligence*. New York: Viking, 1988. Another presentation of the idea of human abilities as opposed to general intelligence.

READINGS ON PERSONAL VISION

Campbell, Angus. *The Sense of Well-Being in America*. New York: McGraw-Hill, 1981.

Cousins, N. *Head First: The Biology of Hope*. New York: Dutton, 1989.

McClelland, David C. "Achievement Motivation Can Be Developed." *Harvard Business Review*, November, 1965.

Myers, David. *The Pursuit of Happiness*. New York: Avon, 1992.

Petri, H. L. *Motivation*. Belmont, Calif.: Wadsworth, 1991.

Seligman, Martin E. P. *Learned Optimism*. New York: Knopf, 1991.

Strack, Fritz, Michael Argyle, and Norbert Schwarz, eds. *Subjective Well-Being: An Interdisciplinary Perspective*. Oxford, England: Pergamon Press, 1990.

Super, Donald. *The Psychology of Careers*. New York: Harper, 1957.

——. *Career Development: Self-Concept Theory*. Princeton, N.J.: College Board, 1963.

——, ed. *Life Roles, Values, and Careers.* New York: Jossey Bass, 1995.

READINGS ON CORPORATIONS AND CORPORATE USES OF DEVELOPMENT

Buckingham, Marcus and Coffman, Curt. *First, Break All The Rules.* New York: Simon & Schuster, 1999.

Cloud, Henry and Townsend, John. *Boundaries.* Grand Rapids: Zondervan, 1992.

Drucker, Peter F. *Management Challenges for the 21st Century.* New York: HarperCollins, 1999.

——, *The Effective Executive.* New York: HarperBusiness, 1993.

Gubman, Edward L. *The Talent Solution.* New York: McGraw-Hill, 1998.

Heskett, Sasser and Schlesinger. *The Service Profit Chain.* New York: Free Press, 1997.

Kaplan, Robert S. and Norton, David P. *The Balanced Scorecard.* Boston: Harvard Business School Press, 1996.

Kotter, John P. *Leading Change.* Boston: Harvard Business School Press, 1996.

Pfeffer, Jeffrey. *The Human Equation.* Boston: Harvard Business School Press, 1998.

Stafford, Tim. "The Business of the Kingdom." Interview with Peter Drucker in *Christianity Today*, November 15, 1999.

A ROCK PILE
CEASES TO BE
A ROCK PILE
THE MOMENT A SINGLE MAN
CONTEMPLATES IT,
BEARING WITHIN HIM,
THE
IMAGE
OF
A
CATHEDRAL.

Saint-Exupery,
Flight To Arras

ALL
OF
A MAN'S TROUBLES
STEM
FROM
HIS INABILITY
TO
SIT
QUIETLY
IN
A ROOM.

Pascal

WHY WE WROTE THIS BOOK—
about the authors

The story of The Highlands Program, the company we created, and our own personal stories are inextricably bound up with each other. We created the company to help people grow and change into roles that fit better and that they would find more fulfilling. But we also created it because we were both at transition points in our own careers and we wanted to grow and change and feel more fulfilled ourselves.

This book is about change and how to learn to live more authentic and balanced lives. One of the basic ideas of this book is that you never find the final answer to your life, but by consciously working on it, you can come closer and closer to balance and meaning. Our own lives are certainly examples of this idea.

We met for the first time as young men in the Army. We were almost exactly the same age, had both grown up in Atlanta, Georgia, and were both Russian linguists. We had each dropped out of college at age twenty-one and joined the Army at the height of the Vietnam War. The reason we dropped out was clear: Neither one of us could figure out what to do with our lives. The Army in Germany in the late 60s and early 70s was a good place and time to think about things.

What connected us then was what has continued to connect us through our friendship of some thirty years. We share a reflective turn of mind and a bullheaded belief that with persistence and effort you can overcome most obstacles—whether external or internal. This belief has been affirmed by our experiences with The Highlands Program. It has been sorely challenged by our personal lives and marriages.

COLLEGE—AND BEYOND

When we left the Army, we both immediately sought to finish our college degrees—at Emory University. At this time—the second Turning Point, college to the work world—neither of us really knew what we wanted to do. Our vision was vague and somewhat typical of young men our age. We thought we might want to teach—Russian seemed like a good option. Bob thought there was probably a way to improve teaching; Don felt that there were good ideas already out there, if we could just make use of them.

We continued discussion on this topic over several months. It is interesting now to look back on this time, because we were struggling toward The Whole Person Technology®, without knowing it. We attacked the problem of what to do with our lives from many different perspectives: What kind of lifestyle did we want? What were our goals in life? What would we enjoy doing? What would we be good at doing? What would feel valuable and worthwhile to do? What about families? We talked to teachers and administrators. In all our talk, one fact became clear. We couldn't quite see ourselves as educators.

Our talents could not be more different. Our approaches to problems are poles apart. Even our approach to staff and leadership is markedly different. Rather than a hindrance, however, this helps us at every turn because we each know and respect the talents of the other.

One day we were walking around the track at Emory, our talk circling back as usual on our lives ahead. Suddenly inspiration struck. Clinical psychology. It seemed like a perfect integration of interests, values, goals, personality and even family background. We talked to psychologists. We got information about graduate schools. Everything we found out was exciting.

The missing element was natural talent. This became totally clear to both of us when we took an introductory psychology course. Bob sat in the lectures and never took notes. Yet he could readily and consistently answer the professor's questions. Don struggled through the text and struggled with the tests and never really got his arms around the material.

Bob rocketed through Emory as a psychology major and then went to graduate school, finishing his coursework and dissertation in three years. Don finished Emory with a degree in Russian language and literature. He had gone back to the idea of teaching and had even accepted a job teaching Russian at a local prep school.

This is another point in the story at which lightning struck. Don's brother in law started a magazine, and wanted Don to help get it started. He decided not to take the teaching job and to help get the magazine launched instead.

At first glance, it might seem like a dizzying leap of faith to jump from Russian literature and a teaching job in hand to selling and running a brand new magazine that no one ever heard of. In fact, it wasn't that big a stretch. Don's father sold insurance and ran his own insurance office. Without knowing it, Don had learned to sell in the family where he grew up. More importantly, he had learned how to get other people to trust him and become enthusiastic about his ideas. He eventually became the publisher of the magazine. It was here that his tremendous natural talents for persuasion and design took hold and began to grow.

Bob's sudden insight about psychology—after years of casting around for a direction in life—was no accident either. His family on both sides had produced helping professionals back to his grandparents. We were both launched into the first phase of our careers by age 25. Exactly on schedule.

LAUNCHED INTO CAREERS

By age 32, Don had quit the magazine and started an advertising agency—an even better fit for his natural talents. Bob had earned his Ph.D. and launched a practice of psychology. He and his wife decided to have a baby. Again on schedule, we both made significant career and life decisions at the Age-30 Assessment. For about the next ten years, we saw less and less of each other.

Don led an increasingly high-powered life as an advertising executive. Pressure, stress, travel and long hours planning pitches took their toll on his personal life and his marriages. Bob launched a very successful private practice in psychology that required much of his energy and creative talent. What energy he had left he threw into his relationship with his children. His marriage gradually grew more distant.

Both of us did well in our separate careers, but by the time we reached 40, we both wanted something different. Quite independently, we both decided to quit our successful jobs. Don sold his ad agency. Bob went on sabbatical from his private practice. These decisions were finalized within a month of each other, even though we had not talked for over a year.

THE HIGHLANDS PROGRAM

It was here that we began talking about The Highlands Program. We were both at Mid Life. Both healthy. Both well enough off financially. And both wanted to do something we felt was worthwhile. Don had had an idea—and had done some research—that it would be good to create a program to help people figure out what to do with their lives. His original thought was that if you could help people when they were in college or just getting ready to graduate, it would benefit them for their whole lives. Bob knew immediately that there was a need in the market for a service like Don described, but not just for college students. He knew from his practice that people deal with this issue at several distinct points in their careers and that the question is never fully resolved. We two were a case in point, of course.

Over the next few months, our discussions about the idea evolved from concept to active research. We started to envision what the business would look like and what the actual service would be that we would offer. After two years of research that involved personally experiencing every program, test, process, and training we could find, Bob sat down at his computer and spent most of a summer writing the program that would become The Whole Person Technology®. We launched The Highlands Program in the fall of 1992. We were both 45.

From the very first seminars we ran, our clients loved the program. They described it as a life-changing event. The Highlands Program wasn't something that people did and forgot about. They couldn't stop talking about how much it helped them. We thought that business success was just around the corner.

Our business partnership, apart from our friendship, has proven a powerful and valuable asset. Our talents could not be more different. Our approaches to problems are poles apart. Even our approach to staff and leadership is markedly different. Rather than a hindrance, however, this helps us at every turn, because we each know and respect the talents of the other. Don has an intuitive, action-oriented style, while Bob is more methodical and careful in his thinking. Don wants to try out idea after idea; Bob wants to work an idea through to get to a conclusion. Neither of us is right or wrong. At different times, the company has benefited hugely from both.

Growing The Highlands Program has been an exciting, frustrating, soul-rending grind of trying to create a viable business from a good idea. At 53, we feel we are on the edge of finally making The Highlands Program work as a business. Having now personally experienced most of the Lemming Conspiracy and the Stress Cycle and having personally experienced the consequences of not attending to a big enough picture of ourselves—even while creating and running a business designed to help people do just that—we both work pretty hard every single day to create and maintain balance in our own personal lives.

Bob: The thing I am most proud of so far is that I feel I have been a good father to my children. I have tried to give up the hubris that the business will live or die depending on what I do. I am convinced it is completely in the hands of God. I try to stay healthy and have enough time to relax and enjoy simple moments in my life. I feel like I've made every mistake you can make in life from the point of view of balance. But I've tried to learn from that and create something better—hopefully it will help my children by example.

Don: Coming up with the idea for The Highlands Program is my proudest business achievement. It is inexplicably satisfying to realize that every single day someone, somewhere is benefiting from our creation. I am also grateful for what I consider to be divine intervention in my life. I feel spiritually connected; have a wonderful relationship with my wife, Lynda; see my family regularly; and have a circle of friends that sustains me. Connection is everything.

Subscribe To Our New Magazine
It's FREE!

HIGHLANDS – THE FIRST WHOLE PERSON E-ZINE™

H I G H L A N D S, the first Whole Person E-zine™, is now available to you as a reader of this book FREE of charge.

Go to our website (www.highlandsprogram.com) and click on the HIGHLANDS magazine subscription icon right on the home page. After subscribing, you will receive, with our compliments, interesting useful articles and essays from some of the country's most accomplished writers, trainers, consultants and educators. Your e-magazine will arrive automatically every two months. Your subscription also entitles you to future Special Offers, including on-line seminars and courses taught by our contributors.

Our goal is to provide you with the tools you need to achieve what matters to you.

Contact Us

INFORMATION ABOUT THE HIGHLANDS PROGRAM

For more information about The Highlands Program or to order a CD of The Highlands Ability Battery™:

- Visit us on the Internet: www.highlandsprogram.com
- Call our offices: (404) 872-9974 or (877) 872-9974, ext. 31.
- E-mail us: u-succeed@highlandsprogram.com
- Write us: The Highlands Program, Suite 1790, 999 Peachtree Street, Atlanta, GA 30309

SCHEDULE BOB & DON TO SPEAK

To schedule Bob and Don for a speaking engagement e-mail us at speakers@highlandsprogram.com or call (877) 872-9974, ext. 48.

MORE INFORMATION ON SEMINARS

To find out about a Whole Person Technology® seminar in your area, e-mail us at psps@highlandsprogram.com or call (877) 872-9974, ext. 31.

LEARN ABOUT OUR CORPORATE PROGRAMS

To learn more about corporate programs and outcomes, e-mail us at corporateprograms@highlandsprogram.com or call (877) 872-9974, ext. 30.

CARRY OUT A RESEARCH PROJECT

If you are interested in carrying out a corporate outcome research project with The Whole Person Technology®, e-mail us at research@highlandsprogram.com.

PURCHASE THIS BOOK IN BULK

To purchase copies of *Don't Waste Your Talent* in bulk for your company or organization, call Longstreet Press (800) 927-1488, ext. 1035.

The Cost of Living Longer

The Cost of Living Longer

National Health Insurance and the Elderly

Stephen M. Davidson
University of Chicago

Theodore R. Marmor
Yale University

with

Janet D. Perloff
Marsha Spear
Nancy Aitken

Lexington Books
D.C. Heath and Company
Lexington, Massachusetts
Toronto

Library of Congress Cataloging in Publication Data

Davidson, Stephen M
   The cost of living longer.

   Includes index.
   1. Insurance, Health—United States. 2. Aged—Medical care—United
States. 3. Medicare. 4. Medicaid. I. Marmor, Theodore R., joint author.
II. Title.
HD7102.U4D277   368.4'2'00973   79-2756
ISBN 0-669-03242-5

This work was financed in part by Grant No. 90-A-1027 from the
Administration on Aging to the University of Chicago.

Published simultaneously in Canada

Printed in the United States of America

International Standard Book Number: 0-669-03242-5

Library of Congress Catalog Card Number: 79-2756

To the memory of Jerome Hammerman

Contents

List of Figures

List of Tables

Preface

The consideration of the current generation of national health insurance (NHI) proposals began in the early 1970s and continues to the present day. This extended period of study has provided an opportunity, one seldom granted, to plan a major public program thoroughly with the advantage of experience from other relevant programs. Making full use of this opportunity will help policymakers avoid some of the unfortunate surprises that followed the enactment and implementation of Medicare and Medicaid.

This book reports the results of a study of the probable impact of national health insurance on health services for the elderly. The study differed from other studies of NHI in four ways.

1. It focused on a single age group, the elderly, who, because they already rely heavily on public sources to finance needed medical services, have the least obvious benefits to gain from a change in public policy.

2. It was not restricted to national aggregates, even for the elderly, but considered differences that are likely to emerge among the states as a result of the administration of any of the leading alternative proposals.

3. It considered implementation issues of particular relevance to the elderly. Chief among them were those arising from the multiple sources of funding envisioned in several proposals.

4. It ignored money estimates in the consideration of the competing proposals, not because they are unimportant—obviously, they are critical. Rather they were omitted in order to highlight and not to distract from other issues which we believe to be central but which often are overshadowed when forecasting the dollar costs of particular plans is a concern.

Any national health insurance program must take into account the fact that almost all elderly Americans receive medical benefits under Title XVIII (Medicare) or Title XIX (Medicaid) of the Social Security Act. A new program will partially or completely replace these sources of benefits. Logically, then, elderly beneficiaries will find themselves in one of three positions: no change from their situation under current law, an improved position (that is, on balance more benefits and/or lower costs), or a worse position (that is, fewer benefits and/or higher costs). Moreover, depending on the particular arrangements enacted and regardless of their substantive entitlements, elderly Americans may confront additional administrative difficulties, brought about by the necessary relationships among multiple programs. If, for example, an NHI law provided less than the combined benefits available under the current Medicare and state Medicaid programs, and even if Medicaid were eliminated, states would be pressured to supplement the NHI benefits up to the present level. In other words, if the national floor on benefits established by NHI turned out to be lower than that available under some Medicaid programs, state supplemental programs would have to be integrated administratively with NHI.

The principal purpose of this study was to shed light on the issues of both equity and practical administration that will arise for elderly Americans were a national health insurance law to be passed. These issues derive principally from the eligibility criteria as they affect the elderly, the benefit packages incorporated, and the administrative implications of the particular NHI plan. Three major prototypical NHI proposals were analyzed in an attempt to identify the likely consequences for the elderly of the passage of NHI.

The results of the study are presented in six chapters. The first chapter provides an overview of the elderly's need for and utilization of health services. The next three chapters present data that illustrate how Medicare and Medicaid eligibility provisions, benefit structures, and administration affect the ability of older Americans to make use of needed medical services. Chapter 5 describes the several prototypical national health insurance proposals, again concentrating on eligibility and benefit provisions, and administrative implications. And, finally, chapter 6 presents comparisons between the present, as represented by Medicare and Medicaid, and the future that would be likely to result from each of the three proposals. The final chapter also includes our conclusions about the relative ability of the elderly to utilize medical services under each of the four sets of conditions discussed.

It is a pleasure to acknowledge our considerable debt to the staff of the Administration on Aging, who not only gave us the opportunity to undertake this study but also provided considerable encouragement throughout. In particular, we wish to thank Byron Gold, former director of the Office of Research, Demonstrations, and Manpower Resources; Harry Posman, chief of the Division of Research and Analysis; and Frances Jacobs, project officer. We share their hope that the final product presented here proves to be useful to those public officials who must decide the future of national health insurance.

Health Services and the Elderly: Needs and Utilization

Any consideration of health care policy occurs against a background of the need for services and the experience of the population using them. This chapter sets the context for our analyses of Medicare, Medicaid, and three national health insurance plans by providing a brief overview of the health care needs of elderly Americans, including data regarding utilization and expenditures.

Acute and Chronic Conditions

Illnesses can be classified as acute or chronic. Although the line separating these two categories may occasionally seem somewhat blurred, the National Center for Health Statistics (NCHS) has defined acute and chronic conditions in the following way (examples of each are listed in appendix A). An acute condition is a condition that has lasted less than three months and has involved either medical attention or restricted activity. A condition is considered chronic if (1) the condition has lasted more than three months or (2) it is one of the conditions identified as chronic in appendix A, regardless of the date of onset. It should be noted that only chronic conditions that limit activity to some degree are addressed in this report.

As can be seen in figure 1-1, older people are comparatively less often afflicted than the young with conditions classified as acute. These trends do not accurately reflect their relative need for services, however; for while the incidence is less, the associated disability and utilization of services are greater,[1] especially since the elderly usually take longer to recover from illness when it does afflict them.[2]

Data from the NCHS surveys show that, as age increases, the percentages of persons in each succeeding age group with activity limitations due to chronic conditions also rise (see figure 1-2). Among persons under 17 years of age in 1974, about 3.7 percent, or one in twenty-five persons, were reported to have some degree of limitation. In the same year 46 percent of the elderly suffered some degree of limitation in their activities because of chronic conditions and an estimated 17.1 percent of all persons 65 years and older were unable to carry on their major activity (working or keeping house).[3]

As can be seen in figure 1-2, the average aged person is twice as likely as a younger person to suffer from one or more chronic conditions, such as heart

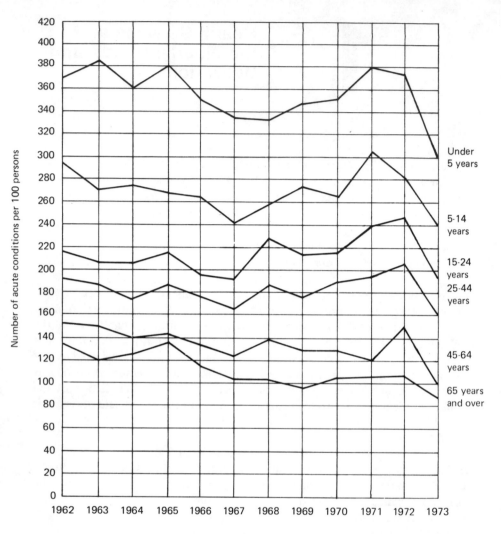

Source: National Center for Health Statistics, Vital and Health Statistics, series 10, #1, 10, 15, 26, 38, 44, 54, 69, 77, 82, 89, 98, 102.

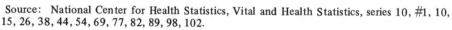

Figure 1-1. Incidence of Acute Conditions by Age, 1962-1973

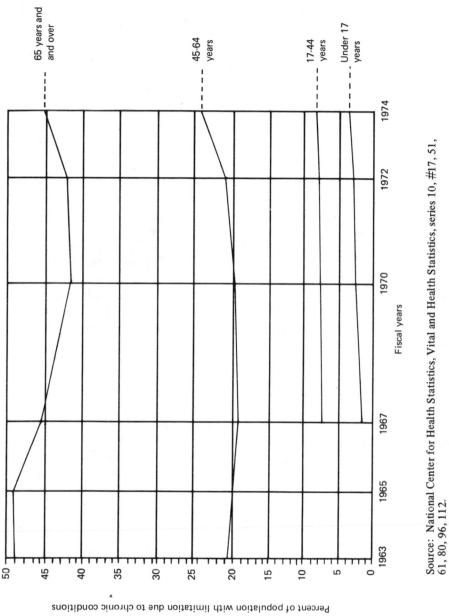

65 years and
and over

45-64
years

17-44
years

Under 17
years

1963 1965 1967 1970 1972 1974

Fiscal years

50 45 40 35 30 25 20 15 10 5 0

Percent of population with limitation due to chronic conditions

Source: National Center for Health Statistics, Vital and Health Statistics, series 10, #17, 51, 61, 80, 96, 112.

Figure 1-2. Percent of Population with Some Degree of Limitation Due to Chronic Conditions by Age for Selected Years

trouble or deafness. He is also much more likely to be limited in activity, to be admitted to hospitals more frequently and for longer stays, and to use physicians' services to a greater extent.[4] Since the over-65 age group is the fastest growing segment of the population, we can expect to see chronic illnesses become an even larger problem in the United States.

Utilization of Health Services

In view of the incidence of illness among the elderly, it is not surprising to learn that they are heavy utilizers of services. A 1977 national survey found that 70 percent of those age 65 and over had seen a physician within the previous six months, almost 13 percent more than for all other people. Moreover, the average person 65 or older had 6.5 physician visits in that year, compared to a mean of 4.6 visits for everyone else.[5] The elderly also have a substantially greater likelihood of being hospitalized and of being in the hospital longer for a spell of illness than others. Eighteen percent of people 65 and over had at least one hospital episode in 1977 compared to only 9.5 percent of all other age groups. Similarly, the elderly had 27.5 discharges per 100 persons, more than three times the rate for everyone else. And, finally, the average length of stay for a hospital episode was 11.1 days for people 65 and older, 4 days longer than that for the under-65 age group.

Institutional services are the most costly and, therefore, are of special concern. For that reason, it is important to know not only that the elderly are heavy users of institutional services but also that, among the elderly, as age increases, so does the proportion of people who are institutionalized. Studies show that 5 percent of all elderly people are in institutions on any given day, mostly in nursing and personal-care homes, and that 16 percent of those age 85 and over are institutionalized.[6] Older people also have more problems with mental illness than the rest of the population. Those over 65 are at least twice as likely to be hospitalized for mental conditions as those 25 to 64 years.[7]

Heavy utilization of medical services, however, depends only in part on the frequency, duration, and type of illness. For example, Shanas pointed out that health-service utilization depends on the organization and staffing of medical-care services, as well as the attitudes and values of those providing the services and of the public in general.[8] Also some people are institutionalized for lack of any other alternative. It is commonly believed, for example, that many people now institutionalized could be cared for at home if well-organized and continuous home health services were available. Atchley found that the institutionalized elderly tend not to have spouses or children and tend to have lived alone. He also found that older people are often able to avoid institutionalization if they have relatives to help in their care and adequate financial resources to draw on.[9] Adding together those who are institutionalized because of lack of home-care services, the bedfast, the housebound, and those who are ambulatory only with difficulty, Shanas calculated that as many as one-fifth of the aged in the United States, or about 4 million older persons, could benefit from some kind of home-care services.[10]

Shanas also found that the individual to whom the average older person would turn for help in a health crisis was a middle-aged woman, either a daughter or other relative, married, and herself the mother of children. Seven of every ten individuals named by older people as sources of aid were women.[11] Yet today's nuclear family often cannot provide someone to care for the sick relative. The size of the nuclear family has been decreasing as the number of persons in the over-65 group has been increasing, which reduces the likelihood that a relative will be available to take care of the elderly person.[12] Also more and more frequently the woman the older person would ordinarily turn to for help is no longer home to care for ill family members. In 1975, 44 percent of the married women in the population were in the labor force, as opposed to only 23 percent in 1950.[13] Finally, increased family mobility has contributed to the inability of adult children to care for elderly family members. Because of these structural changes in the American family, the sick-care function once performed by families has often shifted to care-giving organizations.

In addition, the implementation of Medicare has probably increased hospital utilization by the elderly to some extent. Based on available data, Julian Pettengill noted that a significant redistribution of hospital care has occurred since 1965 between those under age 65 and those 65 and over. For those under 65, days of care and discharges per 1,000 persons declined steadily from 1965 to 1969, while utilization rates of aged persons increased.[14]

Health Care Expenditures

Expenditures are another, less direct, but equally revealing indicator of utilization. In 1977, though the elderly represented only 11 percent of the population, they accounted for 29 percent of personal health-care expenditures.[15] Moreover, per capita expenditures for those 65 and over were $1,745, two and one-half times those for adults 19 to 64 and seven times those for children under age 19 (table 1-1).

To a considerable extent these figures reflect the greater use by the elderly of institutional services noted earlier. Data on the relative distribution of expenditures among the major health-care services confirms this fact. In table 1-2 it can be seen that fully 70 percent of expenditures for the elderly are for institutional care and that the proportion is 20 percent higher than that for the 19 to 64 age group and almost twice as much as for the youngest group.

Table 1-1
Personal Health Care Expenditures, Fiscal Years 1967 and 1977

Fiscal Years	1967 ($)	1977 ($)
Total spent by U.S. for personal health care	41.3 billion	142.6 billion
Average per capita expenditure for persons under 19 years	119	253
Average per capita expenditure for persons 19-64 years	294	661
Average per capita expenditure for persons 65 years and over	681	1,745
Average direct payment by persons under 65	83	164
Average direct payment by persons 65 and over	195	463

Sources: Barbara Cooper and Nancy Worthington, "Medical Care Spending for Three Age Groups, 1966-71," *Social Security Bulletin* 35 (May 1972):14; and Robert M. Gibson and Charles R. Fisher, "Age Differences in Health Care Spending, Fiscal Year 1977," *Social Security Bulletin* (January 1979):3-16.

Even though the elderly account for such large expenditures for health services, they are, on average, poorer than younger people. Sixty percent of the elderly had incomes less than $5,000 in 1970, making them among the least well equipped financially to cope with the financial implications of high medical expenses. Moreover, Gold, Kutza, and Marmor point to an inverse relationship among the elderly themselves between personal income and medical expenses.[16]

Table 1-2
Health Care Expenditures for Three Age Groups, Fiscal Year 1977

	Under Age 19 (%)	Age 19-64 (%)	Age 65 and Over (%)
Inpatient hospital care	35.4	49.3	44.1
Nursing home care	1.9	2.1	25.5
Physician services	27.5	24.1	17.3
Drugs	12.9	8.8	6.9
Other health services	22.3	15.7	6.2

Source: Robert M. Gibson and Charles R. Fisher, "Age Differences in Health Care Spending, Fiscal Year 1977," *Social Security Bulletin* (January 1979):3-16.

That being the case, it is important to consider the sources of payment for those services. In 1977, 67 percent of the bill was paid out of public funds, primarily Medicare and Medicaid, substantially more than for any other age group. Most of the remainder, however, 27 percent of the total, or an average of $613 per person, came directly from the resources of elderly individuals and their families.[17]

Looking only at the major public sources of funds, Medicare, a health insurance program for the elderly established in 1965 as part of the Social Security system, paid 74 percent of the hospital bills and 56 percent of physicians' bills for the elderly, but only 3 percent of the nursing-home expenditures. It is clear from these figures that Medicare leaves uncovered a substantial proportion of expenditures for all services; and further, that it is primarily an acute-care program.[18]

Medicaid, also established under the Social Security Amendments of 1965, is a means-tested program for certain categories of people, including the elderly, whose incomes and resources are low enough for them to qualify. It is financed jointly by state and federal funds and administered by the states. Medicaid covered 17 percent of health care expenditures for the elderly in 1977, but it paid almost 50 percent of the nation's expenditures for long-term-care services.[19]

Conclusion

One of the costs of living longer is the need for large amounts of health services. Medicare pays a major portion of large hospital and medical bills, but leaves much uncovered, especially services in extended-care facilities. Moreover, even with Medicaid, almost half the nursing-home costs are paid directly by the elderly and their families. Undoubtedly the spiraling out-of-pocket expenses that still face the elderly present barriers to utilization of health services.

It is likely that the elderly are not utilizing health services to the extent or of the kind that they probably need, with the possible exception of inpatient hospital care for acute conditions. Hammerman maintained that despite increased social visibility and increased levels of public funding in their behalf, there is ample evidence to indicate that the aged, and particularly the chronically ill and disabled, have not been successful in securing appropriate health services.[20] And, as we have seen, the need is growing.

Notes

1. U.S., Department of Health, Education and Welfare, Public Health Service, National Center for Health Statistics, *Acute Conditions: Incidence and*

Associated Disability: U.S., July 1973-June 1974, series 10, no. 102 (Rockville, Maryland, 1975).

2. Eugene A. Confrey and Marcus S. Caldstein, "The Health Status of Aging People," in *Handbook of Social Gerontology,* ed. Clark Tibbitts (Chicago: University of Chicago Press, 1960), p. 173, as cited in Robert C. Atchley, *The Social Forces in Later Life: An Introduction to Social Gerontology* (Belmont, Calif.: Wadsworth Publishing Co., 1972), p. 114.

3. DHEW, National Center for Health Statistics, "Limitation of Activity Due to Chronic Conditions," *Vital and Health Statistics,* series 10, no. 111 (Hyattsville, Maryland, June 1977).

4. Barbara S. Cooper and Nancy L. Worthington, "Medical Care Spending for Three Age Groups, 1966-71," *Social Security Bulletin* 35 (May 1972):4.

5. DHEW, National Center for Health Statistics, *Current Estimates from the Health Interview Survey: 1977,* series 10, no. 126 (Hyattsville, Maryland, 1978), tables 20 and 21.

6. American Public Health Association, "Home Health Services: Resolution and Position Papers Adopted by the Governing Council of the American Public Health Association," *American Journal of Public Health* 64, no. 2 (February 1974):182; and Atchley, *Social Forces in Later Life,* p. 123.

7. James C. Corman, "Health Services for the Elderly," in *Social Policy, Social Ethics, and the Aging Society,* eds. Bernice L. Neugarten and Robert J. Havighurst (Chicago: University of Chicago, 1976).

8. Ethel Shanas et al., *Old People in Three Industrial Societies* (New York: Atherton Press, 1969), p. 71.

9. Atchley, *Social Forces in Later Life,* p. 123.

10. Ethel Shanas, "Measuring the Home Health Needs of the Aged in Five Countries," *Journal of Gerontology* 26 (1974):39.

11. Ethel Shanas, *The Health of Older People* (Cambridge, Mass.: Harvard University Press, 1962), p. 113.

12. Odin W. Anderson, "Reflections on the Sick Aged and the Helping Systems," in *Social Policy,* eds. Bernice L. Neugarten and Robert J. Havighurst.

13. U.S. Bureau of the Census, *Statistical Abstract of the United States: 1975,* 96th ed. (Washington, D.C., 1975), p. 359.

14. Julian H. Pettengill, "Trends in Hospital Use by the Aged," *Social Security Bulletin* 35 (July 1972):3.

15. Robert M. Gibson and Charles R. Fisher, "Age Differences in Health Care Spending, Fiscal Year 1977," *Social Security Bulletin* 42 no. 1 (January 1979):12.

16. Byron Gold, Elizabeth Kutza, and Theodore R. Marmor, "U.S. Social Policy on Old Age: Present Patterns and Predictions," in *Social Policy,* eds. Bernice L. Neugarten and Robert J. Havighurst.

17. Gibson and Fisher, "Age Differences in Health Care Spending."

18. Ibid.

19. Ibid.

20. Jerome Hammerman, "Health Services: Their Success and Failure in Reaching Older Adults," *American Journal of Public Health* (March 1974):256.

2

Eligibility under Medicare and Medicaid

The nation's elderly benefit more than any other group from public expenditures for medical care. In 1977, Medicare and Medicaid accounted for 61 percent of the $41 billion expended to meet the health needs of the elderly.[1] In spite of the limitations noted in chapter 1, the elderly have increased their use of services throughout the health sector since the introduction of Medicare and Medicaid.[2] Thus over the last decade broad-scale public financing has helped meet the increasing needs of the elderly for health care. Yet problems remain, and new public policy decisions will be taken to try to solve them. Those decisions would benefit from a sound understanding of Medicare and Medicaid. We hope to contribute to the effort with the material presented in this book.

We begin in this chapter by considering how the elderly become eligible for publicly financed health care. Equity issues are examined under two very different programs of public financing, one based on the principles of social insurance and the other on those of public welfare. First, we focus on universal eligibility under Medicare and on recent program changes that have eroded uniform coverage. Then we address the complex and burdensome features of Medicaid eligibility and the problems of vertical and horizontal inequity generated by both administrative and statutory provisions. Finally, we examine joint eligibility under Medicare and Medicaid and the issues connected with state "buy-in" agreements.

Eligibility under Medicare

Title XVIII of the Social Security Act created the Medicare program in 1965 as a federally operated insurance program administered as part of the Social Security contributory system. Eligibility for Medicare generally reflects the program assumption that the services provided are a right, earned by making Social Security contributions throughout one's working life. Most individuals who have earned this right automatically matriculate into the program at age 65, regardless of financial status. Eligibility under Medicare is generally a simple matter, with the designation of beneficiaries based on a universal age criterion.

Hospital Insurance Eligibility

Medicare entitles virtually all persons aged 65 and over to participate in its Hospital Insurance (HI) Program (part A). It is estimated that all but approximately 150,000 of the nation's elderly were included under part A Medicare when the program began. Most were eligible as cash beneficiaries of Social Security or Railroad Retirement programs (the dependents and survivors of such persons were included as well). Others were included under the transitional provisions of Title XVIII. These applied to persons 65 or over who reached age 65 prior to 1968 or became 65 years of age after 1967 with no less than three quarters of Social Security coverage for each year elapsing after 1966 and before the year in which age 65 was attained; for persons who reached age 65 after 1968, the required work credits (quarters of coverage) increased by three quarters each year.[3] Those not included in part A during the early program years were primarily federal employees, who had health insurance protection under the Federal Employees' Health Benefits Program, and aliens.

On July 1, 1966, 19.1 million persons aged 65 and over were enrolled in the Hospital Insurance portion of the Medicare program, and there has been a net yearly increase of 200,000 to 400,000 Medicare enrollees each year thereafter. As of July 1, 1975, 22.5 million persons were entitled to HI benefits.[4] Also as of 1975, fully insured status—that is, having accrued the required number of employed quarters for retired worker benefits—replaced the transitional eligibility provisions as a requirement for obtaining Medicare at age 65. As a result, approximately 1 million persons aged 65 and over are currently not entitled to hospital protection under Medicare. Of these, about one-fourth receive federal civil service retirement benefits.[5]

The Social Security Amendments of 1972 permit aged persons ineligible for part A Medicare, either as cash beneficiaries or under the transitional provisions, to enroll voluntarily in part A Medicare if they also enroll in the Supplementary Medical Insurance (SMI) Program (part B). But there are high monthly individual premiums for voluntary HI—set at $33 a month in 1973 and increased to $69 in 1979—and it seems likely that these costs, which reflect the full actuarial cost of hospital care for a high-risk population, have been a deterrent to participation. This assumption is supported by a comparison of the 15,000 who chose this option and the 318,000 not enrolled in part A who voluntarily purchased part B coverage at a rate less than one-seventh the amount of the HI premium.

Supplementary Medical
Insurance Eligibility

Supplementary Medical Insurance (SMI; part B) is available to all persons over age 65 upon payment of a monthly premium of $8.70. Aged persons entitled to benefits under the hospital insurance program as well as those who do not qualify for HI benefits, (retired federal employees, aliens residing in the United States, and persons not eligible for hospital insurance under the transitional provisions) can participate voluntarily in the SMI program. Of the 19.1 million persons entitled to HI benefits in 1966, 93 percent (17.7 million) enrolled in part B of Medicare.[6] By July 1, 1975, that percentage had risen to 97.4.[7] In addition, of the 1 million elderly excluded from HI coverage in 1975, 318,000 were enrolled in SMI.[8]

To prevent loss or delay of entitlement, the Social Security Amendments of 1972 made the enrollment of persons in SMI automatic as they became eligible for part A Medicare. The premiums of persons receiving Social Security cash benefits, Railroad Retirement, or federal civil service annuities are deducted from their monthly benefit checks. Persons not receiving monthly benefits are billed quarterly for premiums by the Social Security Administration or the Railroad Retirement Board. The aged who are not automatically eligible for HI or SMI coverage are permitted to enroll during initial and general enrollment periods. Initial enrollment is a seven-month period covering the three months prior to and subsequent to the month in which an individual turns age 65. General enrollment periods are annual (January-March), and are intended for individuals who have terminated their coverage and wish to reenroll as well as for those who declined enrollment during their initial enrollment period.

The designation of an aged individual as a "beneficiary" of Medicare is thus dependent on whether the individual has made prior contributions through the Social Security system, has voluntarily chosen to make premium payments, or both. These requirements qualify the individual's entitlement to coverage. Since the abandonment of the transitional provisions, full entitlement has become problematic for many. For persons who fail to meet the employment requirements of the Social Security law, voluntary enrollment is generally prohibited by high premium costs. Those costs are particularly high when coupled with the expense of deductibles and copayments. It appears, then, that for those individuals not eligible for Medicaid, the considerable cost of premiums, deductibles, and copayments serves as a barrier to Medicare coverage.

Eligibility under Medicaid

Medicaid, Title XIX of the Social Security Act, was conceived in 1965 on public welfare principles and these principles underlie the structure of Medicaid eligibility. Characteristically, the program fixes income, resources, and family composition criteria to determine entitlement to medical assistance. In contrast to Medicare's uniform age criterion, the designation of a Medicaid eligible is based on highly complex and variable means tests.

Eligibility under Medicaid is structurally joined to the primary welfare program for the elderly—the Supplemental Security Income (SSI) Program. As illustrated below, much of the variation in eligibility criteria for the elderly which are found in state Medicaid programs can be traced directly to Medicaid's roots in SSI.

Categorically Needy

The Social Security Amendments of 1972 repealed existing provisions of Title I (Aid to the Aged), Title X (Aid to the Blind), Title XIV (Aid to the Permanent and Totally Disabled), and Title XVI (Aid to the Aged, Blind, or Disabled), and added a new Title XVI (Supplemental Security Income). SSI was originally conceived as a federalized replacement for the federal/state programs of aid to the aged, blind, and disabled (OAA, AB, and AD). Implemented in January 1974, the program created a national minimum cash payment standard intended to correct existing state disparities in needs definitions and payment standards. To ensure that there would be no reductions in recipient incomes as a result of the changeover to SSI programs, the law required that the states maintain recipients of OAA, AB, and AD at their December 1973 income levels. In fact, a state's eligibility for Medicaid matching funds was made contingent upon the state's provision of state supplementary payments to achieve this goal.[9] In addition, the states were permitted to make supplements to SSI beyond the required amounts, and they were given full control over the eligibility criteria used to determine the need for these supplements.[10] The implementation of SSI resulted in alterations of Medicaid eligibility criteria for the adult welfare categories. In effect, the creation of a national adult cash-assistance program redefined the basis for establishing Medicaid eligibility among the elderly.

Under the Supplemental Security Income Program, state Medicaid plans are mandated to extend benefit coverage to some class of SSI recipients. This legislative requirement can be met by exercising any one of three options (45 CFR 248.1 [b] [2] [v]):

1. Providing (automatic) Medicaid coverage to all SSI recipients (including persons receiving mandatory state supplements)
2. Extending Medicaid to recipients of both SSI and a state supplementary payment
3. Limiting Medicaid coverage to individuals who meet eligibility standards below the federal SSI level, but not lower than the financial criteria used for medical assistance on January 1, 1972

In the legislative classification of mandatory recipients are also included individuals who (45 CFR 248.1):

1. Were eligible in December 1973 for Medicaid as an "essential spouse" and who continue to live and be essential to the recipient of cash assistance
2. Were eligible in December 1973 as inpatients or residents in medical institutions and would have been, except for inpatient status, eligible to receive cash assistance
3. Were eligible for OAA, AB, APTD, or AFDC in August 1972 and would be

eligible for SSI in the current month except for a 20 percent increase in OASDI payment received in 1972

The choice of options permitted under current legislation has perpetuated earlier variations found in state Medicaid eligibility criteria. As table 2-1 (column 1) illustrates, thirty-five of the fifty Medicaid programs cover all SSI recipients. Arizona has no operating Medicaid program. Fifteen states use eligibility criteria that are more restrictive than the federal SSI standard (called 209B states after the provision of the Social Security Amendments that permit them). In the states that establish Medicaid eligibility at levels lower than the federal standard, all categorically related SSI eligibles must be permitted to "spend down" to a level of eligibility. This provision, which applies only to the five 209B states that do not have medically needy programs (Colorado, Indiana, Mississippi, Missouri, and Ohio), theoretically allows individuals to become eligible for Medicaid when their incomes, less incurred medical expenses, fall below the more restricted standard.

The extent to which the spend-down device is aimed at reducing income to the 1972 eligibility standard is, however, questionable. It is unlikely that many individuals who meet the eligibility criteria of SSI have disposable income beyond the SSI cash-payment level. A review of the Title XIX plans in existing 209B states indicates that restrictions imposed on SSI eligibles are primarily directed toward assets not income. Most of these restrictions focus on resource limitations, such as the transfer of property, the maximum home value, limits on personal property (household goods and personal effects), and automobiles. For example, federal regulations governing SSI eligibility permit individuals to retain $1,500 in personal property, but many of the 209B states place limits on personal property that are at least $500 below that figure. Similarly, the maximum market value of a home is $25,000 under the federal SSI, yet several 209B states establish a market value limit lower than the excluded amount under the federal program.[11]

Tables 2-2 and 2-3 illustrate the states' maximum levels of cash payment to two-person families, living independently. The differences among the payments result from the highly complex and variable state/federal policies governing the administration of mandatory and optional state supplementations. Because of its programmatic links with SSI, Medicaid's eligibility standards reflect enormous state variability. For example, table 2-1 (column 3) shows that in twenty-seven states the elderly who receive optional state supplements are also eligible for Medicaid. California and Massachusetts provide optional state supplements that raise the annual payment levels considerably above the SSI base income (by $3,365 and $2,081, respectively) and automatically provide Medicaid coverage to all SSI recipients (table 2-2, column 2). In contrast, Indiana and Ohio pay an amount equivalent to the minimum cash-assistance level permissible under SSI ($2,839 annually) and, as 209B states, require all cash recipients to meet more

Table 2-1
Medicaid Eligibility, 1977

States	State Covers All Recipients of SSI and Mandatory Supplements	209(B) State with an Automatic Spend-Down	State Covers Recipients of Optional State Supplements Only	State Covers Persons Eligible but Who Have Not Applied for Cash Assistance	State Covers Persons Eligible for Cash Assistance Who Are in Skilled-Nursing or Intermediate Facilities	State Covers Persons in Skilled-Nursing or Intermediate Facilities Who Would Otherwise Not Be Eligible for Medicaid	State Has a Medically Needy Program
	1	2	3	4	5	6	7
Alabama	X		X		X	X	
Alaska	X		X	X	X	X	
Arkansas	X				X	X	X
California	X		X	X			X
Colorado		X	X		X	X	
Connecticut		X	X				X
Delaware	X		X		X		
Dist. of Columbia	X			X	X		X
Florida	X		X	X	X	X	
Georgia	X				X	X	
Hawaii		X	X		X	X	X
Idaho	X						
Illinois		X	X	X	X	X	X
Indiana		X					
Iowa	X		X	X	X		
Kansas	X			X	X		X
Kentucky	X		X	X	X	X	X
Louisiana	X			X	X		
Maine	X		X	X	X	X	X
Maryland	X		X	X	X	X	X
Massachusetts	X		X	X	X	X	X
Michigan	X			X			X
Minnesota		X		X	X		X
Mississippi		X		X	X		
Missouri		X	X		X	X	
Montana	X			X	X		X
Nebraska		X	X		X		X
Nevada	X			X	X		
New Hampshire		X	X	X	X	X	X
New Jersey	X		X	X	X	X	
New Mexico	X				X	X	

	State Covers All Recipients of SSI and Mandatory Supplements	209(B) State with an Automatic Spend-Down	State Covers Recipients of Optional State Supplements Only	State Covers Persons Eligible but Who Have Not Applied for Cash Assistance	State Covers Persons Eligible for Cash Assistance Who Are in Skilled-Nursing or Intermediate Facilities	State Covers Persons in Skilled-Nursing or Intermediate Facilities Who Would Otherwise Not Be Eligible for Medicaid	State Has a Medically Needy Program
New York	x			x	x		x
North Carolina		x	x		x		x
North Dakota	x			x	x		x
Ohio		x			x		
Oklahoma		x	x	x	x	x	x
Oregon	x		x	x	x	x	
Pennsylvania	x			x	x		x
Rhode Island	x		x	x	x	x	x
South Carolina	x		x		x	x	
South Dakota	x		x		x	x	
Tennessee	x						x
Texas	x				x	x	
Utah		x		x	x		x
Vermont	x		x	x	x	x	x
Virginia		x	x		x		x
Washington	x		x	x	x	x	x
West Virginia	x						x
Wisconsin	x			x			x
Wyoming	x				x		
Totals	35	15	27	31	46	24	29

Source: *Medicare-Medicaid Guide*, "State Plans," Commerce Clearing House. The CCH Guide was serially updated between 1975 and 1977; the information in table 2-1 was collected during the spring of 1977.

Table 2-2

A Comparison of the Cash Payment Level and the SSI Base Payment Level for States in Which SSI Recipients Are Automatically Eligible for Medicaid, Fiscal Year 1976

	State Cash Payment Level for Aged Couple Living Independently[b]	Difference between State Cash Payment and SSI Payment Levels ($2,839 for a Two-Adult Family)
	1	2
Alabama[a]	$2,952	+ 113
Alaska[a]	4,596	+1,757
Arkansas	2,935	+ 96
California	6,204[c]	+3,365
Delaware[a]	2,839	
Dist. of Columbia	2,839	
Florida[a]	2,839	
Georgia[a]	2,839	
Idaho[a]	3,432	+ 593
Iowa[a]	2,839	
Kansas	2,839	
Kentucky	2,839	
Louisiana[a]	2,839	
Maine	3,024	+ 185
Maryland	2,839	
Massachusetts	4,920	+2,081
Michigan	3,060	+ 221
Montana	2,839	
Nevada[a]	4,116	+1,277
New Jersey[a]	3,000	+ 161
New Mexico[a]	2,839	
New York	3,756	+ 917
North Dakota	2,839	
Oregon[a]	3,048	+ 209
Pennsylvania	3,204	+ 365
Rhode Island	3,552	+ 713
South Carolina[a]	2,839	
South Dakota[a]	2,839	
Tennessee	2,839	
Texas[a]	2,839	
Vermont	3,456[d]	+ 617
Washington	3,156[d]	+ 317
West Virginia	2,839	
Wisconsin	4,104	+1,265
Wyoming[a]	2,839	

[a]The state has no medically needy program.

[b]U.S., DHEW, Social Security Administration, Office of Research and Statistics, "Selected Characteristics of State Supplementation Programs: The Supplemental Security Income Program for the Aged, Blind, and Disabled," October 1975. The cash payment level represents the highest level of payment available to an aged couple in the state. In states which provide an optional supplement for "basic needs" above the SSI and mandatory supplement levels, the optional payment level is used in the calculations. For states

Table 2-2 *(continued)*

providing no optional supplementation, the SSI monthly payment standard of $237 (rounded) for an eligible couple (effective July 1, 1975) is computed.

Figures for optional supplementation levels were effective January 1975 except in the following states where updated information was available as of July 1975: California, Maine, Montana, New York, Pennsylvania, Rhode Island, Vermont, and Washington. Where the January 1975 level is below the July 1975 SSI payment level, however, the SSI payment level is substituted.

cAn average figure for couples living with cooking facilities and those living without cooking facilities is employed.

dAn average figure is reflected to standardize variation in payment levels on the basis of geographic area.

Table 2-3

A Comparison of the Cash Payment Level and the SSI Base Payment Level for States with a More Restricted Standard for Medicaid Eligibility, Fiscal Year 1976

	State Cash Payment Level for Aged Couple Living Independently[b]	*Difference between State Cash Payment and SSI Payment Levels ($2,839 for a Two-Adult Family)*
	1	*2*
Colorado[a]	$4,452	+1,613
Connecticut	3,648	+ 809
Hawaii	3,180	+ 341
Illinois	2,839[c]	
Indiana[a]	2,839	
Minnesota	3,300	+ 461
Mississippi[a]	2,839	
Missouri[a]	2,839	
Nebraska	3,672	+ 833
New Hampshire	2,839[d]	
North Carolina	2,839	
Ohio[a]	2,839	
Oklahoma	3,492	+ 653
Utah	2,839	
Virginia	2,839	

aThe state has no medically needy program.

bU.S., DHEW, Social Security Administration, Office of Research and Statistics, "Selected Characteristics of State Supplementation Program: The Supplemental Security Income Program for the Aged, Blind, and Disabled," October 1975.

Computed on the basis of SSI payment level effective July 1975. Optional supplementation levels became effective July 1975: Connecticut, Hawaii, Nebraska, and Oklahoma.

cOptional supplementation levels not reported; SSI level has been employed in calculations.

dSSI payment level substituted for antiquated data on optional supplementation level.

restrictive standards of Medicaid eligibility (table 2-3, column 2). To the extent that the disparity in cash payments represents more than a cost-of-living differential, horizontal inequities (defined as the unequal treatment of persons in similar circumstances) appear throughout the SSI and Medicaid interface.

The variations in state Medicaid programs emerging from the option to extend benefits to all recipients of SSI (including persons who receive a mandatory supplement), to recipients of optional state supplements, or to SSI recipients meeting more restricted Medicaid eligibility criteria, are confounded by the legislative provisions that permit inclusion of categorically related individuals. Federal cost-sharing is available under Title XIX for:

1. Individuals who are eligible but have not applied for SSI or an optional state supplementary payment (table 2-1, column 4)
2. Individuals (a) in a medical or intermediate-care facility who would be eligible for SSI or an optional state supplementary payment if they left such a facility (table 2-1, column 5) and, at the states' option, (b) in a medical or intermediate-care facility who if they left the facility would not be eligible for the optional supplementary payment, but who are eligible for Medicaid while in the institution (table 2-1, column 6) (This option is limited to individuals whose income does not exceed 300 percent of the SSI payment level. Also the state cannot elect the coverage of b without the coverage of a.)

The information compiled from reports of the Commerce Clearing House (table 2-1) indicates that the majority of state Medicaid programs have elected to provide coverage to either one or both of the above categories. Thirty-one state Medicaid plans cover individuals in the first optional category—those who could receive, but who have not applied for, SSI or state supplementary payments (column 4). The logic of providing medical assistance to individuals in this category is straightforward: without such assistance, it is likely that many individuals, confronted by high medical expenses, would be forced onto the cash-assistance rolls.

The second optional category is designed to meet the long-term-care expenses of the elderly. This option was made available primarily for the benefit of those states without medically needy programs, where Medicaid eligibility is extended to all recipients of SSI (that is, those states that do not have spend-down provisions). Column 5 shows that forty-six states covered individuals in skilled-nursing and intermediate-care facilities who would be eligible for SSI or an optional supplement if they left such a facility. In addition, twenty-four states (including ten of the sixteen states without spend-down provisions) covered those not eligible for optional supplements, but eligible for Medicaid while institutionalized (column 6).

Political considerations often lie behind a state's decision to provide

Medicaid to categorically related individuals in long-term-care facilities. They can be understood through an examination of the historical effects of Title XIX on the growth of the nursing-home industry. The expansionist character of the original Title XIX provisions permitted states to pay the bills for almost all the elderly in nursing-care homes. They also removed responsibility for the cost of care of the elderly from their children, providing families with greater freedom to institutionalize elderly parents at no expense to them. These factors, together with the Medicare provisions that encouraged the elderly to go to nursing homes after a period of hospitalization, made the potential for nursing-home expansion awesome.[12] Consequently, the elderly recipients and their families and the proprietors of nursing homes have become large and politically powerful interest groups. Both the influence of these constituencies and the stable economic structure of the nursing-home market have hindered development of federal/ state policies directed toward the regulation of nursing-home growth.

Very few generalizations can be made about Medicaid coverage of the categorically needy. Any attempt to answer a question as broad as "Who is eligible?" is complicated by the numerous and frequently subtle variations found in both the medical and cash-assistance programs. The most obvious distinction between Medicaid eligibility practices arises between the 209B states and those in which eligibility is automatic for beneficiaries of Supplemental Security Income, but any attempt to characterize the eligibility process accordingly is frustrated when consideration is given to the "optional" categories. The complex characteristics of eligibility determination as it relates to recipients of cash assistance has implications for the medically needy.

The Medically Needy and the
Spend-Down Provision

The concept of medical indigence is incorporated in Title XIX of the Social Security Act to accommodate individuals who meet all criteria for categorical assistance except income. Under the terms of Section 1902(A)(10), federal funds are available to states to pay part of the cost of medical services used by "all individuals who would, if needy, be eligible for assistance under any such state plan and who have insufficient . . . income and resources to meet the costs of necessary medical or remedial care and services." The intent of this provision is to encourage states to provide medical assistance to persons who, while not qualifying for cash assistance, are subject to the financial consequences of high medical expenses.

Unlike the Title XIX provisions for medical assistance that apply to the AFDC-related medically needy, the SSI-related medically needy provisions are not entirely optional to the state. Rather they may exist because of either state initiative or federal statutory requirement. Under the Social Security Amendments of 1972, if a state elects not to cover all SSI recipients in its medical plan, it has to permit both SSI eligibles and non-SSI eligibles to spend down to the level of eligibility. Where states provide Medicaid automatically with SSI, there need not be a medically needy provision. The following discussion focuses on both types of mechanisms designed to provide Medicaid to the SSI-related indigent: the medically needy program and the spend-down provision.

The Medically Needy Programs. In June 1975, twenty-eight states and the District of Columbia included the SSI-related medically needy in their Medicaid programs. Of the programs that extended coverage to the medically needy, nineteen also extended automatic Medicaid eligibility to all SSI eligibles (table 2-4). The other ten states limited access to adult welfare recipients by instituting more restrictive eligibility standards (table 2-5).

Section 209B of the 1972 Social Security Amendments permits states to treat certain assets differently for Medicaid eligibility than the federal government treats them for SSI eligibility. The ten medically needy programs which use a more restrictive standard of eligibility than SSI all apply the same resource limitations on the medically needy as they do on SSI recipients. The limitations placed on resources in the 209B states (more limiting than those specified under SSI regulations) generally apply to the value of a home or personal property, income deductibles, and the responsibility of the spouse in meeting incurred medical expenses.

All states that elect to cover the medically needy are required to set income criteria for judging the eligibility of individuals who do not receive cash grants. The standard for measuring the amount of income that can be retained in the absence of cash assistance is called the medically needy protected income (MNPI) level. Federal guidelines (45 CFR 248.3) specify broad parameters within which states are given substantial discretion in establishing the MNPI. For two-person families or individuals, the minimum medically needy income level must be the higher of the AFDC payment standards or the highest level of payment generally available to SSI individuals. Since January 1969, the federally supported ceiling on income eligibility levels has been limited to 133 1/3 percent of the maximum cash payments for families of the same size under the AFDC program (45 CFR 248.4).

The process by which states establish eligibility levels for AFDC is highly complex and generates enormous interstate variation. Three concepts are relevant to this process: the need standard, the payment standard, and the maximum amount paid or maximum cash payment. The primary determinant of AFDC eligibility is the "standard of need" defined by each state as the level of money required monthly to meet basic needs for a family of specified size. All states are required to establish such a standard, yet cash payments are frequently made on the basis of only some portion of it. The level for determining cash payments, less a family's nonassistance income and deductions, is known as the "payment standard." In effect, the payment standard is de facto the public assistance eligibility level for families with some source of nonassistance income.

Table 2-4
The Medically Needy Band for Aged Couples in States in Which Medicaid Eligibility Is Automatic with SSI, Fiscal Year 1976

	Medically Needy Protected Income Level	Cash Payment Level for Aged Couple Living Independently	Medically Needy Band (Col.1-Col.2)	Maximum Amount Paid a Two-Person Family under AFDC	133 1/3% of Maximum Amount Paid under AFDC	Difference between 133 1/3% of Maximum Amount Paid and MNPI (Col.1-Col.5)
	1	2	3	4	5	6
Arkansas	$2,000	$2,935	$ -935	$1,320	$1,759	$ +241
California	3,400	6,204[c]	-2,804	3,096	4,127	-727
Dist. of Columbia	2,800	2,839	-39	2,436	3,247	-447
Kansas	4,000	2,839	+1,161	3,288	4,383	-383
Kentucky	2,200	2,839	-639	1,620	2,159	+41
Maine	2,700	3,024	-324	1,968	2,623	+77
Maryland	2,300	2,839	-539	1,872	2,495	-195
Massachusetts	4,300	4,920	-620	3,264	4,351	-51
Michigan	3,400	3,060	+340	3,288	4,383	-983
Montana	3,100[a]	2,839	+261	1,956	2,607	+493
New York	3,400	3,756	+356	3,516	4,687	-1,287
North Dakota	2,400	2,839	-439	2,820	3,759	-1,359
Pennsylvania	2,500	3,204	-704	3,120	4,159	-1,659
Rhode Island	4,000	3,552	+448	3,060	4,079	-79
Tennessee	1,600	2,839	-1,239	1,188	1,584	+16
Vermont	3,450[b]	3,456[d]	-6	3,288	4,383	-933
Washington	3,300	3,156[d]	+144	3,240	4,319	-1,019
West Virginia	2,200	2,839	-639	1,968	2,623	-423
Wisconsin	4,200	4,104	+96	3,600	4,799	-599

Source: Reprinted from "The Status of Aid to the Medically Needy," *Social Service Review* (March 1979):100-101, by Stephen M. Davidson, with permission of the University of Chicago Press; © 1979 by the University of Chicago.

[a]MNPI level represents an average of the income levels established for single-adult and two-adult families.

[b]An average MNPI is reflected in order to standardize current variations in payment levels on the basis of geographic area.

[c]An average figure for couples living with cooking facilities and those living without cooking facilities is employed.

[d]An average figure is reflected to standardize variation in payment levels on the basis of geographic area.

Table 2-5
The Medically Needy Band for Aged Couples in States with a More Restricted Standard for Medicaid Eligibility, Fiscal Year 1976

	Medically Needy Protected Income Level	Cash Payment Level for Aged Couple Living Independently	Medically Needy Band (Col.1-Col.2)	Maximum Amount Paid a Two-Person Family under AFDC	133 1/3% of Maximum Amount Paid under AFDC	Difference between 133 1/3% of Maximum Amount Paid and MNPI (Col.1-Col.5)
	1	2	3	4	5	6
Connecticut	$2,900	$3,648	$ -748	$3,372	$4,495	$-1,595
Hawaii	3,400	3,180	+220	4,440	5,919	-2,519
Illinois	2,400	2,839b	-439	2,592	3,455	-1,055
Minnesota	3,300	3,300	0	3,264	4,351	-1,051
Nebraska	3,000	3,672	-672	2,520	3,359	-359
New Hampshire	3,500	2,839c	+661	3,156	4,207	-707
North Carolina	1,100	2,839	-1,739	1,908	2,543	-1,443
Oklahoma	3,000	3,492	-492	2,196	2,927	+73
Utah	2,800	2,839	-39	2,592	3,455	-655
Virginia	2,800a	2,839	-39	2,676	3,567	-767

Source: Reprinted from "The Status of Aid to the Medically Needy," *Social Service Review* (March 1979):102, by Stephen M. Davidson, with permission of the University of Chicago Press; © 1979 by the University of Chicago.

aReflects average for variation in pay levels on basis of geographic area.

bOptional supplementation levels not reported; SSI level has been employed in calculations.

cSSI payment level substituted for antiquated data on optional supplementation level.

A third relevant standard is the "maximum amount paid" or the maximum monthly payment for basic needs made by states to families with no other income. Some states limit maximum payments to a level below the payment standard. The reasons for this considerable complexity are beyond the scope of this book.

It is around these two standards—the payment standard (for SSI, the cash-payment level) and the maximum cash payment under AFDC—that variation occurs when states establish eligibility criteria for the medically needy. To the extent that differential treatment results for the categorical recipients, so too will it occur for the medically indigent.

Relationship between the MNPI and SSI Cash-Payment Levels: the Medically Needy Band. The federal regulations that require that the MNPI not be less than the "highest level of payment generally available to SSI individuals" set the floor for the MNPI. As noted in the preceding section, the SSI cash-payment levels frequently vary depending on whether a state provides mandatory or optional supplements to the SSI allowance. Whether a state is mandated to provide supplements under Title XVI or merely elects to make optional payments, a higher cash-payment level than SSI will differentially affect eligibility among the medically indigent.

In many of the states with medically needy programs on the books, eligibility for benefits under those provisions of state Medicaid laws is set at dollar figures below eligibility for cash benefits. That is, residents of those states become eligible for cash benefits before they become eligible for medical benefits only. For the adult categories under SSI, this is true for fifteen of the twenty-nine states with medically needy programs. This point is illustrated by comparing the MNPI level with the SSI cash-payment level. When the SSI cash-payment level is subtracted from the MNPI, the resulting difference can be described as the "medically needy band," a band of varying widths and signs.[13]

Table 2-4 contains the information needed to determine the medically needy band for an elderly couple living independently in those states in which Medicaid eligibility is automatic with SSI and in which the medically needy are covered. The medically needy band presented in column 3 is calculated by subtracting the SSI cash-payment level (column 2) from the MNPI level (column 1). Ten of the nineteen states for which data are presented have negative medically needy bands. In other words, ten jurisdictions in which Medicaid eligibility is automatic with SSI set eligibility for the medically indigent at a level below the figure at which an elderly couple would qualify for income maintenance benefits. Seven states have positive medically needy bands, though six have an MNPI less than $500 above the SSI payment level. In two other states the MNPI is identical with SSI eligibility.

A similar comparison of the 209B states is presented in table 2-5. In five of the ten states that use more restricted standards of Medicaid eligibility for SSI recipients, the medically needy band is negative. While two states have positive bands, only one is more than $500 above the SSI cash-payment level. In the remaining three states the MNPI and the SSI eligibility levels are the same.

Relationship of the SSI Cash-Payment Level to 133 1/3 Percent of the Maximum Cash Payment under AFDC. The above analysis suggests that of the twenty-nine jurisdictions that include the medically needy in their Medicaid plans fifteen have in effect eliminated the program for elderly couples by setting eligibility at a level below that for SSI cash benefits. Moreover, in only a few states would the negative band be eliminated by raising the MNPI to its maximum level (133 1/3 percent of the AFDC maximum cash payment). This structural anomaly is created by two incompatible standards governing the MNPI eligibility level. The point is illustrated by examining the relationship of the SSI cash-payment level to 133 1/3 percent of the maximum cash payment under AFDC.

As indicated above, the ceiling placed on the MNPI is 133 1/3 percent of the maximum amount paid to families of comparable size under the AFDC program. Tables 2-4 and 2-5 (column 6) reveal, however, that most states have chosen not to set their eligibility levels at the maximum allowable under the Social Security Amendments of 1967. Of the twenty-nine states with medically needy programs, twenty-three have established eligibility below the maximum standard. Of the remaining six states, four have set the MNPI even with the maximum standard (Kentucky, Maine, Tennessee, and Oklahoma), and two have eligibility levels above the federally supported limit (Arkansas and Montana). It appears from column 6 of tables 2-2 and 2-3 that Kentucky, Maine, Tennessee, and Oklahoma fail to comply with the 133 1/3 percent rule governing the MNPI ceiling. However, federal regulations state that any total annual income level derived by the 133 1/3 percent rule that is not a multiple of $100 should be rounded to the next higher multiple of $100 (45 CFR 248.21 [6] [2] [i]). Noncompliance by Arkansas and Montana with the federally supported ceiling is possible because of errors in federal supervision of state eligibility levels.

Raising the MNPI to the maximum level permissible under federal regulation would extend Medicaid eligibility to a broader segment of the medically indigent elderly; yet it would effectively eliminate the negative bands in only four states. By comparing columns 3 and 6 (tables 2-4 and 2-5), we see that North Dakota, Pennsylvania, Connecticut, and Illinois would be the only states of the fifteen affected by an upward adjustment of the MNPI to 133 1/3 percent of the AFDC maximum cash-payment level; in the remaining eleven states, the MNPI would remain below the SSI cash-assistance level even if the MNPI were raised to the maximum. This anomaly can also be observed in the four states (Kentucky, Maine, Tennessee, and Oklahoma) that currently set the MNPI at the maximum standard. Despite the fact that Medicaid eligibility for the medically indigent is determined in these states using the maximum standard, all have negative bands, ranging from $300 (Maine) to $1,200 (Tennessee).

The MNPI is below the SSI cash-payment level in more than half of the states that cover the medically needy because of the medical assistance tie-in to the AFDC program. Federal regulations fail to specify that AFDC levels be updated periodically, and, in practice, the ceiling on the MNPI has remained fixed while SSI cash-assistance levels have been adjusted upward to compensate in part for increases in the cost of living. The result is that medically needy eligibility criteria, though they started out at higher levels, have not kept pace with increases in the SSI standards.

The Spend-Down Mechanism. Under the medically needy provisions of Title XIX, persons became eligible for medical assistance if their personal income exceeded the MNPI level but they incurred medical expenses that reduced income below the medically needy maximum. This spend-down provision affects all of the twenty-nine states with a medically needy program. In addition, federal statutes require the 209B states to permit all SSI and SSI-related eligibles to spend down to Medicaid eligibility (table 2-3). Five states without medically indigent programs—Colorado, Ohio, Mississippi, Indiana, and Missouri—have spend-down provisions for the aged, blind, and disabled. The eligibility levels in these states are reached when total income, less incurred medical expenses, is less than the 1972 income eligibility standard.

Spend-down can be thought of as protection from catastrophically high medical expenses. In the thirty-four jurisdictions where this provision is in force, the elderly in all income categories can theoretically benefit. However, a special problem arises in the spend-down provision that involves the marginal tax rate faced by SSI-related eligibles. Whatever their income level, the aged must spend down to the MNPI to become Medicaid beneficiaries. Consider the tax rate on an elderly couple earning a monthly income of $500 in a state where the monthly MNPI is $350. If the couple incurred medical expenses of $200 in one month, the state's Medicaid program would provide $50 toward the cost of care. (The administrative process and the problems associated with determining Medicaid eligibility on a monthly basis through spend-down are described more fully in chapter 4.) In effect, the couple would face indirect, 100 percent tax rates on earnings above the MNPI level.

The spend-down device is not available to meet the noninstitutional medical expenses of the elderly who reside in sixteen states where Medicaid eligibility is automatic with SSI and where there is no medically needy program (table 2-2). The result is a "notch effect" under which Medicaid benefits are terminated when income rises above the eligibility cutoff point for SSI. In ten of the sixteen states in this category, the notch occurs at the margin of the annual SSI payment level ($2,839 for a two-person family). The noninstitutionalized medically indigent residing in these states can obtain medical assistance only after they have depleted most of their resources and income and, in effect, become eligible for cash assistance.

The spend-down, as suggested earlier, is a financial device designed primarily to meet the high medical costs of catastrophic or chronic illness. As table 2-1 illustrates, virtually all states offer a spend-down provision to persons in long-term care settings. Since nursing-home costs are very large, eligibility for Medicaid through spend-down means that all income outside a personal-needs allowance, as well as most assets, go toward medical expenses. But since incurred expenses generally exceed these personal contributions states are required to subsidize the burdensome cost of long-term care.

As we have seen, there is considerable variability among states in response to the medically needy. Eligibility is different across states and is based on highly variable MNPI levels. The use of diverse eligibility standards by those states that cover the medically indigent, together with the exclusion of the near-poor in other states, creates an extremely complex and burdensome eligibility pattern. Furthermore, differential barriers exist for aged individuals who must spend down to variable levels of eligibility. Many of the elderly not in long-term-care facilities are never afforded the assistance of Medicaid. In sum, the effects of spend-down are subtly punitive: an older person does not become eligible for medical assistance until he has been struck by serious illness and has depleted income and assets to a point of total dependency.

The Interface between Medicare and Medicaid:
The Buy-In Agreement

The Social Security Amendments of 1965 encouraged the interaction of Medicare and Medicaid in the financing of health care for the elderly. Indeed, it was virtually ensured that overlap would occur for the aged who were unable to meet the combination of costs associated with premiums, deductibles, coinsurance, and exclusions under Medicare. Under section 1843 of Title XVIII, states were permitted to pay the premium of Supplementary Medical Insurance, as well as cover the copayments under part A, for elderly individuals eligible for both Medicare and Medicaid benefits. This was accomplished administratively through a "buy-in" agreement between the states and the Social Security Administration. By January 1, 1970, the closing date for requesting this agreement, forty-five states and the District of Columbia were participating.[14] States were financing the enrollee premiums for 2.3 million aged persons, by 1976;[15] and between fiscal year 1971 and 1975, state payments have averaged 5 percent of the annual medical insurance expenditures under part B Medicare.[16]

Prior to the federalization of the adult welfare categories, buy-in agreements were limited to Medicare eligibles who were also covered under Titles I, X, XIV, and XVI of the Social Security Act. When SSI became effective, the agreements were altered to provide coverage for one of the following three groups at the states' option:

1. Individuals receiving Supplemental Security Income under Title XVI or a state supplement (whether or not federally administered) who are categorically needy under the state Medicaid plan
2. Individuals receiving Supplemental Security Income under Title XVI, a state supplement (whether or not federally administered), or a cash payment under a plan of the state approved under part A of Title IV who are categorically needy under the State Medicaid plan
3. Individuals eligible for medical assistance under a state plan

For recipients of SSI or state supplementary payments, the states share the cost of enrollee premiums with the federal government under standard federal Medicaid matching. With few exceptions, there is no federal matching for the medically indigent elderly covered under state buy-in agreements; the states choosing this option must finance the full premium cost. Federal matching is available to elderly people who retain Medicaid benefits despite the loss of cash assistance which resulted from a 20 percent increase in Social Security payments in 1972.

The Social Security Amendments of 1967 further encouraged a policy of fiscal interaction between Medicare and Medicaid. Beginning in 1970, federal matching was no longer available to meet those expenditures for Medicaid services that would have been paid by Medicare had the individual been covered by Supplementary Medical Insurance. (This is true regardless of whether the individual established eligibility for part B individually or under a buy-in agreement.) This policy gave the states limited financial relief from the rising cost of Medicaid; but compelling states to buy into Medicare was motivated by more than mere benevolence: it was politically expedient for the federal government to implement a policy that would slow the rate of public welfare spending. Thus, though total public health expenditures for the indigent aged continued to grow, a portion of these Medicaid costs was diverted to the Social Security system.

Table 2-6 illustrates that forty-six jurisdictions buy Supplementary Medical Insurance for the categorically needy, an option that is less expensive than the cost of Medicaid coverage without federal financial participation. The number of states that buy Medicare coverage for the medically indigent aged is limited. Only thirteen of the twenty-nine states in which the medically indigent are covered by Medicaid exercise the buy-in option; and several states with traditionally "liberal" Medicaid programs, those that utilize a high MNPI, have chosen not to buy SMI for this group.

Both fiscal and administrative considerations can affect a state's decision to buy Medicare part B coverage for the medically needy population. While part B premiums are relatively low, the deductible and coinsurance burden can be substantial. A considerable number of the medically indigent aged receive Medicaid because they are confined to long-term-care facilities. Since the

Table 2-6
Existing State Buy-In Agreements

States Electing to Buy In for the Categorically Needy	States Not Electing to Buy In for the Categorically Needy	State Medically Needy Programs Electing to Buy In	State Medically Needy Programs Not Electing to Buy In
Alabama	Alaska	Arkansas	Connecticut
Arkansas	Arizona	California	Illinois
California	Louisiana	Dist. of Columbia	Kentucky
Colorado	Oregon	Hawaii	Massachusetts
Connecticut	Wyoming	Kansas	Michigan
Delaware		Maine	Minnesota
Dist. of Columbia		Maryland	Nebraska
Florida		Montana	New Hampshire
Georgia		North Carolina	New York
Hawaii		Tennessee	North Dakota
Idaho		Utah	Oklahoma
Illinois		Virginia	Pennsylvania
Iowa		Washington	Rhode Island
Indiana			Vermont
Kansas			West Virginia
Kentucky			Wisconsin
Maine			
Maryland			
Massachusetts			
Michigan			
Minnesota			
Mississippi			
Missouri			
Montana			
Nebraska			
Nevada			
New Hampshire			
New Jersey			
New Mexico			
New York			
North Carolina			
North Dakota			
Ohio			
Oklahoma			
Pennsylvania			
Rhode Island			
South Carolina			
South Dakota			
Tennessee			
Texas			
Utah			
Vermont			
Virginia			
West Virginia			
Washington			
Wisconsin			

Source: *Medicare-Medicaid Guide*, "State Plans," Commerce Clearing House, 1977 (Spring).

skilled-nursing benefit is limited under Medicare, state expenditures on part B copayments for the elderly in institutions may not finance the cost of long-term care under Medicare.

Administrative costs and complexities may also discourage state participation in the buy-in. Unlike the federal regulations for cash-assistance recipients that permit the Social Security Administration to administer the buy-in option, states alone are responsible for administering the buy-in for the medically indigent. (The administration of the buy-in option is discussed at length in chapter 4.) Since the medically needy are characteristically a transitory population, enrollments and disenrollments in part B Medicare are continuous, and, hence, the administrative paperwork is burdensome. The decision not to buy Medicare part B for the medically indigent is often made because the returns from the buy-in would be less than the investment required to expand a state's administrative machinery.

Conclusion

This chapter has focused on the statutory and administrative provisions that govern entitlement to Medicare and Medicaid benefits. Under Medicare there is universal eligibility for the elderly, contingent on prior contributions made through a social insurance scheme and the payment of premiums, deductibles, and coinsurance. In contrast, to qualify for Medicaid benefits the elderly must pass rigorous state-administered means tests. Although eligibility is conceptually different under Medicare and Medicaid, there has been considerable administrative and fiscal overlap between the two programs since their inception in 1965. Medicaid has, in effect, assumed a residual role by subsidizing the cost of monthly premiums, deductibles, and coinsurance under Medicare for individuals unable to pay. Further integration has been encouraged because of Medicare's narrowly defined benefits, which focus on acute health needs. Medicaid has increasingly come to finance a major portion of the cost of chronic care for the elderly, particularly nursing-home services.

However, not all the elderly poor are afforded the assistance of Medicaid. The statutory provisions of the SSI program and state administration of Medicaid have produced horizontal and vertical inequities and great regional variation in eligibility standards. The option given states to include various categories of SSI eligibles under the Medicaid plan and their designated authority to establish cash-assistance payment levels (above the SSI base) both contribute to variable eligibility levels for categorical and medical assistance recipients. As we have seen, Medicaid benefits are not automatically extended to all SSI eligibles: in the 209B states SSI recipients must meet a more restricted standard of eligibility. Only twenty-nine states operate medically needy programs, and in half of these the MNPI level falls below the level of eligibility for cash-assistance benefits. These vertical inequities stem from the statutory requirements of Title XIX that tie the maximum standard of medical assistance eligibility to the AFDC program, since, in most states, AFDC eligibility standards have not kept pace with increases in SSI benefits. While many of the elderly with incomes greater than the cash-assistance level are able to reach Medicaid eligibility by spending down to the appropriate state standard, the spend-down mechanism is complex and burdensome. Finally, while Medicaid has taken on a residual role to Medicare in the public financing of health care to many of the elderly, some older individuals are not entitled to the protection of either program.

Notes

1. Robert M. Gibson and Charles R. Fisher, "Age Differences in Health Care Spending, Fiscal Year 1977," *Social Security Bulletin* 42, no. 1 (January 1979):14, table 6.

2. U.S., Department of Health, Education and Welfare, Public Health Service, National Center for Health Statistics, "Physician Visits: Volume and Interval since Last Visit, United States—1971," series 10, no. 97 (Rockville, Maryland, 1974).

3. U.S., Social Security Administration, Office of Research and Statistics, *Medicare: Health Insurance for the Aged and Disabled, 1974, Section 2: Enrollment* (Washington, D.C., 1977).

4. Marian Gornick, "Ten Years of Medicare: Impact on the Covered Population," *Social Security Bulletin* (July 1976):4; and Howard West, "Five Years of Medicare—A Statistical Review," *Social Security Bulletin* (December 1971):18.

5. Gornick, "Ten Years of Medicare," p. 4.

6. West, "Five Years of Medicare," p. 18.

7. Gornick, "Ten Years of Medicare," p. 5.

8. Ibid.

9. DHEW, Social Security Administration, Office of Research and Statistics, "The Supplemental Security Income Program for the Aged, Blind, and Disabled: Selected Characteristics of State Supplementation Programs" (Washington, D.C.: DHEW, 1976), p. x.

10. Ibid., p. xi.

11. See State Plans under Title XIX, revised, August 20, 1974.

12. Rosemary Stevens and Robert Stevens, *Welfare Medicine in America* (New York: The Free Press, 1974), p. 62.

13. This discussion is based on Stephen M. Davidson, "The Status of Aid to the Medically Needy," *Social Service Review* (March 1979):92-105; see also Urban Systems Research and Engineering, Inc., *Evaluation of Medicaid Spend-Down,* February 15, 1976.

14. Social Security Administration, *Medicare.*

15. Gibson and Fisher, "Age Differences in Health Care Spending," p. 13.

16. Barbara S. Cooper and Nancy Worthington, "National Health Expenditures, 1929-72," *Social Security Bulletin* 35, no. 1 (January 1973):8; Barbara Cooper, Nancy Worthington, and Paula Piro, "National Health Expenditures, 1929-73," *Social Security Bulletin* 36, no. 3 (March 1974):6; and Nancy Worthington, "National Health Expenditures, 1929-74," *Social Security Bulletin* 37, no. 2 (February 1975):7.

The Benefits Available under Medicare and Medicaid

Having described the eligibility of the elderly under Medicare and Medicaid, we now turn to the next logical topic—the benefits available to eligibles under the two programs. After we enumerate the services that are covered and indicate the scope and duration of that coverage, we will assess the current coverage of the elderly along several dimensions. First, we will consider the comprehensiveness of the health services covered by Medicare and Medicaid and the gaps in current coverage. Second, we will examine the quality of coverage, with special attention to the appropriateness of the covered services for the health care needs of the elderly (as described in chapter 1). Finally, we will discuss uniformity—the extent to which the benefits are available to all Medicare and Medicaid eligibles and variations in the benefit package to which elderly Americans have access.

Medicare Benefits

As noted in chapter 2, the Medicare program provides two types of health insurance for the elderly. Part A, Hospital Insurance (HI), covers inpatient hospital care and posthospital care in skilled-nursing facilities and in the patient's home; part B, Supplementary Medical Insurance (SMI), covers services provided by physicians and other practitioners without relation to a hospital episode.

Under part A, Medicare covers ninety days of inpatient hospital care in a benefit period. A "benefit period" begins when an insured person enters a hospital after his insurance becomes effective and ends after the insured has not been an inpatient in a hospital or skilled-nursing facility for sixty successive days. (There is no limit to the number of benefit periods to which an insured person is entitled.)[1] The coverage applies to the reasonable cost of covered services during the first sixty days, with the exception of an initial inpatient hospital deductible. Table 3-1 indicates that this amount had risen to $104 in 1976. In 1979 the hospital insurance deductible was increased to $160. For the sixty-first through ninetieth days the cost of all covered services are paid by Medicare except for a daily coinsurance amount. Table 3-1 shows that this was $26 in 1976. The daily coinsurance was $40 in 1979. An additional "lifetime reserve" of sixty hospital days may be drawn upon when more than ninety days are needed in a benefit period. For each reserve day all covered services are included, except for the daily coinsurance.[2] Table 3-1 indicates that the

Table 3-1
Medicare Cost-Sharing: Hospital Insurance Deductible and Coinsurance
Amounts, 1966-1976

		Coinsurance Amount per Day		
Effective Date	Inpatient Hospital Deductible	Hospitals Day 61-90[a]	Hospitals 60 Reserve[b]	SNFs Days 21-100[c]
July 1966	$ 40	$10	$20	$ 5.00
Jan. 1967	40	10	20	5.00
1968	40	10	20	5.00
1969	44	11	22	5.50
1970	52	13	26	6.50
1971	60	15	30	7.50
1972	68	17	34	8.50
1973	72	18	36	9.00
1974	84	21	42	10.50
1975	92	23	46	11.50
1976	104	26	52	13.00

Source: Marian Gornick, "Ten Years of Medicare: Impact on the Covered Population,"
Social Security Bulletin (July 1976):13.
[a]1/4 of the deductible; [b]1/2 of the deductible; [c]1/8 of the deductible.

coinsurance on reserve days was $52 in 1976. In 1979 it was $80. Covered under
inpatient hospital services are room and meals in semiprivate accommodations,
regular nursing services, drugs provided on an inpatient basis, supplies and
equipment furnished by the facility, and medical social services. Excluded from
coverage are physicians' services, private duty nurses' services, the cost of three
pints of blood, and any convenience items or services.[3]

In addition, part A covers 100 days in a skilled-nursing facility (SNF) for
eligibles who are in need of skilled-nursing care or skilled rehabilitation services
on a daily basis. All covered services (identical with those of inpatient hospital
care) are paid for the first twenty days of residence. For days twenty-one
through one hundred there is a daily coinsurance amount, which was $13 in
1976 (see table 3-1). The daily coinsurance was $20 in 1979. To be eligible for
this coverage, the patient must be in a hospital for three consecutive days and
must, except for special circumstances, be admitted to the SNF within fourteen
days of hospital discharge.[4]

Finally, part A covers up to 100 days of home health visits within a
one-year period. These visits must follow a three-day stay in a hospital or
discharge from an SNF. The visits may be made by nurses, therapists, and other
health care workers if the beneficiary is under a physician's care and confined to
his home. No coinsurance charge is made for home health care under part A.[5]
The home health services covered are intermittent nursing care; physical,
occupational, or speech therapy; medical supplies and appliances; and medical
social services under a physician's direction. These services are also covered if

they are provided on an outpatient basis by a home health agency through a hospital or SNF.[6]

As noted in chapter 1, the elderly experience acute conditions less often than younger age groups; but acute illness or acute exacerbations of chronic illness are often of a more serious and prolonged nature when they occur in the elderly. Thus a benefit package with coverage of inpatient hospital and posthospital services as extensive as that found in part A is an important resource for older Americans. It should not be overlooked, however, that the out-of-pocket liability of the elderly for the cost of part A services can be substantial. Table 3-2 presents data on total patient and program liability for hospital charges during the period 1968-1977. In 1971 Medicare paid for 74 percent of the total charges. The specific burden of the elderly is most evident in the event of an illness requiring prolonged hospitalization. The cost of deductibles, coinsurance, and noncovered services increases considerably the elderly patients' liability. Thus, despite comprehensive benefits, prolonged hospitalization poses a threat of substantial out-of-pocket costs for the elderly.[7]

The absence of coinsurance on the first twenty days of skilled-nursing care and relatively low coinsurance on the next eighty days provides a less costly alternative for elderly persons who do not require continued hospitalization. The absence of cost-sharing under home health benefits make these financially attractive where the individual's health permits. However, utilization of such alternatives depends, in part, upon the Medicare beneficiaries' access to them. Karen Davis suggests that such factors as the uneven distribution of health care services among geographical areas and racial discrimination may render these and other Medicare services unavailable to many program enrollees.[8]

Unlike part A, part B Medicare is a voluntary program whose benefits are available to the elderly upon payment of a monthly premium.[9] Part B is theoretically available to all the elderly, regardless of their eligibility for part A. Exclusion occurs only for those who cannot afford the premiums, but this is redressed in part by Section 1843 of Title XVIII, which permits enrollment in part B of eligible individuals on whose behalf the state will pay the monthly premiums, as well as any deductibles and coinsurance. (These buy-in agreements are discussed at greater length in chapter 2.)

It is important to recognize that the question of whether a state buys in for its poor elderly introduces variability into the benefits available to this group. Where part B benefits are not purchased by the state, the elderly's access to comparable benefits depends upon the services covered by the state's Medicaid program (discussed in the next section).

Under part B of Medicare the insured pays the first $60 of the cost of covered medical expenses during any calendar year. After this deductible is met, Medicare pays 80 percent of "reasonable costs" for all covered services; the insured incurs liability for the remaining 20 percent. Payment for part B services may be made directly to the physician by the fiscal intermediary (local health

Table 3-2
Hospital Care Expenditures for the Aged: Amounts Covered and Not Covered by Medicare, Fiscal Years 1968-1977

Hospital Care Covered and Not Covered by Medicare	1968	1969	1970	1971	1972	1973	1974	1975	1976	1977
					[In Millions]					
Total	$4,860	$6,048	$6,605	$7,599	$8,812	$9,625	$10,829	$13,289	$15,249	$18,185
Community hospital care	3,735	4,766	5,166	6,026	6,909	7,549	8,505	10,649	12,445	15,117
Covered:										
Medicare reimbursements:										
Inpatient care	3,306	4,224	4,478	5,238	5,926	6,449	7,273	9,080	10,577	12,742
Outpatient care	44	65	95	135	188	205	233	320	436	587
Beneficiary payments for:										
Deductibles and coinsurance:										
Inpatient care	234	271	341	341	405	455	498	624	684	860
Outpatient care	25	45	66	94	131	142	163	178	205	252
Noncovered community hospital care	126	161	186	218	259	298	338	447	543	676
Noncommunity hospital care	1,125	1,282	1,439	1,573	1,903	2,076	2,324	2,640	2,804	3,068
Medicare reimbursements	54	69	71	83	94	103	116	145	169	202
Noncovered care[a]	1,071	1,213	1,368	1,490	1,809	1,973	2,208	2,495	2,635	2,866

Source: Robert M. Gibson and Charles R. Fisher, "Age Differences in Health Care Spending, Fiscal Year 1977," *Social Security Bulletin* (January 1979):16.

[a]Includes small amounts of deductible and coinsurance payments for Medicare covered services.

care insurer who pays claims under contract to the Medicare program). If payment is "assigned" to the physician in this manner, he must accept the level of reimbursement determined by the Medicare carrier, of which 20 percent is then paid by the insured. Where the claim is unassigned, the patient is responsible for the coinsurance amount as well as for the difference between the charges allowable under Medicare and the physicians' billed charges.

The assignment of claims to the physician, then, is clearly in the beneficiary's interest. Assignment limits the beneficiary's liability to the 20 percent coinsurance and relieves him of the responsibility of filing the Medicare claim. However, the proportion of claims for which physicians and suppliers accept assignment has been falling steadily since 1970, when it was 60.8 percent. In 1975, assigned claims were 51.8 percent of all part B claims received by the Social Security Administration.[10]

Where claims are not assigned to the physician, the program's liability remains fixed at 80 percent of allowable charges, but the patient's share is not similarly capped. Here, the out-of-pocket burden upon the elderly can be substantially in excess of the already considerable cost-sharing under part B. The patient's liability for unassigned claims may vary among geographical areas. Where Medicare carriers' judgments of reasonable cost are not acceptable to physicians, patients will face higher out-of-pocket costs. Thus patient liability is one aspect of Medicare that is not uniform for all program beneficiaries.

The medical services covered by part B Medicare are:

1. Physicians' services
2. Services and supplies incident to physicians' services
3. Outpatient hospital services
4. Physical therapy services
5. Speech pathology services
6. Diagnostic x-ray, laboratory, and other diagnostic tests
7. X-ray, radium, and radioactive isotope therapy
8. Surgical dressings and devices for reduction of fractures
9. Rental and purchase of durable medical equipment
10. Ambulance services
11. Prosthetic devices
12. Braces, trusses, and artificial limbs and eyes[11]
13. One hundred home health visits (in addition to any provided under part A) for which the 20 percent coinsurance does not apply[12]

Part B may be used to pay for those inpatient hospital services (such as diagnostic and x-ray services) for which an individual is not covered under part A.[13]

Examination of the part B benefit package shows that the elderly have access to a broad range of partially financed health care services. And when we consider part B together with part A, we can fairly conclude that the elderly already have a substantial national health insurance program. But there are limitations. The major criticisms of the current part B Medicare program include the complete lack of coverage for such key services as prescription drugs on an outpatient basis and limitations on services appropriate to chronic illness requiring institutionalization. Only care received in a skilled-nursing facility following hospitalization is paid for under Medicare. Furthermore, the costly nature of intermediate care, which is not covered at all by Medicare, represents a substantial and often catastrophic expense for the elderly in need of such services. In addition, the magnitude of the part B out-of-pocket costs results in particular financial burdens for elderly persons with chronic illnesses requiring frequent outpatient medical attention. Where such services are necessary, the effort to maintain a healthy state may deplete an older American's financial resources; if such services are foregone, the result may be the deterioration of health and, ultimately, the need for even more costly care. The structure of the benefit package thus dictates a pattern of health-service utilization that may not always be most appropriate to the needs of the elderly.

In sum, Medicare pays some or all of the cost of many medical services needed by the elderly. Its impact is limited to some degree by the imposition of deductibles and coinsurance, the unwillingness of some providers to accept assignment, the special conditions attached to coverage of some of the services, and limitations in the services covered. For some of the patients handicapped by these provisions, Medicaid offers an important supplement.

Medicaid Benefits

The Medicare benefits allowed by the federal government can be described and evaluated succinctly, but the Medicaid program as it is administered by the states permits few simple generalizations. As a federal/state grant-in-aid program, Medicaid gives the states considerable discretion in program decisions, such as the choice of covered services. As a result, the services available to elderly Medicaid eligibles vary widely by state of residence.

Title XIX permits state Medicaid plans to include a broad list of services:

1. Inpatient hospital services
2. Outpatient hospital services
3. Other laboratory and x-ray services
4. Skilled-nursing-facility services (other than in an institution for tuberculosis or mental diseases) for individuals 21 or older
5. Physicians' services rendered in the office, patient's home, hospital, skilled-nursing facility, or elsewhere
6. Early and periodic screening, diagnosis, and treatment of physical and mental defects for individuals under 21

7. Family planning services
8. Medical care, or any other type of remedial care recognized under state law, furnished by licensed practitioners within the scope of their practice as defined by state law (such as podiatrists or chiropractors)
9. Home health care services
10. Private duty nursing services
11. Clinic services
12. Dental services
13. Physical therapy and related services
14. Prescribed drugs, dentures, and prosthetic devices; and eyeglasses prescribed by a physician skilled in diseases of the eye or an optometrist, whichever the patient may select
15. Other diagnostic, screening, preventive, and rehabilitative services
16. Inpatient hospital services and skilled-nursing-home services for individuals aged 65 and over in an institution for tuberculosis or mental diseases
17. Intermediate-care-facility services
18. Inpatient psychiatric hospital services for individuals under 21
19. Any other medical care and any other type of remedial care recognized under state law and specified by the secretary of the Department of Health, Education and Welfare, such as Christian Science nurses' services and skilled-nursing-home services for individuals under 21[14]

Title XIX requires that at least the first seven services listed be provided to the categorically needy. If the state Medicaid plan includes the medically needy, too, it may make available to that group either the first seven services or any seven of the remaining services (except the last).[15] Actually, all thirty-two jurisdictions covering the medically needy do so for the first seven services. States are also bound by the following regulations.

1. Section 249.10(a)(1)-(2) requires that a plan covering the medically needy which includes inpatient-hospital or skilled-nursing-facility (SNF) services must provide physicians' services for these individuals when they are patients in a hospital or SNF, though physicians' services are not otherwise included for the medically needy.

2. Section 249.10(a)(5)(ii) of the 45 CFR requires that provisions be made for ensuring transportation of recipients to and from providers of services and that the state plan describe the methods that will be used.

3. Section 1905(a)(4)(c) of Title XIX requires that family planning services be provided for qualified individuals.

4. Section 249.10(a)(4) of the 45 CFR requires that a state plan must include home health services for any eligible individual who, under the plan, is entitled to SNF services.

Elderly SSI-related Medicaid recipients do, then, have access to a common minimum benefit package but duration of services and coverage of remaining services vary considerably among the states.

State decisions to include or exclude services from Medicaid plans are one form of variation that affects the comprehensiveness and uniformity of the services available to the elderly. Table 3-3 summarizes state decisions in this area. As indicated in column 1, all states cover the services required for the categorically needy and thirty-two jurisdictions cover the basic services for the medically needy as well.

Columns 2 to 18 of table 3-3 indicate the states' decisions regarding the inclusion of optional services in their Medicaid plans. The state may (1) not include a service, (2) cover the service only for the categorically needy, or (3) cover the service for both the categorically and medically needy. The final row of each column indicates the number of states that elect each of the three choices for the optional service listed. The great variability in state decisions makes the table difficult to summarize, but consideration of services that might be salient for the elderly reveals the following.

Physical Therapy and Related Services
(Column 7)

1. Not covered in eighteen plans
2. Covered for the categorically needy in twenty-four plans

Prescription Drugs (Column 9)

1. Not covered in three plans
2. Covered for the categorically needy in twenty-two plans
3. Covered for the categorically and medically needy in twenty-nine plans

Intermediate-Care Facilities (Column 14)

1. Not covered in five plans
2. Covered for the categorically needy in twenty-four plans
3. Covered for the categorically and medically needy in twenty-five plans

Table 3-4 captures the same information from another perspective, giving the number of optional services covered by each state plan. (This information provides a more general indicator of program breadth, and it will be used in the final chapter for comparisons with the national health insurance proposals.) The table indicates that the states again vary widely—from a low of three optional services covered to a high of seventeen.

While the preceding discussion of the benefit package in each Medicaid program provides an overview of the variation in state plans, this is at best a very superficial form of analysis. Though tables similar to table 3-3 have appeared in many congressional documents and HEW publications,[16] they can be quite misleading. Such shorthand disguises the fact that a much more subtle form of variation among states occurs within the broad framework of whether or not a state "covers" a service; this variation arises from what is meant by the term "covered" service for each service, in each state. Section 249.10(a)(5)(i) of 45 CFR indicates the following:

> A state Medicaid plan must specify the amount and/or duration of each item of medical and remedial care and services that will be provided to the categorically needy and to the medically needy, if the plan includes this latter group. Such items must be sufficient in amount, duration, and scope to reasonably achieve their purpose. With respect to the required services for the categorically and medically needy, the state may not arbitrarily deny or reduce the amount, duration, or scope of such services to an otherwise eligible individual solely because of the diagnosis, type of illness or condition. Appropriate limits may be placed on services based on such criteria as medical necessity or those contained in utilization or medical review procedures.

This section permits states to define the parameters of each covered service. This can be done by the establishment of limitations on the duration or scope of services, such as the number of days of inpatient hospital services within a specified time period, that are reimbursable. In addition, the state may require prior authorization—certification by the Medicaid agency—of the medical necessity of a service.

Again there is state variation, this time in the limitations imposed. While they cannot be summarized neatly, table 3-5 describes the variations by state for selected services. We can see, for example, that most states do not limit the duration of skilled and intermediate care, though many states require prior authorization for them. In contrast, twenty states limit the duration of inpatient hospital services. Table 3-6 provides a more general summary of the restrictions imposed by the states on seven basic services.

We find the following for services often used by the elderly.

Inpatient Hospital Services

1. Both limits and prior authorization in six plans
2. Either limits or prior authorization in twenty-eight plans
3. Neither limits nor prior authorization in twenty plans

Outpatient Hospital Services

1. Both limits and prior authorization in one plan

Table 3-3
Optional Services Covered by State Medicaid Programs, 1975

State	Group Covered for Basic Services[a]	Optometrist	Podiatrist	Chiropractor	Clinic	Dental	Physical Therapy	Eyeglasses	Prescription Drugs
	1	2	3	4	5	6	7	8	9
Alabama	x	x						x	x
Alaska	x					x			x
Arkansas	o				x				o
California	o	o	o	x	o	o	o	o	x
Colorado	x		x	o			x		o
Connecticut	o	o	o	o	o	o	x	o	x
Delaware	x		x		x		o	o	o
Dist. of Columbia	o	o	o		o		o		x
Florida	x	x				x		x	x
Georgia	x	x	x			x		x	x
Guam	o	o			o	o	o	o	o
Hawaii	o	o			x	o	o	o	x
Idaho	x	x	x	x	x				o
Illinois	o	o	o	o	o	o	o	o	x
Indiana	x	x	x	x	x	x	x	x	x
Iowa	x	x	x	o	o	x	o	o	o
Kansas	o	o	o		o	o	o		o
Kentucky	o				x				x
Louisiana	x				x				o
Maine	o	o	o	o	o	o	o	o	o
Maryland	o	o	o	o	o	o	o	o	o
Massachusetts	o	o	o	o	o	o	o	o	o
Michigan	o	x	o	o	o	o	o	o	o
Minnesota	o	o			o	o			o
Mississippi	x	x				x		x	x
Missouri	x	x				x		o	x
Montana	o	o	o		o	o	o	o	o

State									
Nebraska	o	o	o	o	o	o	o	o	o
Nevada	x	x	x	x	x	x	x	x	x
New Hampshire	o	o	o	o	o	x	o	o	o
New Jersey	x	x	x	x	x	x	x	x	x
New Mexico	x	x	x	x	x		x	x	x
New York	o	o	o	o	o	o	o	o	o
North Carolina	o	o	o	o	o	o	o	o	o
North Dakota	o	o	o	o	o	o	o	o	o
Ohio	x	x	x	x	x	x	x	x	x
Oklahoma	o	o	o	o	o		o	o	o
Oregon	x	x	x	x	x	x	x	x	x
Pennsylvania	o	o	x	x	o	o	x	o	x
Puerto Rico	o	o		o	o		o	o	o
Rhode Island	o		o	o	o			o	
South Carolina	x	x	x	x	x	x	x	x	x
South Dakota	x	x	x	x	x	x	x	x	x
Tennessee	o			o	o			o	o
Texas	x	x	x	x	x	o	x	x	
Utah	o	o	o	o	o	o	o	o	x
Vermont	o	o	o	o	o		o	o	o
Virgin Islands	o			o	o		o	o	
Virginia	o	o	o	o	o	o	o	o	o
Washington	o	o	o	o	o	o	o	o	o
West Virginia	o	x	o	o	o	x	o	o	o
Wisconsin	o	o	o	o	o	x	o	o	o
Wyoming	x	x		x	o	x		x	x
Summary:	x = 21 o = 32	x = 18 o = 24	x = 15 o = 24	x = 16 o = 29	x = 13 o = 28	x = 11 o = 18	x = 12 o = 24	x = 15 o = 26	x = 21 o = 29

Table 3-3 (continued)

State	Prosthetic Devices 10	Other Diagnostic, Screening, Preventive, Rehab. 11	Inpatient Hospital for Elderly in T.B. Hospital 12	Inpatient Hospital for Elderly in Mental Inst. 13	Intermediate Care 14	Inpatient Psychiatric for under Age 21 15	Emergency Hospital Services 16	Private Duty Nursing 17	Skilled Nursing for under Age 21 18
Alabama	x		x		x	x	x		x
Alaska				x	x	x	x		
Arkansas	x	o	x	x	x	x	x		x
California	o		o	o	o	o	o		o
Colorado	x	o		x	x	x	x		x
Connecticut	o			o	o	o		o	o
Delaware	o	o	x	o	x		o		
Dist. of Columbia	o	o	o	o	o	o	o		o
Florida	x		x	x	x			x	x
Georgia	x	x	x	x	x		o		o
Guam	o						o		x
Hawaii		o			x		o		o
Idaho	o	o			x		x		x
Illinois	o	o	o	o	o	o	o	o	o
Indiana	x	x	x	x	x	x	x	x	x
Iowa	x				x		x		x
Kansas	o		o	o	o	o	o	o	o
Kentucky	o		o	o	o	o	o		o
Louisiana	x	x	x	x	x	x	x		x
Maine	o	o	o	o	o	o	o	o	o
Maryland	o		o	o	o		o	o	o
Massachusetts	o	o	o	o	o	o	o	o	o
Michigan	o	o	o	o	o	o	o		o
Minnesota	o	o	o	o	o	o	o	o	o
Mississippi			x	x	x		x		x
Missouri			x	x			o		
Montana	o		o	o	o	o	o	o	o

State	I	II	III	IV	V	VI	VII	VIII	IX
Nebraska	o		o	o	o		o	o	o
Nevada	x	x	x	x	x	x	x	x	x
New Hampshire	o	o			x		o	o	o
New Jersey	x	x	x	x	x	x	x		x
New Mexico	x			o	x		x	x	x
New York	o	o	o	o	o	o	o	o	o
North Carolina		o	o	o	o	o			o
North Dakota	o	o		x	o	o	o	o	o
Ohio	x	x	x		x	x	x	x	x
Oklahoma				x	o	o			
Oregon	x	x	x	o	x	x	x	x	x
Pennsylvania	x		o		o	x	o		o
Puerto Rico		o	o	o			o		
Rhode Island	o			x	x	x			
South Carolina	x		x		x		x		x
South Dakota	x			x	o		x		o
Tennessee	o	o	o	x	x		o		
Texas		x	x	o	x		x		
Utah	o			o	o	o	o	o	o
Vermont	o			o	o	o	o		o
Virgin Islands	o			o	o				
Virginia	o		o	o	o		o		o
Washington	o	o	o	o	o		o	o	o
West Virginia	o	o	o	o	o			o	o
Wisconsin	x	x		o	o	o	o	o	o
Wyoming		x			x				x
	x = 17	x = 9	x = 13	x = 16	x = 24	x = 10	x = 19	x = 6	x = 16
	o = 25	o = 16	o = 20	o = 24	o = 25	o = 16	o = 24	o = 15	o = 26

x = service offered to categorically needy.

o = service offered to categorically and medically needy.

aThe basic services include inpatient and outpatient hospital services, physicians' services, skilled-nursing-facility services, laboratory and x-ray services, early and periodic screening, diagnosis and treatment services for children (EPSDT), and family planning services.

Source: Stephen M. Davidson, Medicaid Decisions: A Systematic Analysis of the Cost Problem. © 1979 by Ballinger Publishing Co. Reprinted with permission of the publisher.

Table 3-4

Number of Optional Services Included in the State Plans, by State, 1975[a]

Alabama	9	Nebraska	15
Alaska	5	Nevada	16
Arkansas	10	New Hampshire	14
California	16	New Jersey	16
Colorado	9	New Mexico	12
Connecticut	15	New York	17
Delaware	7	North Carolina	13
Dist. of Columbia	14	North Dakota	16
Florida	9	Ohio	16
Georgia	12	Oklahoma	6
Guam	9	Oregon	17
Hawaii	11	Pennsylvania	14
Idaho	8	Puerto Rico	7
Illinois	16	Rhode Island	8
Indiana	14	South Carolina	15
Iowa	11	South Dakota	12
Kansas	16	Tennessee	8
Kentucky	11	Texas	10
Louisiana	10	Utah	15
Maine	17	Vermont	10
Maryland	13	Virgin Islands	5
Massachusetts	16	Virginia	13
Michigan	16	Washington	16
Minnesota	17	West Virginia	15
Mississippi	7	Wisconsin	16
Missouri	7	Wyoming	3
Montana	15		

[a]Summary of data presented in table 3-3.

2. Either limits or prior authorization in nineteen plans
3. Neither limits nor prior authorization in twenty-four plans

Laboratory and X-Ray Services

1. Either limits or prior authorization in twelve plans
2. Neither limits nor prior authorization in forty-two plans

Skilled-Nursing Care (for Eligibles over 21 Years Old)

1. Both limits and prior authorization in six plans
2. Either limits or prior authorization in eighteen plans
3. Neither limits nor prior authorization in thirty plans

Physicians' Services

1. Both limits and prior authorization in two plans
2. Either limits or prior authorization in thirty plans
3. Neither limits nor prior authorization in twenty-two plans

The wide variation in state Medicaid plans makes it difficult to evaluate the comprehensiveness and quality of the benefits available to the low-income elderly. Financial status (that is, eligibility as categorically needy or as medically needy) and state of residence are the major determinants of the Medicaid coverage available. Where services are financed by Medicaid, either alone or as a supplement to Medicare, the scope and duration of that coverage depends upon the individual state plan in question.

It should be noted that for all the elderly Medicaid emerges as particularly important in its coverage of intermediate-care services. These costly services, not covered at all by Medicare, can rapidly deplete the financial resources of the elderly who are in need of them. Therefore this aspect of Medicaid is an important source of financing for long-term care.

Conclusion

Together, Medicare and Medicaid provide a broad spectrum of services to the elderly in all income groups. As we have seen, Medicare coverage is generally comprehensive in the range of services covered, though some gaps were noted, particularly in the treatment of chronic conditions. The high out-of-pocket costs associated with some of the benefits also reduce their accessibility to some degree. And since the elderly live on fixed incomes to a considerable extent, the size of the direct financial burden associated with the use of services, particularly with ongoing care for chronic conditions, cannot be overlooked.

The services financed for the low-income elderly vary widely among the states. Medicaid services are often inclusive of those available under Medicare, though status as either categorically or medically needy may result in access to different lists of services. In addition, limitations on the scope and duration of covered services are often imposed by individual states. Finally, since almost all states have elected to cover intermediate-care services, Medicaid is, again, an important resource for elderly persons in need of long-term care.

Table 3-5

Limitations on Selected Services Offered under Title XIX

State	Inpatient Hospital Services	Skilled-Nursing-Facility Services	Intermediate-Care-Facility Services	Physicians' Services
Alabama	20 days per calendar year.	Preauthorization required.	Preauthorization required.	Prior authorization required, 1 visit per month outside hospital for chronic stable illness: 1 visit per day in hospital.
Alaska	Nonemergency out-of-state hospitalization requires preauthorization.	Do.	Do.	Elective (cosmetic) surgery requires preauthorization.
Arkansas	Limited to 25 days per calendar year with provision for extension based on medical necessity and with prior authorization.	No limitations. Prior authorization required.	No limitations.	18 visits per calendar year in physician's office, patient's home, or nursing home. For hospital emergency room visits, 12 per calendar year.
California	Subject to prior authorization and specified length of stay as approved.	Subject to preadmission authorization and periodic reauthorization.	Subject to preadmission authorization and periodic reauthorization.	Except for services to inpatients of hospitals, nursing homes, and intermediate-care facilities, limited to a total of 2 occasions of service per month unless approval is obtained for an extended treatment plan. Services for cosmetic purposes not covered.
Colorado	Services provided as long as is medically necessary. Emergency hospital services provided when necessary to prevent death or serious impairment of health,	No limitations.	No limitations.	12 home and office calls per calendar year.

State					
Connecticut	even though hospital may not meet conditions for participation under title XVIII.	Prior authorization is required beyond 10 days.	Initial review to determine level of care made by a medical consultant within 14 days of patient's admission to a facility. Periodic patient reviews are made thereafter by a team to determine need for skilled-nursing services.	Level of care is determined within 14 days of patient's admission to facility and the need for continued care in the facility is periodically determined thereafter.	Prior authorization required for services to patients in skilled-nursing homes beyond 1 visit per month for chronic conditions and 5 visits per month for acute conditions.
Delaware		No limitations.	No limitations.	No limitations.	No limitations.
Dist. of Columbia		Services provided in connection with surgical procedures for cosmetic purposes (except for emergency repair of accidental injury) will be included only by prior authorization issued by state agency, services provided in connection with dental or oral surgery will be limited to those required for emergency repair of accidental injury to jaw and related structures.	Items and services furnished by skilled nursing homes maintained primarily for care and treatment of inpatients with TB will be provided only for individuals 65 years of age or older.	Do.	Elective procedures requiring general anesthesia will be provided only when performed in a facility accredited for such procedures. Surgical procedures for cosmetic purposes (except for emergency repair of accidental injury) will be provided only for emergency repair of accidental injury) will be provided only by prior authorization issued by state agency. Ambulatory psychiatric care will be provided only in a formally organized psychiatric clinic which is approved as such by state agency, except when prior authorization for such care has been obtained from state agency.
Florida		45 days per patient per fiscal year.	No limitations.	No limitations.	No specified limitations.

Table 3-5 (continued)

State	Inpatient Hospital Services	Skilled-Nursing-Facility Services	Intermediate-Care-Facility Services	Physicians' Services
Georgia	Prior approval required for renal dialysis and/or kidney transplants except in cases of emergency dialysis which requires a notation on claim form that such treatment was an emergency.	Initial prior approval is required.	Initial prior approval is required.	Outpatient psychotherapy is limited to maximum of $250 per patient per calendar year. Unless medically justifiable need for exception exists, home and office visits limited to 1 per month, nursing-home visits limited to 1 per month, and hospital visits limited to 1 per day.
Guam	Categorically needy—no limitations. Medically needy—not more than 65 days at semiprivate rate. 1 doctor visit per day except for intensive care or consultation. 1st 3 pints of blood.	No limitations.	Not provided.	3 routine visits per month. Not to exceed 36 in 12 mo-period. 2 visits per week in SNF.
Hawaii	Hospital admissions are authorized for following number of days: Medical and surgical—8 days. Confinement and delivery—4 days. T. & A.—2 days. Psychiatric—10 days. Prior authorization is required for any nonemergency admission such as for elective surgery; approval for extension is required for additional days.	Prior authorization required.	Prior authorization required.	For patients in skilled-nursing facilities limited to 2 visits per month except during acute episodes when additional visits are authorized.

State			
Idaho	Limited to 20 days per admission. Abortion-related services will not be provided unless the abortion or abortion-related services are recommended by 2 consulting physicians who state that it is necessary to save the life or health of the mother, or unless the pregnancy is a result of rape or incest as determined by the courts.	Prior authorization is required before payment.	Prior authorization is required before payment.	Physician services related to abortion or abortion-related services will not be provided unless the abortion or abortion-related services are recommended by 2 consulting physicians who state that it is necessary to save the life or health of the mother, or unless the pregnancy is a result of rape or incest as determined by the courts.
Illinois	No limitations.	No limitations.	No limitations.	Do.
Indiana	Do.	Do.	Do.	Do.
Iowa	Do.	Do.	Do.	Do.
Kansas	Do.	Do.	Do.	Do.
Kentucky	21 days per admission.	Preauthorization required.	Preauthorization required.	Initial and extensive visits limited to 2 per patient per physician per calendar year. Preauthorization required for those patients, "locked in" to 1 physician and 1 pharmacy, who require services in excess of 4 prescriptions and 4 physician office visits per month.
Louisiana	No limitations.	No limitations.	No limitations.	Limited to 12 visits per year, with extensions subject to prior approval.
Maine	No limitations. Prior authorization required for private duty nursing, intensive care services, private room, and extension of hospital benefits days beyond 60 days.	No limitations. Prior authorization required for private duty nursing and private room.	Do.	Do.

Table 3-5 *(continued)*

State	Inpatient Hospital Services	Skilled-Nursing Facility Services	Intermediate-Care-Facility Services	Physicians' Services
Maryland	Preauthorization required.	Preauthorization required for all admissions.	Preauthorization required for all admissions.	Preauthorization required for surgery normally considered cosmetic.
Massachusetts	No limitations.	No limitations.	No limitations.	Routine visits to patients shall be limited to 1 visit per month, unless medical justification is submitted to verify need for additional visits. Multiple monthly visits on chronic basis require written approval from regional medical unit.
Michigan	Minimum period necessary in type of facility for the proper care and treatment of patient.	Minimum period necessary in type of facility for the proper care and treatment of patient.	Provided based on level of care appropriate to patient's medical needs.	No specified limitations.
Minnesota	No limitations.	No limitations.	No limitations.	No limitations.
Mississippi	40 days per fiscal year.	Prior authorization required.	Prior authorization required.	Hospital visits—limited to 1 per day; nursing-home visits—limited to 36 per fiscal year.
Missouri	21 days per admission.	Do.	Not provided.	Limited to those that are medically necessary. Payment is not made for cosmetic surgery. Certain recipients who have over-utilized physician's services are limited to service of only 1 physician of their own choosing.
Montana	30 days per fiscal year.	No limitations.	No limitations.	No limitations.
Nebraska	Acute inpatient psychiatric care—14 days with extension.	Do.	Do.	No specified limitations.

State				
Nevada	No limitations.	Do.	Do.	No limitations.
New Hampshire	Requires prior approval for patients who are anticipated to require hospitalization for period longer than 12 days.	Prior authorization required.	Prior authorization required.	1 physician visit per month in ICF; 1 physician visit per week in SNF.
New Jersey	Limited by exclusion of elective cosmetic surgery and diet therapy for exogenous obesity.	Prior authorization required except where patient is transferred to nursing home directly from an acute care facility.	Do.	Prior authorization required for elective cosmetic surgery and for psychiatric treatment when costs exceed $300 in given year.
New Mexico	No limitations.	No limitations.	No limitations.	No limitations.
New York	No limitations. (Revisions under consideration.)	Prior approval except when admitted directly from hospital, another nursing home, or from health-related facility.	Do.	Do.
North Carolina	Prior authorization required for admissions for cosmetic surgery and surgical transplants except bone and tendon transplants.	Prior approval required.	Prior authorization required.	Routine physical exams and routine screening tests are excluded except for EPSDT recipients and an annual examination allowed for recipients in homes for aged, skilled-nursing homes, and intermediate-care facilities. Eye refractions are limited to 1 per year for recipients ages 24 and under, and 1 in 2 years for recipients ages 25 and over. Prior approval required for surgical transplants (except for bone and tendon), cosmetic surgery and more than 2 psychiatric visits.
North Dakota	No limitations.	No limitations.	No limitations.	No limitations.
Ohio	90-day limitation per spell of illness.	Physicians' certification and recertification required every 50 days.	No limitations. Persons must be in need of such care.	10 physician visits per month.

Table 3-5 (continued)

State	Inpatient Hospital Services	Skilled-Nursing Facility Services	Intermediate-Care-Facility Services	Physicians' Services
Oklahoma	10 days per admission.	No limitation.	Preauthorization required.	Categorically needy: Inpatient hospital visits—limited for compensable hospital periods; outpatient—4 office visits per month; 2 visits per month in nursing home. Medically needy: Inpatient limited to hospital visits and surgical services for a compensable period of hospitalization; outpatient—4 home visits per month, nursing homes—2 visits per month.
Oregon	Limited to 21 days.	No limitations.	No limitations.	Prior authorization required for elective and rehabilitative procedures.
Pennsylvania	60 days of intermittent or consecutive care in a benefit period.	Do.	Do.	Prior authorization required for all general and special medical examinations and consultations. Hospital inpatients—consultations limited to 1 per specialty per hospital admission; outpatient—consultation limited to 1 per 12 mo.-period. $200 maximum amount during any 1 period of hospitalization or for a series of recurrent or related surgical procedures.
Puerto Rico	Limited to services provided in public facilities and some private facilities under contract.	Provided in eligible public facilities and in some private facilities under contract.	Not provided.	Available in public facilities and through some physicians under contract.

State				
Rhode Island	Prior authorization required for stays in excess of 15 days per admission for persons under age 65, or in excess of 60 days for persons age 65 or older who are also covered by Medicare.	Prior authorization required for all admissions.	Prior authorization required.	Prior authorization required for visits in excess of 2 per month for chronic illness and in excess of 8 per month for acute illness; inpatient hospital visits in excess of 37 days up to maximum of 100 days, office visits provided by psychiatrists beyond initial evaluation visit.
South Carolina	40 days per fiscal year.	Need for care approved or disapproved by state office.	Need for care approved or disapproved by state office.	Must be medically justified.
South Dakota	30 days per benefit period. 1st 3 pints of blood per benefit period.	No limitations.	No limitations.	Limited to services which are medically necessary and required by patient.
Tennessee	20 days per fiscal year.	Prior authorization required.	Do.	Prior approval required for unusual elective types of surgical procedures.
Texas	30 days per spell of illness.	Level of care determination is required.	Level of care determination is required.	No limitations.
Utah	60 days per spell of illness.	No limitations.	No limitations.	No limitations on number of visits for acute conditions, except psychiatric care is limited to 12 hours of treatment for each acute illness unless prior written approval for additional care is obtained.
Vermont	No specified day limitations.	Authorization is required.	Authorization is required.	Treatment of mental, psychoneurotic, or personality disorders limited to $500 per calendar year.
Virgin Islands	Do.	Service presently being developed. Prior authorization will be required.	Not provided.	No specified limitations.
Virginia	14 days per admission.	No limitations.	No limitations.	No limitations.

Table 3-5 *(continued)*

State	Inpatient Hospital Services	Skilled-Nursing-Facility Services	Intermediate-Care-Facility Services	Physicians' Services
Washington	Approval for admission required.	Prior approval of admission.	Do.	1 visit per month in office, home, skilled-nursing facility, intermediate-care facility for nonemergency conditions. 2 per month in extensive care facility. 2 calls for new and acute conditions. 1 per day in hospital, additional calls must be justified.
West Virginia	No limitations.	No limitations.	Do.	No limitations.
Wisconsin	Do.	No limitations; prior authorization required.	No limitations; prior authorization required.	Do.
Wyoming	14 days per spell of illness.	No limitations.	No limitations.	Physical examinations limited to 1 yearly after 3d year of life; nursing-home visits limited to 1 routine visit per month.

Source: Health Care Financing Administration, Medicaid Bureau, *Data on the Medicaid Program: Eligibility, Services, Expenditures, Fiscal Years 1966-1977* (Washington: Department of Health, Education and Welfare, 1977), pp. 7-11.

Table 3-6
The Use of Limitations and Prior Authorization by States for Seven Mandatory Medicaid Services, June 1975

State	Inpatient Hospital Services	Outpatient Hospital Services	Laboratory and X-Ray	Skilled Nursing	Physicians' Services	EPSDT	Family Planning
Alabama	1	2	2	1	1	1	2
Alaska	2	2	2	1	2	1	2
Arizona	2	2	2	2	2	2	2
Arkansas	1	1	1	2	1	2	1
California	1	1	2	1	1	2	2
Colorado	2	2	2	2	1	1	2
Connecticut	1	1	2	1	1	1	2
Delaware	2	2	2	2	2	2	2
Dist. of Columbia	2	1	1	2	1	2	2
Florida	1	1	1	1	1	1	1
Georgia	2	2	2	2	1	2	2
Guam	2	2	2	2	2	2	2
Hawaii	0	0	1	1	1	1	2
Idaho	1	2	2	2	2	2	2
Illinois	2	2	2	2	2	1	2
Indiana	2	2	2	2	2	1	2
Iowa	2	2	2	1	1	1	2
Kansas	1	2	2	2	1	1	2
Kentucky	0	1	2	2	2	2	2
Louisiana	1	1	2	2	2	2	2
Maine	1	1	2	2	2	1	2
Maryland	1	1	2	1	1	1	2
Massachusetts	2	2	2	2	1	1	2
Michigan	2	2	2	2	2	2	2
Minnesota	2	2	2	2	2	2	2
Mississippi	1	1	2	1	1	1	2
Missouri	1	1	1	1	1	1	2
Montana	1	1	1	2	2	1	2
Nebraska	1	2	2	2	1	2	2
Nevada	0	2	2	0	1	2	2
New Hampshire	0	2	2	0	1	1	2
New Jersey	1	1	2	1	1	1	2
New Mexico	1	2	2	2	1	1	2
New York	1	2	2	1	2	2	2
North Carolina	2	1	2	1	2	2	2
North Dakota	2	2	2	2	2	2	2
Ohio	2	2	2	2	1	2	2
Oklahoma	1	1	1	1	1	1	2
Oregon	1	2	2	2	1	2	2
Pennsylvania	1	1	1	2	2	1	2
Puerto Rico	2	2	2	2	2	1	2
Rhode Island	0	1	2	1	0	2	2
South Carolina	1	2	2	1	2	1	2
South Dakota	1	2	2	2	1	1	2
Tennessee	1	1	1	0	1	1	2
Texas	1	2	2	2	1	1	2
Utah	1	2	2	2	1	1	2
Vermont	2	2	2	0	1	1	2

Table 3-6 *(continued)*

State	Inpatient Hospital Services	Outpatient Hospital Services	Laboratory and X-Ray	Skilled Nursing	Physicians' Services	EPSDT	Family Planning
Virgin Islands	2	2	2	1	2	2	2
Virginia	1	2	2	2	1	2	2
Washington	0	1	1	1	1	1	2
West Virginia	1	2	2	0	2	2	2
Wisconsin	2	2	2	2	2	2	2
Wyoming	1	2	2	2	1	1	2
Summary:	0 = 6	0 = 1	0 = 0	0 = 6	0 = 2	0 = 0	0 = 0
	1 = 28	1 = 19	1 = 12	1 = 18	1 = 30	1 = 29	1 = 2
	2 = 20	2 = 34	2 = 42	2 = 30	2 = 22	2 = 25	2 = 52

Source: Commerce Clearing House, *Medicare and Medicaid Guide*, State Plans, June 1975.

0 = limits and prior authorization.

1 = limits and no prior authorization, or prior authorization and no limits.

2 = no limits and no prior authorization.

Notes

1. See Commerce Clearing House, *Medicare and Medicaid Guide* (Washington, D.C.: Commerce Clearing House, Inc.), p. 819.

2. Glenn R. Markus and Jennifer O'Sullivan, "Medicare-Medicaid," October 5, 1976 (Washington, D.C.: Congressional Research Service, 1976), p. 2.

3. Ibid., p. 4.

4. Ibid.

5. Commerce Clearing House, *Medicare and Medicaid Guide*, pp. 925-926.

6. Ibid., p. 927.

7. Karen Davis, *National Health Insurance* (Washington, D.C.: The Brookings Institution, 1975), p. 55.

8. Ibid., p. 53.

9. Marian Gornick, "Ten Years of Medicare: Impact on the Covered Population," *Social Security Bulletin* (July 1976):13.

10. Ibid., p. 14.

11. Commerce Clearing House, *Medicare and Medicaid Guide*, p. 1225.

12. Markus and O'Sullivan, "Medicare-Medicaid," p. 5.

13. Commerce Clearing House, *Medicare and Medicaid Guide*, p. 811.

14. Ibid., p. 6231.

15. Ibid., p. 6232.

16. See such tables in "Data on the Medicaid Program: Eligibility, Services, Expenditures F.Y. 1966-1976," U.S., House, Committee on Interstate and Foreign Commerce, Subcommittee on Health and the Environment, January 1976, p. 4.

4

Medicare and Medicaid Administration: Implications for the Elderly

In debate about national health insurance consideration of the administrative arrangements implied by the different proposals is all too frequently subordinated to the seemingly more relevant issues of eligibility, benefit packages, and cost. This relative inattention to issues of program administration is a natural product of the political process; administrative issues are not of high political salience to the general public. Most people assume, when they think about it at all, that adequate mechanisms for carrying out the intent of legislation will be fashioned by the organizations to which this responsibility is delegated.

It would be unwise, however, to overlook the impact that the administrative arrangements of a national health insurance plan can have on the population it serves. These arrangements—as they are implicitly or explicitly made in legislation, elaborated in guidelines and regulations, and put into operation by the organizations and actors (public and private) that serve the benefiting public—ultimately determine who will actually get what, and how, and thus, of course, the magnitude of public expenditures.

The experience of the elderly with Medicare and Medicaid since 1965 provides information about the impact of administrative arrangements in the public financing of health care on beneficiaries. Such administrative functions as eligibility determination, payment of claims, quality control, and detection of provider fraud and abuse are common to the two programs, but they have adopted different structures and procedures to accomplish these tasks. This chapter reviews the direct and indirect impact upon the elderly of current administrative arrangements under Medicare and Medicaid, a population widely served by these two programs, with an eye to the implications of these experiences for national health insurance.

The Process of Eligibility Determination

The eligibility of the elderly for Medicare and Medicaid is the central differentiating characteristic of these two programs. Medicare is a federal program of health insurance benefiting most of the nation's elderly. Medicaid is a federal/state medical assistance program with eligibility criteria involving both categorical relatedness and financial need. When comparing the administrative mechanisms for eligibility determination which exist under these two programs, it is important to bear in mind that the character of arrangements that are likely to face the elderly under national health insurance depends upon the extent to which the insurance model or the medical assistance model prevails.

Eligibility Determination: Medicare

The task of determining eligibility for Medicare, performed by the Social Security Administration (SSA), runs smoothly for the most part. In sharp contrast to Medicaid, problems in the determination of eligibility for Medicare are the exception rather than the rule. There are several reasons for this. Chief among them is the fact that fully insured status is governed by simple eligibility criteria: having the required number of quarters of coverage for retirement benefits and the attainment of age 65. Also helpful is the fact that the eligibility of each prospective beneficiary must be established only once. Finally, a centralized administrative structure and the long experience of SSA both contribute to the ease of Medicare eligibility determinations.

Medicare eligibility is automatic with the commencement of Social Security benefits. All Social Security beneficiaries are eligible to receive both part A and part B coverage. Part A coverage is automatic and universal, but part B is optional. The beneficiary must, however, take steps to *decline* program enrollment if part B coverage is *not* desired. Otherwise, the Social Security Administration will deduct the premium amount from the monthly Social Security check.

For those elderly who are not Social Security beneficiaries, Medicare benefits are available for purchase at their full actuarial cost.[1] Persons who desire this coverage must initiate action to obtain it, much like the purchase of private health insurance. It is not clear how widely known the availability of such coverage is among the elderly who are not currently covered, but only 15,000 such individuals purchased part A coverage in 1974.[2] Most of the elderly who are not Social Security beneficiaries are quite poor and thus not in a financial position to purchase Medicare coverage directly. Many of the remainder of this group—the elderly who are not poor (for example, the previously self-employed)—apparently find either that the part A Medicare premiums ($69 a month in 1979)[3] are too costly or the covered benefits too limited for the monthly cost.

The elderly who do wish to purchase Medicare coverage can do so easily. The only criteria brought to bear are age and the payment of monthly premium amounts. Many of the elderly who are not automatically entitled to Medicare part A forego the purchase of this coverage but do purchase part B (318,000 individuals in July 1975). This reflects both the ease of entrance into the program and the low subsidized premium cost of part B ($8.70 monthly in 1979).[4]

In some states the low-income elderly gain access to part B benefits through arrangements between the state Medicaid agency and the Social Security Administration. Section 1843 of Title XVIII permits enrollment in part B of all categorically related Medicaid eligibles over 65 on whose behalf the state will pay the monthly premiums and any deductibles and coinsurance. Under this arrangement, known as a buy-in agreement, Medicare eligibility is predicated upon Medicaid eligibility.

The buy-in is accomplished by an administrative action in which the state notifies SSA that it wishes to buy in for an individual or group. Forty-six states and the District of Columbia buy Medicare part B for the categorically needy. (The agency responsible for initiating the process varies among the states, depending upon whether SSA or the state determines Medicaid eligibility for Supplemental Security Income (SSI) recipients; see the discussion of Medicaid in the next section.) In twenty-six of these forty-seven jurisdictions eligibility for SSI and, in turn, Medicaid is determined by SSA, and SSA then automatically includes these eligibles under part B. In the remaining twenty-one jurisdictions, SSA performs SSI eligibility determinations, but the state performs Medicaid determinations and provides SSA with information about the inclusion of eligibles in part B. All states who buy in for their medically needy provide relevant data for SSA.[5]

Eligibility Determination: Medicaid

As a federal/state program for the provision of medical assistance, Medicaid can be characterized as decentralized. Program administration is guided by the Medicaid statute (Title XIX) and federal regulations, but the primary responsibility for running the program lies with the states. This decentralization has important implications for would-be eligibles. Most fundamental is the fact that the structures and procedures for eligibility determination vary widely and produce different effects on the elderly in different states. In addition, the involvement of several agencies at the federal and state levels adds to the complexity of the process which elderly applicants face. Finally, because Medicaid is an income-tested program, the criteria for Medicaid eligibility are more complex than those for Medicare. These three factors combine to create administrative arrangements for determining eligibility for Medicaid that are very different from those for Medicare.

Supplemental Security Income. The Social Security Amendments of 1972, which created the Supplemental Security Income (SSI) Program, dramatically altered the process of eligibility determination for Medicaid faced by the elderly.

Prior to January 1, 1974—the date when SSI became effective—eligibility of the elderly for Medicaid was tied to eligibility for a state's Title I (Aid to the Aged) program. The criteria of categorical relatedness as an aged person and financial eligibility as a cash welfare recipient were brought to bear by the state agency responsible for Medicaid eligibility determinations: the public welfare department. The pre-SSI administrative structure was relatively streamlined: for each elderly applicant, one agency collected all the required information and made both cash-assistance and medical-assistance eligibility determinations. After implementation, SSI provided for cash payments to financially needy aged, blind, and disabled individuals on the basis of uniform federal eligibility criteria and a national base-payment level.[6] To ensure that an individual suffered no reduction in income as a result of federalization, the law required that the states maintain preexisting cash-grant levels through the use of mandatory supplementary payments. The states could make optional supplementary payments in addition as desired.[7]

As a result of the federalization of the adult welfare categories, there were alterations in Medicaid eligibility. These changes involved primarily the redefinition of the categorical and financial eligibility criteria of adult welfare recipients for medical assistance. Federalization resulted in uniformity at the base-payment level across states, but a disjuncture was created between adult welfare (that is, SSI) and Medicaid eligibility. The states no longer necessarily made all Title I recipients eligible for Medicaid; rather, they retained the right to cover all or only some SSI recipients as long as the eligibility criteria for Medicaid were no more restrictive than those in effect in January 1972. With the advent of SSI, therefore, it was no longer the case that all categorically related cash-assistance recipients were eligible for Title XIX benefits.

One additional change in the Medicaid program as a result of SSI is worth noting. Prior to SSI, most of the elderly gained access to Medicaid as categorical and financial eligibles. However, in those states that also included the medically needy under Medicaid, an elderly individual who was not a cash eligible but incurred high medical expenses—for example, those associated with long-term care—could become eligible for Medicaid when income in excess of the Medicaid eligibility level had been applied to medical expenses. This process—called spending down—involves a complicated eligibility determination described in detail below. It is important to note at this point that the establishment of SSI increased the number of elderly persons whose Medicaid eligibility required spending down. This result occurred because Title XVI required that those states electing not to cover *all* SSI recipients had to deem eligible for Medicaid:

> Individuals who after deducting from their income any SSI payment, mandatory state supplementary payment, and incurred medical expenses, meet a state-established eligibility criterion which is more restrictive than SSI, but no more restrictive than the eligibility criteria in effect in January 1972.[8]

In its effect, this is the same spend-down provision that is made under state medically needy programs, except that it specifically protects income from SSI and mandatory state supplementary payments. Thus whether or not a state had a medically needy program, if it elected to use more restricted criteria for Medicaid eligibility than the federal government used for SSI, the spend-down procedure had to be available to SSI recipients.

Table 2-1 described the state Medicaid eligibility criteria which are brought to bear on the elderly. Columns 1 and 2 indicate whether the state covers all SSI recipients or uses a more restricted eligibility standard and the spend-down, and column 6, whether the state includes the categorically related medically needy. It should be noted that five states—Colorado, Indiana, Mississippi, Missouri, and Ohio—do not have medically needy programs, but make the spend-down available to SSI recipients not included in their Medicaid programs. For these states federalization of the adult cash programs made necessary a complicated process of eligibility determination (spending down) not previously employed.

The nature of the eligibility process an elderly person faces—the criteria that prevail and the agencies involved—is contingent upon (1) the decision about whether to include all SSI recipients in Medicaid, and (2) the administrative arrangements employed in eligibility determination. The nature of the process varies widely across the country, and we will discuss the alternative arrangements separately because each has a different effect on would-be eligibles.

Since the establishment of SSI the simplest cases of Medicaid eligibility are those occuring in states that consider all SSI recipients to be categorically and financially eligible for Medicaid. This is the closest approximation of the previous link between cash-payment and medical-assistance eligibility. Table 2-1 shows that thirty-five jurisdictions extend Medicaid eligibility to the elderly in this manner.

However, because SSI is a federal program, the Social Security Administration makes the cash-eligibility determination for the aged, blind, and disabled. Thus an additional government agency is involved in Medicaid eligibility even in the thirty-five states where it is directly linked to SSI. The removal of the cash-eligibility determination from the state created an obvious problem for state Medicaid programs: access to information about cash-payment eligibles.

To retain a smooth interface between SSI and Medicaid, the 1972 amendments to the Social Security Act gave the states the option of allowing the Social Security Administration to make Medicaid eligibility determinations for SSI recipients. This provision was made "to prevent (1) the payment and the medical assistance eligibility process being separated, (2) the government and the states duplicating administrative work, and (3) individuals being required to provide the same information to both Federal and State agencies."[9] However, because the state Medicaid programs are so complicated and varied, sometimes employing eligibility criteria not used by SSI, the Social Security Administration determines Medicaid eligibility only in those states whose Medicaid eligibility criteria are identical to SSI eligibility criteria and where Medicaid is afforded to all those who meet these criteria, and only for individuals who receive SSI or

SSA-administered mandatory state supplementary payments. Thus Medicaid eligibility of the SSI-related medically needy, for example, is not administered by the Social Security Administration.[10]

The Social Security Administration limited its involvement in Medicaid eligibility determinations because of a belief that it was administratively incapable of doing more.[11] States that do not cover all SSI recipients use a wide variety of Medicaid eligibility criteria (usually differing from SSI on the treatment of resources); such diversity in Medicaid eligibility determinations could not be handled efficiently by SSA data-processing systems. In addition, the inclusion of the SSI-related medically needy would have increased tremendously the number of Medicaid eligibility determinations for which SSA would have been responsible.

As of August 1975, the Social Security Administration was determining the Medicaid eligibility of SSI recipients in twenty-seven programs (see table 4-1, column 1). In such states, the elderly person need only establish eligibility with the Social Security Administration regional office to become eligible for both programs. Though this eases the burden for the elderly, a June 1976 General Accounting Office report noted that the SSA has difficulty in communicating timely and accurate SSI and Medicaid eligibility information to the states,[12] and this may result in delay in the issuance of Medicaid identification cards and in the receipt of benefits. Also a lapse in the transmission of eligibility information undoubtedly makes it necessary that individuals contact both SSA and the relevant state agency, and untangling the confusion is likely to be more difficult than establishing eligibility separately with both agencies would have been.

Faced with these difficulties, the elderly are not likely to understand the source of confusion over their Medicaid eligibility and cannot be expected to advance their cases effectively. Such program interaction problems as those suggested at the SSI-Medicaid interface are surely a source of anxiety for the elderly caught in them, particularly because much-needed medical services may be at stake. Any national health insurance plan that proposes similar interaction between disparate government programs, and does not establish how it is to be achieved effectively, means the perpetuation of the problems now faced by the elderly.

Column 2 of table 4-1 indicates that twenty-three states have retained administrative control of Medicaid eligibility determination; ten of them use Medicaid eligibility criteria identical to those used by SSI. The latter states may implicitly rely on the Social Security Administration simply to transmit lists of SSI eligibles to them for Medicaid purposes. However, Beryl Radin noted in late 1974 that the system of communication of SSI eligibility information to the states—the State Data Exchange—did not function reliably and had created difficulties for the states that chose to make their own Medicaid eligibility determinations.[13] Because Medicaid eligibility in these states is dependent on SSI eligibility, the states cannot determine the former without information from

SSA regarding the latter. Thus, once again, the effort to minimize the reporting and agency-contact burden of the elderly has resulted in program integration problems with consequences similar to those already described.

In the remaining thirteen states that makes their own eligibility determinations, the criteria for Medicaid are more restrictive than those used for SSI. In these states the eligibility processes are completely separate, and the elderly individual faces the information-gathering and verification requirements of both programs. The process of establishing eligibility is thus doubly burdensome. Also, as noted earlier, the state's choice of using criteria more restrictive than SSI must be accompanied by a spend-down provision that is, in itself, extremely complicated to administer. Thus in these thirteen states eligibility determination is particularly difficult along two dimensions. First, it involves the individual's interaction with a state Medicaid agency, above and beyond contact with SSA; and, second, it increases the likelihood that the prospective SSI-related eligible will have to initiate the process of spending down. This administrative arrangement does, however, minimize the need for program interaction between SSI and Medicaid, which may increase the chance that those applying will be granted eligibility without difficulty.

We can see, then, that both the choice of whether to cover all SSI recipients (or, in other words, the definition of the categorically eligible group) and the choice of an administrative arrangement result in eligibility processes with different implications for the elderly. These choices determine whether the eligibility criteria are more or less complicated and whether the elderly have to deal with a smaller or greater number of public agencies and actors.

The process of eligibility determination also varies for the categorically eligible and the medically needy. For categorical Medicaid eligibles (whether all or only some SSI recipients) the process of establishing eligibility with the relevant agency is, at best, complicated. As an income-tested program, Medicaid requires detailed financial information, the provision of which may be particularly difficult for the elderly whose vision, hearing, or memory may be impaired and whose supporting records may be incomplete. Anecdotal data about the complexity of the procedures used in some states suggests that establishing eligibility is rarely easy, and may be even less so for elderly applicants.

Consideration of eligibility determination procedures raises the question whether some of the elderly who might be eligible are discouraged from applying by the ordeal that application may entail. Such a situation is particularly easy to imagine where neither a family member nor a social worker is available to assist the applicant. A closely related question is whether would-be eligibles are aware that they could be receiving medical assistance. This problem is particularly acute for the elderly who may lack knowledge of welfare programs because of their relative isolation. The lack of an outreach component in the Medicaid program may be another factor in any lack of awareness among potential eligibles. Because Medicaid, like most welfare programs, faces fiscal constraints,

Table 4-1
Medicaid Eligibility Criteria and Determining Agency for SSI Recipients

State	Medicaid Eligibility Criteria Same as SSI Eligibility Criteria	Agency Making Medicaid Eligibility Determination
Alabama	x	F
Alaska	x	S[a]
Arkansas	x	F
California	x	F
Colorado		S
Connecticut		S
Delaware	x	F
Dist. of Columbia	x	F
Florida	x	F
Georgia	x	F
Hawaii		S
Idaho	x	S[a]
Illinois		S
Indiana		S
Iowa	x	F
Kansas	x	S[a]
Kentucky	x	F
Louisiana	x	F
Maine	x	F
Maryland	x	F
Massachusetts	x	F
Michigan	x	S[a]
Minnesota		S
Mississippi		S
Missouri		S
Montana	x	F
Nebraska		S
Nevada	x	S[a]
New Hampshire		S
New Jersey	x	F
New Mexico	x	F
New York	x	F
North Carolina		S
North Dakota	x	S[a]
Ohio		S
Oklahoma		S
Oregon	x	S[a]
Pennsylvania	x	F
Rhode Island	x	F
South Carolina	x	S[a]
South Dakota	x	F
Tennessee	x	F
Texas	x	F
Utah		S
Vermont	x	F
Virginia	x	S[a]
Washington	x	F
West Virginia	x	S[a]

Table 4-1 *(continued)*

State	Medicaid Eligibility Criteria Same as SSI Eligibility Criteria	Agency Making Medicaid Eligibility Determination
Wisconsin	x	F
Wyoming	x	F
Summary	36	F = 26 S = 24

Source: Column 1: *Medicare and Medicaid Guide*, "State Plans" (Chicago: Commerce Clearing House); data serially collected 1975-1977. Column 2: U.S., General Accounting Office, "Problems in Administering the Supplemental Security Income Program for the Aged, Blind, and Disabled," Report to Congress, June 1976, appendix III.

F = federal administration; S = state administration.

a = states making Medicaid eligibility decisions using federal SSI criteria.

increasing enrollment is not currently a goal of the program. Thus awareness of potential eligibility for Medicaid depends on individual or family initiative or contact with some other social agency. The latter prospect—referral to Medicaid by another social agency—seems less likely when one considers the relative lack of coordination among agencies that serve the elderly.[14]

Whatever difficulties the SSI categorically needy have in establishing eligibility, things are more difficult for both SSI recipients deemed by a state not to be categorically eligible and the categorically related medically needy in states that have medically needy programs. When compared to the spend-down process required of these two groups of elderly applicants, the eligibility determination process faced by the SSI categorically needy appears relatively simple.

Spend-Down. The process of establishing the eligibility of the elderly through the spend-down provision involves the application of income in excess of the level of Medicaid eligibility to medical expenses. The difficulties in this process arise from two sources. The first is a set of broad and ambiguous federal regulations that have resulted in widely varying state spend-down policies. The second is the fact that state policies are themselves often ambiguous and ill-defined, leaving much to the discretion of caseworkers. Some of the key points of confusion surrounding spend-down applications are described below.

Incurred versus Paid. Title XIX stipulates that "in computing a family's income . . . there shall be excluded any costs (whether in the form of insurance premiums or otherwise) incurred by such family for medical care or for any other type of remedial care recognized under State law."[15] This is, in fact, the only reference the law makes to the spend-down process. But this brief excerpt from Title XIX includes one of the most confusing aspects of the spend-down process—the meaning of the word *incurred.*[16] Interpretations of the "incurred" concept have varied widely. The law has been interpreted in some states to mean that the applicant need not actually have paid for the medical expenses used in satisfying the spend-down liability (the amount of income in excess of the protected income level); in some states it has been interpreted as simply meaning "paid."[17] As a result, this aspect of Title XIX has varied in its implementation, thus affecting the applications of potential elderly spend-downers in uncalculable ways.

Income in Hand, Accounting Periods, and Retroactivity. Federal regulations guide the eligibility determination and spend-down policies adopted by the states. Section 248.3 of Title 45 of the CFR states:

> Only such income and resources will be considered as will be "in hand" within a period, not in excess of six months ahead, including the month in which medical services which are covered under the plan were rendered.

Again there has been confusion and state variation in interpretation, this time in the meaning of in-hand income. A particular problem is the application of the concept of income "in hand" to a retroactive accounting period. There are questions about the spend-down liability if the income that was "excess" during the retroactive period was spent by the applicant before the need for medical assistance arose.[18]

Section 248.3 of Title 45 also provides the states with an option regarding the length of the accounting period, which can vary from one to six months. In addition, Section 206.10 of Title 45 indicates that eligibility can be retroactive (if the individual would have been eligible) for up to three months prior to application. Therefore a nine-month accounting period (three months retroactive and six months ahead) is a possibility, but the states have varied widely in accounting periods chosen.

It should be noted that these components of the spend-down process have important consequences for the elderly Medicaid applicant. The accounting period used, the inclusion or exclusion of a retroactive period, and the state's operationalization of income in hand ultimately determine the amount and duration of the spend-down liability of the applicant. The spend-down strategy used may be either more or less favorable to the individual's chance of successfully establishing eligibility. The effects of the various spend-down procedures on the elderly applicant have not been studied systematically, but two examples should help make the effects of these procedures more clear.

Consider two elderly individuals, both with incomes fixed at $300 a month. Both encounter medical expenses of $400 associated with an incident of illness such as pneumonia, but one's case is considered under a four-month accounting period, the other under a six-month period. Table 4-2 indicates that, when medical expenses are deducted from total income for the accounting period, the individual being considered under the four-month period would have a lower

Table 4-2
The Effects of Different Accounting Periods on Two Elderly
Individuals Encountering $400 of Medical Expenses

	4-Month Account-ing Period ($)	6-Month Account-ing Period ($)
Income per month	300	300
Income per accounting period	1,200	1,800
Medical expenses	−400	−400
Income per accounting period considered in eligibility determination	800	1,400
Monthly income considered in eligibility determination	200	233

monthly income for eligibility determination purposes because incurred medical expenses would be a higher proportion of income under the shorter accounting period. Thus he would be more likely to be eligible for Medicaid benefits.

Consider the same two individuals. Now, however, both encounter $100 in expenses each month in association with a chronic illness requiring ongoing medical attention. Table 4-3 indicates that the four-month accounting period is again more likely to result in eligibility, but the ongoing medical expenses (fixed at one-third the monthly income in this example) would reduce the income of the individual under the six-month accounting period more than did the one-shot medical expenses in the previous example.

While these examples are oversimplified, they demonstrate that factors such as the accounting period, retroactivity, and the definition of income in hand have different effects on the likelihood that two similarly situated individuals

Table 4-3
The Effects of Different Accounting Periods on Two Elderly
Individuals with Ongoing Medical Expenses
of $100 per Month

	4-Month Account-ing Period ($)	6-Month Account-Period ($)
Income per month	300	300
Income per accounting period	1,200	1,800
Medical expenses	−400	−600
Income per accounting period considered in eligibility determination	800	1,200
Monthly income considered in eligibility determination	200	200

will establish Medicaid eligibility. The level of the individual's income, the eligibility level for the state program, and the nature of the medical expenses also interact with these factors to create highly variable outcomes.

The Calculation of Spend-Down Liability. Calculation of the applicant's spend-down liability—the deduction of medical expenses from income in establishing eligibility—is the most complicated aspect of these eligibility determinations. At the same time, it is the heart of the process of spending down.

Federal regulations are intended to shape the process of calculating spend-down liability by establishing the order of priority for incurred medical expenses to excess income. The three-point list, however, leaves the states many options for implementation within this scheme.

The regulations require that, first, funds equal to the medically needy protected income (MNPI) level be set aside for normal living expenses (see chapter 2). Then, income is to be applied to medical insurance premiums, copayments and deductibles, and services which are not included in the state's Medicaid plan. Finally, remaining income and insurance are to be applied to services which are covered by the state plan. When the latter are exhausted (that is, reduced to the MNPI), the applicant is entitled to the benefits of the state plan.

The apparent intent of these regulations is to create objective procedures to reduce the burden of medical expenses. The states frustrate this intent with the actual procedures used, however. For example, in the five states examined in the most complete study to date of the implementation of the spend-down provisions, all local offices visited were found to use screening devices to "filter out applicants with extremely large excess incomes" (defined in one state office as more than $100) even before past, present, or anticipated medical expenses were applied. Further, the individual caseworker was left completely free to determine "the adequacy of medical expenses at this preliminary stage."[19] Because the procedures are complex and personnel often consider themselves to be overworked, it is not surprising to learn they tended to discourage spend-down applicants.

Thus if the steps are taken out of order and the second is omitted during screening, the process may end before it is applied. The result is that some applicants will be unjustly denied eligibility.

Even if the applicants are able to establish their eligibility for benefits, the use of a chronological method of applying medical expenses to income (step two in spending down) may result in reducing the amount of covered expenses. This method increases the applicants' burdens because it requires that they have retained copies of all bills. This may pose difficulty if either the application were not anticipated, or if the provider billing is delayed (for example, if billing is monthly rather than after each visit). Even for eligible applicants, the chronological method may result in reduced benefits when, for example, hospital bills are sufficient to establish eligibility, and bills for prior physician visits, tests, or x-rays are unavailable. If eligibility begins on the date of the hospital admission, the prior services remain the responsibility of the applicant.

The complexity of this process is, however, mitigated by the fact that many medically needy applicants among the elderly are nursing-home residents. For them, accumulated medical expenses arise from a single source, and the application process is simplified considerably. In addition, nursing-home staff presumably facilitate Medicaid application in order to ensure payment on behalf of resident elderly.

Another area of ambiguity that may affect the elderly applicant's success in spending down is in the state's designation of those medical expenses that can be used to meet the liability. Once again, the complexity of state policy on this point promotes confusion and results in errors. If, for example, a caseworker is unaware of or overlooks a directive permitting the application of excess income to health-care-related transportation costs, the result may be that an elderly applicant is unfairly prevented from meeting the calculated spend-down liability.

A final area of confusion is the relationship of other third-party payers to Medicaid. This point is particularly relevant for the elderly, who are likely to have coverage under Medicare (part A, part B, or both). The regulations indicate that Medicaid should *not* pay for services that are reimbursable by another third-party payer. However, ambiguities arise in the relation of third-party liabilities to spend-down liabilities, and in whether the spend-down applicants or Medicaid should benefit from third-party coverage.

Section 248.4 of the regulations indicates that premiums and deductibles can be used in meeting spend-down liability but that services payable by another third party cannot be used. According to the regulations, then, spend-down expenses must be paid out of pocket, and the presence of insurance coverage benefits Medicaid. Problems arise at the time of application, however, in determining which bills might be paid, for example, by Medicare or other third parties, and in what amount. They are recognized in Section 250.31, which indicates that payment on behalf of an individual will not be withheld if the existence or amount of third-party liability cannot be ascertained at the time of application. (Thus a covered expense may be considered a part of the applicant's liability, though it will later be paid by a third party.) Where third-party liability is handled in this way, states need, but often do not have, a reliable means of recouping such expenses from third-party payers.[20]

When the process of AFDC spend-down was studied by Urban Research Systems and Engineering, Inc., it was found that the studied states generally departed from federal regulations in the assignment of liability in spend-down applications, even to the point of complete noncompliance. The key difficulty arises because what is actually a claims-payment function—the assignment of claims to a variety of payers—must become a part of the eligibility determination process. Bills must be collected by the worker and assigned in some manner, often poorly defined by the state. The eligibility worker will usually have difficulty obtaining information about the individual's third-party coverage.

Information beyond premiums and deductibles paid by the applicant often cannot or will not be ascertained. The spend-down process generally requires detailed and complicated work for the caseworker and applicant alike. The degree of thoroughness desired by the federal government is, therefore, not achieved and the states deal with these difficult issues in a variety of ways that have a variety of implications for spend-downers.

What is the specific relevance of the complexity of the Medicaid spend-down in considerations of the elderly applicant? As already mentioned, the use by a state of a more restricted Medicaid eligibility standard for SSI recipients means that in these states spend-down will commonly be used to achieve Medicaid eligibility. In addition, there is evidence to suggest that relatively more spend-downers are found in the SSI-related than in the AFDC-related medically needy population.[21] Thus the spend-down procedures have a particularly great impact on this group. Finally, as a population with a high incidence of prolonged and costly illness, the elderly are more likely to incur the type of "catastrophic" medical expenses that will call into play provisions of the medically needy program. Spending down to Medicaid eligibility is probably most salient as a means of financing, for example, intermediate-nursing-home care for the near-poor elderly.

It is important to note that a national health insurance plan that proposes complexities similar to those found in the spend-down can be expected to perpetuate difficulties for the elderly in establishing eligibility, even if the plan is not income-tested. Such complex procedures admit discretion and error, both of which affect the equity of the program to the extent that they wrongly exclude eligibles or include noneligibles. In addition, complexity may discourage the elderly from applying in the first place. If, for any of these reasons, the elderly unnecessarily forego medical attention, the result may be more serious and expensive forms of medical care than would have been necessary if intervention had occurred earlier.

The Processing of Claims

Another administrative function that must be performed under both Medicare and Medicaid is the processing of claims for payment from providers who have rendered services, but there are differences in the administrative mechanisms employed. Part A Medicare claims are processed either by SSA or through private insurance companies acting as fiscal intermediaries; part B claims are processed by carriers. In some states Medicaid claims are processed by the state itself; in others there is greater reliance on fiscal intermediaries.

These different methods can be thought of as possible arrangements for the processing of claims under national health insurance. In addition, experiences with Medicare and Medicaid indicate that the basis for the reimbursement of institutional providers and physicians, and the provisions made for cost-sharing, can also affect the efficiency of the procedures established for claims payment.

The following discussion of Medicare and Medicaid examines their relative efficiency in containing administrative costs and in processing claims.

Claims Processing: Medicare
Part A

Under the hospital insurance part of Medicare, an institutional provider may file claims in any of three ways for the payment of Medicare services rendered: (1) through an intermediary who has been nominated by a group of providers and approved by the secretary of Health, Education and Welfare, (2) through an approved intermediary other than its association's nominee, or (3) directly with the Social Security Administration. HEW's approval of an intermediary must be consistent with effective and efficient administration of the hospital insurance program. Approval is contingent upon the intermediary's agreement to perform each of the following functions:

1. Paying providers at least monthly, on an estimated-cost basis, for covered services
2. Consulting with providers to ensure that they receive equitable payment under Medicare
3. Serving as a communication conduit between HEW and providers
4. Making necessary audits of providers' records to ensure proper payment
5. Making final annual determinations of the amounts payable to or receivable from providers[22]

Requests for Medicare payment for covered services are generally submitted by the provider and require the beneficiary's signature (or that of someone for him, if he is unable to sign). The provider is reimbursed by the intermediary and bills the beneficiary for deductible and coinsurance amounts as well as for services not covered under part A.[23] Fiscal intermediaries process not only hospital requests for Medicare payment, but also those of skilled-nursing homes, home health agencies, and outpatient hospital service providers where these services are covered under Medicare. Table 4-4 identifies the part A intermediaries in 1973, and the number of providers reimbursed by each. It is worth noting that in 1973 Blue Cross acted as fiscal intermediary for 91 percent of the hospital providers, 54 percent of the skilled-nursing facilities, and 78 percent of the home health agencies. Overall, Blue Cross was intermediary for 77 percent of the part A providers (calculated from table 4-4).

This administrative arrangement for processing part A provider claims is one in which the program beneficiary has a minimal role: he signs the provider claim and is responsible to the provider for cost-sharing amounts. (If the part A beneficiary is also categorically eligible for Medicaid, the provider bills Medicaid for the part A cost-sharing associated with service.) Note, however, that this arrangement (which might be replicated under national health insurance) shifts collection costs from Medicare to the provider. Marmor and Conrad[24] suggest that such an arrangement may burden providers with the expense of collecting

Table 4-4
Hospitals, Skilled-Nursing Facilities, and Home Health Agencies Serviced by All
Intermediaries as of September 30, 1973

Intermediary	Hospitals	Skilled-Nursing Facilities	Home Health Agencies	Total
Total Blue Cross Assoc.	6129	2118	1733	9980
Blue Cross plan, Chicago, Ill. (note a)	(280)	(29)	(80)	(389)
Blue Cross plan, Towson, Md. (note a)	(56)	(18)	(20)	(94)
Mutual of Omaha Insurance Co.	27	661	31	719
The Travelers Insurance Co.	109	559	21	689
Aetna Life and Casualty	154	360	21	535
The Prudential Insurance Company of America	35	80	29	144
National Mutual Insurance Co.	8	70	27	105
Inter-County Hospitalization Plan, Inc.	51	13	7	71
Hawaii Medical Service	26	14	6	46
Kaiser Foundation Health Plan, Inc.	23	3	3	29
Cooperative de Seguros de Vida de Puerto Rico	15	1	2	18
Private intermediary total	6577	3879	1880	12,336
DDR	184	83	343[b]	610[b]
Total	6761	3962	2223	12,946

Source: U.S., General Accounting Office, "Performance of the Social Security
Administration Compared with That of Private Fiscal Intermediaries in Dealing with
Institutional Providers of Medicare Services," September 1975, p. 26.

[a]Numbers in parentheses are included in Blue Cross Association totals.

[b]About 300 home health agencies in 4 states go through state offices and file consolidated
cost reports. Therefore, DDR's total workload for the provider audit and settlement
function is about 320 providers.

cost-sharing amounts and that these may exceed that part of the bill. They
suggest that it provides physicians an incentive to alter billing practices (for
example, raising fees) or to refer patients elsewhere in order to minimize or
eliminate collection costs.

There is also evidence that suggests that the inefficiency of intermediaries in
processing claims and performing other administrative tasks may have an indirect

impact on beneficiaries by resulting in increased program costs. When efficiency is measured in terms of average cost per claim, as was done in a 1975 General Accounting Office (GAO) report, the results presented in table 4-5 were found. The GAO suggested that the higher average cost per claim for SSA's Division of Direct Reimbursement resulted from higher salaries and lower productivity.[25] The low average cost per claim in the Blue Cross plans, compared to the other intermediaries, was thought to be a function of their serving a specific geographic location; because the others serve providers who are geographically dispersed, they require field offices. Finally, the GAO suggested that the Blue Cross plans appeared more efficient because the skilled-nursing-facility bills they processed represented a much smaller proportion of their total than those of the other intermediaries, and such bills, which are more difficult to process than hospital bills, involve higher administrative costs.[26]

While the General Accounting Office report is far from definitive, it is one of the few attempts to assess the relative efficiency of different mechanisms for processing claims found in the literature. We are left with a real question about whether claims processing through the use of intermediaries (Medicare part A) and carriers (Medicare part B) is an efficient administrative arrangement. In fact, a contrary line of reasoning was suggested in a study reported by the Social Security Administration.[27] There it was argued that the agreement between intermediaries and Medicare provides the intermediaries with incentives to maximize Medicare administrative costs, primarily because they are reimbursed for reasonable costs incurred in performing administrative functions.

A staff paper of the Office of Research and Statistics suggests the following:

> The principal economic reason an insurer would want to become an intermediary or carrier under Medicare has to do with economies of scale: if a firm can achieve greater economies in expanding its volume

Table 4-5
Cost per Medicare Claim, Selected Payers, 1975

Payer	Average Cost per Claim
Maryland Blue Cross	$ 3.55
Hospital Service Corporation (Chicago Blue Cross)	3.81
Mutual of Omaha	7.28
Travelers	7.31
Social Security Administration, Division of Direct Reimbursement	12.39

Source: U.S., General Accounting Office, Report to the House Committee on Ways and Means, "Performance of the Social Security Administration Compared with That of Private Fiscal Intermediaries in Dealing with Institutional Providers of Medicare Services" (Washington, 1975), p. 8.

of business by taking on Medicare beneficiaries, it will do so. Further-more, firms can become more competitive in their regular business by allocating as much of their regular business administrative costs as possible to Medicare administrative costs. Because Medicare reimburses the intermediaries and carriers at cost for the administrative functions which they perform, the intermediaries and carriers have an incentive to maximize Medicare administrative costs rather than minimize them.[28]

If this is indeed the case, the burden that Medicare beneficiaries bear (through higher cost-sharing amounts or premiums) as a result of administrative outlays may be larger than necessary. To the extent that private insurance companies continue to process the claims for a portion of the population under national health insurance and are reimbursed at cost, these same incentives can be expected to persist. The staff report suggests that an alternative arrangement would be the payment of capitation administrative costs, which the report suggests would restore the incentive to minimize costs.[29]

A more direct effect on the elderly of the claims-payment process under Medicare part A has resulted from the denial of payment for services already provided to Medicare beneficiaries. It led to the unwillingness of many institutional providers to serve the elderly. The problem—retroactive denials—arose from the intermediaries' increasing role in the early 1970s in efforts to stem rising Medicare costs through utilization review. Although a structure was designed under the original Medicare legislation—provider utilization-review committees—for the purpose of ensuring that Medicare was billed only for covered services that had been deemed medically necessary, this structure was in effect only nominally in the early years of the program. As a result, in 1967 the intermediaries were instructed by HEW to review claims for these characteristics retroactively.[30] Although there is no systematic data for the rate of claims denial in hospitals, with respect to nursing-home services the denial rate rose from 2.7 percent in 1969 to 12.2 percent in the first quarter of 1971.[31]

The consequences of retroactive denials for the elderly were several. The first was that the provider turned to the beneficiary in the hopes of collecting the denied balance of the bill. In addition, since retroactive denial is an ex post facto decision, the beneficiary was afforded neither timely notice of termination of coverage nor adequate means for contesting the administrative decision that overruled the physician's judgment that the care prescribed was medically necessary.[32] Finally, the burden of this system fell most harshly on the poor elderly. Experience with retroactive denials led providers—particularly nursing homes—to refuse service to beneficiaries who had no independent means of ensuring that their bills would be paid if the claims were denied. Other providers responded to the increasing rates of retroactive denial by withdrawing from Medicare.[33] It is clear, then, that claims processing has an indirect but nonetheless powerful impact on part A Medicare program beneficiaries.

Claims Processing: Medicare Part B

Under part B Medicare the secretary of Health, Education and Welfare enters into contracts with carriers to perform the administrative tasks associated with claims payment. Currently, there are forty-seven part B carriers, thirty-two of which are Blue Shield Plans.[34] The carriers are to determine whether charges are allowable (reasonable) and to make payment. The Medicare statute requires that in determining allowed charges carriers take into account the customary charges of each physician and other part B provider, as well as the prevailing charges in the locality for similar services. The law also directs the carrier to take into account the charge for a similar service under similar circumstances to the carrier's own policyholders.

In addition to approving charges and making payments, the carriers also have the authority to determine whether a claim is for a covered service and to deny claims for noncovered items. Once again, the issue of retroactive denials and their implications for the elderly is relevant.

The claims for payment of part B benefits may be submitted by the beneficiary or by the provider. If the patient submits the claim, he receives direct payment of benefits and is responsible to the physician for the bill. Alternatively, the patient may—if the provider is willing—assign the benefits to the provider. In this case the physician agrees to accept the allowable charge determined by the carrier as complete payment for the service rendered. The provider submits the bill and is reimbursed at the rate of 80 percent of the allowed charge; the beneficiary is responsible for the remaining 20 percent as well as the relevant deductible.

In recent years, physicians have increasingly been rejecting the assignment of Medicare claims, that is, refusing to accept the allowed charges as limits on their fees. Karen Davis points out that the Medicare experience demonstrates that "if given an option, many physicians may choose to charge more than the allowed reimbursement"[35] For the elderly this has meant out-of-pocket costs that exceed the premiums, coinsurance, and deductibles of part B which significantly undermine the objective of minimizing the financial burden of medical care on older Americans.

In fact, declining rates of assignment are not the only reflection of provider unwillingness to accept allowed charges as payment in full—breaches of assignment are currently a widespread form of Medicare abuse. A recent report of the Senate Finance Committee indicated that of the 23,000 pending complaints by Medicare beneficiaries about 50 percent pertain to physician failure to live up to the assignment agreement.[36]

Interestingly, the Medicare and Medicaid Anti-Fraud and Abuse Amendments of 1977 make "willfull and repeated assignment violations" a misdemeanor (with a maximum fine of $2,000 and/or imprisonment of up to six months). Until then, the breach of assignment was subject to no civil or criminal penalty.[37] However, unless fees are raised, this approach to the enforcement of assignment agreements seems likely to decrease still further the number of physicians willing to accept assignment in the first place.

Claims Processing: Medicaid

Since Medicaid is administered by the states, claims processing takes a variety of forms. The two dominant administrative structures are the processing of all Medicaid claims directly and contracting with fiscal intermediaries for the performance of all or part of this task. Tables 4-6 and 4-7 show the companies used as fiscal agents by the states in 1977 and 1978 and the services for which they processed claims.

Table 4-6 indicates that fifteen states process all claims themselves and that in seventeen states all claims are processed through intermediaries. The remaining eighteen programs use a combined approach, and the distribution of state and fiscal intermediary administrative responsibilities varies widely.

Medicaid claims-processing systems are most frequently judged on their ability to handle a large number of claims quickly and smoothly, minimizing the rejection of legitimate claims and the resulting delays. In addition, if functioning well, the system has the potential to generate information that can lead to the detection of ineligible recipients, suggest possible instances of fraud and abuse, and facilitate planning for the use of state resources. Thus claims processing is a keystone in Medicaid management.

The states have frequently been criticized in this area since the late 1960s.[38] More recent appraisals suggest that the claims-processing capacity of many states has improved.[39] However, inefficiencies in claims processing, to whatever extent they do persist, have far-reaching implications for the Medicaid programs. In addition to perpetuating the vulnerability of the program to recipient and provider fraud and abuse and to generally weak management performance, the inefficiencies contribute to the unwillingness of providers to participate in the program.[40] The cumbersome billing procedures and the delayed and often unpredictable payments represent substantial disincentives to participation. This, in turn, affects both the quantity and quality of the services available to recipients.[41] To the extent that the poor and near-poor elderly rely on Medicaid for health care financing, inefficient claims processing will reduce their ability to acquire necessary medical care.

The relative efficiency of the states and fiscal agents in processing Medicaid claims has not been studied systematically. One study, executed for HEW in 1973, indicated that the administrative expenses of the Medicaid program have been 30 percent higher in states that contract with fiscal intermediaries.[42] Where this study is cited, it is generally used as an argument in favor of state administration. However, administrative cost cannot be considered the only relevant variable. The speed and accuracy of claims processing, insofar as they facilitate provider willingness to participate, are also relevant, and they may, indeed, be worth paying for. Unfortunately, the states and fiscal intermediaries have not been compared using such performance variables.

Among states that do not use fiscal intermediaries a wide range of relative ability to process claims smoothly and efficiently can be found. Computerized claims-processing systems, and their effective use, are fundamental to effective Medicaid management. In an effort to assist states in developing them, a model claims-payment system was developed by HEW in 1971.[43]

Briefly, the prototypical Medicaid Management Information System (MMIS) is a computerized claims-payment system that is programmed to perform certain control functions and to pay claims that move unimpeded through the computer. In addition to comparing all claims to standards and paying claims that do not deviate from the standards, the system is able to aggregate the data used in processing claims such as the services provided to the different categories of Medicaid recipients and their costs. It can be used to monitor utilization for planning and HEW reporting purposes and to check for fraud and abuse by providers and users alike.

Mechanisms for Quality Control

Quality control as it pertains to public welfare programs refers to the capacity of the particular program to prevent erroneous eligibility determinations and to detect and correct them when they occur. For several reasons, this administrative function is not applicable to the Medicare program. First, as an insurance program, beneficiaries gain coverage by having contributed through payroll taxes or by paying premiums. Furthermore, it stands to reason that concern with error is most likely to arise in a program in which eligibility is difficult to determine, and, as noted earlier, Medicare eligibility criteria are objective and easily applied. Finally, concern with ineligibles is more likely to arise in public welfare than social insurance programs because in the former it is the general tax-paying public whose money is being spent in each state. For these very reasons, quality control is an important administrative function in Medicaid. The first quality-control concern—preventing erroneous eligibility determinations—has been particularly problematic in Medicaid. The federal Medicaid Quality Control staff has estimated that the ineligibility rate for Medicaid is 20 percent (involving some 5 million individuals).[44] It is now commonly believed that the ineligibility problem arises out of the extreme complexity of the criteria used in determinations. These criteria have recently been described as "unadministerable by all but the smallest states with the simplest Medicaid programs."[45] A volume recently published by the Medical Services Administration, *Medicaid: FY 1978-1982,* indicates that the error rates are particularly high where spend-down applications are made, perhaps in excess of 28 percent.[46] (And, as was noted, the spend-down applicant is frequently an elderly person.)

The emphasis in quality control is on detecting Medicaid recipients who are in fact ineligible. This focus ignores the issue of how many erroneous eligibility determinations result in the exclusion of actual eligibles. For obvious reasons,

Table 4-6. Claims Processing Contracts, by Type of Service by Fiscal Agents and Health Insuring Agents

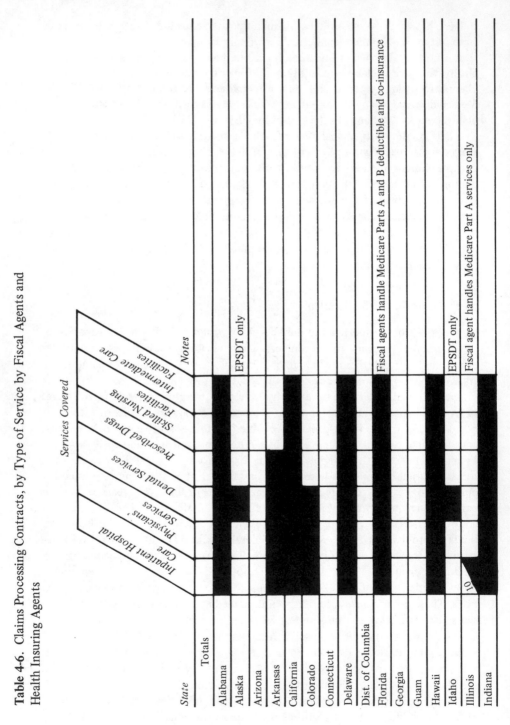

State	Inpatient Hospital Care	Physicians' Services	Dental Services	Prescribed Drugs	Skilled Nursing Facilities	Intermediate Care Facilities	Notes
Totals							
Alabama	■	■	■	■	■	■	
Alaska		■					EPSDT only
Arizona							
Arkansas	■	■		■	■	■	
California	■	■	■		■	■	
Colorado	■	■	■				
Connecticut							
Delaware	■	■	■	■	■	■	
Dist. of Columbia							
Florida	■	■	■	■	■	■	Fiscal agents handle Medicare Parts A and B deductible and co-insurance
Georgia	■	■	■	■	■	■	
Guam							
Hawaii	■	■	■	■	■	■	
Idaho		■					EPSDT only
Illinois							Fiscal agent handles Medicare Part A services only
Indiana	■	■	■	■	■	■	

Fiscal agent handles Medicare SNF crossover claims

Fiscal agent handles crossover claims for Medicare Part A

Fiscal agent handles Medicare Part A and Part B services

Physician services – New York City only. Scheduled for March 1978

Health insuring arrangement for Medicare Part A and Part B crossover claims

State						
Iowa						
Kansas						
Kentucky						
Louisiana			25			
Maine						
Maryland			20	20		
Massachusetts						
Michigan						
Minnesota						
Mississippi						
Missouri						
Montana						
Nebraska						
Nevada						
New Hampshire						
New Jersey						
New Mexico						
New York						
North Carolina						
North Dakota			10	10		
Ohio						
Oklahoma						
Oregon						
Pennsylvania			20			
Puerto Rico						
Rhode Island						
South Carolina						

Table 4-6. *(continued)*

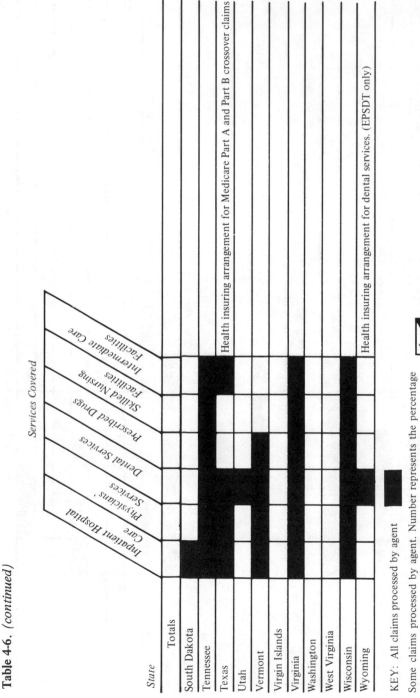

Services Covered

State | Inpatient Hospital Care | Physicians' Services | Dental Services | Prescribed Drugs | Skilled Nursing Facilities | Intermediate Care Facilities

Totals
South Dakota
Tennessee
Texas
Utah
Vermont
Virgin Islands
Virginia
Washington
West Virginia
Wisconsin
Wyoming

Health insuring arrangement for Medicare Part A and Part B crossover claims

Health insuring arrangement for dental services. (EPSDT only)

 15

KEY: All claims processed by agent

Some claims processed by agent. Number represents the percentage of total claims processed by the contractor. Remainder of claims are processed by the State.

Source: Health Care Financing Administration, Institute for Medicaid Management, Data on the Medicaid Program: Eligibility, Services, Expenditures: Fiscal Years 1966-1978. (Washington, 1978). p. 94.

the magnitude of this problem is difficult to measure. Nonetheless, when considering the plight of the elderly under Medicaid, it is an important issue to take into account. Noting that the elderly are frequently involved in complicated spend-down applications, one has cause to suspect that erroneous rejections of applications do in fact take place.

While ensuring that eligibles are determined to be such is not a goal of quality control, efforts to improve the states' error rates may nonetheless advance this goal. The realization that complexity is the source of error has led policymakers to give greater attention to reform of Medicaid eligibility criteria. Such reforms may not only reduce the inclusion of the truly ineligible but may also strengthen the state's ability to detect and correct erroneous ineligibility.[47] It must be pointed out, though, that in this instance Medicaid programs face contradictory imperatives. On the one hand, they want to reduce error rates for the reasons indicated; on the other hand, they want to reduce expenditures. Finding more people eligible for Medicaid benefits is likely to increase program costs and thus to reduce the zeal with which administrators attempt to simplify eligibility criteria and procedures. Nonetheless, if significant reform of eligibility criteria does take place, there is reason to believe that the elderly who are now erroneously excluded may be able to attain eligible status.

Detection of Provider Fraud and Abuse

The ability of both Medicare and Medicaid to detect provider fraud and abuse affects program integrity. Fraud involves misrepresentation with the intent to obtain services, money, or gain to which the provider is not entitled. Abuse involves practice patterns that, while not illegal, have the effect of maximizing financial gain. The latter usually involves unnecessarily increasing or, in the case of prepayment arrangements, reducing the amount of services provided. Thus the detection and prevention of fraud and abuse not only saves tax dollars but also protects the welfare of individuals.

While this administrative function is common to both programs, the strategy for its accomplishment has varied between them. The Social Security Administration's Bureau of Health Insurance has pursued fraud and abuse detection in Medicare directly. In Medicaid, the initiative lies with the states, though state efforts are now more actively influenced by the Health Care Financing Administration.

The magnitude of concern over fraud and abuse is also different in Medicare and Medicaid, with the bulk of the concern expressed for Medicaid. Though it is not clear that Medicare's fraud and abuse problems differ from those of Medicaid, certain factors help to explain the greater attention to Medicaid on this issue. Most fundamental is the concern with rising Medicaid costs. Just as these costs result in part from the program's decentralized operations, they have

Table 4-7
Fiscal Agents and Health Insuring Agencies in the Medicaid Program, January 1978

State	Name of Fiscal Agent(s) or Health Insuring Agency	Types of Claims Handled
Alabama	Blue Cross/Blue Shield of Alabama	All services.
Alaska	Delta Dental Plan of Alaska Incorporated	Dental (EPSDT only).
Arizona	(No Medicaid Program)	
Arkansas	Arkansas Blue Cross/Blue Shield	All services except SNFs and ICFs.
California	Medi-Cal Intermediary Operations (MIO):	
	Blue Cross-North	All institutional claims for Northern California except for 3 counties.
	Blue Cross-South	All institutional claims for Southern California.
	Blue Shield	All noninstitutional claims except dental.
	Redwood Health Foundation[a]	All services except dental for the 3 northern counties of Lake, Sonoma and Mendocino.
	California Dental Service Association[a]	Dental.
Colorado	Colorado Hospital Service, Incorporated	
	Colorado Medical Service, Incorporated (Blue Cross/Blue Shield)	All services except drugs.
Connecticut	No fiscal agent	
Delaware	Blue Cross/Blue Shield of Delaware, Incorporated	All services.
District of Columbia	No fiscal agent	
Florida	Systems Development Corporation Integrated Services, Incorporated	All services including payment of part A and B deductible and coinsurance.
Georgia	No fiscal agent	
Guam	No fiscal agent	
Hawaii	Hawaii Medical Services Association (Blue Cross/Blue Shield)	All services.
Idaho	Delta Dental Plan of Idaho, Incorporated	Dental (EPSDT only).

State	Fiscal agent	Services
Illinois	Health Care Service Corporation (Blue Cross)	Crossover claims for Medicare part A (inpatient hospital services only).
Indiana	Blue Cross/Blue Shield of Indiana	All services.
Iowa	Blue Cross/Blue Shield of Iowa	All services except ICFs.
Kansas	Kansas Hospital Service Association, Incorporated (Blue Cross) and Kansas Blue Shield	All services except ICFs and SNFs; also handles Medicare SNF crossover claims.
Kentucky	No fiscal agent	All services.
Louisiana	Electronic Data Systems Federal Corporation	Drugs.
Maine	Paid prescriptions	Crossover claims for Medicare part A services.
Maryland	Blue Cross	Crossover claims for Medicare part A (inpatient hospital services only).
Massachusetts	No fiscal agent; Blue Cross/Blue Shield of Massachusetts; Pilgrim Health Applications, Incorporated	Drugs, dental, and durable medical equipment.
Michigan	No fiscal agent	
Minnesota	No fiscal agent	
Mississippi	Blue Cross/Blue Shield of Mississippi, Incorporated	All services.
Missouri	No fiscal agent	All services.
Montana	Dikewood Corporation	All services.
Nebraska	No Fiscal Agent	
Nevada	Nevada Blue Shield	
New Hampshire	No Fiscal Agent	
New Jersey	Hospital Service Plan of New Jersey (New Jersey Blue Cross); Prudential Insurance Company of America	Inpatient and outpatient hospital[b], and drugs. All services, including some hospital[b], except drugs, SNFs, ICFs, and institutions for tuberculosis and mental disease.
New Mexico	Electronic Data Systems Federal Corporation	All services.

Table 4-7 *(continued)*

State	Name of Fiscal Agent(s) or Health Insuring Agency	Types of Claims Handled
New York	The Bradford National Corporation (New York City only)	Clinics and physicians. Drug claims scheduled to enter system March 1978; inpatient hospital, SNF, ICF, HIP, and HMO in June 1978. All other claims in September 1978.
North Carolina	Electronic Data Systems Federal Corporation	All services except drugs.
	The Computer Company (T.C.C.).	Drugs.
North Dakota	Blue Cross/Blue Shield of North Dakota.[a]	Crossover claims for Medicare parts A and B services for recipients 65 and over.
Ohio	No fiscal agent.	
Oklahoma	No fiscal agent.	
Oregon	No fiscal agent.	
Pennsylvania	Capital Blue Cross.	All pharmaceutical, medical supplies, equipment, and prosthesis devices.
	Inter-County Hospitalization Plan, Inc.	Inpatient hospital claims for Philadelphia area (Blair, Chester, and Montgomery Counties, etc.).
	Pennsylvania Blue Cross.	Other inpatient hospital claims.
	Blue Shield.	Physicians' inpatient care (medical and surgical) and emergency room services.
Puerto Rico	No fiscal agent.	
Rhode Island	No fiscal agent.	
South Carolina	Blue Cross/Blue Shield of South Carolina.	All services except inpatient and outpatient hospital, drugs, SNFs and ICFs.
South Dakota	Associate Hospital Services (Blue Cross).	Inpatient hospital and home health.
Tennessee	Electronic Data Systems Federal Corporation.	All services including payment of part A and B coinsurance and deductible.

Texas	National Heritage Insurance Company.	All services other than drugs, dental, hearing aids, LTC facilities, EPSDT, and parts A and B deductible and coinsurance.
Utah	Delta Dental Corporation.	Dental.
Vermont	New Hampshire/Vermont Hospitalization Service (Blue Cross/Blue Shield).	All services except SNFs and ICFs.
Virgin Islands	No fiscal agent.	
Virginia	The Computer Company (T.C.C.).	All services.
Washington	Electronic Data Systems Federal Corporation.	All services.
West Virginia	No fiscal agent.	
Wisconsin	Electronic Data Systems Federal Corporation.	All services.
Wyoming	Wyoming Dental Services Incorporated.[a]	Dental (EPSDT only).

Source: Health Care Financing Administration, Institute for Medicaid Management, Data on the Medicaid Program: Eligibility, Services, Expenditures: Fiscal Years 1966-1978 (Washington, 1978), pp. 94-96.

[a]Health Insuring Agency.

[b]Hospitals may contract to send their claims to either fiscal agent.

also resulted in budget disputes at the state and local levels, where the fiscal pressures of Medicaid are most acutely felt.[48] The visibility of Medicaid, its controversial nature, and the resulting preoccupation with fraud and abuse control are best understood as expressions of concern for rising outlays under this state-administered welfare program.

Fraud and Abuse Control: Medicare

The Social Security Administration's Bureau of Health Insurance (BHI) established a Program Integrity Unit for Medicare in 1969. In 1975 the Program Integrity Unit was staffed by 151 persons, assigned to SSA's central office and HEW's regional offices.[49]

The purpose of the unit was to "develop and carry out a program for fraud prevention, detection, reporting and processing."[50] Each year the unit investigates several thousand complaints involving possible fraud and abuse under Medicare. A 1975 General Accounting Office report indicates that, although most fraud complaints prove to be unsubstantiated, from the beginning of Medicare to June 30, 1974, 242 cases of suspected provider fraud were referred by BHI to the U.S. attorney for prosecution. Of these, 118 were prosecuted in federal courts and 102 convictions were obtained.

Efforts to strengthen Medicare's (and Medicaid's) program integrity have relied in large measure upon sanctions expected to discourage fraud and abuse. Existing law considers practices such as the submission of false claims and the acceptance of kickbacks or bribes to be misdemeanors, punishable by a maximum $10,000 fine, up to one year imprisonment, or both. Falsifying statements in order to qualify for certification as a provider is also a misdemeanor, punishable by a maximum $2,000 fine, up to six months imprisonment, or both.

A Senate report on the 1977 Medicare-Medicaid Anti-Fraud and Abuse Amendments indicates that these sanctions have not proven to be adequate deterrents to providers. The report also argues that the sanctions are inconsistent with the existing federal criminal code, which designates similar fraudulent practices to be felonies. Among the amendments is one that would make felonies of fraudulent acts now classified as misdemeanors and impose penalties of a $25,000 maximum fine, up to five years imprisonment, or both. The amendments also require the secretary of HEW to suspend from participation in both programs (for some period) an individual practitioner convicted of a criminal offense related to his involvement in Medicare or Medicaid. The secretary is also directed to notify state licensing authorities and request that investigation and sanctions be invoked.[51]

The utility of stiffening sanctions in the proposed manner may indeed be in their deterrent effect. However, both programs must also have the capacity to detect fraud and to bring cases to prosecution. Turning to Medicaid, we will see that this capacity is not fully realized.

Fraud and Abuse Control: Medicaid

Because state Medicaid programs differ from one another, the criteria for identifying potentially fraudulent or abusive situations differ as well. The federal role in state fraud and abuse efforts was relatively permissive until recently, when federal officials with much larger staffs than they had previously have encouraged states, with whom principal responsibility lies, to undertake aggressive fraud and abuse control programs.

The performance of the states in the detection of fraud and abuse has been hampered by the management weaknesses in the programs noted earlier. One inhibiting factor has been the states' failure to establish MMIS or alternative computerized data systems. The Medical Services Administration estimated provider fraud and abuse at 8 to 15 percent of Medicaid program costs and indicated that "Inadequate claims processing systems at the state level and the lack of information systems which provide data on program utilization and provider participation make detection of such practices limited at best."[52]

Public concern over the issue of fraud and abuse in Medicaid has prompted activity at the federal level to encourage state improvements in this area. Foremost among current efforts is further encouragement of the states to install MMIS. In addition, the establishment of separate statewide investigative bureaus—Medicaid Fraud Control Units—has been encouraged by offers of federal matching funds for expenditures to establish and operate such units. The success of these units where they exist (for example, in the New York Special Prosecutor's Office) has been in increasing the rate of prosecutions and convictions, but few have been established. The 1977 Medicare-Medicaid Anti-Fraud and Abuse Amendments strengthen the incentives to do so by matching state expenditures at a 100 percent rate in 1978, a 90 percent rate in 1979, and a 75 percent rate in 1980 (subject to a quarterly limit of the higher of $125,000 or one quarter of 1 percent of total Medicaid expenditures in the state in the previous quarter).[53] Finally, though this is on the whole a laudatory goal, it should be pointed out that the manner in which the fraud and abuse control function is carried out may also have an impact on honest, competent practitioners. If the data collection procedures are excessively burdensome, for example, providers may be driven from the program, thereby reducing the availability of services to older Americans.

Coordination of Medicare and Medicaid

Provider fraud and abuse in both Medicare and Medicaid may affect the elderly in a variety of ways. As noted, breach of assignment agreements results in financial burdens to Medicare beneficiaries. Medicaid recipients, while less vulnerable to provider attempts to achieve financial gain directly, are more vulnerable to the insidious forms of fraud and abuse associated with profiteering nursing homes[54] and the so-called Medicaid mills.[55] The elderly, who lack protection from fraud and abuse because of programmatic weakness, have been known to receive cursory if not neglectful medical care at times (though provider bills continued to be paid in full).

There has been some indication that the same unlawful providers are defrauding both Medicare and Medicaid. Recommendations that the two programs combine fraud and abuse efforts through greater information-sharing were made by the Senate Finance Committee as early as 1970.[56] However, as recently as 1975 the General Accounting Office reported that such coordination of efforts had not been achieved.[57]

Since reorganization of HEW which resulted in the creation of the Health Care Financing Administration (HCFA), additional steps have been taken to promote greater Medicare-Medicaid integration. The reorganization combined the Social Security Administration's Bureau of Health Insurance and the Social and Rehabilitation Service's Medical Services Administration (as well as other organizational components) under HCFA. It also included a combined Fraud and Abuse Control Unit. While efforts at integrating the two programs have continued during the past several years, fundamental differences between the two programs—for example, differences in eligibility and the importance of the states in Medicaid—have made progress slow and difficult.

Conclusion

This chapter has reviewed the administrative arrangements of Medicare and Medicaid in an effort to make explicit the various consequences these arrangements have for the elderly. Functions such as eligibility determinations, claims payment, quality control, and fraud and abuse detection are common to both Medicare and Medicaid, but their respective administrative strategies have different implications for the older Americans they serve.

There are differences between Medicare and Medicaid along certain dimensions that help to account for some of the different implications that their administrative arrangements have for the elderly. Centralized or decentralized administration, the simplicity or complexity of administrative procedures, and the degree of autonomy or interdependence are all such dimensions.

The consideration of administration means to programmatic ends is usually set aside during the legislative process. Such issues are left to be resolved by program administrators. The experience of Medicare and Medicaid suggests, however, that seemingly simple administrative tasks can prove to be difficult and costly. Further, administrative arrangements can have unanticipated conse-

quences: complicated eligibility criteria that discourage the elderly from applying for Medicaid; higher out-of-pocket costs under Medicare, a program meant to
alleviate the burden of medical-care expenses for the elderly; and cumbersome
billing procedures that contribute to provider unwillingness to serve the elderly.

Notes

1. Glenn R. Markus and Jennifer O'Sullivan, "Medicare-Medicaid," October 5, 1976 (Washington, D.C.: Congressional Research Service), p. 2.

2. Marian Gornick, "Ten Years of Medicare: Impact on the Covered
Population," *Social Security Bulletin* (July 1976):4.

3. U.S., Social Security Administration, "Social Security in Review,"
Social Security Bulletin (January 1979):1.

4. Ibid.; and Gornick, "Ten Years of Medicare," p. 4.

5. Commerce Clearing House, *Medicare and Medicaid Guide,* vol. 2
(Chicago: Commerce Clearing House), paragraph 14,945.

6. Social Security Administration, Office of Research and Statistics, "The
Supplemental Security Income Program for the Aged, Blind, and Disabled:
Selected Characteristics of State Supplementation Programs" (Washington, D.C.:
Department of Health, Education and Welfare, 1976), p. vi.

7. Ibid., p. xi.

8. Commerce Clearing House, *Medicare and Medicaid Guide,* paragraph
14,231.

9. U.S., General Accounting Office, Report to the Congress, "Problems in
Administering Supplemental Security Income for the Aged, Blind, and Disabled"
(Washington, D.C.: GAO, 1976), p. 42.

10. Commerce Clearing House, *Medicare and Medicaid Guide,* paragraph
14,763.

11. General Accounting Office, "Problems in SSI," p. 51.

12. Ibid. p. 50.

13. Beryl A. Radin, "The Implementation of SSI: Guaranteed Income or
Welfare?" *Public Welfare* (Fall 1974):51.

14. Theodore R. Marmor and Elizabeth A. Kutza, "An Analysis of
Legislative Barriers to Coordination under Title III of the Older Americans Act,"
submitted to the Administration on Aging, October 1975.

15. U.S. Code, Title 45, Sec. 1396b (f)(2).

16. Urban Systems Research and Engineering, Inc., *Evaluation of Medicaid
Spend-Down,* vol. 1 (Cambridge, Mass.: Urban Systems Research and Engineering, Inc., 1976), p. 12.

17. Ibid., p. 17.

18. Ibid., p. 23.

19. Ibid., pp. 51-52.

20. Ibid., pp. 83-95.

21. For clarification of this point see Urban Systems Research and Engineering, Inc., *Evaluation,* p. 41.

22. General Accounting Office, "Performance of the Social Security Administration Compared with That of Private Fiscal Intermediaries in Dealing with Institutional Providers of Medicare Services" (Washington, D.C.: GAO, 1975), p. 2.

23. U.S. Congress House Committee on Ways and Means, *National Health Insurance Resource Book* (Washington, D.C.: U.S. Government Printing Office, 1974), p. 432.

24. Douglas Conrad and Theodore R. Marmor, "Cost-Sharing under National Health Insurance: Implementation Forecasts and Policy Choice" (Chicago: University of Chicago, Center for Health Administration, August 1977; unpublished).

25. General Accounting Office, "Performance of the SSA," p. 2.

26. Ibid., p. 8.

27. Social Security Administration, Office of Research and Statistics Staff Paper #21, "Health Insurance Administration Costs" (Washington, D.C.: SSA, 1975).

28. Ibid., p. 10.

29. Ibid., p. 3.

30. Sylvia A. Law, *Blue Cross: What Went Wrong?* (New Haven: Yale University Press, 1976), p. 122.

31. Ibid., p. 123.

32. Ibid., p. 117.

33. Ibid., p. 124.

34. U.S. Congress, Senate Committee on Finance, *Medicare-Medicaid Anti-Fraud and Abuse Amendments of 1977* (Washington, D.C.: U.S. Government Printing Office, 1977), p. 31.

35. Karen Davis, *National Health Insurance* (Washington, D.C.: The Brookings Institution, 1975), p. 77.

36. Senate Committee on Finance, *Medicare-Medicaid,* p. 12.

37. Ibid.

38. U.S., Department of Health, Education and Welfare, "Report of the Task Force on Medicaid and Related Programs" (Washington, D.C., 1970), p. 68.

39. Health Care Financing Administration, Institute for Medicaid Management, "Conference Report on Erroneous Medicaid Payments," February 23, 1977, p. 5.

40. Senate Committee on Finance, *Medicare-Medicaid,* p. 7.

41. Stephen M. Davidson, "A Report from the Special Investigative Committee on Medicaid," Joseph A. Wells, Ph.D., M.D., Chairman (Springfield, Ill., November 1974), p. 11.

42. Davis, *National Health Insurance,* p. 73.

43. General Accounting Office, "Improvements Needed in Medicaid Program Management Including Investigations of Suspected Fraud and Abuse," 1975, p. 35.

44. Medical Services Administration, *Medicaid: FY 1978-1982* (Washington, D.C.: DHEW, 1976), p. 76.

45. Ibid. p. 77.

46. Ibid., p. 58.

47. Ibid., p. 85.

48. Theodore R. Marmor, "Welfare Medicine: How Success Can Be a Failure," *The Yale Law Journal* 85, no. 8 (July 1976):1159.

49. General Accounting Office, "Improvements Needed," p. 11.

50. Ibid.

51. Senate Committee on Finance, *Medicare-Medicaid*, p. 11.

52. Medical Services Administration, *Medicaid*, p. 13.

53. Senate Committee on Finance, *Medicare-Medicaid*, p. 35.

54. U.S. Congress, Senate Special Committee on Aging, Subcommittee on Long-Term Care, Supporting Paper no. 1, "The Litany of Nursing Home Abuse and an Examination of the Roots of Controversy" (Washington, D.C.: Senate Committee Print 1974), p. 225.

55. Senate Special Committee on Aging, "Fraud and Abuse among Practitioners Participating in the Medicaid Program" (Washington, D.C.: Senate Committee Print, 1976), p. 18.

56. Senate Committee on Finance, Staff Report, "Medicare and Medicaid: Problems, Issues, and Alternatives" (Washington, D.C.: Senate Committee Print, 1970), p. 133.

57. General Accounting Office, "Improvements Needed," pp. 12-13.

National Health Insurance Proposals

The following pages highlight the major components of three national health insurance plans: the Comprehensive Health Insurance Plan, the Health Security Plan, and the Catastrophic Health Insurance and Medical Assistance Reform Plan. These plans were chosen not because they are the ones most likely to be enacted, but because they represent three major approaches to national health insurance and incorporate different resolutions of the principal issues. Each plan will be characterized according to its eligibility criteria, services covered, methods of financing, administration, and interorganizational relationships.[1] The features of the three plans are presented in tabular format in appendix B.

The Comprehensive Health Insurance Plan

The Comprehensive Health Insurance Plan (CHIP), proposed by the Nixon-Ford administrations, would establish a three-part national program consisting of (1) an employee health care benefits program requiring employers to offer specified private health insurance to their employees, (2) a state-operated program providing health care coverage for low-income families and for families and employment groups who are high medical risks, and (3) a federal health care program for aged persons, in effect an expanded Medicare program. All programs would offer the same scope of health services and provide protection against the costs of catastrophic illness.

Employee Health Care Insurance Plan

Eligibility. Employers with one or more eligible full-time employees—measured by a test of the number of weeks and hours of work—would be required to offer coverage and contribute toward the premium for a health care plan covering employees and their families. Participation by employees would be voluntary. The law would apply to all employers, including state and local governments, but not the federal government. Employees age 65 and over and aged members of an employee's family would not be eligible under the employee plan.

Benefit Coverage. The required benefits under the Employee Health Care Plan would include services of hospitals, skilled-nursing facilities, and physicians;

home health and diagnostic services; and such additional benefits as prescription drugs, preventive care, and special services for children. A plan could not exclude benefits for preexisting medical conditions, require any waiting period before benefits become payable, or impose maximum limits on the total amount of benefits payable on an annual, lifetime, or any other basis.

Financing. Payment for all covered services, except drugs, would be subject to a common deductible of $150 annually per person, not to exceed $450 annually for any one family. In addition to the deductibles, payment for all covered services would be subject to a coinsurance rate of 25 percent. Cost-sharing would be limited to a maximum of $1,050 in a year for an individual and $1,500 for a family. All covered services above that amount in one year would be provided, with no further payment required of patients or families. With unlimited hospital and other expensive services covered and with a limit on total cost-sharing, the employee plan would protect most covered families against the high costs of catastrophic illnesses. The employer would have to contribute at least 65 percent of the premium cost of the required health care insurance plan for the first three years of the program and at least 75 percent thereafter. Employees would have to contribute the balance of the premium for the required insurance coverage.

Reimbursement. Reimbursement of providers under the CHIP would be on a fee-for-service basis with the rate determined by the states. Providers are classified into one of three categories.

1. Full participating providers would be paid the state rate, including the cost-sharing, as full payment. Hospitals and skilled-nursing facilities must be full participating.

2. Associate participating providers could charge more than the state rate, but would have to collect the extra charges and cost-sharing from the patient.

3. Nonparticipating providers would not qualify for any reimbursement at all.

Administration. Employers could purchase insurance through private carriers or establish a self-insured health plan supervised by the state under federal regulations, or they could provide the required health insurance by enrolling their entire employment groups, if they qualified because of low income or high medical risks, in the Assisted Health Care Insurance Plan.

Assisted Health Care Insurance Plan

Eligibility. The Assisted Health Care Insurance Plan would essentially continue Medicaid, except that the eligibility standards would be set nationally. Workers eligible for an employee plan with income over $5,250 for an individual and $7,500 for a family and aged persons eligible under the federal health care insurance program would be the only ineligibles. In short, the Assisted Health Care Plan is designed for low-income families, employed or unemployed, and for families and employment groups who are high medical risks. Persons age 65 and over not insured under the aged plan could enroll in the assisted plan and pay the cost-sharing premiums applicable to this plan. While these eligibility provisions are relatively broad, the desirability of electing the assisted plan, as opposed to obtaining coverage under another approved plan or under a private plan, would depend on the premium, benefits, and cost-sharing provisions of the various plans, and on the employment, income, and health characteristics of the persons or groups involved.

Benefit Coverage. The health services to be covered under the assisted plan are the same as those under the employer plan, but the cost-sharing varies according to individual or family income. For cost-sharing purposes, individuals and families would be classified in five income classes.

Financing. The costs of the Assisted Insurance Plan would be financed by premium payments from enrollees, with the balance shared by state and federal government general revenues. In calculating premiums, the rate for individuals would be 40 percent of the family rate. The premium rate for enrollees not in employment groups would be based on income, the amount to be calculated from estimated national averages for 1975, with variations among the states according to per capita income. The amount of a state's annual contribution to a plan would be determined by a formula designed to result in states paying about one-quarter of the total federal-state costs of the program, with the proportions varying according to state per capita income.

Administration. The assisted plan would be administered by the states, using private carriers to pay claims under federal regulations. Each state would submit its Assisted Health Insurance Plan to HEW, which would approve qualified plans and designate the state agency responsible for administration. Employed persons eligible under an employee health care plan might find it advantageous to elect the assisted plan, rather than their employee plan, depending on their income level, because of the income-related premiums and cost-sharing provisions of the assisted plan. If the workers or their family members were in poor health and expected to pay high amounts in cost-sharing, the assisted plan would become desirable even at higher-income levels.

Federal Health Care Insurance Plan

Eligibility. Like Medicare, the Federal Health Care Insurance Plan would cover persons who are insured under the Social Security Program. Every citizen who had reached age 65 by the first year of the program would automatically be covered under the plan. After the first year of implementation, eligibility would be extended to additional persons who had specified credits under Social Security, but not enough to meet the regular Medicare requirements. Persons age 65 and over not insured under the federal plan could enroll under the Assisted Health Care Plan and would pay the cost-sharing and premiums applicable to the assisted plan.

Benefit Coverage. The Federal Health Care Insurance Plan would cover the same services as the other plans. Each aged person would be treated as an individual for cost-sharing purposes and would pay the same amounts of cost-sharing—amounts generally less than those required for individuals with comparable incomes under the assisted and employee plans. However, the low-income aged would have reduced cost-sharing. Determination of income would be tied administratively to the Supplemental Security Income (SSI) Program.

Financing. The present Medicare hospital insurance tax levied on wages and self-employment would be continued at the same tax rate and earnings base as scheduled under present law, but would be extended under the Federal Health Care Insurance Plan to cover all federal, state, and local governments and their employees. Each eligible aged person would be required to enroll and pay a premium (the same for all), except for low-income aged, who would pay no premium.

Administration. The federal plan would be administered by HEW in a manner similar to the present Medicare program; the processing of claims would be handled by private carriers under contract with HEW, and Medicare taxes would be collected by the Internal Revenue Service. For all three parts of the CHIP the states would have responsibility for administration of major aspects of the program. HEW would review the state laws, regulations, and administration relating to these functions and certify states qualified under the law.

Relationship to Other Government Programs

As stated previously, Medicare would continue under the CHIP. Federal funds for state Medicaid programs would be limited to the following services: (1) intermediate-care facilities, (2) skilled-nursing facilities for persons age 21 and over, (3) home health services, (4) care in mental institutions for persons under age 21 and over age 65, and (5) medical or remedial care for persons in medical institutions or when needed to reduce institutionalization. Other government programs and private plans would not be affected by the CHIP. The plan would also establish provisions for participation under the program of prepaid health plans.

The Health Security Plan

The Health Security Plan, introduced by Senator Edward Kennedy and Congressman James Corman, would establish a national health insurance program covering the entire population and providing a range of health services with no payment required by the patient for services received. The program would be financed by a federal payroll tax on employers and employees, a tax on unearned income, and federal general revenues. It would be administered by the Department of Health, Education and Welfare. The proposal includes provisions designed to reorganize the delivery of health services, improve health planning, and increase the supply of health care manpower and facilities.

Eligibility

All residents of the United States would be covered, including aliens admitted as permanent residents or for employment. Persons would be eligible for benefits without regard to whether they had contributed to the program.

Benefit Coverage

Benefits would be provided with no cost-sharing for the patient. There would be no limit on coverage of hospital inpatient services, physician services, home health services, laboratory and x-ray, dental care, podiatric services, vision services, hearing services, other personal services (such as physical therapy, psychological counseling, nutrition consultation, and social services), prosthetic devices, medical supplies and equipment, and ambulance services. Payment for prescription drugs would be limited to drugs required for chronic conditions and other specified conditions; however, there would be no limit if these were provided by a Health Maintenance Organization (HMO). In addition, care in a skilled-nursing facility would be covered for only 120 days per spell of illness. Limits would also be set on the period for which mental health services were covered.

Financing

The Health Security Plan is to be financed by:

1. A 1 percent tax on wages of employees
2. A 2.5 percent tax on self-employment earnings
3. A 3.5 percent tax on employers' payrolls
4. A 2.5 percent tax on unearned income

5. Contributions from federal general revenues equal to the total receipts from
    these special taxes

The total income of an individual that would be subject to taxes is limited to an
amount equal to 150 percent of the earning base under the Social Security
Program. (The base under Social Security for 1976 was $15,300 annually, and
the equivalent under the health security proposal was approximately $22,950.)
The total payroll of employers is subject to the employment tax, which applies
to workers under Social Security and to federal, state, and local government
employment Reimbursement of providers of service would be on a capitation,
salaried, or fee-for-service basis. Each year, a national health budget for the
coming year would be established, and funds would be allocated, by type of
medical service, to regions and local areas.

Administration

The Health Security Plan would be administered by a special board in HEW with
regional and local offices to operate the program.

Relationship to Other Government Programs

Under the Health Security Plan Medicare would be abolished. Federal grants for
the cost of covered services for Medicaid, vocational rehabilitation, and maternal
and child health programs would be terminated. HEW would establish by
regulation a new minimum scope of benefits required under an approved state
Medicaid program. These new minimum benefits would be designed to supplement the benefits of the Health Security Program and would include additional
skilled-nursing-home care, dental care, and prescription drugs.

The Catastrophic Health Insurance and
Medical Assistance Reform Plan

The Catastrophic Health Insurance and Medical Assistance Reform Plan, introduced by Senators Russell Long and Abraham Ribicoff, would provide health
benefits for persons in the general population who had incurred unusually large
expenses. A medical assistance plan would cover the low-income population
through a national program with uniform eligibility standards. The two plans
would be administered in a way similar to the Medicare program, which, though
not discussed separately, would continue. The proposal would also establish a
program of federal certification of private health insurance to encourage
insurance carriers to improve basic insurance coverage.

Catastrophic Health Insurance: The
Government Plan

Eligibility. All residents of the United States, including permanent resident aliens, would be eligible for benefits under the program without regard to their contribution to the program.

Benefit Coverage. The program would cover the same services as the Medicare program, and, as under Medicare, the services would be provided under separate hospital insurance and medical insurance parts of the program. The three types of hospital insurance services (hospital inpatient care, skilled-nursing-facility services, home health services) would be covered after the patient had received sixty days of inpatient hospital care during a calendar year. Days spent in the hospital during the last three months of a year would count toward the deductible even if covered by another public health plan or by a private plan. Once the deductible was met, the period of eligibility for covered services (the benefit period) would continue indefinitely until the patient had been out of both a hospital and skilled-nursing facility for a period of ninety consecutive days. After that time, the patient would have to meet another sixty-day hospital deductible before becoming eligible for benefits again. During the benefit period, there would be no limit on the number of covered hospital days or home health visits, and there would be no cost-sharing. However, services in a skilled-nursing home would be limited to 100 days in a year.

Eligibility under the medical insurance part of the program would be on a family basis. The services under medical insurance would be covered for all members of a family after the members together had incurred expenses of $2,000 in a calendar year. Only expenses for the types of services covered under the medical part of the proposal could be counted toward the $2,000 deductible. Expenses covered under another public program or a private health plan would count toward the deductible. Once the deductible was met, the period of eligibility for services (the benefit period) would continue indefinitely until the family had incurred expenses of less than $500 in a ninety-day period. During the benefit period, all the services under medical insurance would be covered without limitation. The amounts shown above for the deductible and the benefit period ($2,000 and $500, respectively) would apply only to the first year of the program. Each year thereafter, these amounts would be adjusted according to the increase in the physician fee component of the consumer price index.

Financing. The program is to be financed by special taxes on employers and self-employed persons. Employers would pay a tax of 1 percent of payroll. The amount of wages subject to tax (the wage base) would be the same as under the Social Security program. The types of employment taxable would also be the same but, in addition, federal, state, and local governments would be covered.

Private employers contributing to the program would be allowed a 50 percent tax credit against federal income tax.

State and local governments would contribute on the same basis as private employers. Self-employed persons would be subject to a tax of 1 percent of earnings, with the earnings base the same as under Social Security. Reimbursement of providers would be the same as under the Medicare program.

Administration. Administration of the program would be similar to that of the Medicare program.

Catastrophic Health Insurance: The
Private Plan

At their option, employers could establish approved private plans as an alternative method of providing coverage for their employees. An approved plan would have to provide the same catastrophic benefits as the government plan. Employees covered under an approved plan would receive the catastrophic benefits under that plan and would not be eligible under the government program.

Eligibility. Employers who elect the private plan would be required to cover all employees and members of the employee's family, except for part-time and temporary employees and employees eligible under the Medicare program.

Benefit Coverage. Employer plans would have to provide the same catastrophic benefits as under the government plan.

Financing. Employers would be required to pay the entire cost of the catastrophic premiums. Employers would not be permitted to require employee contributions to the cost of premiums. Employers with private plans would be subject to the regular 1 percent payroll tax and the 50 percent credit against income tax, but the amount of the tax and credit would be adjusted according to the annual table of the actuarial values of catastrophic health insurance for each state (rather than on the amount of actual premium payments). Thus the tax payable might be reduced, up to its full amount, by the amount of the actuarial value.

Administration. Employers and self-employed people would purchase approved private insurance from approved carriers; HEW would supervise the program.

Medical Assistance Plan for
Low-Income People

Eligibility. The benefits of this program would be available to low-income families and families qualifying under spend-down provisions without regard to age, family status, employment, or state of residence. The types of income counted for eligibility would include both earned and unearned income. In addition, families who met all the requirements for eligibility under a state Medicaid program at the time the assistance plan started would automatically be eligible under the plan if their incomes were within 105 percent of the states' income requirements for Medicaid. While eligibility was based on the family's annual income as indicated above, the determination of the annual income would be based on the rate of income in the two-month period before the date of application for benefits and estimated prospective income for the two months after application. When an application was approved, eligibility for benefits would usually start on the first day of the month in which the application was filed, but eligibility could be extended backward for as many as three months before the month of application, if the family was qualified during this earlier period and incurred covered medical costs.

Benefit Coverage. The program would cover inpatient hospital services (sixty days in benefit period); skilled-nursing facilities and intermediate-care facilities; physicians' services, with a $3 copayment for each of the first ten outpatient visits per family; laboratory and x-ray; home health services; prenatal and well-baby care; family planning, counseling, and supplies; periodic examinations for children under age 18; outpatient physical therapy; immunizations, by regulation; medical supplies and appliances; and ambulance services. There would be neither limits on the amount of services nor any cost-sharing required, except as indicated. The $3 copayment requirement would apply to persons under the Medicare program only to the extent that this amount is less than the regular cost-sharing required under Medicare. The $3 copayment would not apply to any physician visits for well-baby care, health examinations for children, or family planning services. For persons under the Medicare program, the medical assistance program would pay the cost of the premium required to enroll in the Supplementary Medical Insurance part of Medicare.

Financing. The program is to be financed jointly by federal and state general revenues. The state share would be a fixed annual amount based on the state cost under Medicaid for services under the medical assistance plan, with some additions and subtractions. Reimbursement of providers under the medical assistance plan would be the same as for Medicare, but physicians would have to accept the plan's payment as payment in full.

Administration. A new agency would be established under HEW that would administer the Medicare program and the proposed catastrophic insurance, medical assistance, and private health insurance certification programs. The catastrophic program and medical assistance programs would be administered in a manner similar to the Medicare program.

Relationship to Other Government Programs

Catastrophic benefits would be payable without regard to coverage under other programs. Medical assistance benefits, however, would be secondary to all other programs and plans. Medicare would continue to operate as it does now.

Note

1. The primary source of information for this chapter is the publication entitled *National Health Insurance Proposals, Provisions of Bills Introduced in the 94th Congress as of February, 1976,* compiled by Saul Waldman (USDHEW Publication [SSA] 76-11920, March 1976).

National Health Insurance and the Elderly

The elderly in the United States are now affected by public medical programs to a very large extent, and to a much greater extent than other age groups. Almost all are covered by Medicare, Medicaid, or a combination of the two. On a per capita basis, they use health services worth three times the amount used by other adults and 67 percent of their bill is paid by government sources (principally Medicare and Medicaid), in comparison to only 29 percent of the medical expenditures of adults under 65.

Because the elderly so much are affected by public programs, it is important that people interested in their welfare know what would be likely to happen to them if a national health insurance plan were adopted. To make such an assessment, it is necessary to know their present experience, to be able to predict the likely occurrences under a new plan, and to compare the two. The previous chapters laid the groundwork for comparisons by providing information about the present and about the likely effects of three prototypical new plans. In this chapter, we present the comparisons.

Four plans are compared.

1. The current system has two components, Medicare and Medicaid. Medicare is the federally administered national health insurance program for the elderly. Hospital benefits are paid out of a health insurance trust fund financed by contributions from employees, employers, and self-employed persons. Other benefits are available under a supplemental program financed by premiums paid by beneficiaries of the program. Claims are submitted to and bills are paid by insurance companies acting as fiscal intermediaries under contract with the Social Security Administration. Medicaid is the state-administered medical assistance program for low-income people. It is tied to the means-tested welfare system and is financed by federal and state (and sometimes local or county) taxes. For the elderly, eligibility is usually related to the federally operated Supplemental Security Income (SSI) Program.

2. The Comprehensive Health Insurance Plan (CHIP) is a combined public-private proposal sponsored by the Nixon-Ford administrations. It consists of three parts: an employee plan, a plan for low-income and high-medical-risk people, and a plan for the elderly.

3. The Health Security Plan is a proposal for a publicly financed, publicly administered, comprehensive, compulsory program introduced by Senator Edward Kennedy and Congressman James Corman.

4. The Catastrophic Health Insurance and Medical Assistance Reform (CHIMAR) Plan is a proposal, sponsored by Senators Russell Long and Abraham Ribicoff, for providing coverage for financially catastrophic medical-care episodes under two plans, and for reforming Medicaid for the poor by federalizing it under Medicare. In addition, it would retain the present Medicare program for the elderly.

The four plans are compared on several key issues, each of which affects or would affect benefits to the elderly. The issues are eligibility criteria, services covered, financing arrangements, and administration. The four plans are ranked on each question according to their effect on the elderly. Following the assessments of the four plans on each issue, a summary and conclusions are presented.

Eligibility

The combination of Medicare and Medicaid covers almost all elderly Americans. The Hospital Insurance component of Medicare (part A) includes all elderly Old Age, Survivors, and Dependents Insurance (Social Security) beneficiaries; and the Supplementary Medical Insurance Program (part B) covers all the elderly who pay a monthly premium. Medicaid covers the elderly poor, with income and asset tests administered by the states. Thirty-five states cover all Supplemental Security Income (SSI) recipients at the SSI grant level of $2,839 for an elderly individual; another eight states set the cash eligibility level between $2,839 and $3,500; seven states have established eligibility floors above $3,500. Fifteen states exercise their option of applying a more restricted standard (which was in effect on January 1, 1972, prior to the implementation of SSI) for elderly SSI recipients. This more restricted standard generally consists of stricter asset tests than those required by the federal SSI cash-assistance program. Twenty-nine states provide coverage for the medically needy, people who do not receive cash assistance but whose medical expenses reduce their net incomes to state-established eligibility levels. As noted in chapter 2, however, in eighteen of those twenty-nine states the income level is less than the SSI grant level. Nonetheless, this category is important, particularly to the elderly and their families, because of the extent to which it is used for individuals receiving care in nursing homes. The expense of such care is such that, through the spend-down mechanism, it often reduces income even to the less-than-SSI level required in some of the states and thus causes people to become eligible for Medicaid benefits.

The Comprehensive Health Insurance Plan would essentially continue Medicare (as the Aged Plan) and Medicaid (as the Assisted Plan), except that the eligibility standards would be set nationally. The covered income levels in the original bill, introduced in 1974, are $5,250 for individuals and $7,500 for families. Those levels are higher than any state's Medicaid cash eligibility level then in effect, and higher than the medically needy eligibility levels in the twenty-nine states with medically needy programs. (Also asset tests in some of those states may be more burdensome than that contemplated by the CHIP proposal.)

The Health Security proposal would eliminate Medicare and Medicaid except, in the latter case, as needed to supplement coverage for the poor. All U.S. residents would be covered. There would be neither age and retirement tests (as under Medicare) nor an income test (as under Medicaid).

The Catastrophic Health Insurance and Medical Assistance Reform proposal would cover low-income individuals and families under the Medical Assistance Reform provisions. All persons meeting the income test would be eligible without regard to age, family status, employment, or state of residence. The income level established in the 1976 proposal was $3,600 a year for a family of two, higher than the SSI eligibility level in forty-four of the fifty jurisdictions with Medicaid programs. Other residents would be eligible if they spent down to that level. Medicare would continue for the elderly.

Under the catastrophic insurance provisions, all residents would be eligible for benefits once they met the rather large deductibles of sixty days of inpatient hospital care or $2,000 in other covered expenses.

The Health Security Plan must be ranked first among the four programs on the basis of eligibility provisions affecting the elderly, since it represents the ultimate coverage: it has no income or age restrictions, all would be covered. The CHIP program ranks second because it would cover all the elderly under Social Security, as at present under Medicare. It would also cover the poor elderly under separate provisions that are a distinct improvement over Medicaid in two ways: first, the standards would be set nationally instead of by the states; and second, the standards would be set at levels higher than those in any state. The Catastrophic and Medical Assistance Reform proposal is ranked third because it would continue Medicare and would improve coverage of the elderly poor over Medicaid by setting a national standard higher than that used in forty-four of the fifty states. Thus it is better than the present system, but not quite as good as the CHIP proposal. The present combination of Medicare and Medicaid ranks last because, even though it covers all the elderly eligible for Social Security and most of the elderly poor who receive SSI benefits, both the CHIMAR and CHIP proposals improve on the provisions for the elderly poor by setting national standards at higher levels than state standards in effect in most states.

Covered Services

Each program specifies covered services and, by omission, excluded services. Although there are differences among the four plans, it is important to note their similarity in covering, at least to some degree, the seven Medicaid services of relevance to the elderly (as well as family planning):

1. Inpatient hospital care
2. Outpatient hospital services
3. Laboratory and x-ray services
4. Skilled-nursing-facility services
5. Physician services
6. Home health services
7. Transportation to and from services

But some programs are more inclusive than others. Moreover, the same service may be covered quite differently by two plans; both the amount of the service and the conditions under which it is covered may vary.

Under the present system, home health services, for example, are provided in all states, but some states limit reimbursable care to visiting nurse associations, some limit it to persons discharged from hospitals, and some limit the numbers of visits and the personnel (for example, nurses, but not home health aides). The net effect is to make the distribution of care quite uneven and still largely unavailable in some states. To some extent these results could be altered by public policies that removed restrictions or liberalized payments to providers. Changes of this nature would undoubtedly stimulate the development of home health service providers, but they would probably develop first in the large population centers best able to support them. Thus even with changes in coverage, the availability of some of the services of importance to the elderly would continue to be limited and to vary by region.

Among other services of importance, prescription drugs available on an outpatient basis are of particular interest. Under Medicaid, this is an optional service available in forty-seven of the fifty jurisdictions with Medicaid programs; but it is not a covered service under Medicare, except in cases where the drugs are provided by the physician and the cost incorporated in his fee. Under the CHIP proposal, prescription drugs would be provided without limit to eligibles. The Health Security proposal would cover drugs without limit if they were provided by an HMO, but would otherwise limit coverage to drugs used in treating specified chronic conditions for which the drugs are costly. The CHIMAR plan would cover drugs on an outpatient basis only if they were required to avoid institutional care.

Clearly, then, a full comparative assessment of the services covered by the four plans would be extremely complex. Moreover, much of the data regarding the scope and duration of benefits necessary for a complete analysis would not be specified until the implementation phase. Therefore we have based this comparison on the number of optional Medicaid services covered by each plan.

Under Medicare, five of the optional services permitted under Medicaid are covered. Under Medicaid itself, two states provide fewer than five optional services, eleven provide five to nine services, sixteen provide ten to fourteen services, and the remaining twenty-two states provide fifteen or more optional services.[1] (That is, thirty-eight states provide ten or more optional services.) Under CHIP, nine would be covered; under Health Security, twelve would be covered; and under CHIMAR, three or four would be covered, depending on the particular subplan.

The Health Security Plan again ranks first because it would cover twelve Medicaid optional services throughout the country and with fewer limits than the other plans. CHIP is ranked second because it would provide only nine Medicaid optional services and because the states would have major administrative responsibilities, including cost-sharing and reimbursement rates, which could affect the willingness of providers to participate. The current Medicare/ Medicaid system ranks third even though thirty-eight states cover more optional services under their Medicaid programs than the top-ranked Health Security Plan. This is in part a result of the fact that although the comprehensiveness of coverage has been increasing in recent years, thirteen states still cover fewer than ten Medicaid optional services, and in part a result of the fact that Medicare, which affects millions more of the elderly than Medicaid, covers only five Medicaid optional services. Moreover, Medicare is essentially an acute-care program even though it is their chronic conditions that set the elderly apart from other age groups. Finally, CHIMAR is ranked fourth because it would leave the Medicare restrictions intact and increase the Medicaid restrictions (that is, only four optional services would be covered).

Financing

The financing of any health insurance plan is a major issue because it may affect who becomes eligible for benefits as well as how many benefits can be used. In this section, the focus is on two principal aspects of this issue: first, the major source of revenue for the health care financing proposal; and second, provisions for cost-sharing, if any, and limits to patient liability. The two are taken up separately.

Major Revenue Source

Medicare consists of part A, Hospital Insurance, and part B, Supplementary Medical Insurance. The first is financed by a trust fund created from taxes paid by employers, employees, and the self-employed. It is not financed by people who are currently elderly and thereby eligible for its benefits, but rather by workers and their employers against the time when those workers will be elderly and eligible for benefits. Part B is financed primarily by a separate trust fund including monthly premiums paid by elderly people who choose to be enrolled in the program and an equal amount from federal general revenues. It is thus financed by people who are currently eligible for benefits. The current monthly premium is $8.70.

Medicaid is supported by federal and state (and sometimes local) taxes. The federal share varies from 50 to 78 percent of the total, with the rate determined by a formula based on the state's relative per capita income. To the extent that the elderly pay taxes, they pay for Medicaid, but it is unlikely that many elderly Medicaid beneficiaries support the program directly because to become eligible they must either meet a low-income and asset test or spend down to a minimum income level.

CHIP consists of several parts, each of which is financed separately. Those of interest to the elderly are the Assisted Plan (comparable to Medicaid), which would be financed by income-graduated premium payments from enrollees and state and federal taxes. The plan stipulated, in 1975 when it was proposed, that the lowest two income groups, with incomes up to $5,000, would pay no premium; the three groups above $5,000 would pay from $300 to $900 annually.

The Aged Plan under CHIP would be financed as Medicare is currently, out of taxes paid by employees, employers, and self-employed persons. In addition, elderly enrollees with incomes over $3,500 would pay an annual premium of $90 (approximately $7.50 per month); those with incomes below $3,500 would pay nothing. Federal and state general revenues would make up the balance, with state tax rates varying with the state's ability to pay and the level of benefits paid. The elderly would contribute to the support of the program beyond premiums paid to the extent that they paid taxes.

The Health Security proposal would be financed as follows: half would come from federal general revenues and half from contributions from employers (3.5 percent of payrolls), self-employed persons (2.5 percent of earnings), unearned income (2.5 percent), and a tax on employees' wages (1 percent). The elderly would pay into the funds to the extent that they paid federal taxes, had unearned income, or were employed.

Financing of the CHIMAR proposal would vary among its several parts. One-half of the government Catastrophic Health Insurance Plan would be financed by 1 percent taxes on employers' payrolls and self-employed individuals' earnings, and the remaining half would come from federal general revenues. Contributors would receive a 50 percent federal income tax credit. The private Catastrophic Health Insurance Plans would be financed by employers (who would receive a 50 percent tax credit) and by the general revenue. The elderly would contribute to the extent that they were employers or self-employed or paid taxes.

The Medical Assistance part of the plan would be supported by federal and state taxes. The initial state share would be based on Medicaid expenditures, but a particular state's share would not rise in future years even if expenditures under the program rose. The elderly would contribute to the extent that they paid taxes. Under CHIMAR, Medicare would continue, as would its financing mechanisms.

On the basis of major revenue source, the Health Security Plan ranks first because the elderly beneficiaries of the program would not contribute to its revenues except to the extent that they paid federal taxes, had earned income, or were employed. Of all the plans, it is thus the most beneficial for the elderly. All the other plans require or would require some premium contributions from elderly beneficiaries. CHIP is ranked second, however, because its contributions to the Assisted Plan are graduated by income, with the poorest people paying nothing at all, and because people remain eligible beyond the Medicaid levels. Also even though enrollees would be required to make a contribution to the Aged Plan, that too is graduated by income, again with the poorest people paying nothing. Therefore under both parts of CHIP the elderly are better off than under Medicare/Medicaid. Finally, the elderly would fare about the same under CHIMAR as they do currently under Medicare/Medicaid. CHIMAR's proposed medical assistance plan would be financed by federal and state taxes just as Medicaid is, and Medicare would be retained without change. Both programs are ranked third.

Cost-Sharing and Limits of Patient Liability

Medicare requires cost-sharing under parts A and B. Current rates for part A (Hospital Insurance) are $160 deductible for inpatient hospital care and $80 deductible (half the inpatient deductible) for outpatient hospital care, with an additional $40 a day copayment after the sixtieth day in the hospital, a 20 percent copayment for outpatient services, and $20 a day copayment after twenty days in an extended-care facility. Part B (Supplementary Medical Insurance), which requires payment of a monthly premium discussed above, also calls for a deductible of $60 a year and copayments of 20 percent of reasonable charges for physicians' services and of reasonable costs for other services. These cost-sharing provisions continue to run without limit for beneficiaries under Medicare. Medicaid requires no deductible or copayment, except to the extent that people who are initially above the income-eligibility levels must spend down to establish their eligibility for services. Except for spend-downers, whose liability is limited to the amount required to establish eligibility, there is no recipient liability.

Under CHIP's assisted plan, a deductible based on income, ranging from $0 to $150, is required, along with a separate $0 to $50 deductible for drugs. In addition, copayments of 10 to 25 percent for individuals and families are called for, but again they are graduated by income. Maximum liability, which also varies with income, ranges from nothing for the poorest individuals and families to a maximum of $1,050 for individuals with incomes above $7,000 and families with incomes above $10,000.

CHIP's aged plan includes deductibles of $0 to $100 for elderly individuals and a separate deductible of $0 to $50 for drugs. Copayments vary from a minimum of 10 percent to a maximum of 20 percent. Maximum liability is limited to $750 for individuals with incomes over $5,250.

The Health Security proposal contains no deductible and no copayment and therefore contains a maximum liability above taxes of 0.

Under CHIMAR's catastrophic plans, liability is limited to the deductible, which is $2,000 per family for medical insurance and sixty inpatient days per hospitalized individual. The plan calls for no copayment beyond the deductibles. Under the private catastrophic plans, these deductibles may be lower but cannot be higher.

CHIMAR's assisted plan calls for $3 copayments for each family for each of the first ten physician visits (except for well-baby, child-health examinations, and family-planning visits). In addition, for individuals not in families, after the first sixty days in a long-term-care facility, the copayment is equal to the patient's monthly income minus $50. Medicare would be retained for the elderly, with its present cost-sharing and maximum liability provisions.

Health Security ranks first among the four programs, since it imposes no cost-sharing burden above taxes on elderly beneficiaries. All the other plans require copayments (except for the present Medicaid program), but the CHIP plan ranks second because its cost-sharing provisions vary progressively with income and set definite maximums. Copayments under CHIMAR's assisted plan are even more limited for the poor than those of CHIP, but CHIMAR ranks third because it continues the cost-sharing arrangements used by Medicare for the elderly, and these are more onerous than those proposed by the aged plan under CHIP. These copayments are less burdensome than Medicare itself, however, since the catastrophic component of the plan would limit inpatient liability to the sixty days covered by Medicare. Medicare/Medicaid is ranked last because of the burdensome copayment and cash liability provisions of Medicare.

Administration

In addition to the issues of who is covered, for what services, and at what price, a very important set of questions arises under the heading *administration.* While administrative matters are not always spelled out in a piece of legislation or even in the regulations that guide its implementation, the manner in which a program actually functions independently affects the success with which it achieves its stated goals. To be maximally effective, a health care financing program must not discourage appropriate participation by key people. It should be administratively simple for both beneficiaries and service providers, its necessary inter-relationships with other programs should be minimal, and those that are unavoidable should be smooth. We will consider administrative issues under headings of administrative simplicity and interrelationships with other programs.

Administrative Simplicity

Certain functions must be performed in all programs of this type: eligibility of claimants must be determined, coverage of particular services must be determined, and claims for services rendered must be paid.

Eligibility Determination. Under Medicare, a person who once establishes eligibility for Health Insurance (part A) retains that eligibility continuously. Eligibility for Supplementary Medical Insurance (part B), in contrast, must be renewed monthly and is contingent on payment of the monthly premium. But since virtually all Medicare eligibles are Social Security beneficiaries, the premium can be deducted from the monthly Social Security checks of most participants. Thus eligibility for even part B Medicare is relatively simple administratively.

Medicaid is another story altogether. Eligibility is means-tested and is done on a monthly basis. That is, fluctuations in a person's nonpublic-assistance income determine his eligibility for Medicaid benefits. Much of this job is performed by the Social Security Administration in its operation of the Supplemental Security Income (SSI) Program. In fifteen states, however, eligibility for Medicaid is subject to a more restricted treatment of assets than that required for federal SSI benefits. Thus in those states, applicants must file twice, once for SSI benefits and once for Medicaid, and eligibility for the latter requires additional documentation and processing. Moreover, the interface between SSI and the state Medicaid agency must be smooth to ensure that people who establish eligibility for SSI are not delayed or unduly burdened in establishing their eligibility for Medicaid as well. In sum, Medicaid fares poorly on this question for two principal reasons: eligibility is a monthly affair, and, for the elderly, it depends to a considerable extent on smooth and prompt communication between federal SSI officials and state Medicaid staff.

Under CHIP, the program for the aged would be similar to Medicare and the program for the low-income population would be similar to Medicaid. Thus the problem discussed above applies here too, except that national eligibility criteria would remove the state-to-state variation. Also higher-income levels would probably affect the design of the procedures: since more would be eligible, it might not be necessary to design safeguards as burdensome as at present.

Since the Health Security proposal would cover everyone, eligibility determination would be quite simple. No one could be excluded for failing to meet certain criteria. Instead of an eligibility determination process, a much simpler registration process could be designed.

The CHIMAR plan would be similar to the current Medicare/Medicaid programs and to the CHIP proposal, and the comments concerning them therefore apply here as well. There are two relatively minor differences. First, since the income levels for CHIMAR would be lower than those for CHIP (though higher than Medicaid), the procedures would have to be stricter to exclude the larger number of noneligibles. But because categorical restrictions would be eliminated under the national eligibility standards set for the assisted component, the procedures could be simplified further. If Medicare beneficiaries had to demonstrate that they had met the deductibles for the catastrophic plan, information would have to be transferred between the Medicare administration and the catastrophic plan administration. Since both organizations would be part of Medicare, this might involve fewer problems than that caused by the creation of SSI. The difficulties might be increased, however, by the use of either private catastrophic plans or private supplementation plans to fill the gaps left in benefit coverage by the basic plans.

The Health Security plan ranks first on the simplicity of eligibility determination, followed by CHIP and CHIMAR in that order but with little separating them. Finally, the present Medicare/Medicaid programs rank last primarily because of the complexity of eligibility procedures in state Medicaid programs.

Benefits Coverage. The question here is to what extent covered services are limited such that a provider may not be sure whether or not a particular service will be reimbursed and to what extent the amounts of services that are reimbursable are limited so that a provider may not know whether a patient has used his allotment of that service. In general, the more restrictions placed on coverage of a service, the more complicated the administration becomes.

The four programs are essentially similar on this score. All are fairly omprehensive in the scope of services covered, yet all employ some limitations that will cause confusion. While some are more restrictive than others, there is no good basis at this stage to say that one will cause greater problems than another.

Claims Payment. In a largely private, largely fee-for-service system like the American medical-care system, providers typically submit statements to patients or third parties claiming that particular services have been provided and that a stated fee is due. The administrative question raised by this fact is how quickly and reliably such claims can be processed and checks issued in payment for the services rendered. (The important question of the rate of payment is beyond the scope of this volume.)

Under Medicare, payment may be made either to the provider, who agrees to regard Medicare's payment as the complete fee for the service (assignment), or to the beneficiary, who must pay the provider directly. Institutional providers, like hospitals and nursing homes, must accept assignment; individual providers, like physicians, need not. In the latter case, the check is sent to the patient who then pays the practitioner, who may in turn charge the patient more than the Medicare program is willing to pay. Administratively, the issue is keeping assigned claims and others separate, technically not a very difficult matter. It does, however, lead to misunderstanding and hard feelings on the part of both practitioners and their patients, when, for example, practitioners expect to be paid at higher rates than Medicare deems appropriate (fees are based on usual, customary, and reasonable charges in the area), or when patients expect that their entire bills will be paid and are disappointed and angered to find that they must pay their practitioners some money.

Under Medicaid, providers are paid in full by the state or a fiscal intermediary under contract to the state. Providers must accept the fee paid as the full fee.

Difficulty has arisen in both programs when payers—a government or its intermediaries—have not paid providers promptly or predictably. Medicaid files are full of complaints from physicians, pharmacists, and others that say they do not understand why one claim was paid and another, for an identical service, was disallowed or paid at a different rate. Some state programs have been criticized for late payments, resulting from either inefficient processing systems or politically inspired efforts to reduce state costs by withholding payments, sometimes until the next budget year begins. The effect is to create considerable ill will, to cause providers to overprovide and overbill in the hope of collecting what they consider to be a fair share, and to reduce the number of providers willing to participate. All these results can reduce the effectiveness of the program and increase its cost. All have been charged to Medicaid and, to a lesser extent, Medicare.

The CHIP proposal would call for an essentially similar system as operates at present. The assisted plan would be administered by the states and, therefore, subject to variability similar to that found in Medicaid now. The amount of state-to-state variation might decrease slightly, however, by virtue of the fact that benefits would be the same in all states, thus permitting greater uniformity among them. But the basic problem of establishing a processing system and finding the money to pay the bills would remain.

The Health Security plan is the most complicated on this score, at least in the beginning, because it would require processes and tasks not now performed. The proposal calls for a national health budget established at the beginning of the year and divided among the areas of the nation on the basis of a formula. Local health planning organizations would have control of the local allotments and would budget funds among the several types of services and the many providers. The procedures to accomplish these tasks would be difficult to design and would require a testing period before they could be expected to operate smoothly.

Moreover, they would require special arrangements with providers. For example, hospitals would have to establish annual budgets, uniform accounting systems, and full compensation of hospital-based physicians (that is, radiologists, anesthesiologists, and pathologists). Physicians in general or family practice could be paid on a fee-for-service basis according to a fee schedule, capitation, or salary. These latter procedures are likely to generate opposition in the provider community, at least until it can be demonstrated that practitioners are not likely to be hurt by them. Once the system is designed, installed, and debugged, it should be no more complicated to operate than any other; and it might be simpler because the lid on expenditures would be known in advance, and this would permit adjustments that at first would be difficult but later should be manageable.

Under the CHIMAR plan, the government would either pay the physician directly (assignment) and in full or would pay the beneficiary who would then be responsible for paying the provider. The exception is the Medical Assistance program which, though it would be operated by Medicare, would require that the physician accept the program's payment as the full fee. The private plan would be administered by private insurance companies and monitored by HEW.

Since many of the claims-payment problems under the present system stem either from the states' efforts to cope with their limited financial capacity or from Medicare's efforts to limit its expenditures by tightening up on claims payment (through such devices as retroactive denials, that is, refusing to pay for covered services after they have been rendered on the grounds that they were unnecessary), all the programs that borrow from the present system will be prey to the same problems. The Health Security plan would not have such problems once a national health budget was established, but in the beginning it would face the formidable tasks involved in determining the budget and its distribution among the health service areas and, within those areas, among providers. Thus in the short run, no plan has much of an advantage over another; in the long run, the Health Security proposal will be simpler administratively. On balance, however, at this stage it must be considered a toss-up; all the programs will very likely present substantial problems.

Interrelationships with Other Programs

The fewer the relationships necessary to the smooth operation of the program, the easier it will be for administrators to manage. Problems that arise will be within the administrators' own control, and will not require perhaps lengthy negotiations with counterparts in other organizations.

Eligibility for Medicare is determined by the Social Security Administration through a rather simple process that needs to be done only once for each applicant. Premiums for the SMI portion of Medicare can be deducted from monthly Social Security checks. Administratively, therefore, the functions are performed in different, but by now closely related, parts of the federal Department of Health, Education and Welfare. Even when other sources, like Medicaid, pay part of the patient's bill, since Medicare pays first its need for interorganizational relationships is limited. Somewhat more complicated arrangements are needed, however, for people for whom state Medicaid programs pay the SMI premiums.

For Medicaid the need for relationships is greater. Moreover, since eligibility is a monthly process, the relationships must be ongoing. Principally, they are of two types. First, since elderly people usually demonstrate eligibility for Medicaid by showing they are eligible for federally administered SSI benefits, SSI officials must transfer to state Medicaid officials data tapes of SSI beneficiaries living in their state each month. Delays in transmission of the tape and errors in the content create considerable hardship for sick people. Many of the bugs in the relationship appear to have been worked out, but, in the beginning especially, the problems were large. Second, many elderly people are eligible for both Medicaid and Medicare. When they use services, the question becomes how to ensure that providers are paid what they are owed in a timely manner and that there be no double payments. Medicare pays first, but for Medicaid to pay its share it must know what Medicare has paid and what is still owed. This, too, requires the timely exchange of information and thus carries the potential for delays, errors, and bad feelings.

CHIP would continue many of the same relationships required now under Medicare and Medicaid, but with several possible improvements. The Assisted Plan would tie eligibility to income, which would require relationships with SSI, as at present. Moreover, if the state supplements SSI benefits or uses a more restricted standard for Medicaid eligibility, additional relationships would be required with other state-level units, as at present. However, if eligibility were established for an entire year at a time, as would be possible, administration would be simplified. Although Medicare would end, the proposed plan for the aged appears to be very similar, and eligibility would continue to be tied to Social Security. People would enroll in only one plan, thereby eliminating the need for information regarding partial payment for services covered by more than one agency. The exception is that Medicaid would continue to supplement federally supported services for eligible poor people, but this supplement would be limited to intermediate-care facilities, skilled-nursing facilities, home health services, and care in mental institutions.

The Health Security plan would require none of the Medicare/Social Security or Medicaid/SSI relationships discussed above since eligibility would extend automatically to all residents regardless of age or income, and the public program would be inclusive. To the extent that private plans were used to supplement gaps in benefits, this issue would remain important. Still, Medicaid would continue to supplement covered services for poor people and would thus continue to have an eligibility function and a claims-payment function. It would have to establish relationships with the federal health insurance agency to receive information about benefits paid and with the federal SSI agency or the state public assistance department regarding client eligibility. But the program would be much smaller than at present and so, presumably, would be the interrelationship problems. The extent to which the Health Security program would call for relationships with health planning bodies at national, state, and local levels is not clear at this point. It might simply be a matter of telling the health planners how much money is available to them with no further relationship necessary. Or the amount might be determined in part by negotiation, thus necessitating a continuing and perhaps problematic relationship.

The CHIMAR plan would retain Medicare and its present interrelationships. Medicaid would be abolished, and the replacement program would be simpler to operate because the national eligibility standards would be divorced from age, family status, and residence criteria. Moreover, once eligibility was established, it would continue for an entire year unless family income increased by more than 20 percent. Nonetheless, the low-income medical program would require continuing relationships with SSI for information about eligibles.

The Health Security plan ranks first because it would require no continuing relationships with other health insurance plans regarding eligibility or benefits, and its relationship with a much smaller Medicaid program that would supplement benefits would be an improvement over the present situation. CHIP is rated second because, though it would continue some of the current relationships, it would result in substantial improvements. CHIMAR too would result in improvements, largely because of its national eligibility criteria for the low-income program and its year-at-a-time eligibility. Since people could still be eligible under more than one program, however, continuing relationships would be required to avoid duplicate and late payments. Medicare and Medicaid rank last principally because of the monthly nature of Medicaid eligibility and its relationship to SSI.

Conclusion

Table 6-1 summarizes the rankings presented in this chapter. The ratings are rather crude because they attach equal weight to all the factors and allow no degree of difference among the plans (for example, if plans 2 and 3 are close to each other but both are much superior to plan 4, those gradations will not be captured in the rankings). Nonetheless, we believe they provide a useful way to sort out the mass of information about the several programs and to arrive at a general impression of how they compare. Also we considered the programs only in terms of their impact on the elderly. Policymakers will have to consider other questions, including the impact of the plans on appropriate utilization of services, on participation of providers, on potential for monitoring quality and

Table 6-1
Summary of Ratings of Four National Health Insurance Plans for Their
Impact on the Elderly

Criteria	Plans			
	Medicare/ Medicaid	CHIP	Health Security	CHIMAR
Eligibility	4	2	1	3
Covered services	3	2	1	4
Financing				
Major revenue source	3	2	1	3
Cost-sharing and maximum liability	4	2	1	3
Administration				
Eligibility	4	2	1	3
Benefit coverage	1	1	1	1
Claims payment	1	1	1	1
Interorganizational relations	4	2	1	3
Totals	24	14	8	21

fraud and abuse, and, perhaps most important from a political viewpoint, on the ability to contain expenditures for medical care.

With these caveats in mind we think it is clear that the Health Security plan would benefit the elderly considerably more than the other plans. It ranked first on every count. It includes more eligibles and more covered services, its financing plans are least burdensome to the elderly, it requires no cost-sharing by elderly people (many of whom are on limited fixed incomes), and it is likely to be simpler administratively than the other plans.

The CHIP proposal ranks second on all counts. It essentially tinkers with the present system without solving its underlying problems. The Catastrophic Health Insurance and Medical Assistance Reform Act also removes some of the worst aspects of the present system, but leaves it fundamentally intact. Thus it too is a limited improvement.

Perhaps the clearest finding of all is that the elderly would be better off under any of these national health insurance proposals than they are now under Medicare and Medicaid. Under all these plans eligibility would be broader and less burdensome to establish, more services would be covered (except in states with the most generous Medicaid programs) and they would be less heavily weighted toward acute care, cost-sharing would be reduced, and administration would be simplified.

While the findings are remarkably consistent from item to item, they should be read for the general impression they create rather than their precision. With that in mind, there can be no doubt that the elderly would benefit by a change in our method of financing health care.

Note

1. Figures are for 1975. See Stephen M. Davidson, "Variations in State Medicaid Programs," *Journal of Health Politics, Policy and Law* (Spring 1978):54-70.

Appendix A
Acute and Chronic Conditions

Acute Conditions

Infective and parasitic diseases

    Common childhood diseases
    Virus not otherwise specified
    Other infective and parasitic diseases

Respiratory conditions

    Upper respiratory conditions
        Common cold
        Other upper respiratory conditions
    Influenza
        Influenza with digestive manifestations
        Other influenza
    Other respiratory conditions
        Pneumonia
        Bronchitis
        Other respiratory conditions

Digestive system conditions

    Dental conditions
    Functional and symptomatic upper gastrointestinal disorders
        not elsewhere classifiable
    Other digestive system conditions

Injuries

    Fractures, dislocations, sprains, and strains
        Fractures and dislocations
        Sprains and strains
    Open wounds and lacerations
    Contusions and superficial injuries
    Other current injuries

All other acute conditions

    Diseases of the ear
    Headaches
    Genitourinary disorders
    Deliveries and disorders of pregnancy and the puerperium
    Diseases of the skin
    Diseases of the musculoskeletal system
    All other acute conditions

Chronic Conditions

Tuberculosis, all forms
Malignant neoplasms
Benign and unspecified neoplasms
Diabetes
Mental and nervous conditions

Heart conditions
Cerebrovascular disease
Hypertension without heart involvement
Varicose veins
Hemorrhoids
Other conditions of circulatory system
Chronic bronchitis
Emphysema
Asthma, with or without hay fever
Hay fever, without asthma
Chronic sinusitis
Other conditions of respiratory system
Peptic ulcer
Hernia
Other conditions of digestive system

Diseases of kidney and ureter
Other conditions of genitourinary system
Arthritis and rheumatism
Other musculoskeletal disorders
Visual impairments
Hearing impairments
Paralysis, complete or partial
Impairments (except paralysis) of back or spine
Impairments (except paralysis and absence) of upper extremities and shoulders
Impairments (except paralysis and absence) of lower extremities and hips

Condition not specified:
    Old age
    Other

Source: National Center for Health Statistics, Data from the National Health Survey, series 10, numbers 96, p. 50, and 126, p. 52 (Hyattsville, Maryland, 1974 and 1978).

Appendix B
National Health
Insurance Proposal
Summaries

CHIP

Subject	Provisions		
	Employee Plan	**Assisted Plan**	**Plan for Aged**
General concept and approach	A 3-part program including: (1) a plan requiring employers to provide private health insurance for employees, (2) an assisted plan for the low-income and high-medical-risk populations, and (3) an improved federal Medicare program for the aged. The states would supervise providers of health service and insurance carriers, under federal guidelines. Supported by the administration in the 93d Congress.		
Coverage of the population	Full-time employees, including employees of state and local governments.	Low-income families, employed or nonemployed. Also, families and employment groups who are high-medical risks.	Aged persons insured under Social Security.

Benefit structure	No limits on amount of benefits listed below, except where indicated:
	Institutional services:
	  Hospital inpatient and outpatient.
	  Skilled nursing facility: 100 days per year.
	Personal services:
	  Physicians.
	  Dentists: For children under age 13.
	  Laboratory and x-ray.
	  Home health services: 100 visits per year.
	  Family planning, maternity care, and health examinations; by regulation.
	Other services and supplies:
	  Prescription drugs.
	  Medical supplies and appliances.
	  Eyeglasses and hearing aids (and eye and ear exams): for children under age 13.
	
	Deductible of $150 per person and 25 percent coinsurance, but total cost sharing limited to $1,500 annually per family ($1,050 for individuals).
		Maximum cost sharing provisions are same as employee plan, but reduced according to individual or family income.	Deductible of $100 per person and 20 percent coinsurance, but total cost sharing limited to $750 per person annually. Reduced cost sharing according to individual income for low-income aged.

	Insurance through private carriers (or self-insured arrangements) supervised by states, under federal regulations.	Administered by states, using private carriers to administer benefits, under federal regulations.	Administered by federal government in way similar to present Medicare program.
Administration	Insurance through private carriers (or self-insured arrangements) supervised by states, under federal regulations.	Administered by states, using private carriers to administer benefits, under federal regulations.	Administered by federal government in way similar to present Medicare program.
Relationship to other government programs	Medicare: Program continues as the federal plan for the aged. Medicaid: No federal matching funds for covered benefits (or for premiums or cost sharing) under new program, but continues for specified noncovered services (such as intermediate-care facilities).		
Financing	Employer-employee premium payments, with employer paying 75 percent of premiums (65% for first 3 years). Temporary federal subsidies for employers with usually high increases in payroll costs. Special provisions to assure coverage for small employers.	Premium payments from enrollees according to family income (none for lowest income groups). Balance of costs from federal and state general revenues, with state share varied according to state per capita income.	Continuation of present Medicare payroll taxes and premium payments by aged (but no premiums for low-income aged). Federal and state general revenues used to finance reduced cost sharing and premiums for low-income aged.
Standards for providers of services	Similar to Medicare, with additional standards for participation of physicians' extenders.		
Reimbursement of providers of services	Reimbursement rates established by states, according to federal procedures and criteria. Providers of service who elect as "full participating" would be paid the state-established rates, including the cost-sharing, as full payment of their charges. Providers who elect as "associate participating" could charge more than the state rate for employee plan patients, but must collect the extra charges and cost-sharing from the patients. However, all hospitals and SNFs must be full participating providers.		
Delivery and resources	Prepaid practice plans: Under all plans, option available to enroll in approved prepaid group or individual practice plans (which meet special standards). Regulation of insurance carriers: By state, including approval of premium rates, enforcement of disclosure requirements, annual CPA audit, and protection against insolvency of carriers. Regulation of providers: By state, including standards for participation in program, approval of proposed capital expenditures, and enforcement of disclosure requirements. Professional Standard Review Organization (PSRO): Applies to all services under program.		

Source: Saul Waldman, *National Health Insurance Proposals: Provisions of Bills Introduced in the 94th Congress as of February 1976*, publication number (SSA) 76-11920 (Washington: Social Security Administration), p. 7.

Health Security Plan

Subject	Provisions
General concept and approach	A program administered by federal government and financed by special taxes on earned and unearned income and by federal general revenues. Supported by Committee for National Health Insurance and AFL-CIO.
Coverage of the population	All U.S. residents.

Benefit structure	Benefits with no limitations, except as noted. No cost-sharing by patient.
	Institutional services:
	  Hospital.
	  Skilled-nursing facility: 120 days.
	Personal services:
	  Physicians.
	  Dentists: For children under age 15; scheduled extension to age 25; eventually to entire population.
	  Home health services.
	  Other health professionals.
	  Laboratory and x-ray.
	Other services and supplies:
	  Medical appliances and ambulance services.
	  Eyeglasses and hearing aids.
	  Prescription drugs needed for chronic illness and other specified diseases.

Administration	Federal government: Special board in DHEW, with regional and local offices to operate program.
Relationship to other government programs	Medicare: Abolished. Medicaid and other assistance programs: Would not pay for covered services. Other programs: Most not affected.
Financing	Special taxes: On payroll (1.0% for employees and 3.5% for employers), self-employment income (2.5%) and unearned income (2.5%). Income subject to tax: Amount equal to 150% of earning base under social security (i.e., $22,950 in 1976). Employment subject to tax: Workers under Social Security and federal, state, and local government employment. Federal general revenues: Equal to amount received from special taxes.

Standards for providers of services	Same as Medicare, but with additional requirements: Hospitals cannot refuse staff privileges to qualified physicians. Skilled-nursing facilities must be affiliated with hospital which would take responsibility for quality of medical services in home. Physicians must meet national standards; major surgery performed only by qualified specialists. All providers: Records subject to review by regional office. Can be directed to add or reduce services in a new location.
Reimbursement of providers of services	National health budget established and funds allocated, by type of medical services, to regions and local areas. Hospitals and nursing homes: Annual predetermined budget, based on reasonable cost. Physicians, dentists, and other professionals: Methods available are fee-for-service based on fee schedule, per capita payment for persons enrolled, and (by agreement) full- or part-time salary. Payments for fee-for-service may be reduced if payments exceed allocation. Health maintenance organizations: Per capita payment for all services (or budget for institutional services). Can retain all or part of savings.
Delivery and resources	Health planning: DHEW responsible for health planning, in cooperation with state planning agencies. Priority to be given to development of comprehensive care on ambulatory basis. Health resources development fund: Will receive, ultimately, 5 percent of total income of program, to be used for improving delivery of health care and increasing health resources. Health maintenance organizations: Grants for development, loans for construction, and payments to offset operating deficits. Manpower training: Grants to schools and allowances to students for training of physicians for general practice and shortage specialties, other health occupations, and development of new kinds of health personnel. Personal-care services: Demonstration projects to provide personal care in the home, including homemaker, laundry, meals-on-wheels, transportation, and shopping services.

Source: Saul Waldman, *National Health Insurance Proposals: Provisions of Bills Introduced in the 94th Congress as of February 1976*, publication number (SSA) 76-11920 (Washington: Social Security Administration), p. 10.

CHIMAR

Subject	Provisions		
		Catastrophic Insurance	*Medical Assistance Plan*
		Government Plan	*Private Plans*	
General concept and approach	Proposal includes (1) a catastrophic illness insurance program for the general population provided through a federally administered plan or alternatively under approved private plans and (2) a federal medical assistance program for the poor and medically indigent. Also includes provisions for federal certification of qualified private basic health insurance.		
Coverage of the population	All U.S. residents, except persons under private plans.	Employees (and their families) of employers who voluntarily elect private plan. Self-employed who voluntarily elect.	Without regard to age or employment, low-income families and families qualifying under "spend-down" provisions.
Benefit structure	After person spends 60 days in the hospital, following benefits become available: Additional hospital days, skilled-nursing facility (100-day limit), and home health services. After family spends $2,000 on medical expenses, following benefits become available to all members of family: Physicians services, laboratory and x-ray, home health services, medical supplies and appliances. No limit on amount of services (except SNF) and no cost-sharing.		No limits on services and no cost sharing except as indicated: *Institutional services:* Hospital (60 days), skilled-nursing and intermediate-care facilities. *Personal services:* Physicians ($3 a visit for first 10 visits), laboratory and x-ray, family planning, maternity, and exams for children. *Other:* Medical supplies and appliances.
Administration	Similar to Medicare program.	Employers and self-employed purchase approved private insurance from approved carriers. DHEW supervises program.	Similar to Medicare program.

Relationship to other government programs	Catastrophic benefits payable without regard to coverage under other government programs or private plans. Medical assistance benefits secondary to all other programs and plans. Medicare program continues and Medicaid abolished.	
Financing	Payroll tax of 1% on employers, including federal, state, and local governments; employers allowed a credit against their federal income tax of 50% of the tax. Similar provisions for self-employed.	Employers are subject to regular 1% payroll tax, but this tax is reduced by the actuarial value of their private coverage; also receive the 50% tax credit. Similar provisions for self-employed.	Financed by federal and state general revenues. State share is fixed annual amount based on state cost under Medicaid for types of services under new program, with some additions and subtractions.
Standards for providers of services	Same as Medicare.	
Reimbursement of providers of services	Same as Medicare.	Determined by carrier.	Same as Medicare, but physicians must accept plan's payment as payment in full.
Delivery and resources	Government catastrophic program and medical assistance plan incorporate HMO and PSRO provisions now applicable to Medicare.	
Encouragement of basic insurance	Under provisions designed to encourage improved basic health insurance, DHEW would certify private policies meeting specified standards (including coverage of 60 hospital days and first $2,000 in medical services). States would arrange marketing of this insurance through pools and reinsurance arrangements. DHEW would offer certified insurance in states where not available.	

Source: Saul Waldman, *National Health Insurance Proposals: Provisions of Bills Introduced in the 94th Congress as of February 1976*, publication number (SSA) 76-11920 (Washington: Social Security Administration), p. 19.

Glossary

AB Aid to the Blind, a public assistance category.

AFDC Aid to Families with Dependent Children, a public assistance category.

APTD Aid to the Permanently and Totally Disabled, a public assistance category.

HCFA Health Care Financing Administration, that part of the Department of Health, Education, and Welfare with responsibility for Medicare and Medicaid.

HI Hospital Insurance, part A of Medicare, the federal health care insurance program for the elderly and disabled.

HMO Health Maintenance Organization, another term for prepaid group practice.

MSA Medical Services Administration, a former part of the Social and Rehabilitation Service with responsibility for Medicaid.

NHI National Health Insurance.

OAA Old Age Assistance a public assistance category.

OASDI Old Age, Survivors, and Disability Insurance, the Social Security program.

SMI Supplementary Medical Insurance, part B of Medicare, the federal health care insurance program for the elderly and disabled.

SRS Social and Rehabilitation Service, the part of the Department of Health, Education, and Welfare which formerly had responsibility for Medicaid at the federal level.

SSI Supplemental Security Income, the federal income assistance program which replaced the former federal/state public assistance programs of AB, APTD, and OAA.

Index

About the Authors

Stephen M. Davidson, who received the Ph.D. from the University of Chicago, has taught health policy and planning at the University's School of Social Service Administration since 1971. He is one of the leading students of Medicaid and is currently finishing a book-length analysis of that major public program. He is principal investigator of a thirteen-state study of physician participation in Medicaid. His papers include studies of major health policy issues and have appeared in leading medical care, public policy, and social welfare journals. In addition to his health policy work, he is coauthor of the book *Effective Social Services for Older Americans*, published in 1976 by the University of Michigan Institute of Gerontology.

Theodore R. Marmor, Ph.D., now at Yale where he is professor in the Department of Political Science and the School of Epidemiology and Public Health and chairman of the Center for Health Studies, is one of the country's most prominent public policy analysts. His book, *The Politics of Medicare* (Aldine, 1973), is the standard analysis of the passage of the Medicare and Medicaid legislation. His numerous papers have appeared in most of the major professional journals. "Rethinking National Health Insurance," which appeared in *The Public Interest* in 1977, was selected as the best article on health issues by the Policy Studies Association.

Janet D. Perloff, **Marsha Spear**, and **Nancy Aitken** were graduate students in health policy and planning at the University of Chicago School of Social Service Administration at the time this book was written. Ms. Perloff is the full-time project manager of a thirteen-state study of physician participation in Medicaid and a Ph.D. candidate at the University of Chicago. Ms. Spear received the M.A. degree in 1978 from the University of Chicago and is now at work there on the Ph.D. Ms. Aitken, who also received the M.A. in 1978, is a planning specialist in the Region V office (Chicago) of the Department of Health, Education and Welfare.